Gill & Macmillan
Hume Avenue
Park West
Dublin 12
www.gillmacmillan.ie

978 07171 6043 3

Design by Mike Connor Design & Illustration
Print origination by Carole Lynch
Printed by GraphyCems, Spain

The paper used in this book is made from the wood pulp of managed forests. For every tree felled, at least one tree is planted, thereby renewing natural resources.

A catalogue record is available for this book from the British Library.

Contents

Assignment 2: Pizza Perfection Database

Assignment 3: Riverside Rugby Club Database

Assignment 4: Distance Learning Database

SECTION 2: INTERMEDIATE DATABASE ASSIGNMENTS

Assignment 5: National Railways Database

SECTION 3: ADVANCED DATABASE ASSIGNMENTS

Assignment 8: Southside Motor Tests Database

Assignment 9: Southern Estate Agents Database

About This Book

The assignments in this book were written specifically for Microsoft Access 2010 and Access 2007, but all of the tasks in the book can be completed using Access 2003. However, as Access 2003 doesn't use the Ribbon system, there will be instances where references are made to commands that don't exist in Access 2003. It is a 'learning through practice' book with lots of practical assignments for the student. No previous knowledge of databases is needed, as the assignments start at a very basic level. The book contains four sections:

- Section 1: Beginners Database Assignments
- Section 2: Intermediate Database Assignments
- Section 3: Advanced Database Assignments
- Section 4: Introduction to Relational Databases

There are 10 practical database assignments, which are graded by level of difficulty. Each assignment introduces new concepts and, with the exception of Assignment 1, enables you to consolidate what you have learned in previous assignments.

Students who have no previous database experience should start at Section 1. Students already familiar with Microsoft Access will be able to use this book as an independent study guide and may wish to start at Section 2. However, these students can practise and consolidate existing database skills by completing Section 1.

By completing all the assignments contained in Sections 1, 2 and 3 together with the first part of the assignment in Section 4, you will have covered all the necessary course material required to successfully complete the NFQ Level 5 Database Methods Module. Students who are studying NFQ Level 6 Relational Databases or who simply wish to learn about relational databases should also complete all of Section 4 of *Step by Step Databases*.

Teachers have the option of downloading the records for each database assignment from the Gill & Macmillan website. This cuts out the data entry phase and saves time in the classroom. Full solutions for each of the 10 database assignments are also available online, as well as project guidelines and sample exams.

New versions of Microsoft Access will be introduced over time. Because the assignments in this workbook deal more with the principles of databases than the features of Microsoft Access, I am confident that except for a few minor inconsistencies, they will also work with future versions of Microsoft Access.

The following symbols are used throughout the book.

Tip	**Note**	**Rule**	**Cross-reference**	**Shortcut**	**Hint**	**Important Point**	**Theory Section**

Introduction

WHAT IS A DATABASE?

We all use databases in everyday life, sometimes without even being aware of it. The most common example of a database is the telephone directory. These days, search engines are running in a close second place. If you have used Google or Bing, then you have used a database. If you use the Internet to buy products and services online, then you have used a database. When you search for a song on iTunes or for a book on Amazon, a database does the searching in the background. Whether you like it or not, your details are stored in at least one database. The following is a list of databases that you may find yourself in:

- Customer database for a bank.
- Loyalty card database for a supermarket.
- National database of PPS numbers.
- National database of registered vehicles.
- Database of any company from which you bought goods or services online.

The main function of a database is to store data. The data is stored in a particular order and is divided into sections. For example, in the telephone directory, the stored data is in alphabetical order of name and is divided into three sections – name, address and phone number, as shown in Table 0.1.

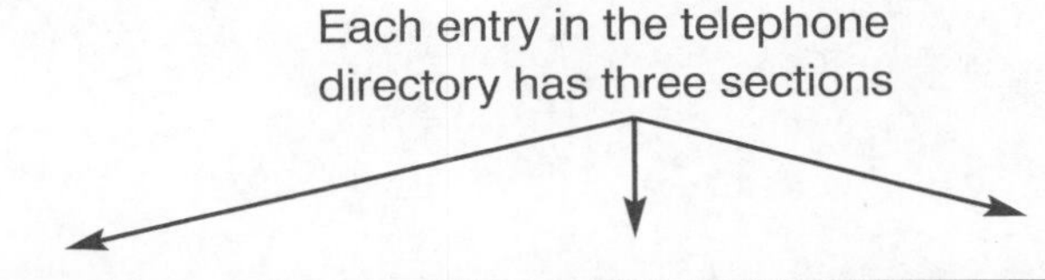
Each entry in the telephone
directory has three sections

Name	Address	Phone Number
Dunne, Adam	27 Killiney Towers	2682931
Dunne, Aileen	7 Park Drive	2076878
Dunne, Alan	32 Mount Anville Grove	2271883

Data in the telephone directory is in ascending alphabetical order of name

Table 0.1

So, a database allows us to store data:

- With a specific structure.
- In a particular order.

A database can be recorded on paper or stored in a computer. The telephone directory is an example of a database recorded on paper (it is also available online). One of the disadvantages of paper-based databases is that it is time consuming to find specific data and to view the data in different ways. Imagine trying to compile a list of all the people who live in Dublin 4 from the telephone directory! You would first have to look through every address and make a note of Dublin 4 addresses. Then you would have to write out the name, address and telephone number of people with a Dublin 4 address in a new list. In practice, it is not possible to do this in a paper-based database as big as the telephone directory.

HISTORY OF DATABASES

Unlike a spreadsheet, you don't need a computer to use a database. Consequently, databases have been around a lot longer than spreadsheets. The first proper database was developed in 1876 by Melvil Dewey to categorise books in a library. As computers didn't exist in 1876, Dewey's database was paper based. It wasn't until the 1960s, with the advent of mainframe computers, that computerised databases became part of everyday life. Mainframe computers were used by large organisations such as banks to store and retrieve business data. Databases became available to the wider public when IBM launched the first mass-market PC in 1981. The IBM PC came pre-loaded with application software. The database application was dBase II. Figure 0.1 shows the menu screen in dBase II.

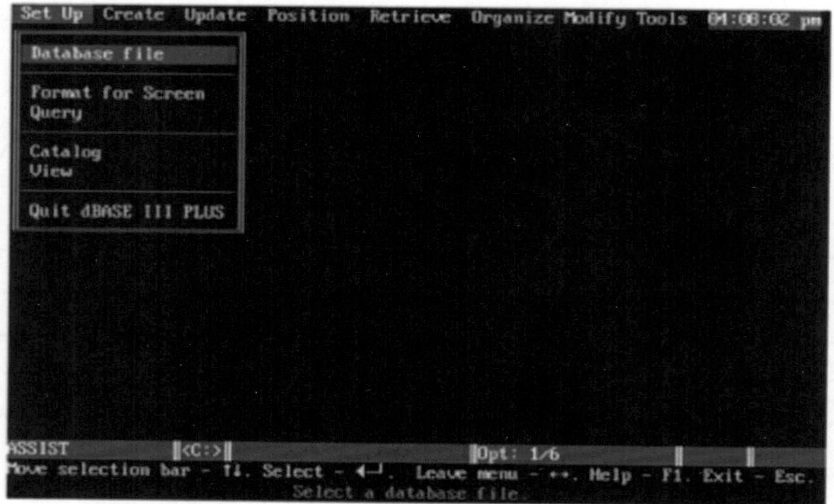

Figure 0.1: dBase II on the IBM PC

The dBase program was very popular with PC users during the 1980s, and new upgraded versions, dBase III and dBase IV, were introduced. When Microsoft launched the first version of Access in 1992, it quickly became the database of choice for PC users.

ADVANTAGES OF COMPUTERISED DATABASES

Computerised databases offer great flexibility in the way you view data and also allow you to find specific data in a matter of seconds. Data can also be sorted into different orders (in ascending or descending alphabetical order or in ascending or descending numerical order).

The main differences between a database recorded on paper and a computerised database are summarised in Table 0.2.

	Database Recorded on Paper	Computerised Database
Data in a structured format	✔	✔
Data in a particular order	✔	✔
Find specific data quickly	✘	✔
View data in different orders	✘	✔
Quickly perform calculations on groups of data	✘	✔

Table 0.2

From Table 0.2, it can be seen that computerised databases offer greater flexibility than databases stored on paper.

This book introduces the learner to computerised databases using Microsoft Access. The learner will be guided through a series of graded assignments. Each assignment introduces new concepts and tasks while building on concepts and tasks learned in previous assignments. For the remainder of the book, the term 'database' will be used when referring to a computerised database.

WHAT A DATABASE CAN DO FOR YOU

If, in the course of your work, you need to keep track of large amounts of data and that data is constantly changing or being updated, then a database will save time and reduce errors. For example, a school principal could use a database to store information about students and subjects. This database could produce reports on students currently in the college and the subjects they are studying. This information can be used by the school principal when making decisions such as how many teachers should be employed, how many classrooms are needed and how many exam scripts are required for each subject.

Mail Merge is an important feature of Access. It is used by direct mail and marketing companies to create customised letters for customers stored in a database. The letters are sent to customers to promote products and services offered by a company. Many companies now communicate with their customers by linking their customer database with an email application. This is much cheaper than using surface mail.

Companies such as the National Car Testing Service (NCTS) would find it very difficult to keep track of all the data they need to process without the help of a database. Using a database, NCTS can determine which vehicles are due to be tested in the next month. The database generates customised test notifications that inform each vehicle owner of their forthcoming test.

With the growth of e-commerce, where products and services are sold via the Internet, databases are becoming more and more important. All e-commerce sites, such as iTunes and Amazon, rely on powerful databases to store details of their products and orders made by customers. Without databases, these companies would not be able to function efficiently.

In the course of business, people make decisions. The quality of the decision depends on the information on which the decision is based. Business decisions based on accurate database Reports, which are available at the click of a button, will be better decisions.

An important point to note is that the database is only as good as the information it stores. If you don't update the database by entering new data as it occurs, the Reports produced by the database will be inaccurate.

STRUCTURE OF A DATABASE

A database consists of objects. There are four main object types that can be used in an Access database: Tables, Queries, Forms and Reports. Access displays a list of the objects in your database in the Navigation Pane (Figure 0.2). Each object carries out a different function within the database and should be given a unique name. The database itself must also have a name. At the very least, a database must have a Table so that it can store data. The number of objects in a database depends on the complexity of the database. More complex databases will have more objects.

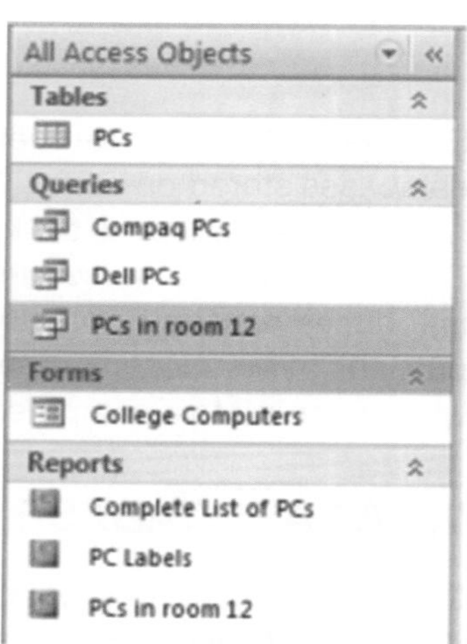

Figure 0.2: The Navigation Pane

CREATING A DATABASE

Before you can create objects such as Tables and Forms, you must create a database to store the objects. The database is like a container. Initially it is empty, but as you work through the assignments you will add Tables, Forms, Queries and Reports to each database you create. It is important to note that you must name your database before you start adding objects to it.

The way in which a database is named differs from other popular applications such as word processing and spreadsheets. You can create a new word processing document and start working on it before you save it. You may have two or three pages of typed text before you click the *Save* button.

Access, on the other hand, will not allow you to work with your database unless you give it a name. If you forget to name your database, Access names it for you! (Normally Access will assign the name **Database1.accdb** to your database.)

N Access uses the *.accdb* file extension, which is an abbreviation of *Access database*. Earlier versions of Access used the *.mdb* file extension.

Database Example

I will use an example of a tennis club database to explain each of the four objects in an Access database. To keep things simple, the club has only six members. Figure 0.3 shows the Navigation Pane, which lists the objects in the database. Data relating to the tennis club is stored in the *Club Members* Table.

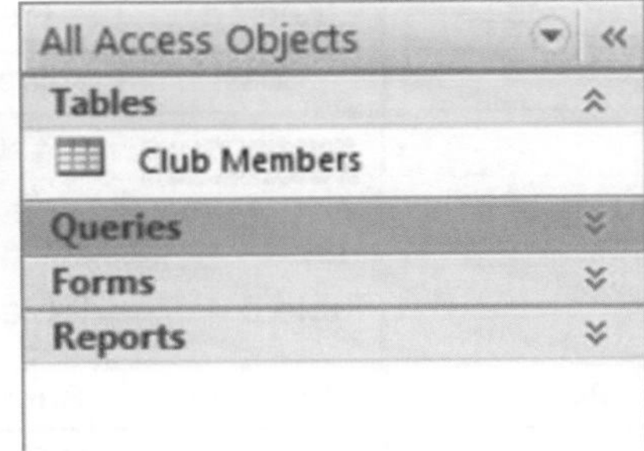

Figure 0.3: Tennis club database

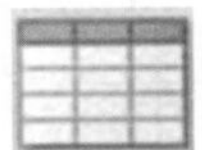

TABLES

The Table is the most important object in the database. The function of the Table is to store data. Data stored in the Table must be broken down into smaller pieces of data, called fields. This is shown in Table 0.3.

Data stored in the Table is divided into columns, which in database terminology are called fields. The field names are in the top row of the Table.

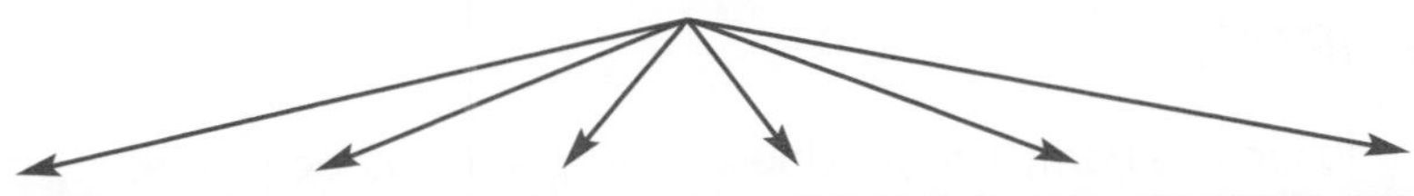

Member No	Firstname	Surname	Gender	Phone	Date of Birth
1	Paul	Moore	Male	2036558	20/06/1982
2	Deirdre	O Connell	Female	5440291	15/10/1988
3	Konrad	Frejek	Male	8795412	03/01/1987
4	Ross	Mooney	Male	4590298	28/02/1986
5	Cathy	Duffy	Female	8701593	21/08/1985
6	Geraldine	Abbey	Female	3390217	12/12/1989

All the information relating to one club member is called a record

Table 0.3

QUERIES

A Query allows us to find specific records in the Table. For example, a Query could find all records of female club members, as shown in Table 0.4 and Table 0.5.

Member No	Firstname	Surname	Gender	Phone	Date of Birth
1	Paul	Moore	Male	2036558	20/06/1982
2	Deirdre	O Connell	Female	5440291	15/10/1988
3	Konrad	Frejek	Male	8795412	03/01/1987
4	Ross	Mooney	Male	4590298	28/02/1986
5	Cathy	Duffy	Female	8701593	21/08/1985
6	Geraldine	Abbey	Female	3390217	12/12/1989

Table 0.4: The Table stores records of all club members

Member No	Firstname	Surname	Gender	Phone	Date of Birth
2	Deirdre	O Connell	Female	5440291	15/10/1988
5	Cathy	Duffy	Female	8701593	21/08/1985
6	Geraldine	Abbey	Female	3390217	12/12/1989

Table 0.5: The Query displays only female club members

In the example, the Query has searched through the Table, record by record. Each time it finds a female club member, that record is extracted from the Table and displayed in a separate list. The completed Query displays three female club members.

FORMS

The main function of a Form is to provide a convenient method of entering data into the Table. A Form can also be used to edit or add to data already stored in the Table. The Form is linked to the Table. When you enter data in the Form, it filters down into the Table.

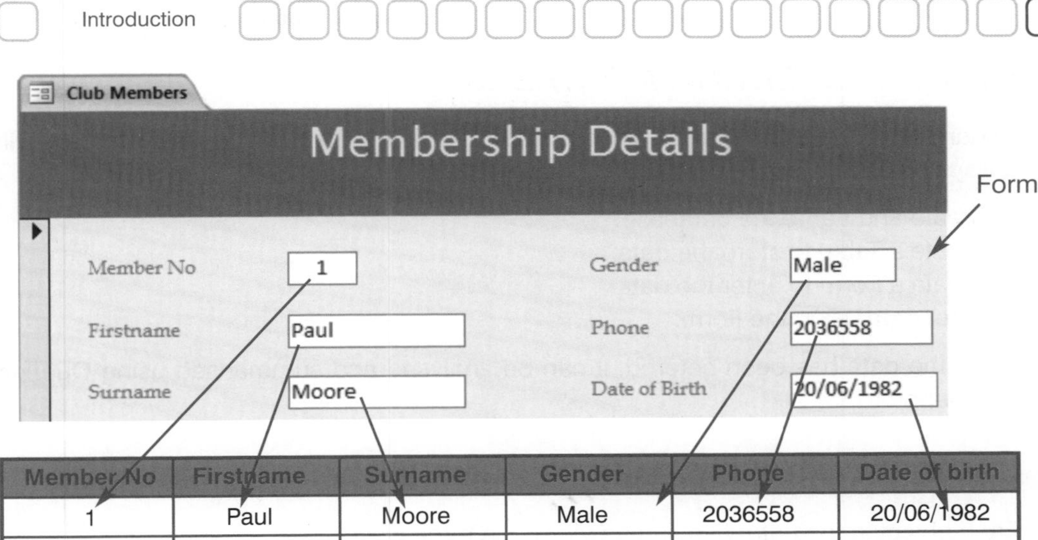

Member No	Firstname	Surname	Gender	Phone	Date of birth
1	Paul	Moore	Male	2036558	20/06/1982

Figure 0.4: Data is transferred from the Form to the Table

In Figure 0.4, Paul Moore's record has been entered in the Form. Because the Form is linked to the Table, Paul's record filters down to and is stored in the Table. The arrows indicate how data is transferred from the Form to the Table. The function of the Form is to facilitate data entry. The function of the Table is to store data.

REPORTS

People in business base their decisions on data they receive while they are at work. This data can come from lots of different sources, such as business transactions, news reports and colleagues. Many business decisions are based on data retrieved from databases. The reporting facility in Access provides a means of presenting data so that it can be easily interpreted by the decision maker. In an Access Report, data can be summarised, formatted and presented in a way that makes it easy to understand. In the tennis club database, we could use a Report to create a member contact list, as shown in Figure 0.5.

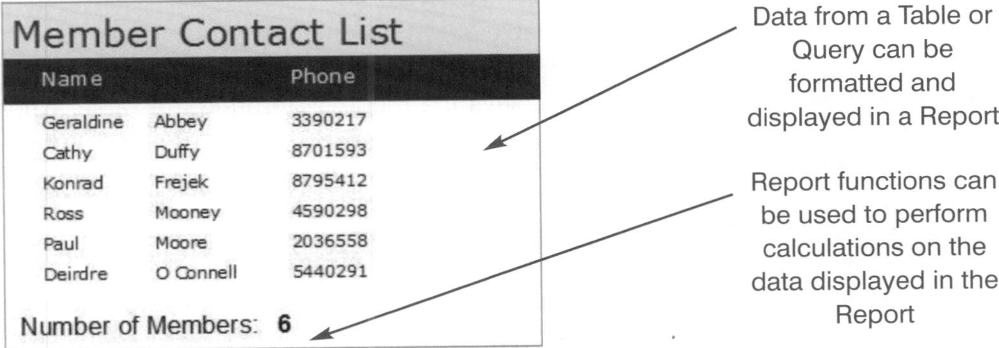

Member Contact List

Name		Phone
Geraldine	Abbey	3390217
Cathy	Duffy	8701593
Konrad	Frejek	8795412
Ross	Mooney	4590298
Paul	Moore	2036558
Deirdre	O Connell	5440291

Number of Members: 6

Data from a Table or Query can be formatted and displayed in a Report
Report functions can be used to perform calculations on the data displayed in the Report

Figure 0.5: An Access Report

STEPS IN CREATING A DATABASE

Regardless of how complex a particular database assignment is, the first four steps will always be as follows:

1. Create and name the database.
2. Create a Table to store the data.
3. Create a Form to enter the data.
4. Enter data using the Form.

Once the data has been entered, it can be analysed and summarised using Queries and Reports.

USING DATABASE OBJECTS

Each object in the database can be viewed in three ways.

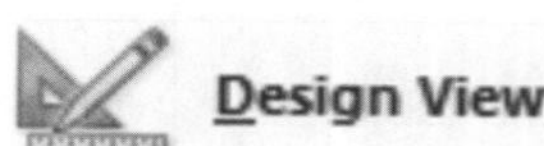

1. First, you can look at how an object is designed. Use this option if you want to change the format or layout of a Table, Form, Query or Report. Design view is generally used when you first create an object. When you are in design view, you will only see the structure of the object. You cannot view or enter data in design view.

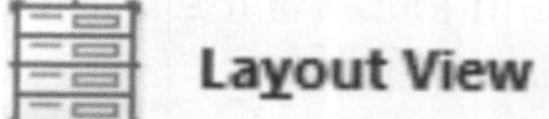

2. Layout view only applies to Forms and Reports. This view allows you to change the design of an object while viewing the data in the object. For example, you could adjust the column widths in a Report while viewing the data displayed in the Report. Layout view is useful for fine tuning the design of a Form or Report.

3. Finally, once an object has been designed and fine tuned, you will want to use the object. Each object has its own specific view (Table 0.6).

Table	Query	Form	Report
Datasheet View	Datasheet View	Form View	Report View

Table 0.6

Opening a Table in datasheet view displays the records stored in the Table. Query datasheet view displays the records found by the Query. Opening a Form in Form view allows you to enter and edit data. Report view displays the data contained in a Report.

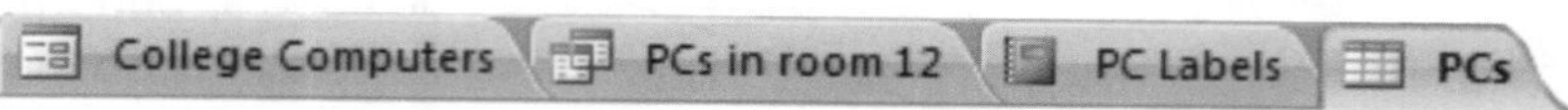

Figure 0.6: Tabbed objects in Access

The name of each object that is currently open is displayed in a separate tab. In Figure 0.6, the *College Computers* Form, *PCs in room 12* Query, *PC Labels* Report and *PCs* Table are open. You can quickly switch between objects by clicking the tabs. Access uses different icons to represent Tables, Queries, Forms and Reports. These icons, which are displayed in each of the tabs in Figure 0.6, are explained in Table 0.7.

Icons Used in Access			
Table	Query	Form	Report

Table 0.7: Icons used to represent Tables, Queries, Forms and Reports

ACCESS WIZARDS

Each time you create a new object in Access, you have the option of either:

1. Getting help from a wizard.
2. Doing all the work yourself by creating the object in design view.

Most of the wizards in Access are very good and can save you a lot of time by doing the basic set-up of an object for you, giving you more time to work on the finer details. However, some of the wizards are a little confusing, particularly for new database users. As you work through the assignments in this book, you will learn how to create Tables, Queries, Forms and Reports. Each time you are required to create an object, I will recommend whether you should get help from a wizard or create the object in design view.

THE NAVIGATION PANE

The Navigation Pane, which appears on the left of the screen, allows you to access and manage the objects in your database. The Navigation Pane has a separate section for Tables, Queries, Forms and Reports, as seen in Figure 0.7. Each section can be expanded to display a list of objects by clicking the double down arrow.

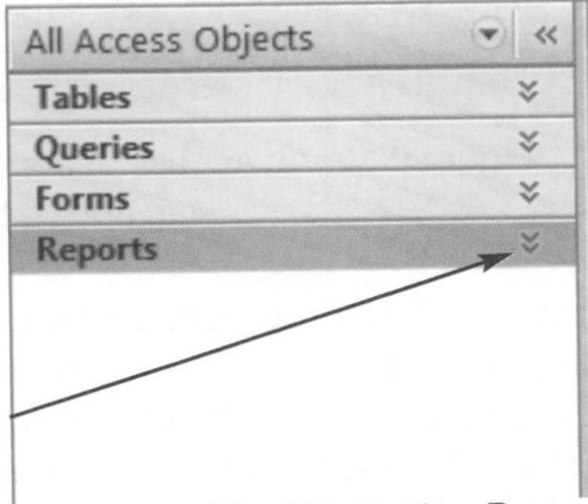

Figure 0.7: The Navigation Pane

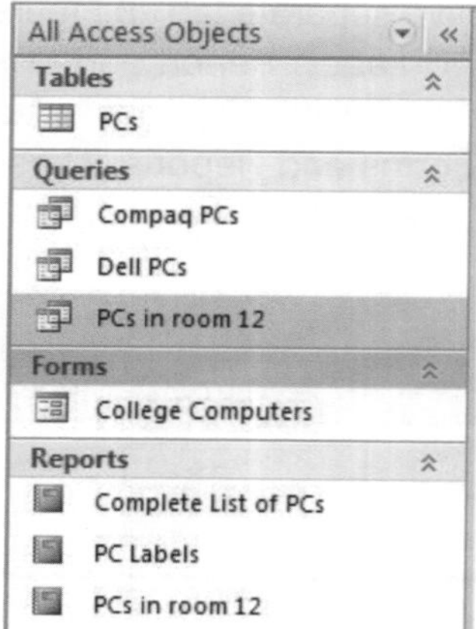

Figure 0.8

Figure 0.8 is an example of the Navigation Pane displaying all Access objects. The Navigation Pane can be hidden by clicking the << symbol displayed at the top right-hand side of the Navigation Pane. This makes the full screen available for your database.

THE RIBBON

In Access 2007, the menus and toolbars were replaced by the Ribbon, which helps you quickly find the commands that you need to complete a task.

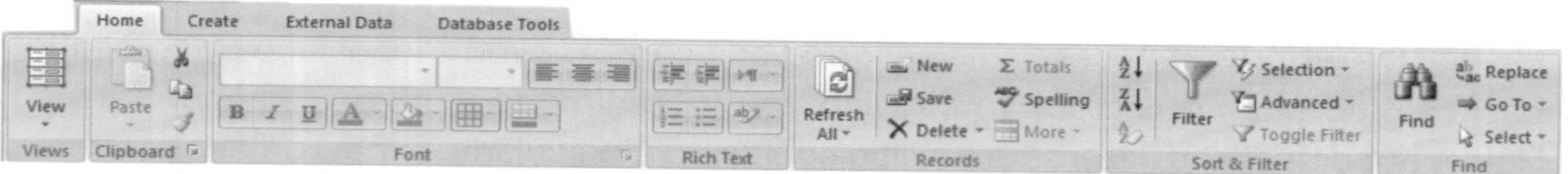

Figure 0.9: In Access 2007, commands in the Ribbon are organised into four basic groups

In Access 2010, Microsoft updated the Ribbon to include the File tab (Figure 0.10).

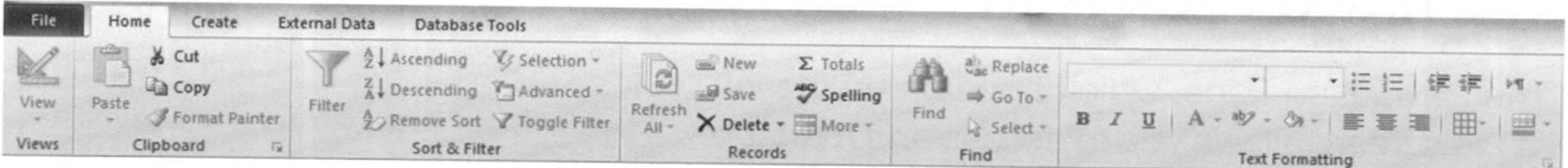

Figure 0.10: As Access users were confused by the Office button, the File tab was added to the Ribbon in Access 2010

Using the Ribbon is very intuitive. Commands in the Ribbon are organised into four basic groups: Home, Create, External Data and Database Tools (Figure 0.9 and Figure 0.10). As objects in the database are opened, additional groups of commands are displayed in the Ribbon. For example, when you open a Table, the Datasheet group is added to the four existing groups in the Ribbon. Groups are also added to the Ribbon as you change the way you view an object.

Figure 0.11: The Ribbon when an Access Form is opened in design view

In Figure 0.11, three additional groups appear in the Ribbon when you open a Form in design view. The additional Design, Arrange and Format groups contain commands to help you design and format your Access Form.

A specific group of commands in the Ribbon can be selected by clicking the appropriate tab. Each group in the Ribbon is divided into sections of related buttons. Figure 0.10 displays the commands in the Home section of the Ribbon, which is displayed by default. It contains the Views, Clipboard, Sort & Filter, Records, Find and Text Formatting sections. Commands in the Home section of the Ribbon can be used for formatting, copying and pasting, finding and editing records as well as sorting records in your database.

If you like using shortcut key combinations, you can access Ribbon commands by pressing *ALT* on the keyboard. Once you press *ALT*, letters representing each Ribbon group are displayed together with the letter F, which represents the Office button (Access 2007) or File tab (Access 2010). This is displayed in Figure 0.12 and Figure 0.13. The buttons in the Quick Access Toolbar are represented by numbers.

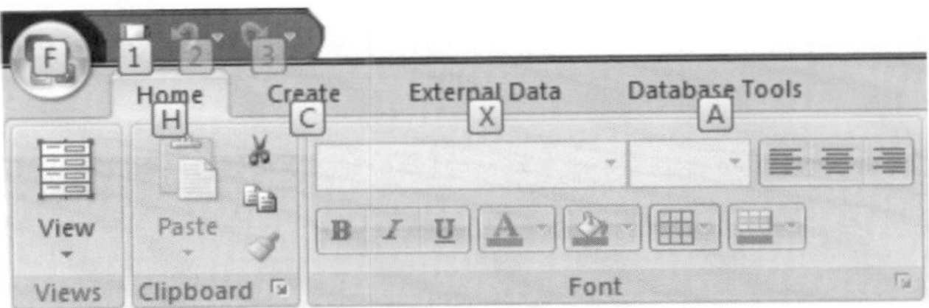

Figure 0.12: Keyboard shortcuts in Access 2007

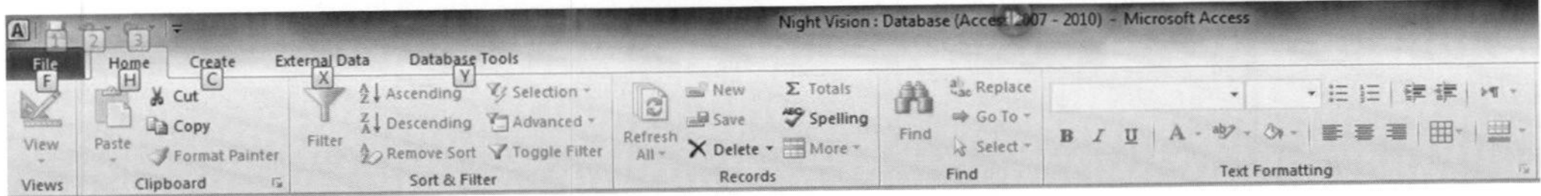

Figure 0.13: Keyboard shortcuts in Access 2010

Shortcut key combinations for the commands in a specific Ribbon group can be displayed by typing the appropriate letter on the keyboard. For example, pressing *H* displays the shortcut key combinations for the Home group, as shown in Figure 0.14.

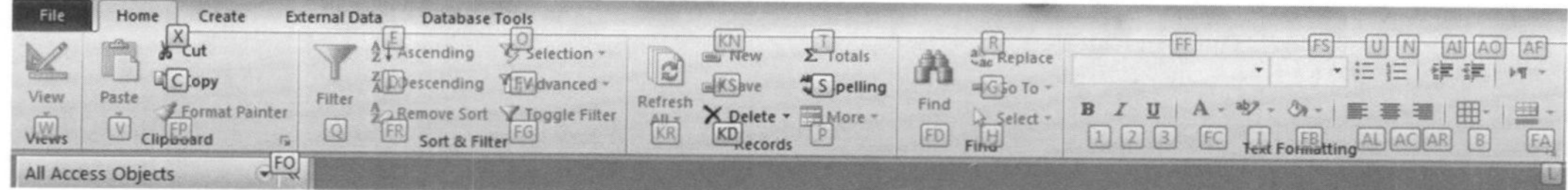

Figure 0.14: Shortcut key combinations in the Home group

In Figure 0.14, the keyboard shortcuts for the Home group of commands are displayed. Each keyboard shortcut can be used to access a specific command or button. For example, typing *1* will format the selected item to bold. The complete sequence of commands is *ALT+H+1*. If you use these keyboard combinations frequently, they can speed up many tasks.

Commands that are available in the Ribbon will depend on the view you are in and the task you are completing. Keyboard shortcuts for commands that are currently unavailable will appear dimmed. For example, in Figure 0.14, paste is currently unavailable. The associated shortcut key, *V*, is dimmed.

THE OFFICE BUTTON AND FILE TAB

In Access 2007 the File menu was replaced by the Office button. Commands to create or open database files do not appear in the Ribbon and are instead accessed by clicking the Office button, as shown in Figure 0.15.

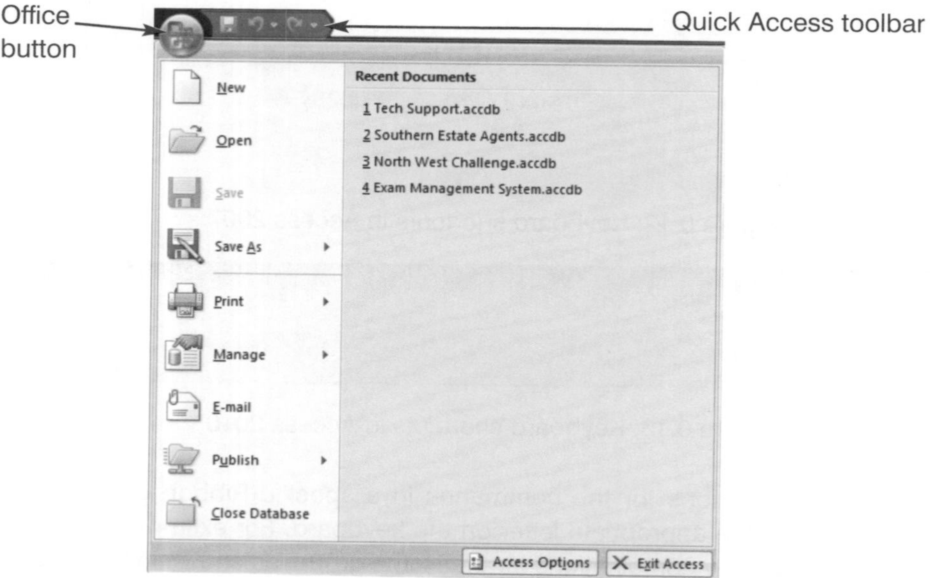

Figure 0.15: In Access 2007, common commands and recently used databases are accessed by clicking the Office button

The Recent Documents panel can be used to quickly open the databases you have recently been working on.

The Office button caused confusion amongst computer users who were accustomed to managing their documents via the File command. The confusion was so great that in Access 2010, Microsoft replaced the Office button with the File tab. Clicking the File tab displays the options shown in Figure 0.16.

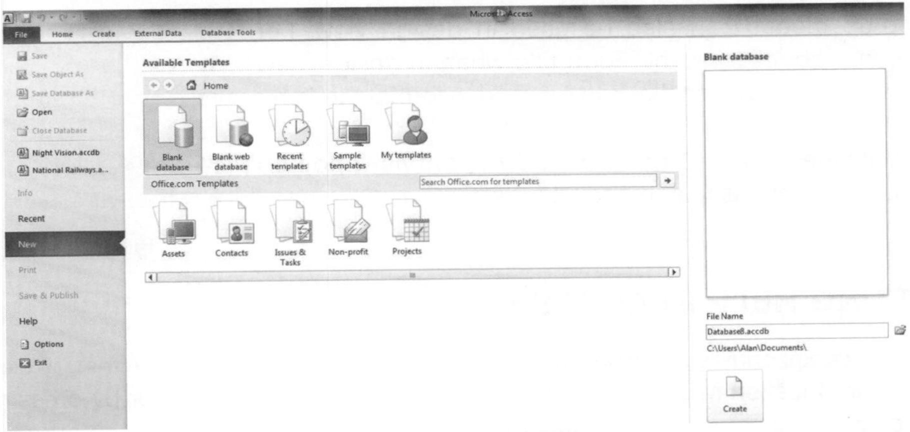

Figure 0.16: In Access 2010, file management tasks are grouped under the File tab

QUICK ACCESS TOOLBAR

The Quick Access Toolbar (Figure 0.17) contains frequently used commands. It appears to the right of the Office button and is used to quickly access buttons for common tasks, such as opening an existing database or creating a new database. The *Undo* and *Redo* buttons also appear in the Quick Access Toolbar.

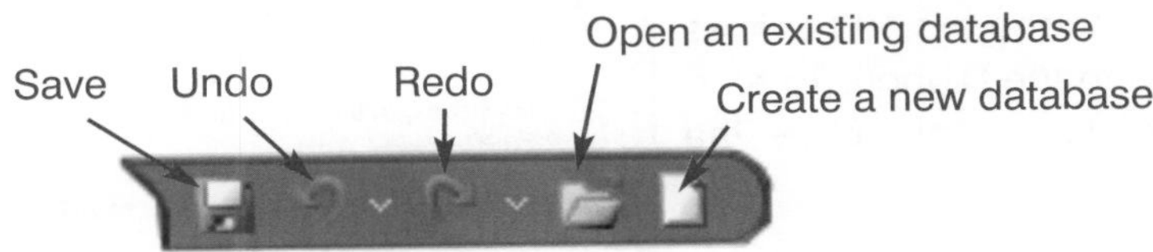

Figure 0.17: The Quick Access Toolbar

Because the Quick Access Toolbar is always visible, adding buttons that you frequently use to this toolbar makes the buttons readily available.

POP-UP MENUS

Pressing the right mouse button will display a pop-up menu in Access. Different pop-up menus will appear depending on where the mouse pointer is on the screen. Right clicking on an object name in the Navigation Pane displays the menu shown in Figure 0.18.

Using the options displayed in Figure 0.18, you can open the object or view it in design or layout view. You could also rename, delete, cut, copy, hide or export the object to another database as well as viewing the properties of the object.

Pop-up menus can also be used in design view. For example, right clicking the Form title when in design view displays a list of options that can be used to format the Form title.

In datasheet view, Form view and Report view, pop-up menus have options to sort and filter data.

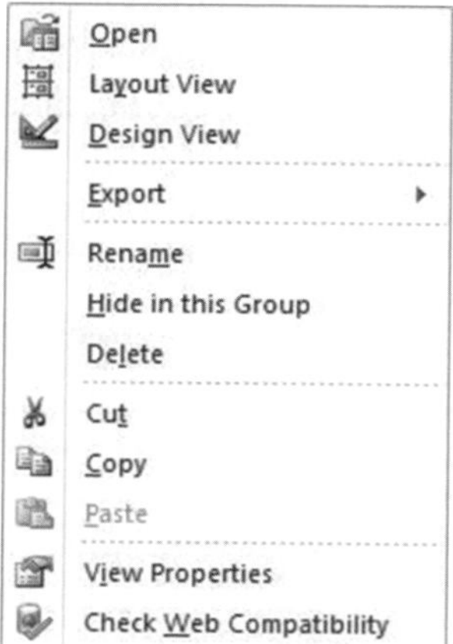

Figure 0.18

GETTING HELP IN ACCESS

Access contains a powerful help feature that can be accessed either by clicking the question mark in the top right-hand corner of the screen or by pressing *F1* on the keyboard.

To search for help on a particular aspect of Access, type your search term into the search box and then click the *Search* button. Figure 0.19 is an example of using the help feature to find information on the Ribbon.

In Figure 0.19, Access is displaying the top 100 articles related to the Ribbon. To read an article, simply click the article title.

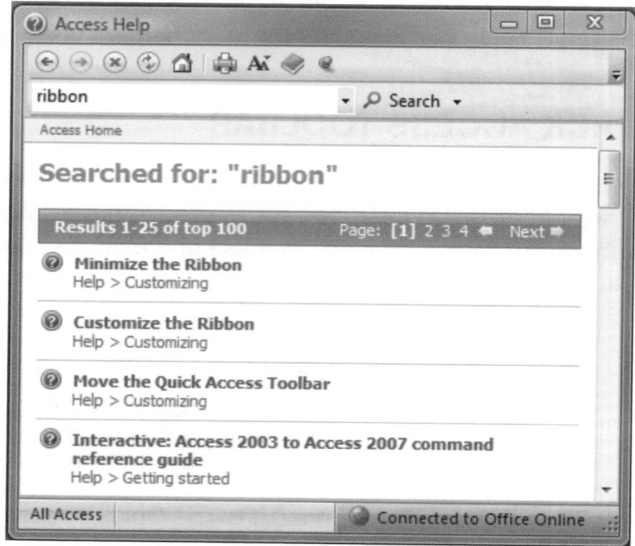

Figure 0.19: An example of searching for help on the Ribbon

ACCESS SECURITY WARNINGS

Each time you open an Access database, you will see a security warning (Figure 0.20).

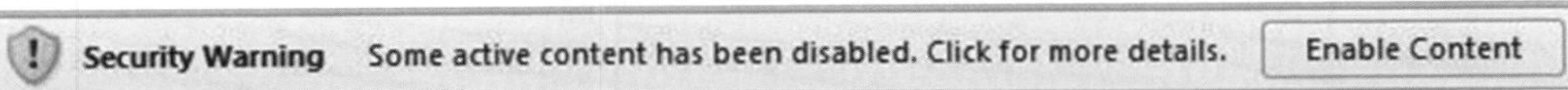

Figure 0.20: Security warning upon opening an Access database

The following items in an Access database can pose security risks:

1. Action queries: A Query which finds and updates records.
2. Macros: A computer program generated by Access.
3. VBA code: A computer program written by a database programmer.

This book does not deal with VBA code. However, action queries and macros are introduced in Section 4 of the book. When working through the assignments in Sections 1, 2 and 3 it is perfectly safe to ignore the security warnings as long as you are opening a database assignment that you created yourself. The best way to do this is to click the *X* that appears to the right of the warning (Figure 0.20).

LIMITS OF ACCESS

Access is a great database application designed to work on PCs, laptops and tablets and on network servers. It works really well for standard record-keeping and reporting in an office. In general, Access functions efficiently as long as the database is smaller than 2 gigabytes. (You'd need a huge amount of records for the database to get this big!) However, for database applications that need to store digital content (e.g. photos, videos, music) or keep track of huge volumes of orders on a commercial website, Access may not be the best choice. More powerful databases, such as Oracle, are generally used for these types of business applications.

ACCESS VS. EXCEL

Many students find it difficult to understand the difference between a database and a spreadsheet. Databases are great for storing large amounts of data and then retrieving that data very quickly. Spreadsheets are all about numbers and calculations. To use an analogy, a database is a bit like a computerised telephone directory and a spreadsheet is like a computerised pocket calculator.

HOW IT ALL WORKS TOGETHER

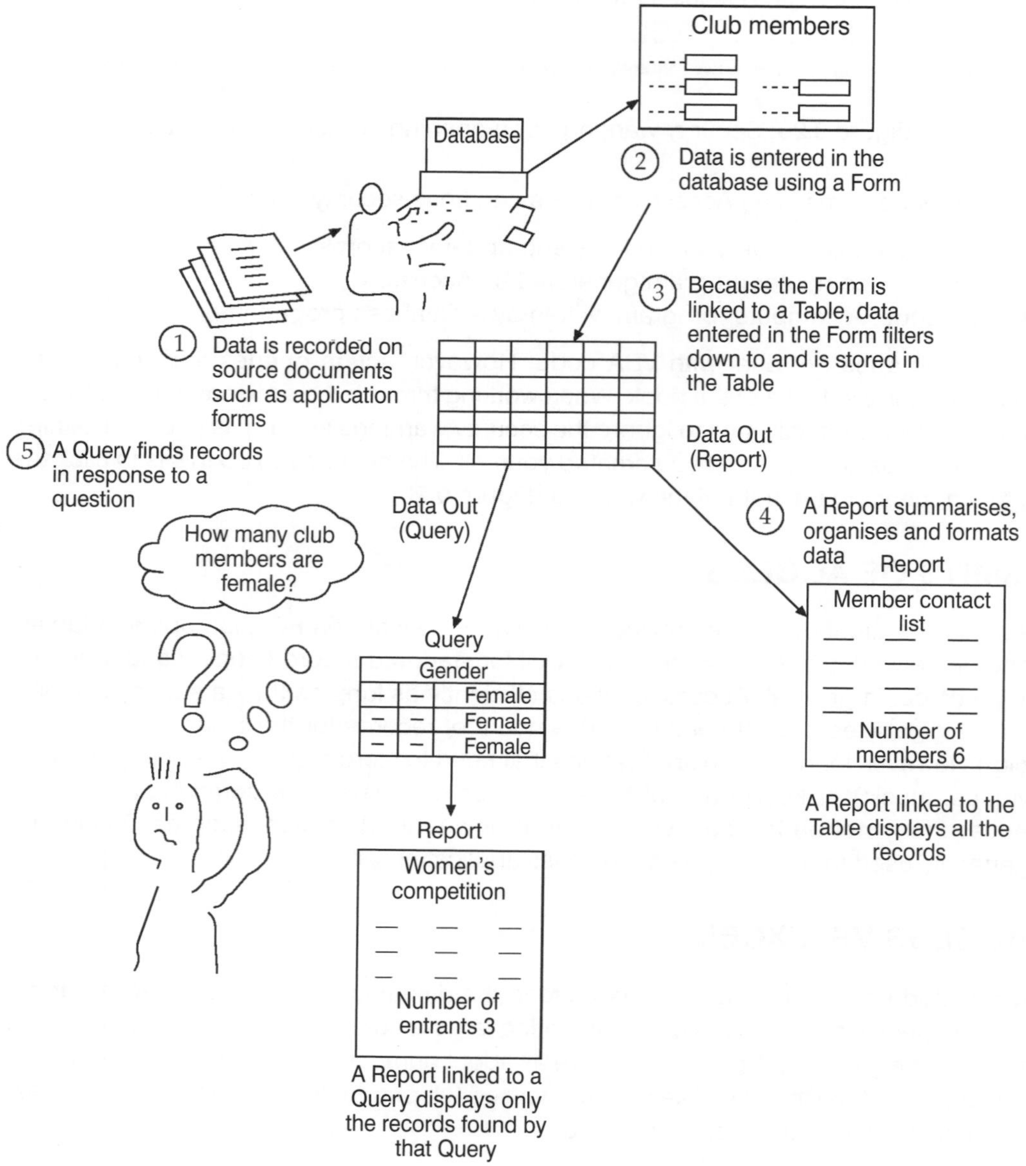

Club members

Database

(2) Data is entered in the database using a Form

(1) Data is recorded on source documents such as application forms

(3) Because the Form is linked to a Table, data entered in the Form filters down to and is stored in the Table

Data Out (Report)

(5) A Query finds records in response to a question

How many club members are female?

Data Out (Query)

(4) A Report summarises, organises and formats data

Report

Member contact list

Number of members 6

A Report linked to the Table displays all the records

Query

		Gender
–	–	Female
–	–	Female
–	–	Female

Report

Women's competition

Number of entrants 3

A Report linked to a Query displays only the records found by that Query

SECTION 1

Beginners Database Assignments

Assignment 1: College of E-Commerce Database

Assignment 2: Pizza Perfection Database

Assignment 3: Riverside Rugby Club Database

Assignment 4: Distance Learning Database

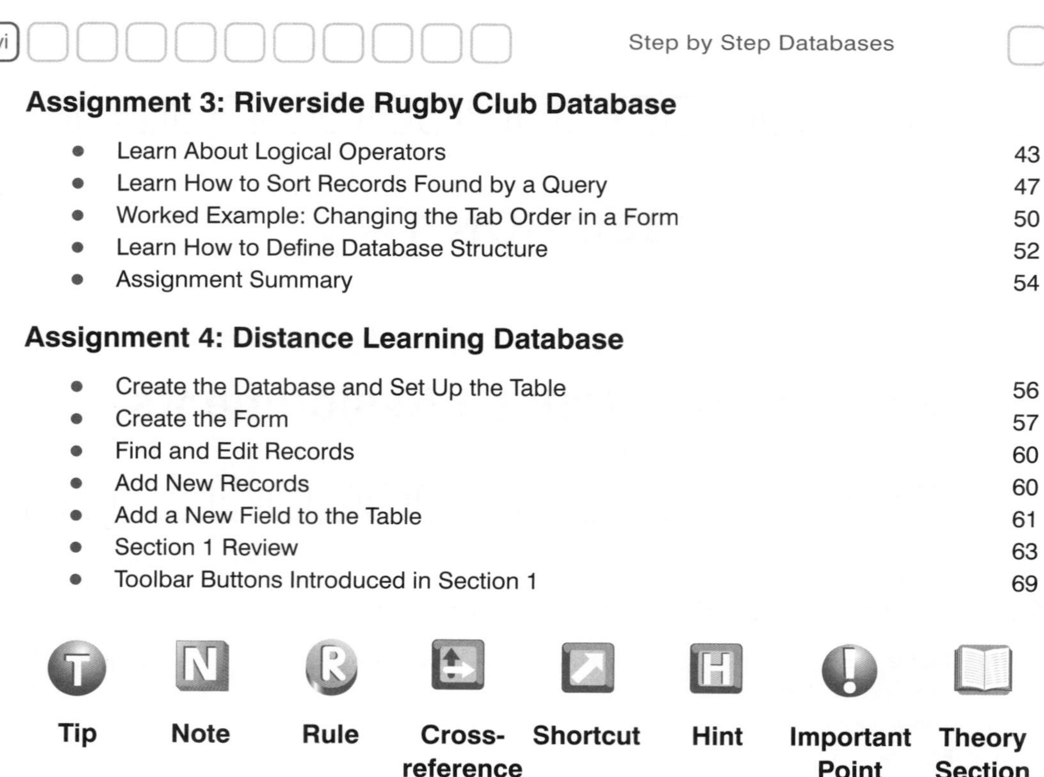

1 College of E-Commerce Database

SCENARIO

The College of E-Commerce runs night classes in a number of different subjects ranging from Administration to Web Design. In Assignment 1 you will create a database to store and update data relating to students currently attending the college.

By completing this assignment, you will learn how to:

- Create a database.
- Create a Table to store data.
- Create a Form to enter data.
- Enter data using a Form.
- Make basic changes to Form design.
- Use a Form to find, edit and delete records.

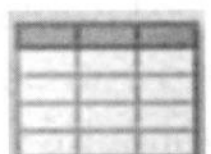

TABLES

The Table is the most important object in a database. Its task is to store data. A database cannot function without a Table. The Table is divided into columns and rows. The columns are called *fields* and the rows are called *records*. All records in the Table must have the same number of fields. A record is a collection of data about a single item. In Table 1.1, each record stores data about an individual student. Table 1.1 displays the data that you will enter in the College of E-Commerce database later on in this assignment.

All the information relating to one student is called a **record**

Student Code	Student Name	Age	Course	Date Started	Teacher
BS001	Peter Dunne	18	Admin	02/09/2014	Tadhg Allen
BS002	Mark Connolly	17	Admin	02/09/2014	Tadhg Allen
BS003	Dave O Neill	21	Finance	02/09/2014	Gerry Browne
BS004	Maura Keegan	18	Finance	02/09/2014	Gerry Browne
BS005	Ann Murphy	20	Admin	02/09/2014	Tadhg Allen
CP001	Enda Doyle	19	Web Design	09/09/2014	Noelle Duffy
CP002	Seamus Lowry	18	Database	09/09/2014	Liam Kearney
CP003	Tetyna Maryshko	18	Database	09/09/2014	Liam Kearney
CP004	Christine O Donnell	20	Web Design	09/09/2014	Noelle Duffy
CP005	Martin Murray	19	Database	09/09/2014	Liam Kearney

The data is divided into six columns, each of which is called a **field**

Table 1.1

Tables are the most important part of any database. The Table stores data. Before data can be stored in a Table, it must be organised so that each record has the same structure. In Table 1.1 the data has been divided into six columns, which are called fields.

CREATING A TABLE

The top row of the Table contains the field names: Student Code, Student Name, Age, Course, Date Started and Teacher. Rows of records appear below the field names. All the data relating to a specific student is called a record.

The fields define the structure of the Table. Before we can enter data in the database, each field must be set up in the Table. When setting up a field, you must name the field and specify what type of data you intend to store in that field. Field names and data types for the *Student Details* Table are displayed in Table 1.2.

Field Name	Data Type
Student Code	Text
Student Name	Text
Age	Number
Course	Text
Date Started	Date/Time
Teacher	Text

Table 1.2

Selecting a Data Type

Table 1.2 contains three different data types: Text, Number and Date/Time.

1. Text Data Type

The Text data type is used to store letters and combinations of letters and numbers. Common examples would be a person's name and car registration number. Phone numbers including area codes, e.g. (021) 6689017, are also stored in Text fields. This is because brackets cannot be entered in Number fields. Numbers with leading zeros, e.g. 00200102, will also need to be stored in Text fields, as Access removes the leading zeros when they are entered in a Number field.

2. Number Data Type

The Number data type is used to store numbers. In later assignments, you will learn about the Byte, Integer, Long Integer and Single Number types. It is important to note that Access will not allow you to enter letters or symbols in a field with a Number data type.

3. Date/Time Data Type

The Date/Time data type is used to store dates and times. When entering dates, the days, months and years are separated using the forward slash (/). When entering times, hours, minutes and seconds are separated using the colon (:).

You will learn more about data types in later assignments.

PRIMARY KEY

Each time you create a new Table, Access automatically sets up a primary key field. A primary key field differs from other fields in the Table in a number of important ways.

1. Once a field has been identified as the primary key field, Access will not allow you to duplicate data in that field. For example, if the *Order Number* field is the primary key field, each unique order number can only be entered once. If you attempt to enter an order number that is already stored in the Table, Access will display an error message.

2. While the fields define the structure of each record in the Table, the primary key determines the order of records in the Table. Records in the Table are automatically stored in ascending order of the primary key field, even if they are not entered in this order.

Access will not allow you to complete data entry of a record unless you have entered data in the primary key field. The primary key allows Access to uniquely identify each record. This is particularly important in large databases. For example, in a customer database, the primary key allows Access to distinguish between two customers who have the same first name and surname. Sometimes the primary key will occur naturally in the data. For example, in a database that stores details of cars for sale, the obvious candidate for the primary key field is the car registration number. This is because each car has its own unique registration number. In many databases, the database designer has to make up the primary key to ensure that each record can be uniquely identified. For example, your bank account number is a primary key generated by the bank's database. It ensures that each customer's bank account has a unique identification code. This is particularly important in cases where some customers have the same name. Other common examples of primary keys are PPS numbers, club membership numbers, credit card numbers, medical card numbers and order numbers.

FORMS

The Form is an important object in the database. Its main function is data entry. As data is entered in the Form, Access transfers it to the Table record by record. An example of this is shown in Figure 1.1.

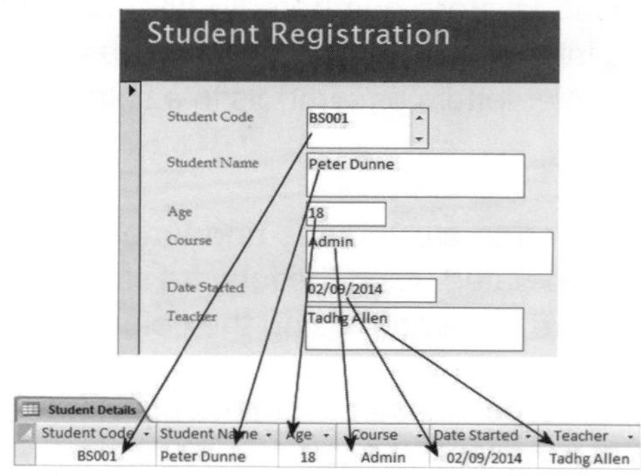

Figure 1.1:
Each record entered in the Form is automatically transferred to the Table

In Figure 1.1, Peter Dunne's record has been entered in the Form. As the Form is linked to the *Student Details* Table, Access automatically transfers this data from the Form and stores it in the *Student Details* Table.

Data is transferred from the Form to the Table record by record and not field by field. This means that the record that you are currently entering in the Form is not actually transferred to the Table until you move on to the next record, either by pressing the *Tab* or *Enter* key on the keyboard or by clicking the *Next Record* button in the Form.

An Access Form may be thought of as a digital version of a paper form such as a job application form. Forms make the task of data entry easier, quicker and more accurate for a number of reasons:

- Rather than typing data, it can often be selected from a list, e.g. selecting the flight destination from a drop-down list when booking a flight on the Internet.
- Forms can be made attractive and easier to use through the use of formatting.
- Titles, images and explanatory text can be added to a Form.

As well as entering data, Forms can also be used to edit records that are stored in the Table. Later on in this assignment you will use a Form to edit and delete records.

Students new to databases often enter data directly in the Table. It is more efficient to use the Form for data entry, as it was specifically set up for this purpose.

STRUCTURE OF A FORM

Forms created using the Form Wizard have two sections: the Form header and detail section.

1. The Form Header

Figure 1.2

The Form header (Figure 1.2) normally contains the Form title. Other items, such as company logos and graphics, can also be added to the Form header.

2. The Detail Section

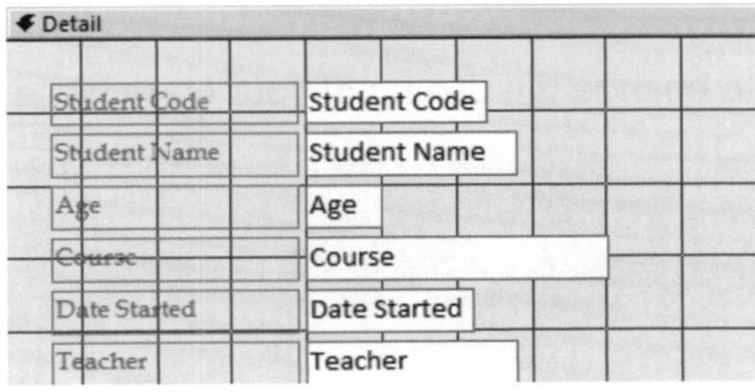

Figure 1.3

The detail section (Figure 1.3) is the main section of the Form. It normally contains all the fields that are included in the Form. The detail section is used for data entry and is the most important section of the Form.

A third section, called the Form footer, can also be added to the Form. The Form footer appears at the bottom of the Form and can be used to display summary information. It could also be used to display the date or time.

VIEWING AN ACCESS FORM

There are three ways to view an Access Form: Form view, design view and layout view.

1. Form View

Use this view to enter new records and edit existing records.

Figure 1.4 displays the *Student Registration* Form in Form view. Data relating to Peter Dunne has been entered using the Form.

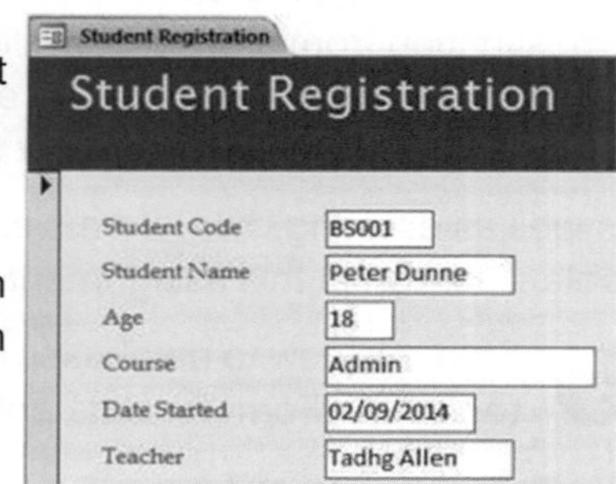

Figure 1.4

2. Design View

Use this view to change the design, layout and formatting of your Form.

Figure 1.5 displays the *Student Registration* Form in design view. Field names appear instead of data when you are in design view. For example, Student Code is displayed instead of BS001 and Student Name is displayed instead of Peter Dunne.

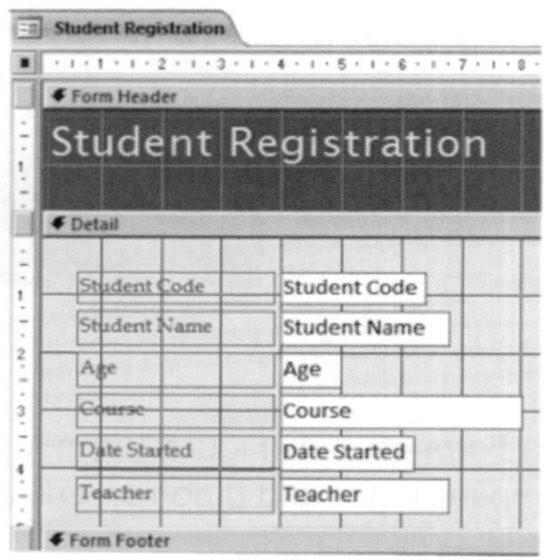

Figure 1.5

3. Layout View

Use this view to change the design of your Form while viewing the data.

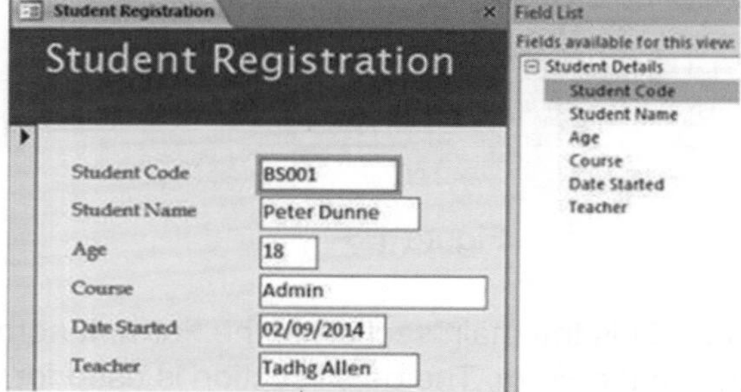

Figure 1.6

Figure 1.6 displays the *Student Registration* Form in layout view. Layout view is a combination of Form view and design view. In layout view, you can make changes to the design of the Form while viewing the data. However, in layout view you cannot see the detailed structure of the Form, which is displayed in design view. Although you can see existing data in layout view, you cannot enter new data.

STRUCTURE OF AN ACCESS FORM

An Access Form has two main sections: the Form header and the detail section (Figure 1.7).

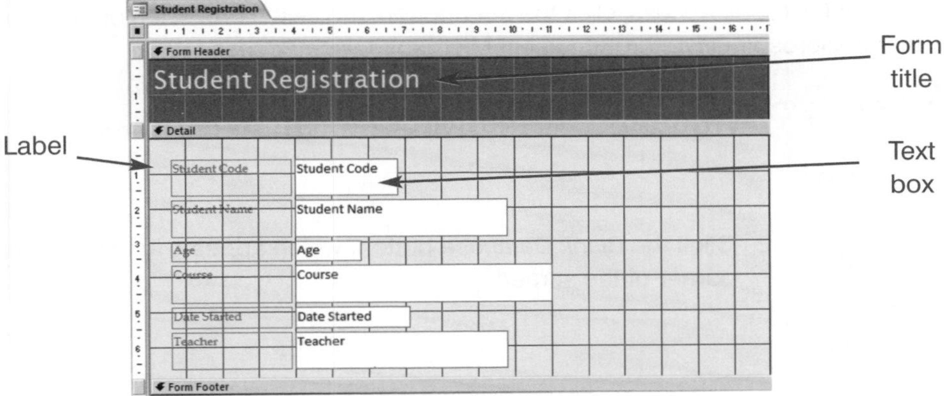

Figure 1.7:
Design view of the *Student Registration* Form, created later on in this assignment

Figure 1.7 displays the *Student Registration* Form in design view. You will create this Form later on in this assignment. The Form title is displayed in the Form header. The detail section displays a series of labels and text boxes. Each label/text box combination represents a specific field in the Table.

N Before starting this assignment, ensure that Access is set up to display Tables, Forms, Queries and Reports as tabbed documents.

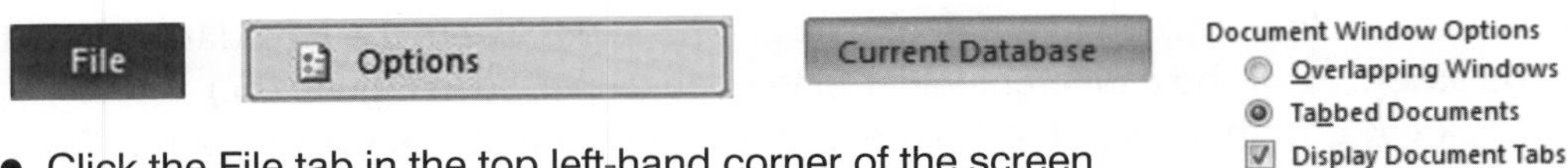

- Click the File tab in the top left-hand corner of the screen.
- Select Options.
- Select Current Database from the list of options.
- In Document Window Options, select Tabbed Documents.

N If you are using Access 2007, click the Office button, select Access Options and then select Current Database from the Access Options list. In Document Window Options, select Tabbed Documents and tick the Display Document Tabs check box.

DATABASE SET-UP

Setting up the College of E-Commerce database is completed in five distinct stages.

1. Create a new database.
2. Create the Table.
3. Create the Form.
4. Fine tune the Form layout.
5. Enter data.

Create a New Database

1. To start Microsoft Access, click the *Start* button and select *Programs* or *All Programs*. In the Microsoft Office group, select Microsoft Office Access.

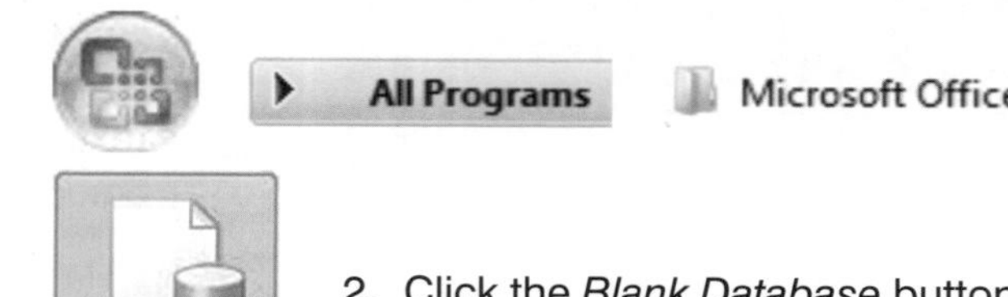

2. Click the *Blank Database* button, which appears in the top left-hand corner of the screen.

3. Enter *College of E-Commerce* as the file name (Figure 1.8).

Figure 1.8: Creating a new database

4. Click the folder icon (Figure 1.8) and select the folder where the new database will be saved. (It will be a different folder to the one displayed in Figure 1.8.)
5. Click *OK* and then click the *Create* button. A new database opens, with a Table already set up.

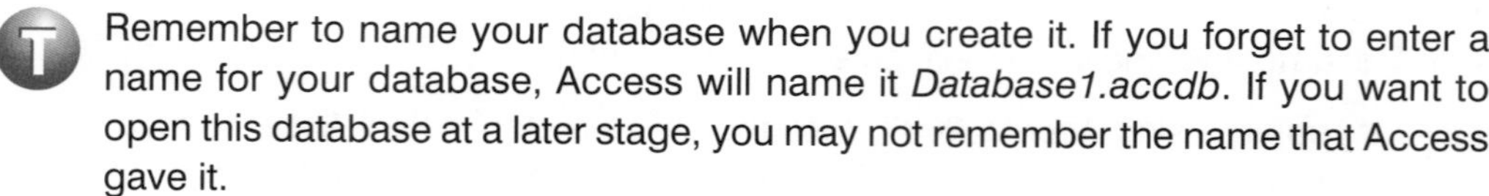

Remember to name your database when you create it. If you forget to enter a name for your database, Access will name it *Database1.accdb*. If you want to open this database at a later stage, you may not remember the name that Access gave it.

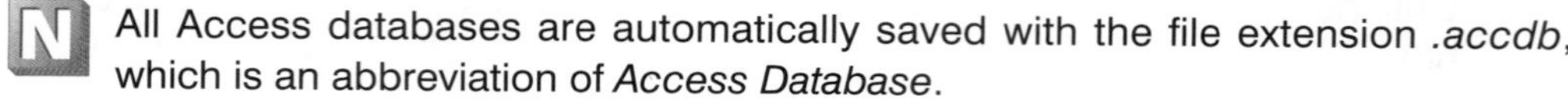

All Access databases are automatically saved with the file extension *.accdb*, which is an abbreviation of *Access Database*.

Create the Table

Each time you create a new database in Access, a new blank Table is displayed in datasheet view (Figure 1.9). Note that Access has already set up an ID field. This is the primary key field.

1. Click the *Save* button, either in the Quick Access Toolbar or in the Office Menu. Alternatively, right click the tab for *Table1* and select Save from the pop-up menu. The Save As dialog box is displayed (Figure 1.9).

Figure 1.9: *Student Details* has been entered as the Table name

2. Enter *Student Details* as the Table name in the Save As dialog box, as shown in Figure 1.9.
3. Click *OK* to name and save the Table.

4. In the Home section of the Ribbon, click the *Design View* button.

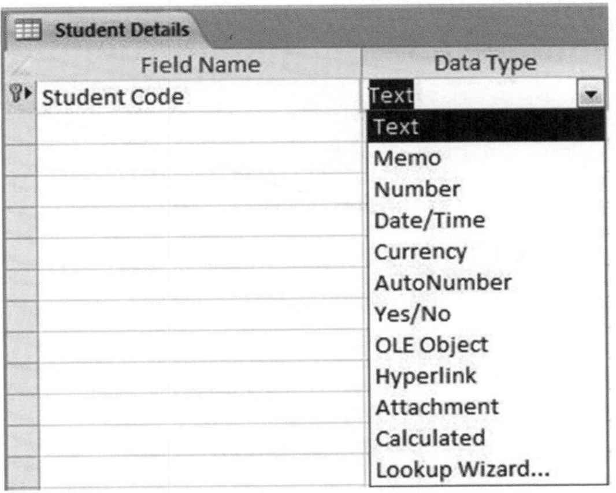

Figure 1.10: Design view of the *Student Details* Table

5. Change the field name of the *ID* field to *Student Code*, as shown in Figure 1.10. Select *Text* from the list of data types for the *Student Code* field.

6. Set up the remaining fields and select the data types, as shown in Figure 1.11.

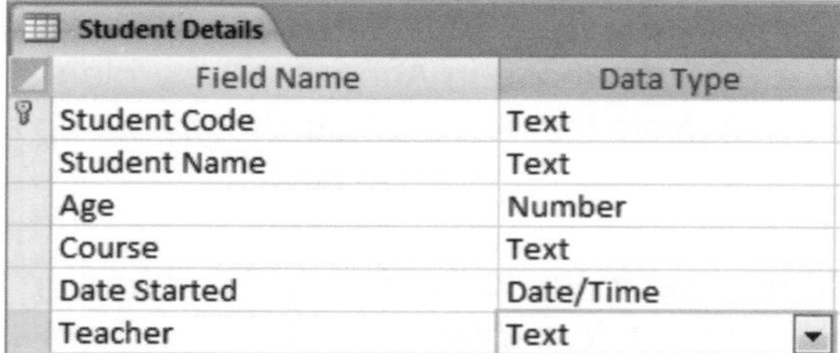

Student Details

Field Name	Data Type
Student Code	Text
Student Name	Text
Age	Number
Course	Text
Date Started	Date/Time
Teacher	Text

Figure 1.11: Field names and data types in the *Student Details* Table

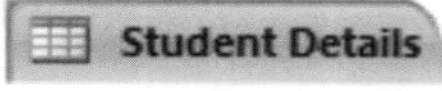

7. Right click the tab for the *Student Details* Table and select Save from the menu.

8. Close the *Student Details* Table.

Create the Form

1. In the Create section of the Ribbon, select *Form Wizard* from the More Forms drop-down list (Figure 1.12).

N In Access 2007, the Form Wizard is in the More Forms drop-down list.

2. Add all fields in the *Student Details* Table to the Form by clicking the double arrow. Fields that have been added to the Form will appear in the Selected Fields box (Figure 1.12).

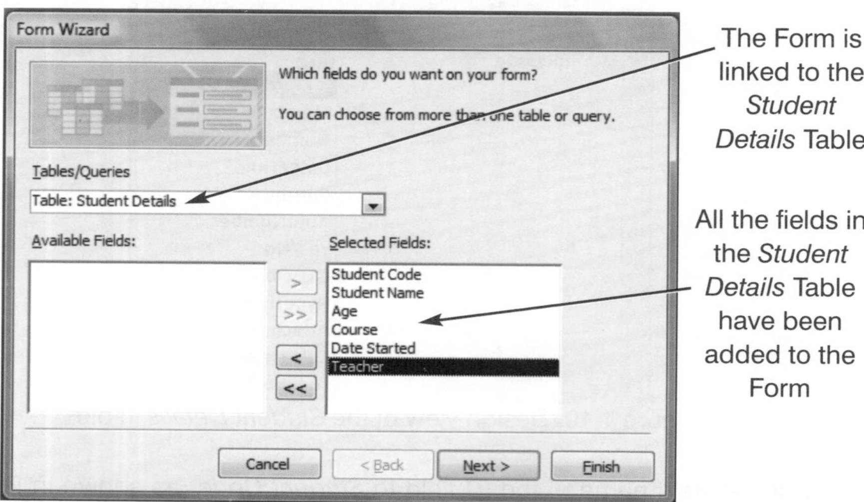

Figure 1.12: All fields in the *Student Details* Table have been added to the Form

3. Click the *Next* button.
4. Accept Columnar as the Form layout by clicking the *Next* button once again.
5. Enter *Student Registration* as the Form title. Click *Finish*.

Access users should refer to the note at the end of this section.

Fine Tune the Form Layout

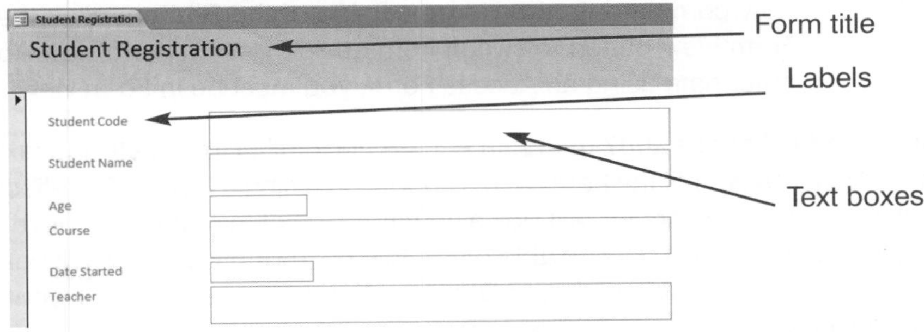

Figure 1.13: The completed *Student Registration* Form

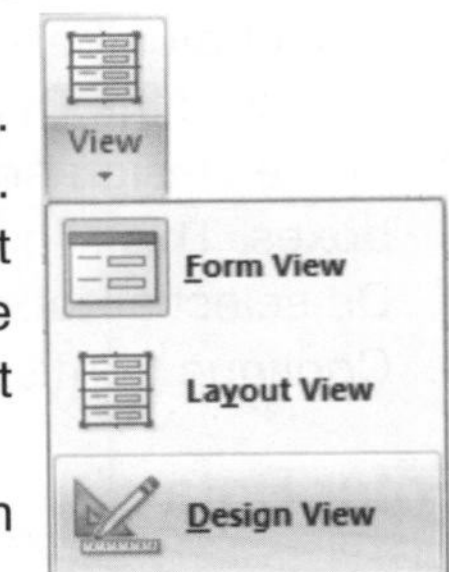

1. Figure 1.13 displays the completed *Student Registration* Form. Some of the text boxes are too wide and must be adjusted. Changes to the design of an Access Form can be made in layout view or design view. While layout view is very useful for fine tuning Form design, the initial set-up and design of a Form is best done in design view.

   In the Home section of the Ribbon, select design view from the View drop-down list.

2. Select and resize each text box individually. Point at the dot at the right-hand side of the selected text box. Drag to the left when the mouse pointer changes to a double horizontal arrow. Figure 1.14 demonstrates the resizing of the *Student Code* text box using this method. Resize all other text boxes so that they appear like Figure 1.14.

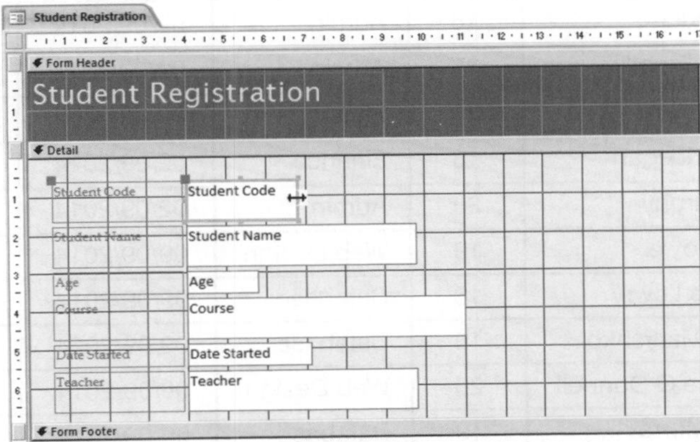

Figure 1.14: Use the double arrow mouse pointer to resize a text box

 Adjusting the width of a text box in a Form has no effect on the field size of the corresponding field in the Table.

3. Right click the *Student Registration* tab and select Save from the pop-up menu.

4. Adjustments to the design of the *Student Registration* Form are now complete. In the Home section of the Ribbon, click the *Form View* button to switch from design view to Form view. To enter data using an Access Form, you must be in Form view.

Important note for Access 2007 users: In Access 2007, all of the labels and text boxes in the Detail section of the Form were grouped in a single layout. The effect of this is that resizing a particular text box also resizes all of the other text boxes in the Detail section. You will only be able resize text boxes individually once you remove the labels and text boxes in the Detail section from the existing layout. Follow these steps.

1. Select all labels and text boxes by clicking the cross symbol in the top left-hand corner of the Detail section (to the left of the Student Code label).
2. In the Design section of the Ribbon, click the *Remove* button to ungroup the text boxes. This allows each text box to be resized independently.
3. De-select all labels and text boxes by clicking in a blank area of the Detail section.
4. Continue from step 2 in the 'Fine Tune the Form Layout' section.

Enter Data

With the *Student Registration* Form in Form view, enter all the records shown in Table 1.3. To move to the next field, press the *Tab* key on the keyboard.

If necessary, adjust the width of text boxes (using layout view) as you enter the data.

Student Code	Student Name	Age	Course	Date Started	Teacher
BS001	Peter Dunne	18	Admin	02/09/2014	Tadhg Allen
BS002	Mark Connolly	17	Admin	02/09/2014	Tadhg Allen
BS003	Dave O Neill	21	Finance	02/09/2014	Gerry Browne
BS004	Maura Keegan	18	Finance	02/09/2014	Gerry Browne
BS005	Ann Murphy	20	Admin	02/09/2014	Tadhg Allen
CP001	Enda Doyle	19	Web Design	09/09/2014	Noelle Duffy
CP002	Seamus Lowry	18	Database	09/09/2014	Liam Kearney
CP003	Tetyna Maryshko	18	Database	09/09/2014	Liam Kearney
CP004	Christine O Donnell	20	Web Design	09/09/2014	Noelle Duffy
CP005	Martin Murray	19	Database	09/09/2014	Liam Kearney

Table 1.3

 You can make adjustments to your Form as you are entering the data using layout view.

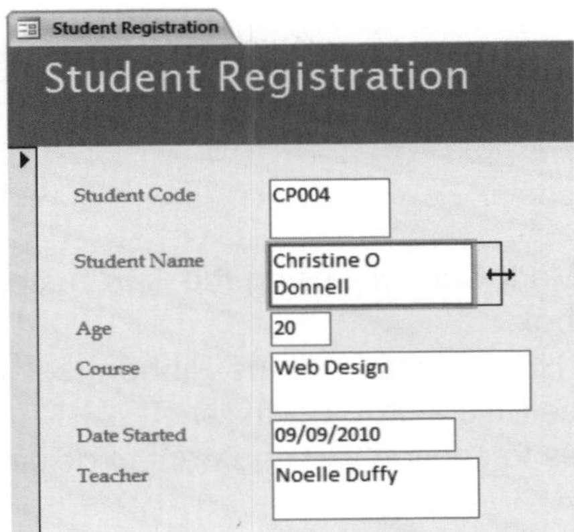

Figure 1.15: Adjusting the *Student Name* text box in layout view

Layout view allows you to view the data you have entered while making adjustments to the design of the Form. In Figure 1.15, the *Student Name* text box is being adjusted to prevent the text from wrapping. You can't enter data in layout view, so you will need to click the *Form View* button when you have finished adjusting your Form.

 Data is saved automatically as it is entered in a Form. There is no need to click the *Save* button to save the records you have entered. You only need to click the *Save* button when you make adjustments to the design of a Form.

Use the Form to Edit Data

1. Edit Existing Records

Maura Keegan has switched from the Finance course to the Web Design course. This information needs to be updated in the database.

1. With the *Student Registration* Form open in Form view, click in the text box containing the Student Name.
2. In the Home section of the Ribbon, click the *Find* button.
3. Type *Maura Keegan* in the Find What box.
4. Click *Find Next*. Maura Keegan's record is now displayed on the screen.
5. Change Maura's course from Finance to Web Design.

 You can quickly display the Find and Replace dialog box using the *CTRL + F* keyboard combination.

Edit the following records using the *Student Registration* Form:

 Click in the *Student Name* text box before clicking the *Find* button.

- Ann Murphy started on 16/9/2014.
- Martin Murray's age is 20.
- Tetyna Maryshko is in the Finance course.
- Enda Doyle started on 02/09/2014.

2. Delete a Record

1. Find the record for Mark Connolly using the *Find* button. Close the Find and Replace dialog box.

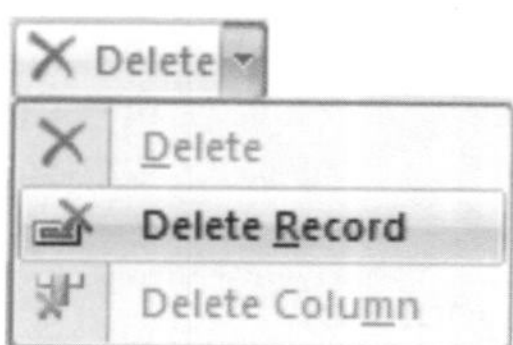

2. In the Home section of the Ribbon, select Delete Record from the Delete drop-down list.
3. Click *Yes* to confirm that you want to delete this record.

3. Add a New Record

Click the *New Record* button on the toolbar and enter the following information:
A new student, Keith Little, aged 19, has joined the Admin course. His start date is 24/09/2014. His teacher will be Tadhg Allen and his Student Code is BS006.

ASSIGNMENT SUMMARY

Basic Concepts	
Table	A database object that stores data. It is divided into rows and columns. The rows are called records. The columns are called fields.
Field	A specific column in the Table, e.g. Student Name. The data type of a field reflects the data that it stores, e.g. text, number, date/time.
Record	A specific row in the Table.
Primary Key	A special field in a Table where data cannot be duplicated. Records in the Table are stored in ascending order of the primary key field.
Form	A database object designed to facilitate data entry. The Form is linked to the Table. Data entered in the Form filters down to and is stored in the Table.
Label/Text Box	Each label/text box combination in the Form is linked to a specific field in the Table. Data is entered in the text boxes. Descriptive text is displayed in the labels.

Potential Pitfalls

- An Access Form is specifically designed for data entry. Although data can be entered directly in the Table, it is best to use the Form for data entry.
- Once a particular field has been identified as the primary key, Access will not allow you to duplicate values in that field.
- Access will not allow you to enter letters or symbols in a field with a Number data type.

Useful Shortcut	
Keyboard Combination	**Action**
CTRL + F	Find records in a Form

Table 1.4

Log on to www.gillmacmillan.ie to download review questions for Assignment 1.

2 Pizza Perfection Database

SCENARIO

Pizza Perfection takes orders from customers over the telephone and delivers within the local area. The manager, Gavin Donnelly, is finding it difficult to keep track of orders and amounts owed by customers. Orders are getting mixed up and some customers have been charged the wrong price. In Assignment 2 you will create a database to help Gavin manage his pizza delivery business.

By completing this assignment, you will learn how to:

- Configure data types in the Table.
- Add a new field to a Table.
- Reposition labels and text boxes on a Form.
- Align data in text boxes.
- Edit a Form using the field list.
- Find specific records using a Query.

LEARN ABOUT DATA TYPES IN ACCESS

TEXT DATA TYPE

The Text data type is used to store:

1. Text entries, i.e. data consisting entirely of letters and spaces, e.g. John, Red, Technical College.
2. Alpha-numeric entries, i.e. a combination of letters and numbers, such as 09KY2298, 6089932F, (087)2337802.
3. Numbers with leading zeros, e.g. 00205619.
4. Numbers including spaces, e.g. 506 2334 1, 01 2076698.

Figure 2.1 displays the *Current Deliveries* Table (created later on in this assignment) in design view. A data type of Text has been selected for the *Pizza Type* field. Access automatically sets the field size to 255.

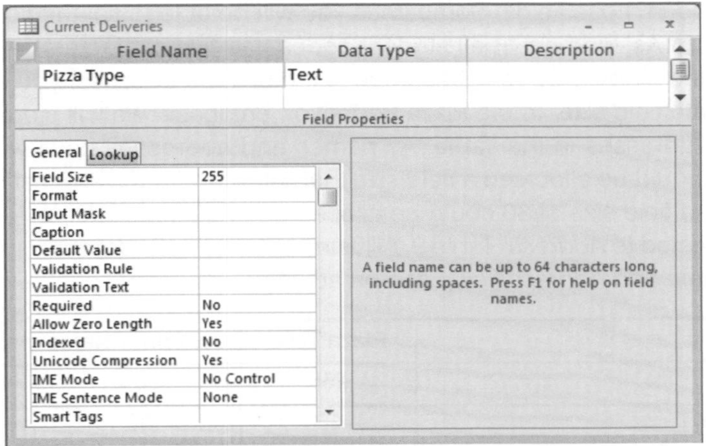

Figure 2.1: Setting up a Text data type in Table design

Adjusting the Field Size of a Text Field

Each character stored in a Text field requires one byte of computer storage. By default, Access sets the field size of all Text fields to 255. In practice, this means that you could continue entering data into a Text field until you had typed a total of 255 characters and spaces. The majority of Text fields store names, addresses and descriptions and rarely use the full allocation of 255 characters and spaces. In fact, it would be unusual to come across a person's name containing more than 30 characters.

Each time you enter data in a Text field, Access uses up all of the 255 bytes of computer storage allocated, even though the data you entered is only taking up a small proportion of those 255 bytes. In Figure 2.2, *Ham and Mushroom* has been entered in the *Pizza Type* field. This requires 16 bytes of storage (14 letters and two spaces). In the *Pizza Type* field, 239 of the 255 bytes of storage remain unused.

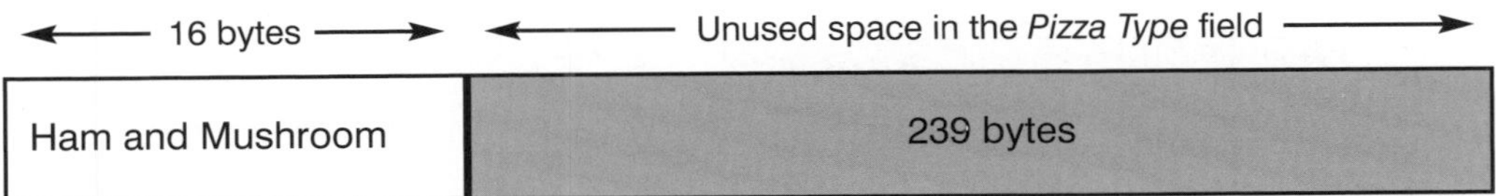

Figure 2.2

This isn't an issue in a database storing a small number of records. However, in large commercial databases storing hundreds of thousands of records, unused space in Text fields can eat up lots of storage space.

In the early days of computing, the cost per megabyte of disk storage was much more expensive than it is now. As modern PCs have large and relatively cheap hard drives, the issue of field sizes and inefficiently used disk storage is less critical than it was in the past. However, it is good practice to reduce the field size of Text fields to reflect the data stored in those fields. Sometimes you will be able to set the field size exactly. For example, in Assignment 1, all student codes had five characters, e.g. BS001. The field size for the *Student Code* field can be set to 5. In other cases, you will have to set an approximate field size. In the Pizza Perfection database, we will store the customer names and addresses in the Table. As names and addresses have varying lengths, these fields should be allocated a field size that will allow for the longest possible entry. For example, a field size of 30 could be allocated to *Customer Name*. A field size of 60 could be allocated to *Address*. Table 2.1 illustrates how the field sizes for the *Pizza Type*, *Customer Name* and *Address* fields can be adjusted.

	Pizza Type	Customer Name	Address
Original field size	255	255	255
Adjusted field size	16	30	60
Storage saved per Record (bytes)	239	225	195

Table 2.1: Adjusted field sizes of Text fields in the Pizza Perfection database

The field size for the *Pizza Type* field has been set to 16, as no pizza in the Table has more than 16 characters and spaces.

From Table 2.1, it can be seen that adjusting the field sizes of the Text fields in the Pizza Perfection database results in saving a total of 659 bytes per record (239 + 225 + 195). In a database with 10,000 records, this would save 6 megabytes of disk storage.

Reducing the size of Text fields improves the efficiency of a Query. Smaller field sizes allow Access to store the records closer together, which in turn speeds up the searches performed by Queries.

DATE/TIME DATA TYPE

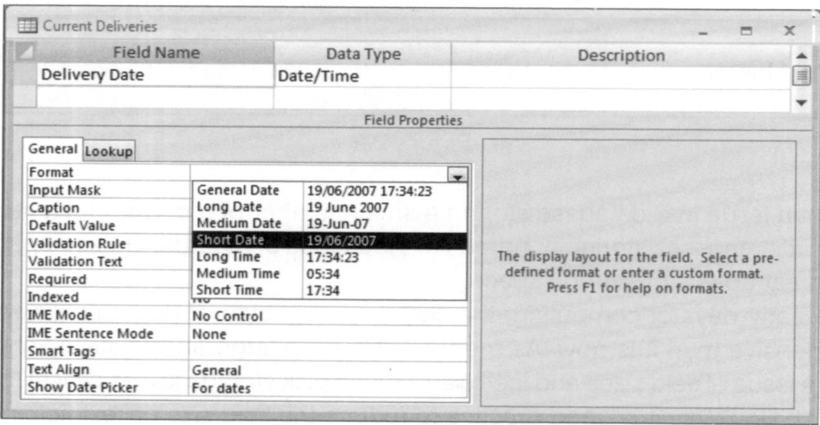

Figure 2.3: Setting up a Date/Time field in Table design

As the name suggests, the Date/Time data type is used to store dates or times in a field. Figure 2.3 shows the design of the *Current Deliveries* Table. A data type of Date/Time and a format of Short Date have been selected for the *Delivery Date* field.

When setting up a Date/Time field, it is important to select an appropriate format for the data stored in that field. Access provides four formats for dates (see Table 2.2).

Date Format	Explanation	Example
General Date	This is the default setting for a Date/Time field. With this format you can enter a date, a time or a date/time combination. Seconds are displayed in times even if you don't enter them. When entering a date/time combination, a space is required between the date and the time.	18/09/2014 10:25:00 18/09/2014 10:25:00
Long Date	Displays a date with a non-abbreviated month name. Enter 18/09/14 and Access will display 18 September 2014.	18 September 2014
Medium Date	Displays a date with an abbreviated month name using two digits for the year. Enter 18/09/14 and Access will display 18-Sep-14.	18-Sep-14
Short Date	Displays a date with the month represented by a number and the year represented by four digits.	18/09/2014

Table 2.2: Date formats available in Access

Access provides three formats for times (see Table 2.3).

Time Format	Explanation	Example
Long Time	This reflects the time setting in the Regional and Language options of your PC, laptop or tablet. The default setting is HH:MM:ss, i.e. two digits for hours, minutes and seconds, respectively. Enter 9:01 and Access displays 09:01:00.	09:01:00
Medium Time	Displays hours and minutes using two digits for each. Times entered using the 24-hour clock are automatically converted to the corresponding time from the 12-hour clock, e.g. 23:17 becomes 11:17.	11:17
Short Time	Displays hours and minutes using two digits for each in 24-hour clock format.	23:17

Table 2.3: Time formats available in Access

Each date or time stored in a Date/Time field requires 8 bytes of storage space.

When entering a date, you have the option of typing the date or using the calendar smart tag, which appears to the right of the text box in the Form (Figure 2.4). To use the calendar smart tag, simply click the calendar icon. Scroll through the calendar and select the date you require. The calendar cannot be used to enter times.

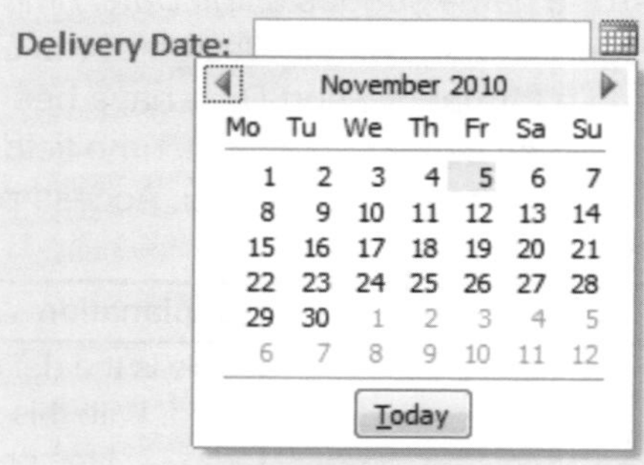

Figure 2.4: Calendar smart tag

Hours and minutes are separated by a colon (:). If you enter a full stop between the hour and minute, Access will replace it with a colon, e.g. enter 9.01 in a Date/Time field and Access will automatically change it to 09:01.

NUMBER DATA TYPE

The Number data type is used to store numbers. Access will not allow you to enter letters or other text characters in a Number field.

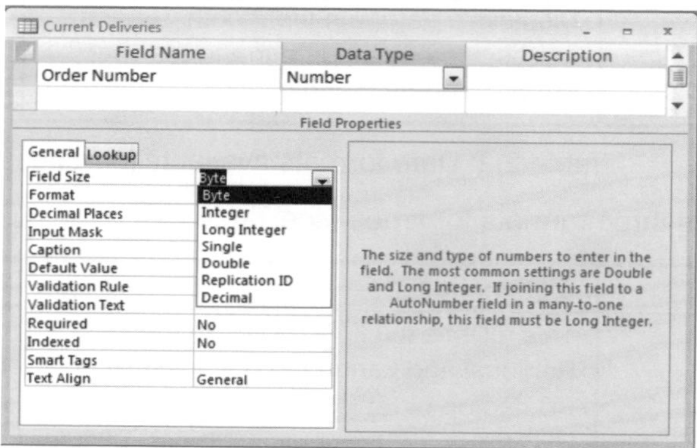

Figure 2.5: Setting up a Number field in Table design

In Figure 2.5, a data type of Number has been selected for the *Order Number* field. Each time you set up a Number field, you should select the field size appropriate to the type of number that will be stored in that field. In Figure 2.5, a field size of Byte has been selected. Selecting a specific field size for a Number field affects three important factors:

1. The range of numbers that can be stored in that field.
2. The maximum number of digits allowed to the right of the decimal place.
3. Storage space, in bytes per record, required to store a number in that field.

Settings for the Byte number type are displayed in Table 2.4.

Byte Number Type	
Range of numbers	0–255
Decimals?	No
Storage required per field entry	1 byte

Table 2.4

A field size of Byte should be selected for a number when you are certain that all the numbers entered in that field will be in the range 0 to 255 and will always be whole numbers, i.e. no decimal places. In the *Current Deliveries* Table, the highest order number is 12 and none of the order numbers have decimal places. The field size of the *Order Number* field can be set to Byte. Another common example of a number that could be stored in a Byte field is a person's age. A person's age cannot be a negative number, doesn't have decimal places and will never be greater than 255.

As you work through the assignments in this book, you will also learn about the Integer, Long Integer and Single data types.

If you enter numbers with decimals in a Byte field, the number will either be rounded up or down. For example, 3.6 would become 4 and 3.3 would become 3.

In a commercial pizza delivery database, setting the field size of the *Order Number* field to Byte would cause a problem, as you would not be able to enter order numbers higher than 255. In this case, a data type of Integer or Long Integer should be selected.

CURRENCY DATA TYPE

The Currency data type is used to store financial data. Numbers are displayed with a euro (€) sign and with two decimal places, e.g. enter 22.1 in a Currency field and Access displays €22.10.

The format of a Currency field can be set to Currency or Euro. When you set the format to Currency, Access will use the currency symbol specified in the Regional and Language options of your PC, laptop or tablet, which may be a euro (€) sign but could be a dollar ($) sign if your device is set up incorrectly.

In Figure 2.6, a data type of Currency has been selected for the *Total Due* field and the Format has been set to Euro. Each number stored in a Currency field requires 8 bytes of storage space.

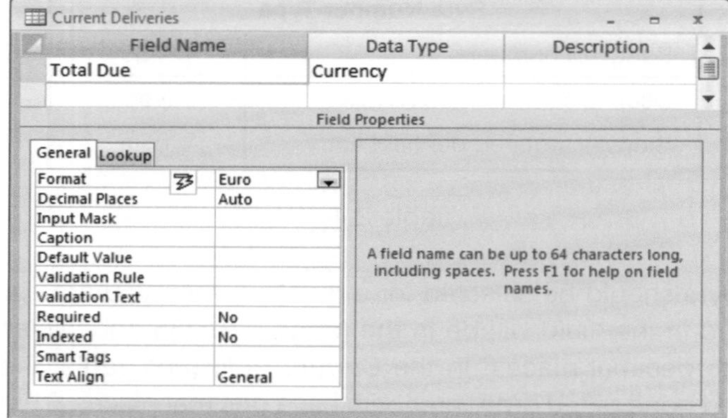

Figure 2.6: Setting up a Currency field in Table design

YES/NO DATA TYPE

The Yes/No data type is used when one of two possible items can be entered in a field. Three combinations are allowed in a Yes/No field:

1. Yes/No.
2. True/False.
3. On/Off.

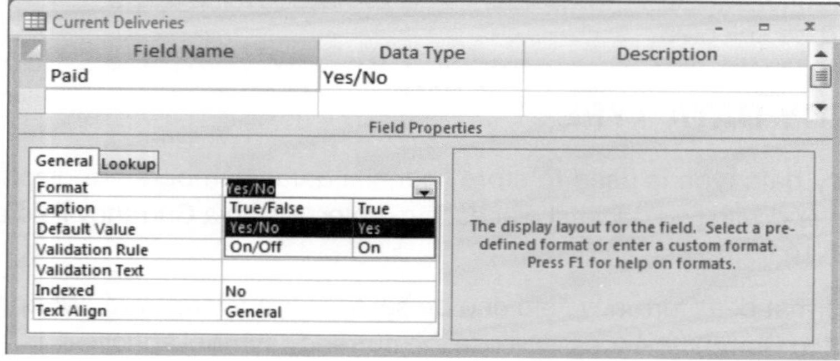

Figure 2.7: Setting up a Yes/No field in Table design

Data stored in a Yes/No field requires 1 byte of storage per record. In Figure 2.7, a data type of Yes/No has been selected for the *Paid* field, which is a common example of a field requiring a Yes/No data type. In a customer database, *Yes* would be entered in the *Paid* field for customers who have settled their account. *No* would be entered for customers who haven't paid.

By default, Access uses a check box control for the Yes/No data type. This means that a Form linked to the *Current Deliveries* Table displayed in Figure 2.8 will have a check box for the *Paid* field.

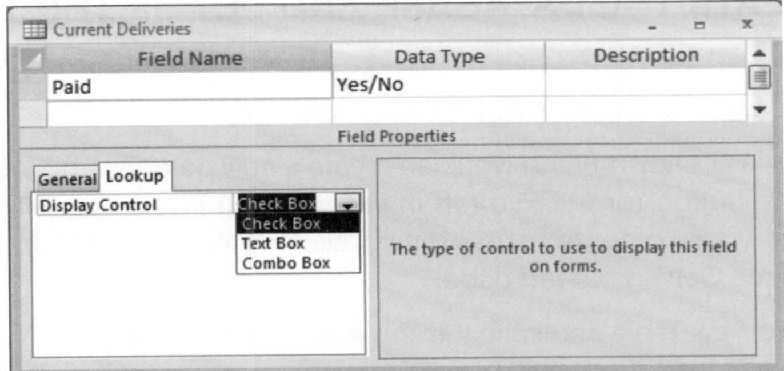

Figure 2.8: Check box is the default setting for Yes/No fields

Figure 2.9 shows the *Pizza Perfection* Form, which is linked to the *Current Deliveries* Table. Access automatically creates a check box for the Paid field because the data type of this field has been set to Yes/No in the Table.

Figure 2.9

 To enter *Yes* in the *Paid* field, tick the box.

☐ Not ticking the box enters a default of *No* in the *Paid* field.

Although data is entered in a Yes/No field by ticking or not ticking a check box, you must enter *Yes* as a Query condition to find all records where the check box was ticked. Type *No* as a Query condition to find all records where the check box wasn't ticked.

SUMMARY OF DATA TYPES USED IN THE PIZZA PERFECTION DATABASE

Data Type	Field Size	Comments
Text	Maximum of 255. The field size should be adjusted to reflect the data stored in each Text field.	Stores text, alpha-numeric data, numbers with leading zeros and numbers including spaces.
Date/Time	8 bytes	Stores dates or times.
Number, Byte	1 byte	Stores whole numbers ranging from 0 to 255 inclusive. No decimal places are allowed. Numbers with decimals will be rounded up or down.
Currency	8 bytes	Displays numbers with a currency symbol and two decimal places.
Yes/No	1 byte	Stores Yes/No, True/False or On/Off in a field.

Table 2.5

CREATE THE DATABASE AND SET UP THE TABLE

Task 1: Create a new database named *Pizza Perfection.*

If Access is already running, you can create a new database by clicking the Office button (or the File tab in Office 2010) in the top left-hand corner of your computer screen, then clicking the *New* button. This displays the *Getting Started* page.

Task 2: Create a new Table and save the Table as *Current Deliveries.*

- Using the data displayed in Table 2.6, create fields with appropriate data types in the *Current Deliveries* Table.

Order Number	Delivery Date	Pizza Type	Customer Name	Address	Total Due
1	03/11/2014	Spicy Cheese	Harry O Leary	15 Main Street	€8.95

Table 2.6

For a detailed explanation of primary keys, refer to pages 3–4 in Assignment 1.

- Set up the *Order Number* field as the primary key.
- Set the format of the *Delivery Date* field to Short Date.
- Select appropriate field sizes for the Text fields.
- Do not enter data in the Table at this point.

- Save the *Current Deliveries* Table.

Set the field size of each Text field to allow for the longest possible entry in that field. Setting the field size too low can cause problems later on.

WORKED EXAMPLE: CREATING AND EDITING AN ACCESS FORM

Part 1: Create the Form

1. Create a new Form linked to the *Current Deliveries* Table using the Form Wizard.

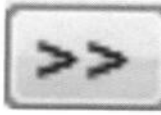

2. Add all the fields from the *Current Deliveries* Table to the Form.
3. Select *Columnar* as the Form layout.
4. Enter *Pizza Perfection* as the Form title. Click *Finish*.

5. View the Form in layout view. In design view of the Ribbon, click the *Themes* button and select *Aspect* from the list of Themes.

In Access 2007, the Form Theme is selected when following the steps in the Form Wizard.

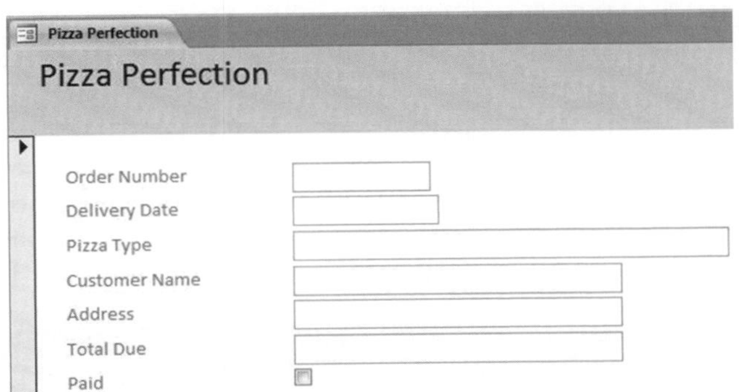

Figure 2.10: Completed *Pizza Perfection* Form using the Form Wizard

The completed Form is displayed in Figure 2.10. In a Form created using the Form Wizard, the labels and text boxes are arranged in a single column and the Form title is aligned to the left. Continuing with the worked example, you will:

- Resize text boxes.
- Rearrange the labels and text boxes in two columns.
- Align the Form title in the centre.

Each item in an Access Form is called a *control*, i.e. the label boxes, text boxes and the label box containing the Form title. In later assignments you will add image controls to an Access Form.

Part 2: Modify the Form Design

1. Select design view from the View drop-down list in the Home section of the Ribbon.

2. Select all labels and text boxes by clicking the cross symbol, which appears to the left of the *Order Number* label.

3. In the Arrange section of the Ribbon, click the *Remove* button to ungroup the selected labels and text boxes.

Access uses a layout to arrange the controls in your Form. This means that resizing one label or text box resizes all the other labels and text boxes as well. It also means that labels and text boxes can only be moved as a single unit and cannot be moved independently of each other. Removing the controls from the layout allows you to resize and move labels and text boxes independently.

4. Deselect all labels and text boxes by clicking in a blank area of the detail section.

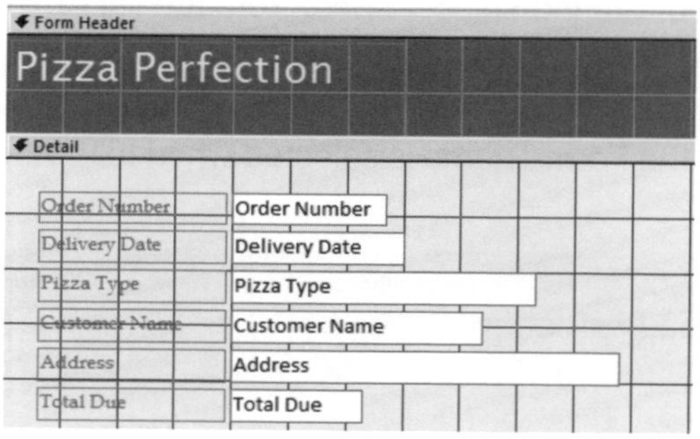

Figure 2.11: Text boxes have been resized

5. Select and resize the text boxes so that they appear like Figure 2.11.

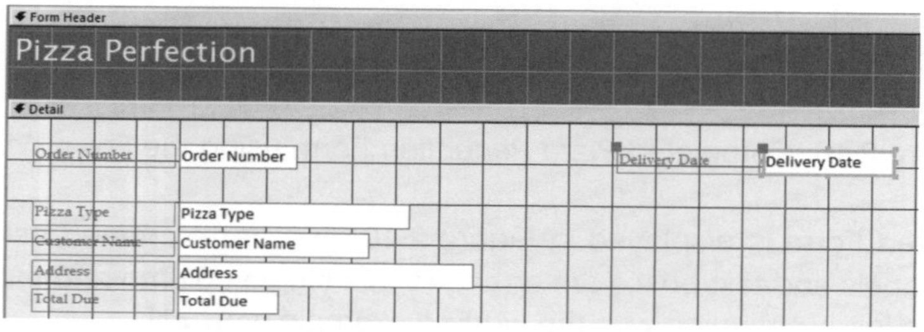

Figure 2.12: Form has been widened, with Delivery Date controls in new location

6. With the mouse pointer in the shape of a double-headed horizontal arrow, increase the width of the Form by dragging its right edge towards the right of the screen. Ensure that the Form is not wider than your computer screen.

7. Move the label and text box for the *Delivery Date* field and position as shown in Figure 2.12. (Click the Delivery Date text box once to select it. Release the mouse button and point at the edge of the selected Delivery Date controls. When the mouse pointer changes to a black cross/white arrow, move the controls by dragging.)

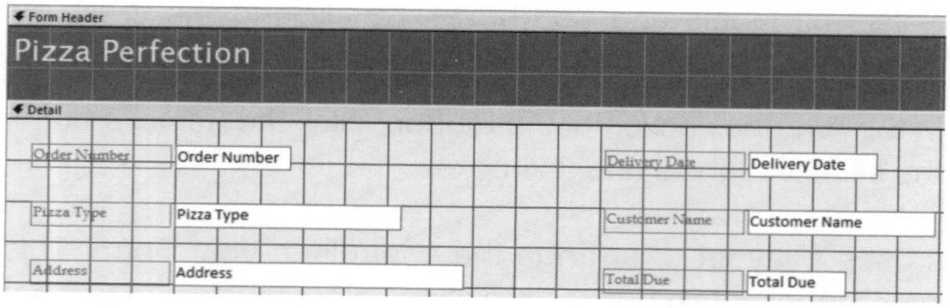

Figure 2.13: Delivery Date, Customer Name and Total Due controls have been moved to their new positions

8. Move the *Customer Name* and *Total Due* controls to their new positions, as shown in Figure 2.13.

Use the grid to line up the controls in the Form.

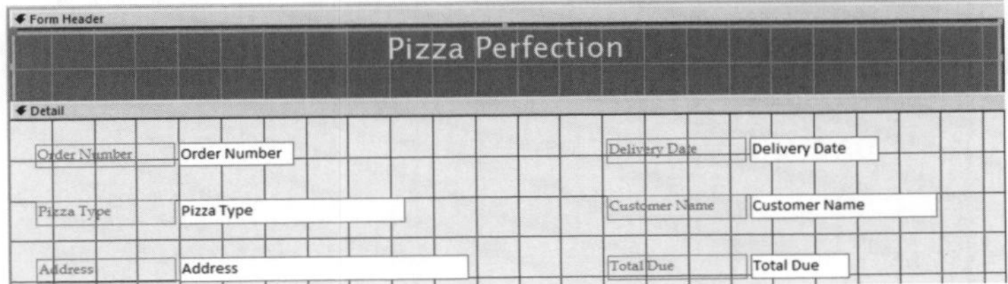

Figure 2.14: Centred heading in the *Pizza Perfection* Form

9. In the Form header, select the label box containing the heading.

10. Resize the label box until it is roughly the width of the Form (see Figure 2.14).

11. Centre the text in the label box using the *Center* button, which is in the Home section of the Ribbon.

12. Save the *Pizza Perfection* Form.

LEARN ABOUT LABELS AND TEXT BOXES

When you create an Access Form using the Form Wizard, each field that you add to the Form is represented by a label and a text box.

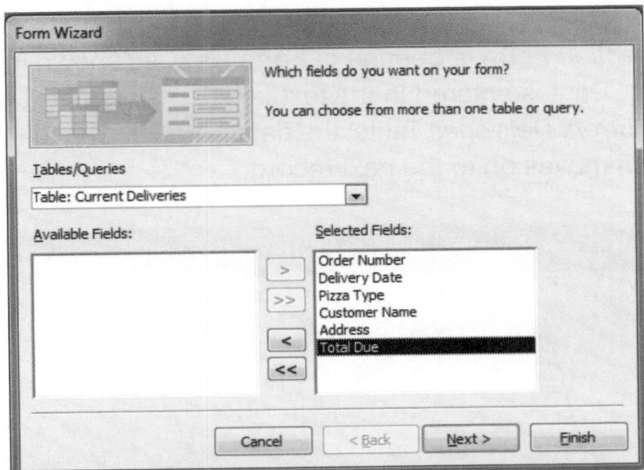

Figure 2.15: Using the Form Wizard to add fields to a Form

In Figure 2.15, all fields from the *Current Deliveries* Table have been added to the *Pizza Perfection* Form. Each of these fields is represented by a label and a text box in the completed Form.

Figure 2.16: Design view of the *Pizza Perfection* Form

Figure 2.16 displays the completed *Pizza Perfection* Form in design view. Each of the six fields in the *Current Deliveries* Table is represented by a label and a text box. In each label/text box pair, the labels are on the left and the text boxes are on the right.

Each text box is linked to a specific field in the Table. For example, in Figure 2.16, the *Delivery Date* text box is linked to the *Delivery Date* field in the *Current Deliveries* Table. The labels contain descriptive text. The text boxes contain field names.

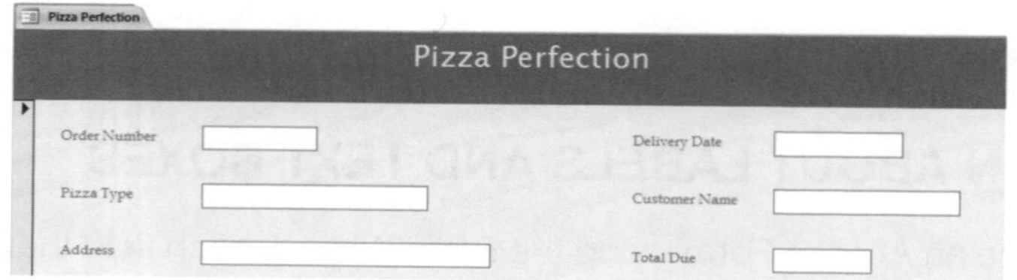

Figure 2.17: *Pizza Perfection* Form in Form view

When the *Pizza Perfection* Form is opened in Form view, as shown in Figure 2.17, the text boxes are empty. Data is entered in the text boxes. As each text box is linked to a specific field in the *Current Deliveries* Table, the data is transferred to the Table once the *Pizza Perfection* Form moves on to the next record.

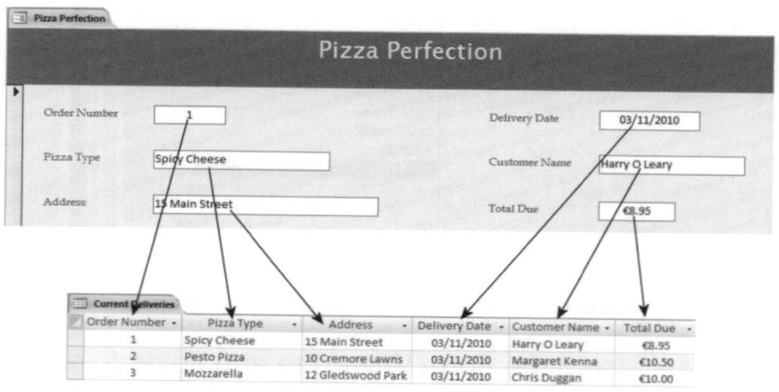

Order Number	Pizza Type	Address	Delivery Date	Customer Name	Total Due
1	Spicy Cheese	15 Main Street	03/11/2010	Harry O Leary	€8.95
2	Pesto Pizza	10 Cremore Lawns	03/11/2010	Margaret Kenna	€10.50
3	Mozzarella	12 Gledswood Park	03/11/2010	Chris Duggan	€10.00

Figure 2.18: How each text box links to a specific field in the Table

Figure 2.18 demonstrates how data in the text boxes is transferred from the Form to the Table record by record. This process happens automatically each time the Form moves on to a new record.

When in Form design, never change the text in a text box displaying a field name, as this will break the link to the Table.

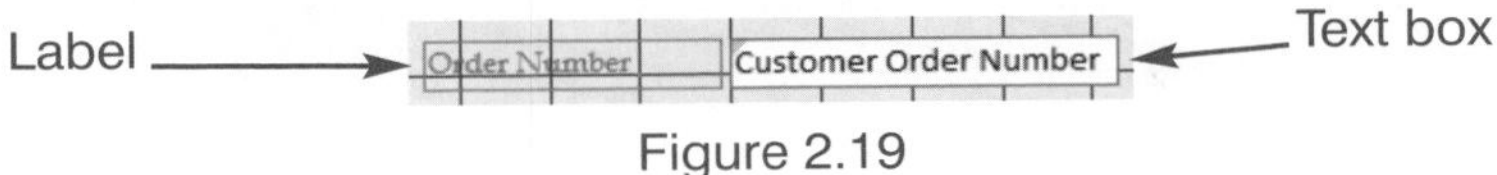

Figure 2.19

In Figure 2.19, the field name in the text box has been incorrectly changed to *Customer Order Number*. A triangle is displayed in the top left-hand corner of the text box, indicating a problem. When the Form is displayed in Form view, Access displays the error message shown in Figure 2.20, as it cannot find a field named *Customer Order Number* in the *Current Deliveries* Table. The correct field name is Order Number.

Figure 2.20

It is OK to edit the text in a label. Database designers generally abbreviate fields in Table design and then edit the labels in a Form to make them more descriptive.

Figure 2.21

In Figure 2.21, the text in the label has been changed from *Order Number* to *Customer Order Number*. Editing labels in a Form like this can make the Form easier to understand and use.

In an Access Form, never change the text in a text box displaying a field name.

WORKED EXAMPLE: ALIGNING LABELS AND TEXT BOXES

Although the vertical grid lines that appear in Form design can be used to line up labels and text boxes, it is difficult to line them up exactly using the naked eye.

1. Open the *Pizza Perfection* Form in design view if it is not already open.

Figure 2.22: Selecting labels and text boxes in design view

2. Click and drag to draw a rectangle around the *Delivery Date*, *Customer Name* and *Total Due* controls, as shown in Figure 2.22. When the left mouse button is released, these controls are selected (Figure 2.23).

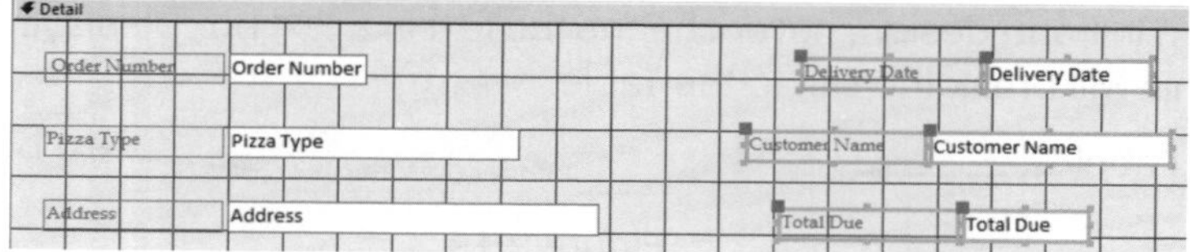

Figure 2.23: *Delivery Date, Customer Name* and *Total Due* controls are selected

3. In the Arrange section of the Ribbon, click the *Align* button and select left.

4. Save the *Pizza Perfection* Form.

In Access 2007, the *Align* buttons are not part of a drop-down list.

WORKED EXAMPLE: ALIGN DATA IN TEXT BOXES

In the previous example, you aligned the labels and text boxes in relation to each other. We must now align the data displayed in the text boxes. Access aligns data in text boxes to the left by default. This works well for Text fields. For Number, Date/Time and Currency fields, it is best to set the alignment of text boxes to Center.

1. Open the *Pizza Perfection* Form in design view if it is not already open.
2. Select the *Order Number*, *Delivery Date* and *Total Due* text box controls, as shown in Figure 2.24.

Holding down the *Shift* key while left clicking allows you to select multiple controls using the mouse.

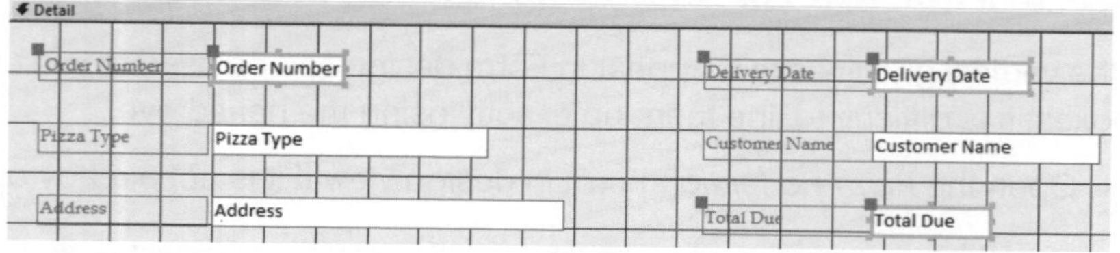

Figure 2.24: Hold down the *Shift* key while clicking the *Order Number, Delivery Date* and *Total Due* controls

3. In the Home section of the Ribbon, click the *Center* button to align data that will be entered in the selected controls.

4. Save the *Pizza Perfection* Form.

ENTER DATA

Task 3: Open the *Pizza Perfection* Form in Form view and enter the records shown in Table 2.7. To move to the next text box, press the *Tab* key on the keyboard.

If necessary, adjust the width of text boxes, using layout view, as you enter the data.

There is no need to type the euro sign. Access does this for you as the data type of the *Total Due* field is set to Currency.

Use the *CTRL* + 2 keyboard combination to copy the delivery date from the previous record.

Order Number	Delivery Date	Pizza Type	Customer Name	Address	Total Due
1	03/11/2014	Spicy Cheese	Harry O Leary	15 Main Street	€8.95
2	03/11/2014	Pesto Pizza	Margaret Kenna	10 Cremore Lawns	€10.50
3	03/11/2014	Mozzarella	Chris Duggan	12 Gledswood Park	€10.00
4	03/11/2014	Ham and Mushroom	Crisan Dumitro	15 Grange Park	€10.95
5	03/11/2014	Vegetarian	Diane O Connor	101 Kings Road	€11.50
6	03/11/2014	Four Seasons	Mary Smith	15 Woodpark	€10.95
7	03/11/2014	Pepperoni	Eamonn Buckley	27 The Pines	€10.50
8	04/11/2014	Vegetarian	John Murphy	5 The Gallops	€11.50
9	04/11/2014	Spicy Cheese	Declan Keane	33 Meadowvale	€8.95
10	04/11/2014	Pepperoni	Emma Daly	101 Glenview Drive	€10.50

Table 2.7

LEARN ABOUT QUERIES

A Query is a very important object in the database. Its function is to search for specific records in the Table. The speed at which a Query can find records is one of the major advantages of a computerised database. Examples of Queries regularly used in everyday life include:

- Checking available flights to a particular location on an airline website.
- Searching for songs by a particular band or artist on iTunes.
- Searching for a specific book on Amazon.

The database user gives instructions to the Query telling it how to find the records. These search instructions are called conditions. For example, in the Pizza Perfection database we might instruct the Query to "Find all Pepperoni pizzas" using a condition. Conditions are entered in the Criteria row of the Query design grid.

Field:	Order Number	Delivery Date	Pizza Type	Customer Name	Address	Total Due
Table:	Current Deliveries	Current Deliveries	Current Deliveries	Current Deliveries	Current Deliveries	Current Deliveries
Sort:						
Show:	☑	☑	☑	☑	☑	☑
Criteria:			"Pepperoni"			
or:						

Figure 2.25: The Query design grid

N When creating Queries, you don't need to type the double quotes. Access does this for you.

Figure 2.25 displays the Query design grid. *Pepperoni* has been entered as the condition for the *Pizza Type* field. When the Query is run, it searches through the Table, record by record. Each time it finds a record with *Pepperoni* stored in the *Pizza Type* field, it copies this record into a separate list. When the Query has finished searching through the Table, the list of records found by the Query, which is called a datasheet, is displayed on the computer screen. These records are shown in Table 2.8.

Order Number	Delivery Date	Pizza Type	Customer Name	Address	Total Due
7	03/11/2014	Pepperoni	Eamonn Buckley	27 The Pines	€10.50
10	04/11/2014	Pepperoni	Emma Daly	Glenview Drive	€10.50

Table 2.8: Records found by a Query searching for Pepperoni pizzas

Conditions can be added to a Query to refine the way it searches for records. The more conditions you add to a Query, the more specific its search becomes. For example, as well as specifying Pepperoni as a condition in the *Pizza Type* field, we could specify 04/11/2014 as a second condition in the *Delivery Date* field (Figure 2.26).

Field:	Order Number	Delivery Date	Pizza Type	Customer Name	Address	Total Due
Table:	Current Deliveries	Current Deliveries	Current Deliveries	Current Deliveries	Current Deliveries	Current Deliveries
Sort:						
Show:	☑	☑	☑	☑	☑	☑
Criteria:		#04/11/2014#	"Pepperoni"			
or:						

Figure 2.26: A second condition has been added to the Query

There are now two conditions. The Query will only display records where both conditions are satisfied, i.e. Pepperoni pizzas delivered on 04/11/2014. The single record found by the updated Query is shown in Table 2.9.

N When you enter a date in the Query design grid, Access automatically encloses dates in hash signs.

Order Number	Delivery Date	Pizza Type	Customer Name	Address	Total Due
10	04/11/2014	Pepperoni	Emma Daly	101 Glenview Drive	€10.50

Table 2.9: Record found by a Query searching for Pepperoni pizzas delivered on 04/11/2014

Adding a second condition to the Query has made the search more specific. The Query finds only one record where both conditions are satisfied.

As you work through the assignments in the book, you will learn how to create more complex Queries.

Although you can search for a record using the *Find* button in an Access Form, the Form will only display one record at a time. Queries are required for searches that find multiple records. Searches created using a Form are temporary, so if you close the database and open it again, you will have to set up the search condition again. One of the great advantages of Queries is that the search conditions are saved with the Query, so you only have to enter them once.

WORKED EXAMPLE: CREATE A QUERY TO FIND VEGETARIAN PIZZAS

1. In the Create section of the Ribbon, click the *Query Design* button. The Show Table dialog box is displayed.
2. Add the *Current Deliveries* Table to the Query design grid by clicking the *Add* button in the Show Table dialog box.
3. Click the *Close* button to close the Show Table dialog box.
4. Add the fields in the *Current Deliveries* Table to the Query design grid, either by:

- Double clicking each field name in turn;

or

- Dragging each field from the *Current Deliveries* Table and dropping in the Query design grid;

or

- Double clicking the title bar of the *Current Deliveries* Table, dragging the highlighted fields and dropping in the first column of the Query design grid.

Figure 2.27 shows the Query design grid after adding fields from the *Current Deliveries* Table.

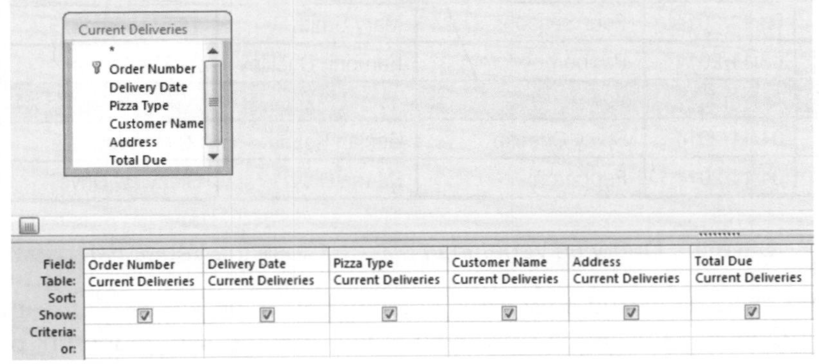

Figure 2.27: The Query design grid

Field:	Order Number	Delivery Date	Pizza Type	Customer Name	Address	Total Due
Table:	Current Deliveries	Current Deliveries	Current Deliveries	Current Deliveries	Current Deliveries	Current Deliveries
Sort:						
Show:	☑	☑	☑	☑	☑	☑
Criteria:			"Vegetarian"			
or:						

Figure 2.28: Finding Vegetarian pizzas

5. To find Vegetarian pizzas, type *Vegetarian* in the Criteria row of the *Pizza Type* column, as shown in Figure 2.28. Press Enter. As the *Pizza Type* field has a data type of Text, Access encloses the condition in double quotes.

Incorrect spelling in a Query condition usually results in the Query finding no matching records. For example, if you type *Vegatarian* instead of *Vegetarian*, the Query would not find any records. Also, entering "Vegetarian Pizzas" in the Query design grid will not find any records, as this does not exactly match what is stored in the table.

Run

6. Click the *Run* button to see the records found by the Query, which are highlighted in Figure 2.29.

Field:	Order Number	Delivery Date	Pizza Type
Table:	Current Deliveries	Current Deliveries	Current Deliveries
Sort:			
Show:	☑	☑	☑
Criteria:			"Vegetarian"
or:			

Figure 2.29: How a Query condition finds records in the Table

Order Number	Delivery Date	Pizza Type	Customer Name	Address	Total Due
1	03/11/2014	Spicy Cheese	Harry O Leary	15 Main Street	€8.95
2	03/11/2014	Ham and Mushroom	Margaret Kenna	10 Cremore Lawns	€10.50
3	03/11/2014	Mozzarella	Chris Duggan	12 Gledswood Park	€10.00
4	03/11/2014	Ham and Mushroom	Crisan Dumitro	15 Grange Park	€10.95
5	03/11/2014	Vegetarian	Diane O Connor	103 Kings Road	€11.50
6	03/11/2014	Four Seasons	Mary Smith	15 Woodpark	€10.95
7	03/11/2014	Pepperoni	Eamonn Buckley	27 The Pines	€10.50
8	04/11/2014	Vegetarian	John Murphy	5 The Gallops	€11.50
9	04/11/2014	Spicy Cheese	Declan Keane	33 Meadowvale	€8.95
10	04/11/2014	Pepperoni	Emma Daly	Glenview Drive	€10.50

7. Save the Query as *Vegetarian pizzas*. Close the *Vegetarian pizzas* Query.

If you make a spelling error when entering data in an Access Form, it will affect your Queries later on. For example, if you entered five Pepperoni pizzas but incorrectly entered one of them as *Peperoni*, a Query condition that searches for

Pepperoni in the *Pizza Type* field will only find four records. This is why accurate data entry is so important.

There is no need to type the double quotes when entering a Query condition in a Text field. Access does this for you.

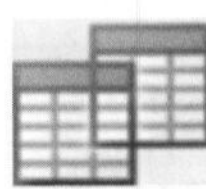

CREATE QUERIES

Task 4: Create a new Query that finds records of pizzas delivered on 03/11/2014. Save the Query as *03/11/2014 deliveries.*

Task 5: Create a new Query to find records of pizzas where the Total Due is €11.50. Save the Query as *Special pizzas.*

Never type the euro symbol (€) when you are creating a Query condition in a Currency field.

If you include a euro (€) symbol in a Query condition for a Currency field, Access displays the message "Data type mismatch in criteria expression". This is because the euro (€) symbol is text and cannot be included in a condition for a Currency field, which stores numbers.

Task 6: Create a new Query to find records of customers who ordered Spicy Cheese pizzas. Save the Query as *Spicy Cheese.*

Task 7: Create a new Query to find records of pizzas costing €10.95 delivered on 03/11/2014. Save the Query as *Premium deliveries*.

FIND AND EDIT RECORDS

Task 8: Open the *Pizza Perfection* Form. Use the *Find, Delete Record* and *New Record* buttons to make the following changes.

Click in the *Customer Name* text box before clicking the *Find* button. If you forget to select the appropriate text box, Access will not find the record.

1. Margaret Kenna's order was incorrectly taken and should be a Spicy Cheese pizza.
2. Diane O Connor's correct address is 103 Kings Road.
3. Crisan Dumitro ordered a Vegetarian Pizza.
4. Emma Daly lives at 101 Glenview Dale and not 101 Glenview Drive.
5. Declan Keane's order has been cancelled. Delete this record.

Don't confuse the *Delete* button with the *Delete Record* button. The *Delete* button only deletes data in the currently selected text box. The *Delete Record* button deletes the entire record currently displayed by the Form.

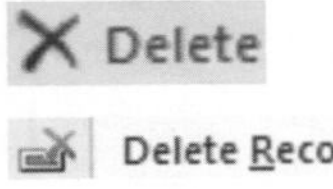

ADD NEW RECORDS

- Click the *New* button and add the records displayed in Table 2.10 using the *Pizza Perfection* Form.

Order Number	Delivery Date	Pizza Type	Customer Name	Address	Total Due
11	04/11/2014	Vegetarian	Mairead Moore	21 Woodpark	€11.50
12	04/11/2014	Spicy Cheese	Natalija Gasewski	2a Main Street	€8.95

Table 2.10

- Open the *Vegetarian pizzas* Query. Verify that the Query now finds Mairead Moore's and Crisan Dumitro's record.
- Open the *Spicy Cheese* Query. Verify that the Query now finds Margaret Kenna's and Natalija Gasewski's records.

THE FIELD LIST

The field list displays a list of all fields in the Table that the Form is linked to. The *Pizza Perfection* Form is linked to the *Current Deliveries* Table. Displaying the field list, in either design or layout view of the *Pizza Perfection* Form, will display a list of fields in the *Current Deliveries* Table, as shown in Figure 2.30.

The field list can be used to update your Form to reflect changes you have made in the Table. For example, if you add a new field to the Table, this new field can be added to the Form using the field list.

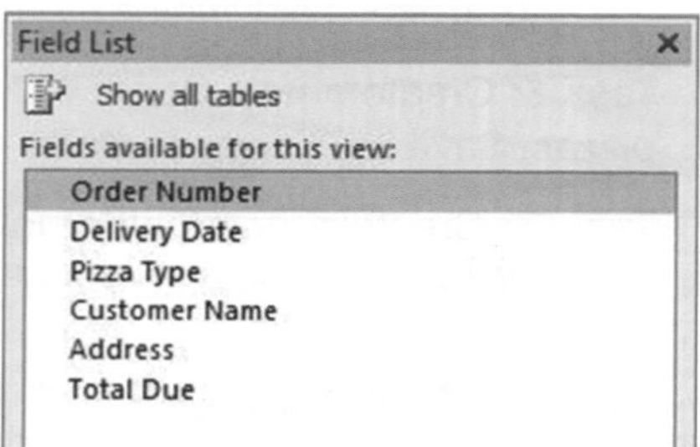

Figure 2.30

WORKED EXAMPLE: ADDING A NEW FIELD TO THE TABLE AND FORM

1. Open the *Current Deliveries* Table in design view.
2. Add a new *Paid* field to the Table, as shown in Figure 2.31.
3. Set the data type of the *Paid* field to Yes/No.
4. Save and close the *Current Deliveries* Table.

Current Deliveries

Field Name	Data Type
Order Number	Number
Delivery Date	Date/Time
Pizza Type	Text
Customer Name	Text
Address	Text
Total Due	Currency
Paid	Yes/No

Figure 2.31: Adding a new field in Table design

5. Open the *Pizza Perfection* Form in design view.
6. To display the field list, click the *Add Existing Fields* button.
7. Drag the *Paid* field from the field list and drop in the detail section of the *Pizza Perfection* Form, as shown in Figure 2.32.

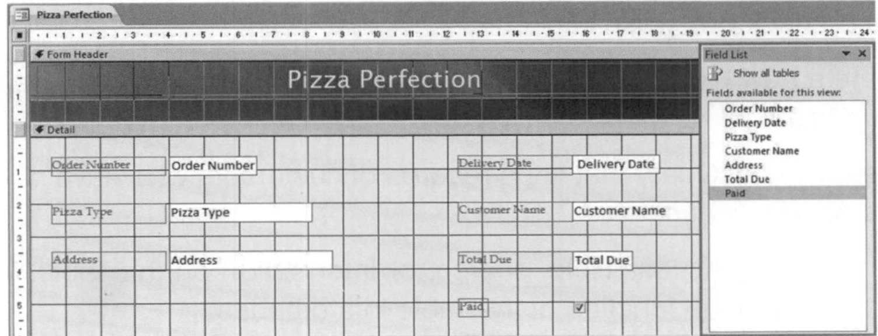

Figure 2.32: The *Paid* field has been added to the detail section

8. Position the *Paid* label on the left of the check box and align with existing labels, as shown in Figure 2.32.

9. Save the *Pizza Perfection* Form.

10. Click the *Form View* button and enter the *Paid* data displayed in the shaded cells in Table 2.11.

Order Number	Customer Name	Paid
1	Harry O Leary	No
2	Margaret Kenna	Yes
3	Chris Duggan	Yes
4	Crisan Dumitro	Yes
5	Diane O Connor	No
6	Mary Smith	Yes
7	Eamonn Buckley	Yes
8	John Murphy	Yes
10	Emma Daly	No
11	Mairead Moore	Yes
12	Natalija Gasewski	Yes

Table 2.11

Press the *Page Down* button to quickly advance the Form to the next record.

Ticking the *Paid* check box is equivalent to entering *Yes*, while not ticking the check box is equivalent to entering *No*.

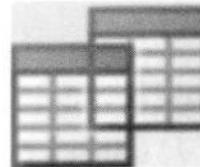

CREATE QUERIES

In a Query, entering *Yes* as a condition for the *Paid* field finds all records where the *Paid* check box was ticked. Entering *No* as a condition finds records where the *Paid* check box wasn't ticked.

Task 9: Create a new Query that finds records of customers who have paid. Save the Query as *Paid in full.*

Task 10: Create a new Query that finds records of customers who have not paid. Save the Query as *Accounts due.*

Task 11: Using Access Help, search for information on the Table. Write a brief report outlining the function of the Table in a database.

REVIEW YOUR WORK

Use the checklist below to verify that you have completed all the tasks in the Pizza Perfection database.

		Completed (√)
Table:	• Current Deliveries	☐
Form:	• Pizza Perfection	☐
Queries:	• 03/11/2014 deliveries	☐
	• Accounts due	☐
	• Paid in full	☐
	• Premium deliveries	☐
	• Special pizzas	☐
	• Spicy Cheese	☐
	• Vegetarian pizzas	☐

ASSIGNMENT SUMMARY

Basic Concepts	
Data Type	The data type of a field determines the type of data that can be stored in that field. • The Text data type is used to store letters, combinations of letters and numbers (alpha-numeric), numbers with leading zeros and numbers with spaces. • The Number data type is used to store numbers. Access will not allow you to enter text in a Number field. However, you can enter numbers in a Text field.

	• The Date/Time data type is used to store dates and times. Days, months and years are separated using the forward slash (/). Hours and minutes are separated using a colon (:). • The Currency data type is used to store monetary data. Access adds a currency symbol to numbers entered in a Currency field. To get the correct currency symbol, you must ensure that the country is set correctly in the Regional and Language options of your PC, laptop or tablet.
Field Size	The field size is the amount of storage space, in bytes, required to store data in a particular field. The field size of a Text field is set by the database designer. For all other field types, the field size is determined by Access. Date/Time fields and Currency fields require 8 bytes of storage per record. The Yes/No data type requires 1 byte of storage per record.
Byte	One of a number of possible field sizes that can be selected for a Number field. A Number field set to Byte can store whole numbers from 0 to 255 inclusive. Numbers entered with decimals will be rounded up or down.
Query	An object in an Access database. The function of a Query is to find records matching the condition(s) entered in the Query design grid. The Query searches through the Table, record by record. Any records that satisfy the Query condition(s) are copied into a separate datasheet, which is then displayed on the screen.
Condition	An expression entered in the Criteria row of the Query design grid for a specific field. Conditions allow us to specify exactly what records we are searching for.

Potential Pitfalls

- Spelling errors at the data entry stage can often result in Queries not finding all of the relevant records.
- If there is a spelling error in a Query condition, it is most likely that the Query will not find any records.
- Even if your condition is correct, the Query will not find any records if you have entered the condition in the wrong field.
- When creating a Query condition for a Currency field, never type the euro (€) sign.

Log on to www.gillmacmillan.ie to download review questions for Assignment 2.

3 Riverside Rugby Club Database

SCENARIO

Paddy Johnson is coach to Riverside Rugby Club. In order to improve their performance, he has been analysing player statistics from recent matches but is finding this very difficult and time consuming. In Assignment 3 you will create a database to store and analyse data relating to players and their match performances.

By completing this assignment, you will learn how to:

- Use logical operators in Query conditions.
- Sort records found by a Query.
- Adjust the tab order in a Form.
- Define database structure.

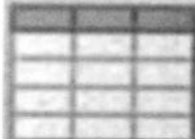

CREATE THE DATABASE AND SET UP THE TABLE

Task 1: Create a new database named *Riverside Rugby Club.*

Task 2: Create a new Table and save the Table as *Players.*

- Using the data displayed in Table 3.1, create fields with appropriate data types in the *Players* Table.

Player Number	Player Name	Position	No of Tackles	No of Passes	No of Errors	Player Rating
1	Darragh Foley	Forward	5	2	3	6

Table 3.1

- Set the *Player Number* field as the primary key.
- Select appropriate field sizes for the Text fields.
- Do not enter data in the Table at this point.

- Save the *Players* Table.

As there are only three positions stored in the Table – forward, back and centre – the field size for the *Position* field can be set to exactly match the data.

For a detailed explanation of setting the field size of a Text field, refer to pages 17–18 in Assignment 2.

It is important to get your data types correct at this stage. Setting a data type incorrectly in Table design can cause errors in Queries and Reports later on. For example, if the *No of Tackles* field was given a data type of Text instead of Number, the following problems could occur:

1. Use of the logical operators <, <=, > or >= in Queries may produce incorrect results. For example, <2 could potentially find *1*, *10*, *11*, *12*, *13*, *14*, *15*, *16*, *17*, *18* and *19* in the *No of Tackles* field.
2. Sorting by the *No of Tackles* field will not display data in ascending or descending numerical order. Data would be displayed in the following order: *1*, *10*, *11*, *12*, *13*, *14*, *15*, *16*, *17*, *18*, *19*, *2*, *20*, *21*, etc.

CREATE THE FORM

Task 3: Using the Form Wizard, create a Form including all fields from the *Players* Table. Information relating to the design of the Form is displayed in Table 3.2.

Form Layout	Columnar
Form Title	Match Statistics

Table 3.2

Use layout view to make the following adjustments to the Form.

- Apply the *Trek* theme to the Form.
- Set up labels and text boxes in two columns and adjust the width of text boxes as shown in Figure 3.1.
- Edit the No of Tackles, No of Errors and No of Passes labels so that they appear like Figure 3.1.

Do not change the text in any text boxes.

For a detailed explanation of how to modify the design of an Access Form, refer to pages 25–7 in Assignment 2.

In Access 2007, selecting all labels and text boxes and then clicking the *Remove* button (in the Arrange section of the Ribbon) allows you to move and resize labels and text boxes independently of each other. This is not necessary in Access 2010.

Click a label box and then click its associated text box while holding down the *Shift* key. Now you can move the label and text box together.

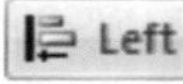

- Line up *the Player Number*, *Player Name*, *No of Tackles* and *No of Errors* label and text box controls using the *Align Left* button in the Arrange section of the Ribbon (see Figure 3.1).

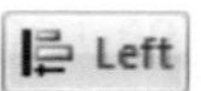

- Line up the *Position*, *No of Passes* and *Player Rating* label boxes using the *Align Left* button.

- Line up the *Position*, *No of Passes* and *Player Rating* text box controls using the *Align Right* button.

- Centre the Form heading (see Figure 3.1).
- Set the alignment of the *Player Name* and *Position* text boxes to Left.
- Set the alignment of all other text boxes to Center.

- Save the *Match Statistics* Form.

A text box does not need to be wide enough to display the field name in design view. It only needs to be wide enough to accommodate the data.

Figure 3.1 is an example of the completed *Match Statistics* Form.

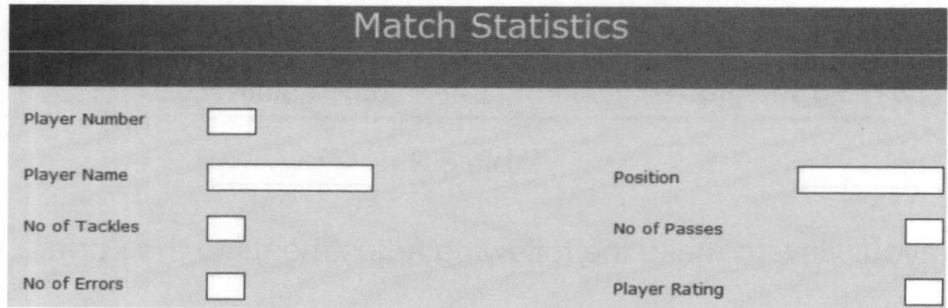

Figure 3.1: The completed *Match Statistics* Form

ENTER DATA

Task 4: Using the *Match Statistics* Form, enter all the records displayed in Table 3.3. To move to the next field, press the *Tab* key on the keyboard.

If necessary, adjust the width of text boxes, using layout view, as you enter the data.

The *CTRL + 2* key combination can be used to copy data from a field in the previous record. For example, when the cursor is in the *Position* text box for the second record, holding down the *CTRL* key and typing *2* automatically enters *Forward*.

Player Number	Player Name	Position	No of Tackles	No of Passes	No of Errors	Player Rating
1	Darragh Foley	Forward	5	2	3	6
2	Shay Lunny	Forward	9	4	4	7
3	Eddy Moran	Forward	6	2	1	6
4	Nick O Kelly	Forward	10	3	2	8
5	Declan Hennesey	Forward	8	1	3	6
6	Sean Hayes	Forward	11	2	1	8
7	Tom Wood	Forward	10	5	1	9
8	Aidan Clohosey	Back	5	2	2	7
9	Mick Moloney	Back	7	40	2	8
10	Gerard Byrne	Back	4	12	4	7
11	Fionn O Sullivan	Centre	4	5	1	10
12	James O Driscoll	Centre	9	2	0	8
13	Ciaran Higgins	Back	3	5	1	8
14	Paul Murray	Back	1	2	1	6
15	Graham Nolan	Back	3	3	0	7

Table 3.3

LEARN ABOUT LOGICAL OPERATORS

Logical operators are used when creating Query conditions for Number fields. They allow us to specify exactly what range of numbers we want the Query to find. The list of logical operators that can be used in an Access Query is shown in Table 3.4.

Logical Operator	Meaning
<	Less than
<=	Less than or equal to
=	Equal to
<>	Not equal to
>	Greater than
>=	Greater than or equal to
Between	Finds numbers ranging from a lower to an upper limit

Table 3.4

Logical operators can be combined with numbers to form logical expressions. Examples of logical expressions are shown in Table 3.5.

Logical Expression	Meaning
>=1 and <=10	From 1 to 10 inclusive
Between 1 and 10	From 1 to 10 inclusive
>1 and <10	From 2 to 9 inclusive
>=1 and <10	From 1 to 9 inclusive
>1 and <=10	From 2 to 10 inclusive

Table 3.5

The Between logical operator is inclusive. Between 1 and 10 means *From 1 to 10 inclusive*. Between 5 and 15 means *From 5 to 15 inclusive*.

Table 3.6 details the records found using logical expressions in the *No of Tackles* field. Depending on which logical operator is used in the Query condition, different sets of records are found by the Query.

Logical Operator	**Meaning**	**Example (based on conditions entered in the *No of Tackles* field in the Query design grid)**	**Number of Records Found**
<	Less than	**<5** finds 4, 4, 3, 1 and 3	5
<=	Less than or equal to	**<=5** finds 5, 5, 4, 4, 3, 1 and 3	7
=	Equal to	**5** finds 5 and 5	2
>	Greater than	**>5** finds 9, 6, 10, 8, 11, 10, 7 and 9	8
>=	Greater than or equal to	**>=5** finds 5, 9, 6, 10, 8, 11, 10, 5, 7 and 9	10
<>	Not equal to	**<>5** finds 9, 6, 10, 8, 11, 10, 7, 4, 4, 9, 3, 1 and 3	13
Between	Records within a range including the highest and lowest number	**Between 5 and 8** finds 5, 6, 8, 5 and 7	5

Table 3.6: Records found by logical operators entered in the *No of Tackles* field

The logical operator **Not** can be used instead of <>. Entering **Not 5** as a condition in the *No of Tackles* field also finds 13 records. *Not* is widely used in database programming, while <> is generally used in Queries.

The following examples demonstrate how to use logical operators in a Query.

Example 1: Logical operator used in one field

Field:	Player Number	Player Name	Position	No of Tackles
Table:	Players	Players	Players	Players
Sort:				
Show:	☑	☑	☑	☑
Criteria:				<5
or:				

Figure 3.2

Entering the logical operator shown in Figure 3.2 finds players who made less than 5 tackles. The records found by this Query are displayed in Table 3.7.

Player Number	Player Name	Position	No of Tackles	No of Passes	No of Errors	Player Rating
10	Gerard Byrne	Back	4	12	3	7
11	Fionn O Sullivan	Centre	4	5	1	10
13	Ciaran Higgins	Back	3	5	1	8
14	Paul Murray	Back	1	2	1	6
15	Graham Nolan	Back	3	3	0	7

Table 3.7: Five records found by entering <5 as a condition in the *No of Tackles* field

Example 2: Logical operator used in two fields

In this example, two conditions have been entered in the Query design grid to find players who made less than 5 tackles and whose rating was greater than 7. Both conditions include logical operators.

Including more than one condition in a Query, as shown in Figure 3.3, refines the search and in most cases will result in the Query finding fewer records.

Field:	Player Name	Position	No of Tackles	No of Passes	No of Errors	Player Rating
Table:	Players	Players	Players	Players	Players	Players
Sort:						
Show:	☑	☑	☑	☑	☑	☑
Criteria:			<5			>7
or:						

Figure 3.3

Because both conditions are in the Criteria row in Figure 3.3, Access interprets the conditions as being linked. In the above example, the Query finds players who made less than 5 tackles **and** whose rating is greater than 7. Including a second condition has reduced the amount of records found by the Query from five records to two records, which are displayed in Table 3.8.

Player Number	Player Name	Position	No of Tackles	No of Passes	No of Errors	Player Rating
11	Fionn O Sullivan	Centre	4	5	1	10
13	Ciaran Higgins	Back	3	5	1	8

Table 3.8: Two records found by entering <5 as a condition in the *No of Tackles* field and >7 as a second condition in the *Player Rating* field

Example 3: Using Between as a logical operator

In Example 3, *Between* is used as a logical operator to find players who made between 5 and 8 tackles inclusive, as shown in Figure 3.4.

Field:	Player Name	Position	No of Tackles	No of Passes
Table:	Players	Players	Players	Players
Sort:				
Show:	☑	☑	☑	☑
Criteria:			Between 5 And 8	
or:				

Figure 3.4

N Typing *>=5 and <=8* achieves the same result as *Between 5 And 8.*

The records found by this Query are displayed in Table 3.9.

Player Number	Player Name	Position	No of Tackles	No of Passes	No of Errors	Player Rating
1	Darragh Foley	Forward	5	2	3	6
3	Eddy Moran	Forward	6	2	1	6
5	Declan Hennesey	Forward	8	1	3	6
8	Aidan Clohosey	Forward	5	2	2	7
9	Mick Moloney	Back	7	40	2	8

Table 3.9: Five records found by entering *Between 5 and 8* as a condition in the *No of Tackles* field

N Logical operators can also be used in Text fields. Entering **<"d"** as a condition in the *Player Name* field finds **A**idan Clohosey, **B**rendan Byrne and **C**iaran Higgins.

The use of logical operators with Date/Time fields will be explained in Assignment 5.

LEARN HOW TO SORT RECORDS FOUND BY A QUERY

Records found by a Query will be in ascending order of the primary key field unless you specify otherwise. In examples 1, 2 and 3, the records are in ascending order of the *Player Number* field, as this is the primary key field in the *Players* Table. You will often want to sort the records found by a Query in a different order. In Example 3, where the Query finds players who made between 5 and 8 tackles inclusive, it is easier to read the results of the Query when the records are in ascending order of the *No of Tackles* field.

Field:	Player Number	Player Name	Position	No of Tackles
Table:	Players	Players	Players	Players
Sort:				
Show:	☑	☑	☑	Ascending
Criteria:				Descending
or:				(not sorted)

Figure 3.5: Setting the sort order for the *No of Tackles* field

To sort by a particular field, simply specify a sort order for that field using the *Sort* row of the Query design grid. In Figure 3.5, a sort order of *Ascending* has been selected for the *No of Tackles* field.

Player Number	Player Name	Position	No of Tackles	No of Passes	No of Errors	Player Rating
1	Darragh Foley	Forward	5	2	3	6
8	Aidan Clohosey	Forward	5	2	2	7
3	Eddy Moran	Forward	6	2	1	6
9	Mick Moloney	Back	7	40	2	8
5	Declan Hennesey	Forward	8	1	3	6

Table 3.10

The records found by this query are no longer in ascending order of *Player Number* and are now in ascending order of the *No of Tackles* field (see Table 3.10). As the *No of Tackles* field is where we entered the *Between 5 and 8* condition, sorting by this field makes the output of the Query easier to interpret.

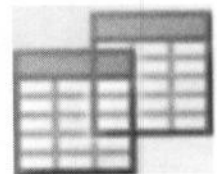

CREATE QUERIES

Create a separate Query for each task described in Table 3.11. Save each Query using the name provided.

For a detailed explanation of how to create a Query, refer to pages 31–5 in Assignment 2.

	Purpose of Query	Sort Order	Query Name	Records Found
Task 5	Find records of players who made less than 2 errors	Ascending order of No of Errors	Made less than 2 errors	8
Task 6	Find records of players who made less than 3 passes	Ascending order of No of Passes	Made less than 3 passes	7
Task 7	Find records of players with a rating of 7 or less	Descending order of Player Rating	Player rating of 7 or less	8
Task 8	Find records of players who made only 1 error	–	Made 1 error	6
Task 9	Find records of players who made more than 6 tackles	Descending order of No of Tackles	Made more than 6 tackles	7
Task 10	Find records of players who made more than 5 passes	–	Made more than 5 passes	2
Task 11	Find records of players with a rating of 8 or more	Descending order of Player Rating	Player rating of 8 or more	7
Task 12	Find records of players who are not Centres	Ascending order of Position	All players excluding Centres	13
Task 13	Find records of players whose rating is between 6 and 8 inclusive	Descending order of Player Rating	Player rating from 6 to 8	13
Task 14	Find records of Forwards who made 8 or more tackles	Descending order of No of Tackles	Forwards who made 8 or more tackles	5
Task 15	Find records of Backs who made between 2 and 6 tackles inclusive	–	Backs who made between 2 and 6 tackles	4

Table 3.11

Task 16: Create a Query to find players who made between 7 and 10 tackles inclusive. Sort the Query in ascending order of the *No of Tackles* field. Save the Query as *Made between 7 and 10 tackles*. Print the records found by this Query. (Records found: 6.)

Preview the Query before you print it. If all the data does not fit on a page in portrait orientation, click the *Landscape* button in the Ribbon.

FIND AND EDIT RECORDS

Task 17: With the *Match Statistics* Form open, use the *Find* and *New Record* buttons to make the following changes.

1. Aidan Clohosey is a Forward and not a Back, as recorded.
2. Tom Wood made 12 tackles.
3. Gerard Byrne made 3 errors.
4. Nick O Kelly's player rating is 7.

ADD NEW RECORDS

- Brendan Byrne came on as a sub during the match. Enter his details, shown in Table 3.12.

Player Number	Player Name	Position	No of Tackles	No of Passes	No of Errors	Player Rating
16	Brendan Byrne	Forward	5	0	2	6

Table 3.12

√

- Open the *Made less than 3 passes* Query. Verify that this Query finds Brendan Byrne's record. ☐
- Verify that the following Queries find Brendan Byrne's record:
  - *Player rating of 7 or less* ☐
  - *All players excluding Centres* ☐
  - *Player rating from 6 to 8* ☐
- Verify that the *Player rating of 7 or less* Query now finds Nick O Kelly's record. ☐

ADD A NEW FIELD TO THE TABLE

Add a new field called *Points Scored* to the *Players* Table, using an appropriate data type and field size (see Table 3.13 on page 51).

1. Open the *Match Statistics* Form in design view.
2. Add the *Points Scored* field to the Form using the *Add Existing Fields* button.
3. Position the *Points Scored* controls to the right of the *Player Number* label and text box controls.
4. Resize the new control to fit the data.
5. Line up the *Points Scored* label with the *Position*, *No of Passes* and *Player Rating* labels using the *Align Left* button.
6. In the same way, line up the *Points Scored* text box using the *Align Right* button.
7. Set the alignment of the *Points Scored* text box to Center.
8. Save the *Match Statistics* Form.

WORKED EXAMPLE: CHANGING THE TAB ORDER IN A FORM

The tab order determines the order in which the cursor moves from text box to text box in a Form as you press the *Tab* key. There should be a direct relationship between the order of fields as they appear on the Form, the tab order of the Form itself and how the data exists on paper before it is entered using the Form. If all three are synchronised, the task of data entry is much easier. Often you will have to change the tab order to ensure that the cursor moves through the Form in a particular sequence. When a new field is added to the Form, it is automatically placed last in the tab order list. This usually means that the sequence of the tab order does not match the sequence in which data is entered. The tab order is displayed by selecting *Tab Order* from the *Arrange* section of the Ribbon when the Form is in either layout or design view.

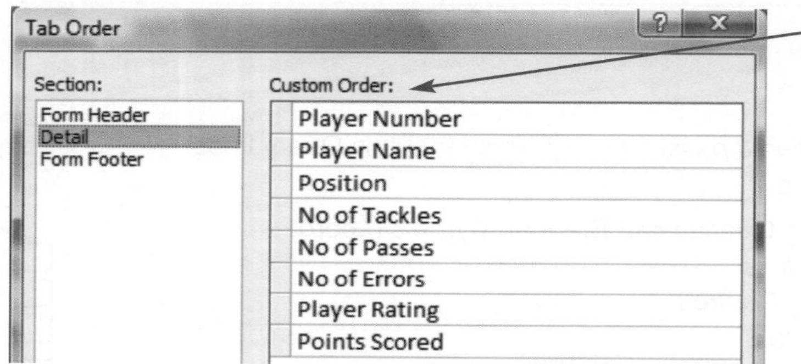

Figure 3.6: Tab order of the *Match Statistics* Form

Figure 3.6 displays the tab order of the *Match Statistics* Form. The new *Points Scored* field is out of sequence. It is last in the tab order list but appears second in the Form. Once data is entered in the *Points Scored* text box, pressing the *Tab* key will cause the cursor to jump to the next record instead of moving to the *Player Name* text box.

- Open the *Match Statistics* Form in design view.
- Click the *Tab Order* button in the Design section of the Ribbon.
- Rearrange the tab order list so that it matches the sequence of fields on the Form, as shown in Figure 3.7.

- Save the *Match Statistics* Form.
- Click the *Form View* button in the Home section of the Ribbon and enter the *Points Scored* data displayed in the shaded cells in Table 3.13.

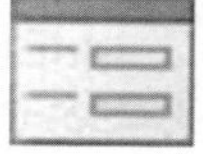

In Access 2007, tab order is in the Arrange section of the Ribbon.

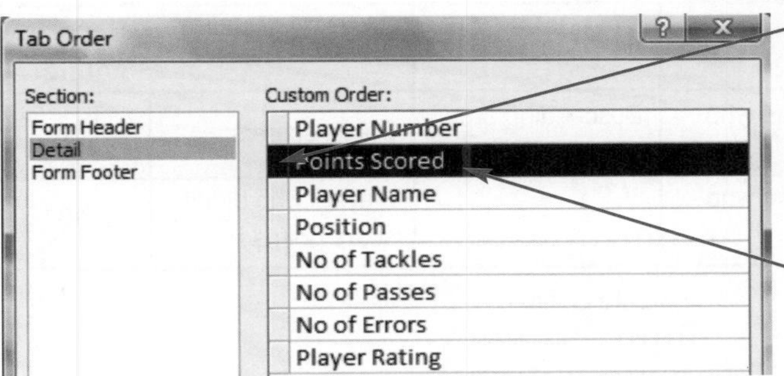
Tab Order
Section:
Form Header
Detail
Form Footer
Custom Order:
Player Number
Points Scored
Player Name
Position
No of Tackles
No of Passes
No of Errors
Player Rating
Click on the box to the left of the field name. Release the mouse button and then drag upward or downward to move a field to a different position in the tab order.
Points Scored has been moved to appear second in the list. The order of fields in the tab order now matches the order of fields as they appear on the Form.

Figure 3.7: Adjusting the tab order

Press the *Page Down* key to quickly advance to the next record.

Player Number	Player Name	Points Scored
1	Darragh Foley	0
2	Shay Lunny	5
3	Eddy Moran	0
4	Nick O Kelly	0
5	Declan Hennesey	0
6	Sean Hayes	0
7	Tom Wood	0
8	Aidan Clohosey	0
9	Mick Moloney	0
10	Gerard Byrne	10
11	Fionn O Sullivan	0
12	James O Driscoll	0
13	Ciaran Higgins	0
14	Paul Murray	0
15	Graham Nolan	5
16	Brendan Byrne	0

Table 3.13

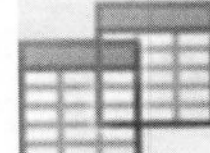

CREATE QUERIES

Create a separate Query for each task described in Table 3.14. Save each Query using the name provided.

	Purpose of Query	Sort Order	Query Name	Records Found
Task 18	Find records of players who scored points	Descending order of Points Scored	Points scorers	3
Task 19	Find records of players who didn't score points	–	Players who didn't score points	13

Table 3.14

LEARN HOW TO DEFINE DATABASE STRUCTURE

It is good database practice to keep a record of the structure of your database in a separate word processing document. This is called the database structure form. You will need to refer to this document if you are making alterations to the database, if you haven't worked with a particular database for a period of time and need to refresh your memory or if you have been assigned responsibility for a database that was designed by someone else.

In a single Table database, we need to specify the field names, field sizes (in bytes) and data types. This information can be found in design view of the *Players* Table, as shown in Figure 3.8.

Field Name	Data Type
Player Number	Number

General Lookup

Field Size Byte

Figure 3.8: Design view of the *Players* Table

Using the information in Figure 3.8, we can fill in the first line of the database structure form, as shown in Table 3.15.

Database Structure Form		
Field Name	**Data Type**	**Field Size**
Player Number	Number	Byte (1)

Table 3.15

For Number fields, the field size in bytes is not given in Table design. When the data type of a Number field is set to Byte, Access automatically sets the field size to 1.

Details of the next field in the *Players* Table are shown in Figure 3.9.

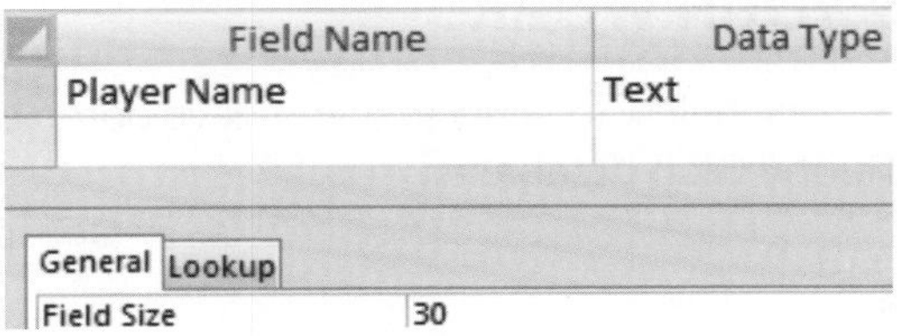

Field Name	Data Type
Player Name	Text

General | Lookup

Field Size 30

Figure 3.9

In the *Player Name* field, the default Text field size of 255 has been reduced to 30 to save disk space. Although there are no players on the team with a name long enough to use up 30 bytes of storage, a field size of 30 has been selected to allow for future players with longer names. Remember that 1 byte is required for each letter or space stored in a Text field.

Continuing the example, we can fill in the information relating to the *Player Name* field as shown in Table 3.16.

Database Structure Form		
Field Name	**Data Type**	**Field Size**
Player Number	Number	Byte (1)
Player Name	Text	30

Table 3.16

Task 20: Create a new Word document. Complete the database structure form shown in Table 3.17 for the remaining fields in the *Players* Table.

Database Structure Form		
Field Name	**Data Type**	**Field Size**
Player Number	Number	Byte (1)
Player Name	Text	30
Position		
No of Tackles		
No of Passes		
No of Errors		
Player Rating		
Points Scored		

Table 3.17

In Microsoft Word, save this file as *Riverside Rugby Structure Form.*

Task 21: Using Access Help, search for information on comparison operators. Write a brief report outlining the function of the operators you have learned about in this assignment. For each operator, give an example of its use in a Query condition.

REVIEW YOUR WORK

Use the checklist below to verify that you have completed all the tasks in the Riverside Rugby Club database.

		Completed (√)
Table:	• Players	☐
Form:	• Match Statistics	☐
Queries:	• All players excluding centres	☐
	• Backs who made between 2 and 6 tackles	☐
	• Forwards who made 8 or more tackles	☐
	• Made 1 error	☐
	• Made between 7 and 10 tackles	☐
	• Made less than 2 errors	☐
	• Made less than 3 passes	☐
	• Made more than 6 tackles	☐
	• Made more than 5 passes	☐
	• Player rating from 6 to 8	☐
	• Player rating of 7 or less	☐
	• Player rating of 8 or more	☐
	• Players who didn't score points	☐
	• Points scorers	☐
Other:	• Database structure form	☐

ASSIGNMENT SUMMARY

Basic Concepts	
Yes/No Data Type	Used when a combination of either Yes and No, True and False or On and Off are the only values that can be entered in a field. By default, Access sets up a check box in a Form for each Yes/No field. For new records, the check box is not ticked by default. Ticking a check box is equivalent to entering "Yes".
Logical Operator	Used in Query conditions to instruct the Query to search for a specific range of numbers in a particular field. The logical operators are:

	• Less than (<) • Less than or equal to (<=) • Equal to (=) • Not equal to (<>) • Greater than (>) • Greater than or equal to (>=) • Between Logical operators are combined with numbers to create Query conditions, e.g. **<=6**. They can also be used with Text fields, e.g. entering **<"d"** as a condition in a *Surname* field would find all surnames beginning with a, b or c.
Database Structure Form	Used to record the way that fields have been set up in the Table. This is a useful reference when updating a database you have designed in the past or when working with a database designed by someone else. The field name, data type and field size are recorded for each field in the Table.

Potential Pitfalls

- Data is entered in a Yes/No field by ticking or not ticking a check box. However, you must enter *Yes* as a Query condition to find all records where the check box was ticked. Type *No* as a Query condition to find all records where the check box wasn't ticked.
- When the field size of a Number field is set to Byte, any numbers entered with decimals will be either rounded up or rounded down.
- When creating Query conditions for Text fields, the condition must match the data in the Table rather than reflecting the way the question is phrased, e.g. *Find all players who are Forwards.* The correct Query condition is **"Forward"**. Some students incorrectly enter **"Forwards"** as the condition.

Log on to www.gillmacmillan.ie to download review questions for Assignment 3.

4 Distance Learning Database

SCENARIO

Debbie Riordan is responsible for the organisation of hardware and software provided for students studying by distance learning. She is finding it difficult to keep track of students who have PCs belonging to the college. Recently she couldn't find DVDs containing applications software and course work and was unable to determine which student has them at present. In Assignment 4 you will create a database to help Debbie manage the allocation of hardware and software.

By completing this assignment, you will practise the following skills:

- Setting up the Table.
- Creating and formatting a Form.
- Editing existing records using a Form.
- Finding records using Queries.
- Adding a new field to a Table and a Form.
- Completing a database structure form.

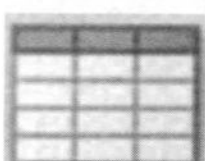

CREATE THE DATABASE AND SET UP THE TABLE

Task 1: Create a new database named *Distance Learning.*

Task 2: Create a new Table and save the Table as *Students.*

- Using the data displayed in Table 4.1, create fields with appropriate data types in the *Students* Table.

Student Number	Firstname	Surname	Phone	PC	Email	MS Office	ECDL DVD	Current	PC No
001	Michael	Noonan	(01) 2043980	Own	mnoo @eircom.net	Yes	Yes	No	6

Table 4.1

- Set the *Student Number* field as the primary key.
- Select appropriate field sizes for the Text fields.
- Set up *MS Office*, *ECDL DVD* and *Current* as Yes/No fields.
- Do not enter data in the Table at this point.

- Save the *Students* Table.

If you set the data type of the Student Number field to Number, the leading zeros won't be displayed.

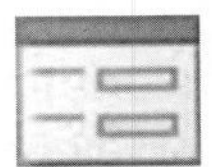

CREATE THE FORM

Task 3: Using the Form Wizard, create a Form including all fields from the *Students* Table. Information relating to the design of the Form is displayed in Table 4.2.

Form Layout	Columnar
Form Title	Student Information

Table 4.2

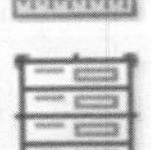

1. In design view, increase the width of the Form so that it fits exactly on your screen.
2. Use layout view to make the following adjustments to the Form.
   - Apply the *Flow* style to the Form.
   - Delete the *Surname* label.

In Access 2007, remove the Form controls from the existing layout before deleting the *Surname* label.

3. Move the Surname text box to the right of the Firstname text box.
4. Edit the Firstname label so that it reads *Student Name.*
5. Edit the PC No label so that it reads *PC Number.*
6. Reposition labels and text boxes and adjust the width of text boxes so that they appear like Figure 4.1.
7. Set the alignment of the *Student Number*, *PC* and *PC No* text boxes to Center.
8. Centre the Form title.

Use the *Align Left* button to line up the Form controls.

Figure 4.1 is an example of the completed *Student Information* Form.

Student Information

Student Number

Student Name

Phone

PC

Email

MS Office

ECDL DVD

PC Number

Current

Figure 4.1: The completed *Student Information* Form

Task 4: Using the *Student Information* Form, enter all the records displayed in Table 4.3.

If necessary, adjust the width of text boxes, using layout view, as you enter the data.

Ticking the *MS Office*, *ECDL DVD* and *Current* check boxes is equivalent to entering *Yes* in each of these fields, while not ticking the check boxes is equivalent to entering *No*.

You can increase the amount of available space on the screen by hiding the Navigation Pane. Click the double left arrow in the top right-hand corner of the Navigation Pane. To display the Navigation Pane again, click the double right arrow.

«

»

Student Number	Firstname	Surname	Phone	PC	Email	MS Office	ECDL DVD	Current	PC No
001	Michael	Noonan	(01) 2043980	Own	mnoo @eircom.net	Yes	Yes	No	6
002	Anne	Ward	(045) 8209396	Loan	anne200 @yahoo.com	Yes	No	Yes	2
003	Avril	Kearney	(086) 8338017	Loan	avrilk @indigo.ie	Yes	Yes	No	12
004	Jelena	Rozova	(01) 4992266	Own	jroz @yahoo.com	No	No	Yes	9
005	John	Delaney	(01) 2993676	Loan	jdl55 @hotmail.com	No	No	Yes	1
006	Susan	Mc Grath	(086) 2886134	Loan	smg @gmail.com	Yes	No	Yes	10
007	Hugh	O Keefe	(087) 4510501	Own	hok @gmail.com	Yes	Yes	Yes	5
008	Erica	Sullivan	(085) 6264457	Loan	erica @hotmail.com	No	No	Yes	7
009	Pamela	Galvin	(041) 8333359	Own	pgalvin @yahoo.com	Yes	Yes	Yes	11
010	Fran	Byrne	(057) 8944055	Own	fran3000 @gmail.com	No	Yes	No	3
011	Daniel	Conroy	(086) 2962138	Loan	dconroy @eircom.net	No	No	No	8
012	Jacob	Wielgosz	(01) 8936274	Loan	jwielgosz @gmail.com	No	No	Yes	4

Table 4.3

Task 5: Table 4.4 is the database structure form for the *Students* Table. Complete the database structure form by recording the field names, data types and field sizes for all fields in the *Students* Table.

For a detailed explanation of how to complete a database structure form, refer to pages 52–3 in Assignment 3.

Field Name	Data Type	Field Size
Student Number		
Firstname		
Surname		
Phone		
PC		
Email		
MS Office		
ECDL DVD		
Current		
PC No		

Table 4.4

Ensure that the field sizes of Text fields specified in design view of the *Students* Table match those specified in the database structure form.

CREATE QUERIES

Create a separate Query for each of the tasks described in Table 4.5. Save each Query using the name provided.

	Purpose of Query	Sort Order	Query Name	Records Found
Task 6	Find records of students currently on the course	Ascending order of Surname	List of current students	8
Task 7	Find records of current students who have their own PC	Ascending order of Surname	Current students with own PC	3
Task 8	Find records of students who have finished the course and still have the ECDL DVD	Ascending order of Surname	ECDL DVDs to be returned	3
Task 9	Find records of current students who need to have MS Office installed on their PCs	Ascending order of Surname	MS Office installations	4
Task 10	Find records of current students who have PCs 1 to 6	Ascending order of PC No	Location of PCs 1 to 6	4
Task 11	Find records of current students who have PCs 7 to 12	Ascending order of PC No	Location of PCs 7 to 12	4

Table 4.5

Task 12: Print the records found by the *Location of PCs 1 to 6* Query and the *Location of PCs 7 to 12* Query.

FIND AND EDIT RECORDS

Task 13: Open the *Student Information* Form. Use the *Find* and *New Record* buttons to make the following changes.

When searching for a record using a Form, Access will only find the record if it finds an exact match. Searching for *Fran Byrne* will not find any records, as the student names are stored in two separate fields. Either search for the first name or the surname.

1. Fran Byrne has not finished the course.
2. Anne Ward is no longer on the course.

Do not delete Anne Ward's record. Change the value in the *Current* field.

3. John Delaney's email address is jdl54@hotmail.com.
4. Hugh O Keefe doesn't have the ECDL DVD.
5. Jacob Wielgosz's phone number is (01) 8836274.

Completed (√)

- Verify that the *List of current students* Query now finds Fran Byrne but no longer finds Anne Ward. ☐

ADD NEW RECORDS

New

- A new student has started. Click the *New* button and enter the data displayed in Table 4.6.

Student Number	Firstname	Surname	Phone	PC	Email	MS Office	ECDL DVD	Current	PC No
013	Ciaran	Murphy	(086) 2012339	Loan	cmpy @gmail.com	No	No	Yes	2

Table 4.6

- Verify that the following Queries find Ciaran Murphy's record. **Completed (√)**
  - *List of current students* ☐
  - *MS Office installations* ☐
  - *Location of PCs 1 to 6* ☐

ADD A NEW FIELD TO THE TABLE

1. Add a new field named *Completed Modules* to the *Students* Table, using an appropriate data type and field size (see Table 4.7).
2. Open the *Student Information* Form in design view.
3. Add the *Completed Modules* field to the Form using the *Add Existing Fields* button.
4. Position the *Completed Modules* controls to the right of the *Surname* control.
5. Resize the *Completed Modules* text box to fit the data and set the alignment to center.

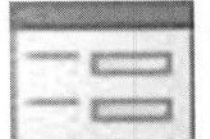

6. Adjust the tab order so that *Completed Modules* is fourth in the list.
7. Using the *Student Information* Form, enter the data relating to completed modules displayed in the shaded cells in Table 4.7.

Press the *Page Down* button on the keyboard to quickly advance to the next record.

Student Number	Firstname	Surname	Completed Modules
001	Michael	Noonan	7
002	Anne	Ward	7
003	Avril	Kearney	7
004	Jelena	Rozova	6
005	John	Delaney	4
006	Susan	Mc Grath	1
007	Hugh	O Keefe	0
008	Erica	Sullivan	3
009	Pamela	Galvin	5
010	Fran	Byrne	7
011	Daniel	Conroy	4
012	Jacob	Wielgosz	2
013	Ciaran	Murphy	0

Table 4.7

CREATE QUERIES

Create a separate Query for each of the tasks described in Table 4.8. Save each Query using the name provided.

	Purpose of Query	Sort Order	Query Name	Records Found
Task 14	Finds records of students who have finished the course and who have 7 ECDL modules	Ascending order of Surname	Past students with full cert	3
Task 15	Finds records of current students who have completed 2 or more ECDL modules	Descending order of Completed Modules	Current students with 2 or more modules	6

Table 4.8

Task 16: Using Access Help, search for information on "Primary Key". Write a brief report outlining the function of the primary key.

REVIEW YOUR WORK

Use the checklist below to verify that you have completed all the tasks in the Distance Learning database.

		Completed (√)
Table:	• Students	☐
Form:	• Student Information	☐
Queries:	• Current students with 2 or more modules	☐
	• Current students with own PC	☐
	• ECDL DVDs to be returned	☐
	• List of current students	☐
	• Location of PCs 1 to 6	☐
	• Location of PCs 7 to 12	☐
	• MS Office installations	☐
	• Past students with full cert	☐
Other:	• Database structure form	☐

Log on to www.gillmacmillan.ie to download review questions for Assignment 4.

SECTION 1 REVIEW

Database

A database is used to store, organise and retrieve data. A database can be paper based, such as the telephone directory, or computerised. Computerised databases are much more efficient, as specific data can be found instantly and records can be quickly sorted into different orders. An Access database consists of four main objects: Tables, Queries, Forms and Reports. Each object carries out a specific function.

The Table

The Table is the most important object in a database. It is responsible for storing data. A Table is divided into columns and rows. The columns are called fields. The rows are called records.

All the information relating to one student is called a record

Student Code	Student Name	Age	Course	Date Started	Teacher
BS001	Peter Dunne	18	Admin	02/09/2014	Tadhg Allen
BS002	Mark Connolly	17	Admin	02/09/2014	Tadhg Allen
BS003	Dave O Neill	21	Finance	02/09/2014	Gerry Browne

Each record in this Table is divided into six fields

Table 4.9

The Table – Important Concepts

Field	A specific column in the Table, e.g. *Student Name*.
Data Type	The data type of a field specifies the type of data that can be stored in that field. • The Text data type is used to store letters, combinations of letters and numbers (alpha-numeric), numbers with leading zeros and numbers with spaces. When numbers are stored in a Text field, Access treats them as characters. This means that they cannot be sorted in ascending or descending numerical order.

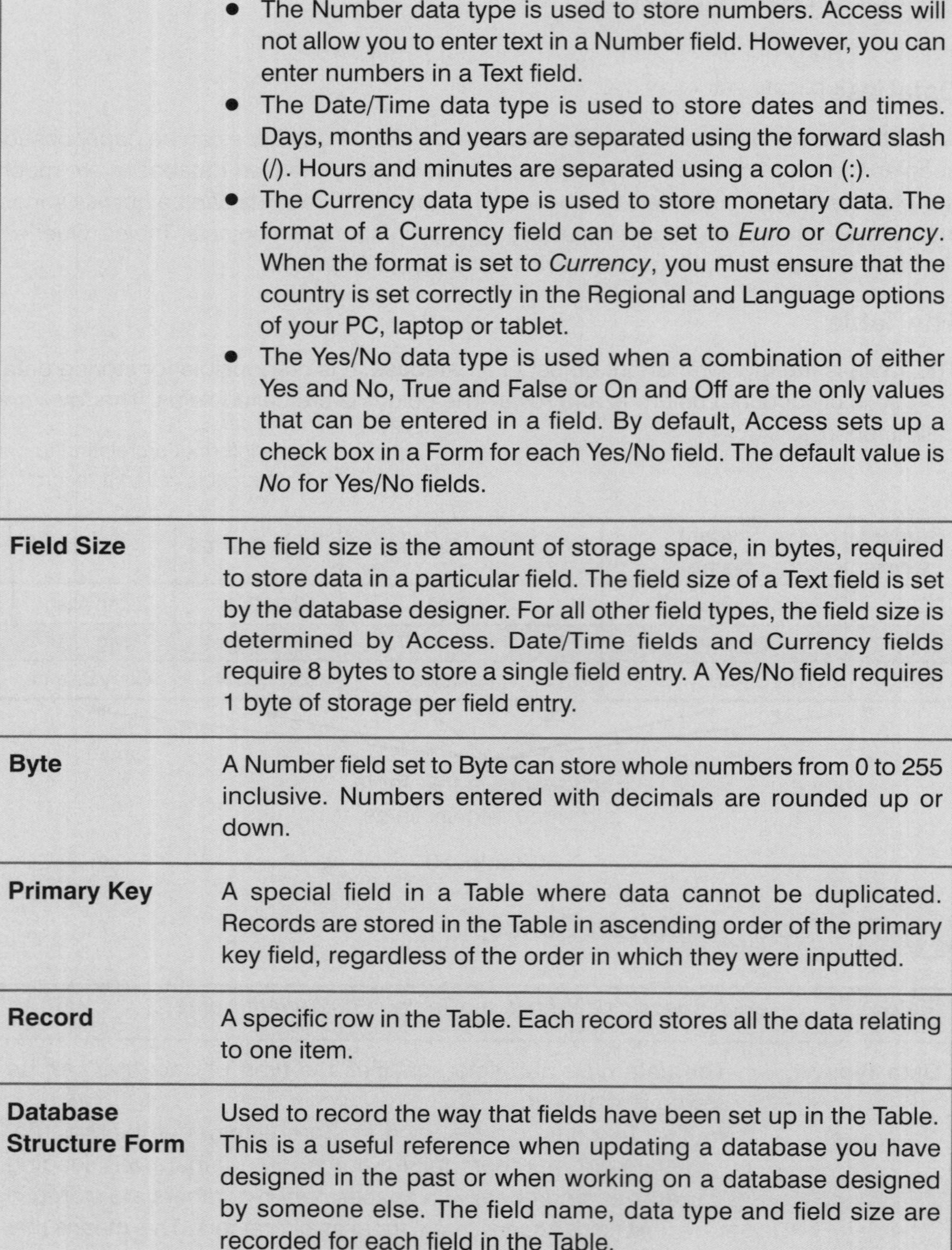

	• The Number data type is used to store numbers. Access will not allow you to enter text in a Number field. However, you can enter numbers in a Text field. • The Date/Time data type is used to store dates and times. Days, months and years are separated using the forward slash (/). Hours and minutes are separated using a colon (:). • The Currency data type is used to store monetary data. The format of a Currency field can be set to *Euro* or *Currency*. When the format is set to *Currency*, you must ensure that the country is set correctly in the Regional and Language options of your PC, laptop or tablet. • The Yes/No data type is used when a combination of either Yes and No, True and False or On and Off are the only values that can be entered in a field. By default, Access sets up a check box in a Form for each Yes/No field. The default value is *No* for Yes/No fields.
Field Size	The field size is the amount of storage space, in bytes, required to store data in a particular field. The field size of a Text field is set by the database designer. For all other field types, the field size is determined by Access. Date/Time fields and Currency fields require 8 bytes to store a single field entry. A Yes/No field requires 1 byte of storage per field entry.
Byte	A Number field set to Byte can store whole numbers from 0 to 255 inclusive. Numbers entered with decimals are rounded up or down.
Primary Key	A special field in a Table where data cannot be duplicated. Records are stored in the Table in ascending order of the primary key field, regardless of the order in which they were inputted.
Record	A specific row in the Table. Each record stores all the data relating to one item.
Database Structure Form	Used to record the way that fields have been set up in the Table. This is a useful reference when updating a database you have designed in the past or when working on a database designed by someone else. The field name, data type and field size are recorded for each field in the Table.

The Table – Potential Pitfalls

- Once a particular field has been identified as the primary key, Access will not allow you to duplicate values in that field.
- Access will not allow you to enter letters or symbols in a field with a Number data type.
- When the field size of a Number field is set to Byte, any numbers entered with decimals will be either rounded up or rounded down.

Queries

The function of a Query is to search for records in the Table. Search instructions are given to the Query by the conditions entered in the Query design grid. The Query searches through the Table, record by record. Any records that satisfy the Query condition(s) are copied into a separate datasheet, which is then displayed on the screen. Queries are dynamic in that they automatically pick up new records entered in the database, as long as those records satisfy all the conditions in the Query. However, when a new field is added to the Table, it is not automatically picked up by the Query. The new field must be added to the Query using the Query design grid.

Field:	Order Number	Date	Pizza Type
Table:	Current Deliveries	Current Deliveries	Current Deliveries
Sort:			
Show:	☑	☑	☑
Criteria:			"Vegetarian"
or:			

Figure 4.2: How a Query condition finds records in the Table

Order Number	Delivery Date	Pizza Type	Customer Name	Address	Total Due
1	03/11/2014	Spicy Cheese	Harry O Leary	15 Main Street	€8.95
2	03/11/2014	Ham and Mushroom	Margaret Kenna	10 Cremore Lawns	€10.50
3	03/11/2014	Mozzarella	Chris Duggan	12 Gledswood Park	€10.00
4	03/11/2014	Ham and Mushroom	Crisan Dumitro	15 Grange Park	€10.95
5	03/11/2014	Vegetarian	Diane O Connor	103 Kings Road	€11.50
6	03/11/2014	Four Seasons	Mary Smith	15 Woodpark	€10.95
7	03/11/2014	Pepperoni	Eamonn Buckley	27 The Pines	€10.50
8	04/11/2014	Vegetarian	John Murphy	5 The Gallops	€11.50
9	04/11/2014	Spicy Cheese	Declan Keane	33 Meadowvale	€8.95
10	04/11/2014	Pepperoni	Emma Daly	Glenview Drive	€10.50

In Figure 4.2, the condition in the Query design grid instructs the Query to search through the Table record by record and extract records where the Pizza Type is *Vegetarian*. This Query finds two records, which are shaded in Figure 4.2.

Queries – Important Concepts

Condition

An expression entered in the Criteria row of the Query design grid. Conditions allow us to specify exactly what records we are searching for.

Field:	Order Number	Delivery Date	Pizza Type	Customer Name	Address	Total Due
Table:	Current Deliveries	Current Deliveries	Current Deliveries	Current Deliveries	Current Deliveries	Current Deliveries
Sort:						
Show:	☑	☑	☑	☑	☑	☑
Criteria:		#04/11/2014#	"Pepperoni"			
or:						

Figure 4.3: Query conditions

In Figure 4.3, two conditions have been entered in the Query design grid. These conditions instruct the Query to search for records where the Date is *04/11/2014* and the Pizza Type is *Pepperoni*. The Query will only find records where both conditions are satisfied.

Logical Operator

Used in Query conditions to instruct the Query to search for a specific range of numbers in a particular field. The logical operators are:

- Less than (<)
- Less than or equal to (<=)
- Equal to (=)
- Not equal to (<>)
- Greater than (>)
- Greater than or equal to (>=)
- Between

Logical operators are combined with numbers to form Query conditions, e.g. **<=6**.

Field:	Player Name	Position	No of Tackles	No of Passes	No of Errors	Player Rating
Table:	Players	Players	Players	Players	Players	Players
Sort:						
Show:	☑	☑	☑	☑	☑	☑
Criteria:			<5			>7

Figure 4.4: Using logical operators in a Query

In Figure 4.4, the *less than* logical operator is used in the *No of Tackles* field and the *greater than* logical operator is used in the *Player Rating* field. The Query will search through the Table for records of players who have made less than 5 tackles <u>and</u>

whose rating is greater than 7. It will only display records where both of these conditions are satisfied.

Field:	Player Name	Position	No of Tackles	No of Passes
Table:	Players	Players	Players	Players
Sort:				
Show:	☑	☑	☑	☑
Criteria:			Between 5 And 8	
or:				

Figure 4.5: The *Between* logical operator

In Figure 4.5, the *Between* logical operator is used to find all players who made between 5 and 8 tackles inclusive. An alternative method would be to use the following expression: ***>=5 and <=8***

Logical operators can also be used with Text fields, e.g. entering **<"d"** as a condition in a surname field would find all surnames beginning with a, b or c.

Queries – Potential Pitfalls

- A single spelling error at the data entry stage will often result in multiple Queries not finding all the relevant records.
- If there is a spelling error in a Query condition, the Query will not find any records.
- Even if your condition is correct, the Query will not find any records if you have entered the condition in the wrong field.
- Data is entered in a Yes/No field by ticking or not ticking a check box. However, you must enter *Yes* as a Query condition to find all records where the check box was ticked. Type *No* as a Query condition to find all records where the check box wasn't ticked.
- When creating a Query condition for a Currency field, never type the euro (€) sign.
- When numbers are stored in a Text field, you will get unexpected results when you query that field using a logical operator.

The Form

The main function of a Form is to facilitate data entry. The Form is linked to the Table. Data entered in the Form filters down to and is stored in the Table.

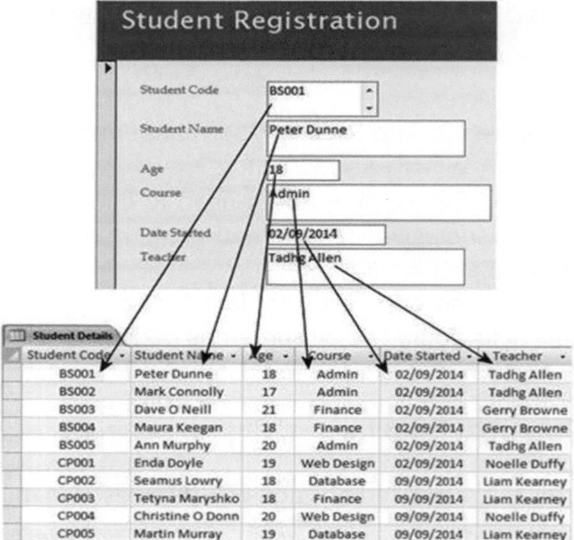

Student Code	Student Name	Age	Course	Date Started	Teacher
BS001	Peter Dunne	18	Admin	02/09/2014	Tadhg Allen
BS002	Mark Connolly	17	Admin	02/09/2014	Tadhg Allen
BS003	Dave O Neill	21	Finance	02/09/2014	Gerry Browne
BS004	Maura Keegan	18	Finance	02/09/2014	Gerry Browne
BS005	Ann Murphy	20	Admin	02/09/2014	Tadhg Allen
CP001	Enda Doyle	19	Web Design	02/09/2014	Noelle Duffy
CP002	Seamus Lowry	18	Database	09/09/2014	Liam Kearney
CP003	Tetyna Maryshko	18	Finance	09/09/2014	Liam Kearney
CP004	Christine O Donn	20	Web Design	09/09/2014	Noelle Duffy
CP005	Martin Murray	19	Database	09/09/2014	Liam Kearney

Figure 4.6: Data entered in the Form is transferred to the Table record by record

Figure 4.6 demonstrates how data entered in the *Student Registration* Form is transferred to the *Student Details* Table, record by record. A Form can also be used to find and delete individual records as well as basic editing of data, such as correcting spelling errors.

Label/Text Box Each label/text box combination in the Form is linked to a specific field in the Table. Data is entered in the text boxes. Descriptive text is displayed in the labels.

Useful Shortcut	
Keyboard Combination	**Action**
CTRL + F	Find records in a Form

Table 4.10

TOOLBAR BUTTONS INTRODUCED IN SECTION 1

	Design View Button: Used to enter design view of a database object, such as a Form. Once you are in design view, you can make adjustments to the appearance and functionality of a database object.
	Layout View Button: Used to view a Form or Report in layout view. Using layout view, you can make changes to the design of your Form or Report while viewing live data.
	Form View Button: Click this button when you want to enter records using a Form.
	Form Wizard Button: Click this button to start the Form Wizard, which helps you to create a new Form.
	Center Button: Centres data in a selected label or text box when in either design or layout view of a Form.
Left	**Align Left Button:** Clicking this button while in either design or layout view of a Form will align selected controls to the left.
Right	**Align Right Button:** Clicking this button while in either design or layout view of a Form will align selected controls to the right.
	Horizontal Resize: When the mouse pointer takes this shape, click and drag to the left or right to resize a label or a text box in a Form. This only works when you are in either layout or design view.
	Move: The mouse pointer takes this shape when you point at the edge of a selected control in design view of a Form or when you point at any Form control in layout view. Click and drag to move the selected control. When all the controls in the Form are grouped in a layout, moving one label or text box will also move all the other labels and text boxes.
	Adjust Width: The mouse pointer takes this shape when you point at the right-hand edge of a Form in design view. Drag to the right to increase the width of the Form. Drag to the left to decrease the width of the Form.
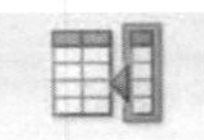	**Add Existing Fields Button:** Clicking this button when in either design or layout view of a Form will display the field list. The field list is a complete list of fields in the Table that the Form is linked to. Use the field list to add fields to your Form.
	**Save Button:** Click this button to save any design changes made to a Form or Table. There is no need to click the *Save* button as you enter records in a Form, as these are saved automatically.

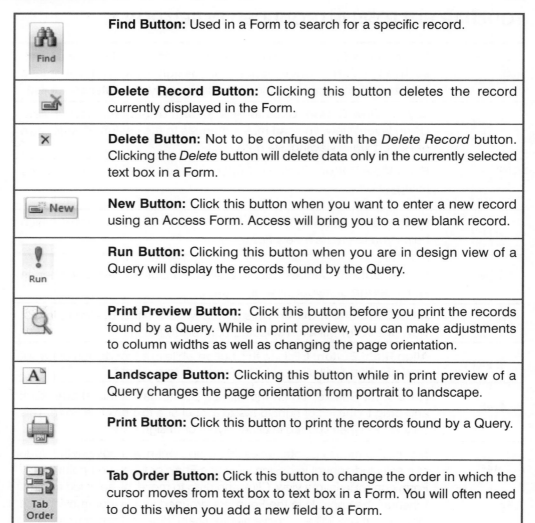

Find	**Find Button:** Used in a Form to search for a specific record.
	Delete Record Button: Clicking this button deletes the record currently displayed in the Form.
×	**Delete Button:** Not to be confused with the *Delete Record* button. Clicking the *Delete* button will delete data only in the currently selected text box in a Form.
New	**New Button:** Click this button when you want to enter a new record using an Access Form. Access will bring you to a new blank record.
Run	**Run Button:** Clicking this button when you are in design view of a Query will display the records found by the Query.
	Print Preview Button: Click this button before you print the records found by a Query. While in print preview, you can make adjustments to column widths as well as changing the page orientation.
A	**Landscape Button:** Clicking this button while in print preview of a Query changes the page orientation from portrait to landscape.
	Print Button: Click this button to print the records found by a Query.
Tab Order	**Tab Order Button:** Click this button to change the order in which the cursor moves from text box to text box in a Form. You will often need to do this when you add a new field to a Form.

SECTION 2

Intermediate Database Assignments

Assignment 5: National Railways Database

Assignment 6: Night Vision Database

Assignment 7: Technical Zone Database

Tip | Note | Rule | Cross-reference | Shortcut | Hint | Important Point | Theory Section

5 National Railways Database

SCENARIO

Luke Thomas is the manager of the customer information service in a large railway station. He would like to provide customers with up-to-date information regarding the expected arrival time of trains.

In Assignment 5 you will create a database to store data relating to trains arriving at the station. The Queries and Reports in the database will help Luke to find information on specific routes.

By completing this assignment, you will learn how to:

- Create an index.
- Create a combo box to enter data in a Form.
- Create a Report linked to a Table.
- Create a Report linked to a Query.
- Use layouts to organise Report controls.
- Create Query conditions in Date/Time fields.

LEARN ABOUT NUMERIC FIELD TYPES IN ACCESS

In the Riverside Rugby Club database, we introduced the Byte number type, which stores whole numbers in the range 0 to 255. A complete list of the number types that we will encounter in the remaining assignments in this book is displayed in Table 5.1.

Number Type	Description	Max No. of Decimals	Storage Size per Field Entry
Byte	Stores whole numbers from 0 to 255	None	1 byte
Integer	Stores whole numbers from –32,768 to +32,767	None	2 bytes
Long Integer	Stores whole numbers from –2,147,483,648 to +2,147,483,648	None	4 bytes
Single	Stores numbers with decimals	7	4 bytes

Table 5.1

Table 5.1 can be summarised as follows:

- For whole numbers, select a field size of Byte, Integer or Long Integer, depending on the highest and lowest value that you expect to store in a particular field.
- Select a field size of Single when you need to store numbers with a decimal element.

N If you need to store numbers bigger than 2,147,483,648, the Single field size can store numbers to a maximum of 3.4×10^{38}. That's 3.4 multiplied by 10 thirty-eight times, which is a very big number!

Examples of the Byte, Integer, Long Integer and Single field sizes are displayed in Table 5.2.

Data Stored in Field	Example	Field Size
A person's age	32	Byte
Seat numbers in a 10,000-seat stadium	8946	Integer
Kilometres on a car's odometer	78904	Long Integer
A person's weight, in kilograms	72.5	Single
A golfer's score, which can be above or below par	-4	Integer
Distances in kilometres in the AA Route Planner	520	Integer
Number of bedrooms in a house	4	Byte
Circulation figure for a national newspaper	51292	Long Integer
Speed of a PC's processor, in gigahertz	3.2	Single

Table 5.2

N Each time you create a Number field in an Access Table, the field size is set to Long Integer by default.

CREATE THE DATABASE AND SET UP THE TABLE

Task 1: Create a new database named *National Railways.*

Task 2: Create a new Table and save the Table as *Train Schedule.*

- Using the data displayed in Table 5.3, create fields with appropriate data types in the *Train Schedule* Table.

Code	Journey Date	Departure Time	From	Due in at	No of Stops	First Class	Restaurant Car	Tickets Sold	Notes
CD001	25/08/2014	07:05	Cork	09:46	3	Yes	Yes	275	Running 10 mins late

Table 5.3

For a detailed explanation of data types in Access, refer to pages 16–23 in Assignment 2.

- Set the *Code* field as the primary key. Set the field size of this field to an exact number, as all codes have the same number of characters.
- Set the format of the *Journey Date* field to Short Date.
- Set the format of the *Departure Time* and *Due in at* fields to Short Time.
- The field size for the *From* field can be set exactly, as trains depart from five different towns and cities: Cork, Galway, Kildare, Tralee or Westport.
- Select appropriate field sizes for the *No of Stops* and *Tickets Sold* fields.
- Set the data type of the *First Class* and *Restaurant Car* fields to *Yes/No.*
- Do not enter data in the Table at this point.

- Save the *Train Schedule* Table.

LEARN ABOUT INDEXES

Indexes are used to speed up searches in a database. Indexes are not only used in databases. They are commonly found at the back of educational or technical books. An index allows you to quickly find what you are looking for. For example, if you want to find sections of a database book that deal with Reports, you could look under *R* in the index. Each listing for Reports will have an associated page number. You can then go directly to that page number without having to read any of the preceding pages. Without an index, it would be very time consuming to find all the references to Reports, as you would effectively have to scan through the entire book.

In an Access database, indexes work in a similar way when you are searching for records with a Query. The index file is much smaller than the Table, so the Query can search through the index faster than searching through the entire Table.

Each time you set up a primary key, the Table is automatically indexed on the primary key field. A primary key is a special type of index that doesn't allow duplicate values. In addition to the primary key index, creating an index on a field that you regularly search will speed up your Queries. Without an index, Access has to search through the entire Table, record by record, each time a Query is run. In large databases, this can be slow.

An indexed search is much faster, as the index only contains a single field, which is sorted. The fact that the index is sorted helps Access to find the correct value more quickly. In the example on page 76, an index has been created for the *Course* field. In a Query to find students on the *Admin* course, the Query searches the index instead of searching the entire Table. Each reference to *Admin* in the index points to the corresponding record in the Table.

Example: Searching an index file for references to "Admin"

Course Index

Admin
Database
Finance
Finance
Admin
Web Design
Admin
Database
Web Design
Admin

Searching through the index is much faster than searching through the entire Table.

Students Table

Student Code	Student Name	Age	Course	Date Started	Teacher
BS001	Peter Dunne	18	Admin	02/09/2014	Tadhg Allen
BS002	Mark Connolly	17	Database	02/09/2014	Tadhg Allen
BS003	Dave O Neill	21	Finance	02/09/2014	Gerry Browne
BS004	Maura Keegan	18	Finance	02/09/2014	Gerry Browne
BS005	Ann Murphy	20	Admin	02/09/2014	Tadhg Allen
CP001	Enda Doyle	19	Web Design	09/09/2014	Noelle Duffy
CP002	Seamus Lowry	18	Admin	09/09/2014	Liam Kearney
CP003	Tetyna Maryshko	18	Database	09/09/2014	Liam Kearney
CP004	Christine O Donnell	20	Web Design	09/09/2014	Noelle Duffy
CP005	Martin Murray	19	Admin	09/09/2014	Liam Kearney

The advantage of the index is that the Query only has to search through a single field – the *Course* field. Without the index, the Query would have to search every field in every record. The more records there are in the Table, the slower the search becomes.

Indexes should be used in databases with large Tables or when the performance of Queries has slowed down. You should only set up indexes on fields that you regularly search. One drawback of setting up an index is that it will slow down updates to your database. In the example above, each time a new record is added to the *Students* Table, Access also has to update the *Course* index. The more indexes you have, the slower updates become.

The databases that you will create in this book don't really require indexes. This is because they are small enough to work efficiently without indexes. However, in each of the remaining assignments, you will be required to set up indexes so that you can practise this important task.

WORKED EXAMPLE: CREATE AN INDEX

1. Open the *Train Schedule* Table in design view.
2. Select the *No of stops* field.

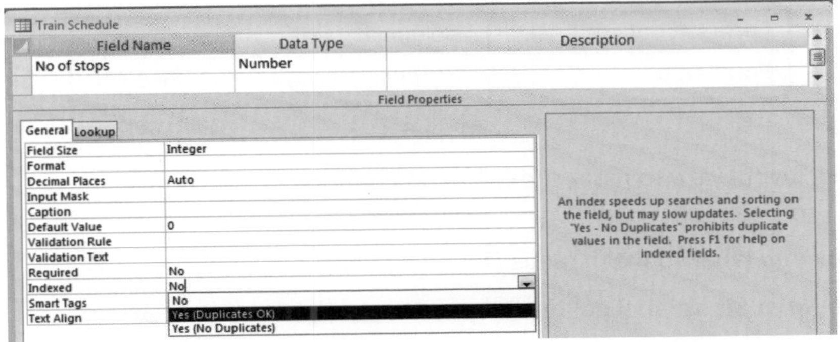

Figure 5.1: Creating an index for the *No of stops* field

3. In the *Indexed* property of the *No of stops* field, select *Yes (Duplicates OK)*, as shown in Figure 5.1.

4. Click the *Indexes* button in the Design section of the Ribbon. The list of indexes currently defined in the *Train Schedule* Table is displayed (Figure 5.2).

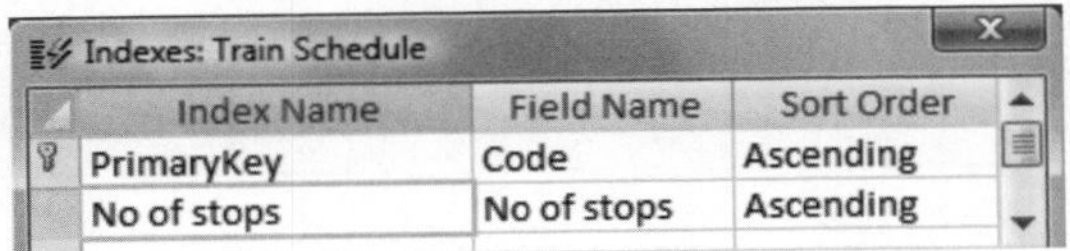

Indexes: Train Schedule

Index Name	Field Name	Sort Order
PrimaryKey	Code	Ascending
No of stops	No of stops	Ascending

Figure 5.2: Indexes in the *Train Schedule* Table

Notice how Access has already created an index for the *Code* field, which is the primary key field. Access indexes primary key fields by default. The newly created index on the *No of stops* field appears below the *PrimaryKey* index in Figure 5.2. The effect of setting up this index is that searches on the *No of stops* field will be faster. However, updates will be slower, as both the *PrimaryKey* and *No of stops* indexes must be updated each time a new record is added.

5. Save and close the *Train Schedule* Table.

In a primary key index, duplicates are not allowed. This forces the data entry operator to enter a unique value in the primary key field of each record. In all other cases, you will need to select *Duplicates OK* when setting up an index.

CREATE THE FORM

Task 3: Using the Form Wizard, create a Form including all fields from the *Train Schedule* Table. Information relating to the design of the Form is displayed in Table 5.4.

Form Layout	Columnar
Form Title	National Railways Train Schedule

Table 5.4

Use layout view to make the following changes to the Form:

- Edit the *From* label so that it reads *Departing From.*
- Edit the *No of Stops* label so that it reads *Number of Stops.*

- In design view, adjust the width of the Form so that it takes up the full width of the PC screen.
- The completed Form should look something like Figure 5.3.

- Save the *National Railways Train Schedule* Form.

National Railways Train Schedule

Code	CD001	Journey Date	25/08/2014
Departure Time	07:05	Departing From:	Cork
Due in at	09:46	Number of stops	3
First Class	☑	Restaurant Car	☑
Tickets Sold	275	Notes	On Time

Figure 5.3: *National Railways Train Schedule* Form in tabular layout

LEARN ABOUT COMBO BOXES

One of the advantages of Forms is that they can make the task of data entry easier. A combo box is a particularly useful tool that provides the data entry operator with a drop-down list of selectable items. Instead of typing data, the operator selects the required item from the combo box list. Combo boxes are commonly found on commercial websites. Figure 5.4 is an example of a combo box from the Aer Lingus website.

Figure 5.4: A combo box commonly seen on holiday booking websites

In Figure 5.4, you can select the month of departure from the combo box list rather than typing it. This has a number of advantages:

- It is faster and easier than typing the data.
- Data entry errors are eliminated.
- The database designer can restrict data entry to items in the list.

In an Access database, you can create a combo box for fields where data entry is limited to a fixed number of items, e.g. selecting the colour of a new car from a list of 10 available colours or selecting an exam result where the result can only be distinction, merit, pass or fail. In the National Railways database, we can create a combo box for the *From* field, as each train originates from one of five different towns and cities.

WORKED EXAMPLE: CREATE A COMBO BOX

Note to Access 2007 users: You will need to remove the controls for the *From* field from the existing layout before starting this worked example.

1. Open the *National Railways Train Schedule* Form in design view.

Figure 5.5: Controls in the right-hand layout have been selected

2. Select the *From* text box. Delete this text box by pressing the *Delete* key on the keyboard.

3. In the Design section of the Ribbon, click the *Combo Box* button.

4. Display the field list using the *Add Existing Fields* button.

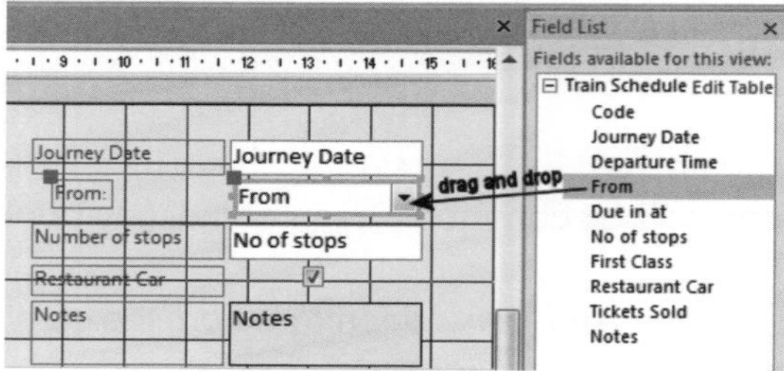

Figure 5.6: Dragging a field from the field list

5. Drag the *From* field from the field list and drop in the detail section of the Form, as shown in Figure 5.6.

If the Combo Box Wizard doesn't start, delete the combo box, click the *Use Control Wizards* button and start again from step 8.

6. In the Combo Box Wizard, select *I will type in the values that I want*. Click *Next*.
7. Type the list shown in Figure 5.7.

Use either the *Tab* key, the right arrow or the down arrow key to move on to the next line of the combo box list. Pressing the *Enter* key is equivalent to clicking the *Next* button and will advance you to the next step of the Combo Box Wizard.

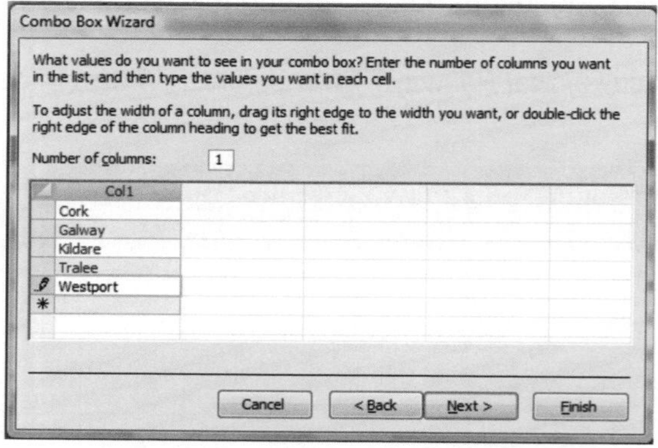

Figure 5.7: Creating a combo box list

8. Click *Next* to move on to the next step.
9. This is an important step in the Combo Box Wizard. Each time a value is selected in the combo box, Access needs to know where to store that value in the Table.

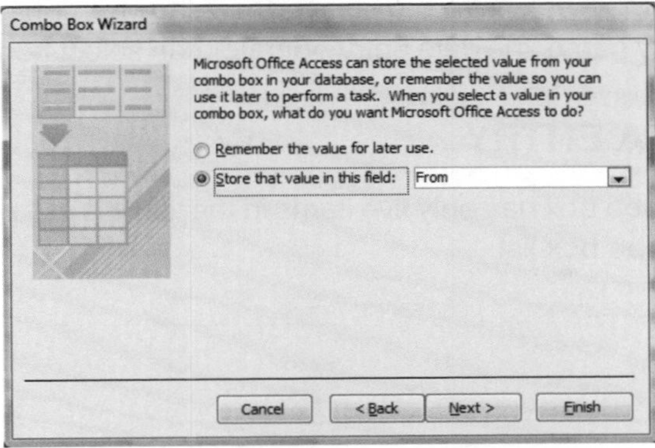
Combo Box Wizard

Microsoft Office Access can store the selected value from your combo box in your database, or remember the value so you can use it later to perform a task. When you select a value in your combo box, what do you want Microsoft Office Access to do?

- Remember the value for later use.
- Store that value in this field: From

Cancel | < Back | Next > | Finish

Figure 5.8: Ensuring that the combo box is linked to the correct field in the Table

Figure 5.8 indicates that the town or city selected in the combo box will be stored in the *From* field in the *Train Schedule* Table. Before moving on to the next step, ensure that the *From* field is selected, as shown in Figure 5.8. Click *Next*.

10. Type *From* as the label for the combo box. Click *Finish*.

FINE TUNE AND TEST THE COMBO BOX

1. View the *National Railways Train Schedule* Form in design view.

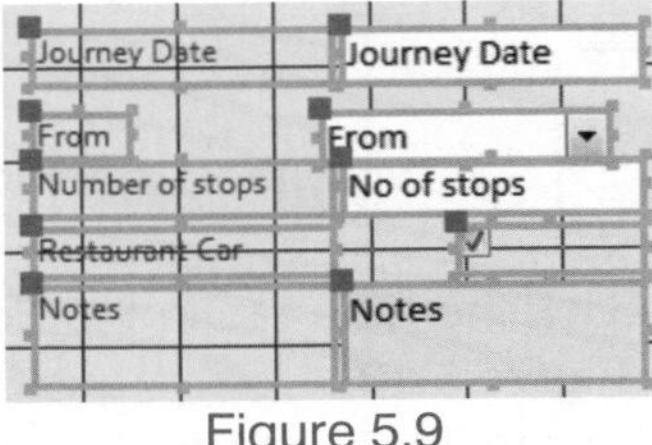

Figure 5.9

2. Select controls as shown in Figure 5.9.

Using the mouse, drag to draw a rectangle around the controls. All controls inside the rectangle are automatically selected.

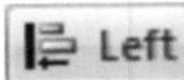

3. Click the *Left* button in the Arrange section of the Ribbon.
4. Move the *From* combo box so that it is an equal distance from the *Journey Date* and *No of stops* controls.
5. Set the alignment of the *From* combo box to Center.
6. Edit the label box so that it reads *Departing From*.
7. View the *National Railways Train Schedule* Form in Form view.
8. Click the down arrow at the right of the *From* text box.

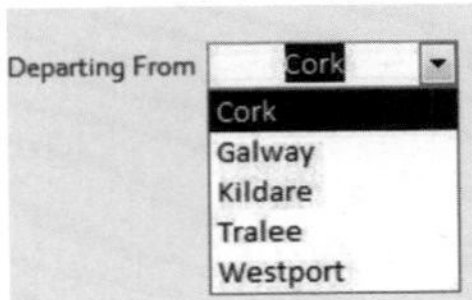

Figure 5.10: The completed combo box

The values in the combo box list are displayed, as shown in Figure 5.10. Rather than typing the town or city name, the data entry operator can select from the combo box list.

RESTRICT DATA ENTRY

Even though the combo box has only five items in the list, it is still possible to enter data that is not in the combo box list.

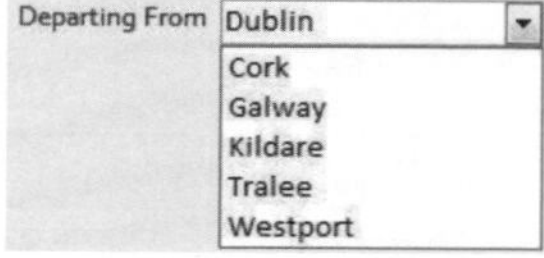

Figure 5.11: Entering a value that is not in the combo box list

In Figure 5.11, the database user has ignored the combo box list and entered *Dublin* in the *From* text box. Currently, there is nothing to stop this from happening. It is important to trap as many of these data entry errors as possible to prevent incorrect data from getting into the Table. Data entry can be restricted to the items listed in the combo box by turning on the *Limit to List* property.

1. View the *National Railways Train Schedule* Form in design view.

2. View the properties of the *From* combo box.

3. Click the *Data* tab in the Property Sheet (Figure 5.12).
4. Locate the *Limit to List* property and select *Yes* from the drop-down list, as shown in Figure 5.12. Turning on the *Limit to List* property means that only items listed in the combo box can be entered in the *From* field.
5. In the line immediately below the *Limit to List* property, change the *Allow Value List Edits* property from *Yes* to *No*.

6. Click the *Form View* button. Click the *New Record* button. Enter *Dublin* in the *From* text box and then press the *Tab* key. Access displays the error message shown in Figure 5.13.

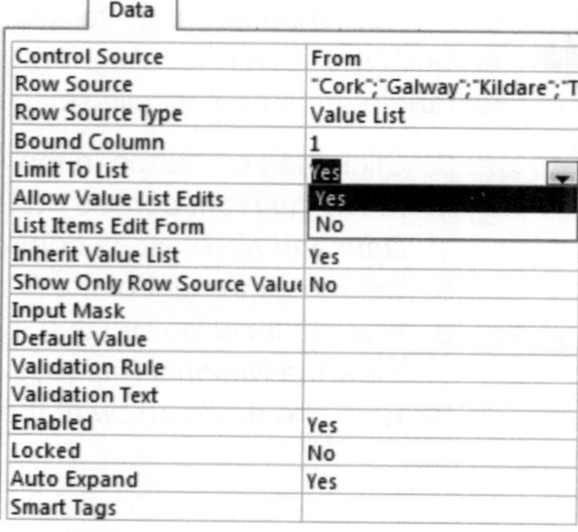

Data
Control Source From
Row Source "Cork";"Galway";"Kildare";"T
Row Source Type Value List
Bound Column 1
Limit To List Yes
Allow Value List Edits Yes
List Items Edit Form No
Inherit Value List Yes
Show Only Row Source Valu No
Input Mask
Default Value
Validation Rule
Validation Text
Enabled Yes
Locked No
Auto Expand Yes
Smart Tags

Figure 5.12: Turning on *Limit to List*

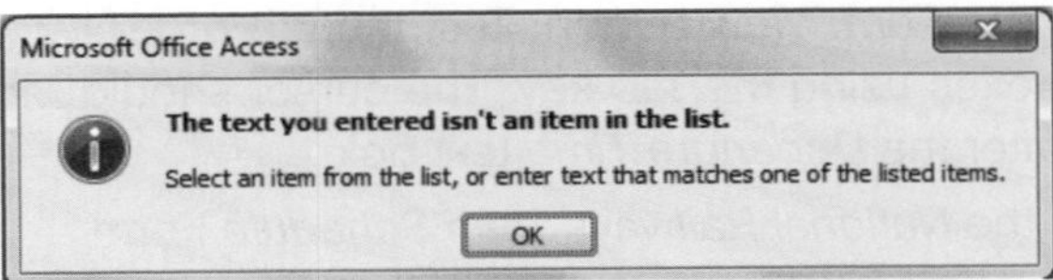

Figure 5.13: *Limit to List* has prevented Dublin from being entered

As Dublin is not in the combo box list, it cannot be entered in the *From* field. Only the five items listed in the combo box can be entered. It is good practice to set the *Limit to List* property to *Yes* each time you create a combo box. Doing so reduces the number of data entry errors.

7. Press the *Esc* key repeatedly to remove the dialog box and cancel the data entry.

8. Save the *National Railways Train Schedule* Form.

If you don't set the *Allow Value List Edits* property to *No*, Access will allow the database user to add items to the combo box list, even if *Limit to List* is set to *Yes*.

ADJUST THE TAB ORDER

Each time you create a combo box, the order in which the cursor moves through the text boxes in the Form is affected. The *From* field is now last in the tab order list but is the fourth text box in the Form. When the tab order is out of sync with the Form layout, data entry can become tedious.

1. Open the *National Railways Train Schedule* Form in design view.
2. Click the *Tab Order* button in the Arrange section of the Ribbon. The *From* field appears last in the list.

Tab Order

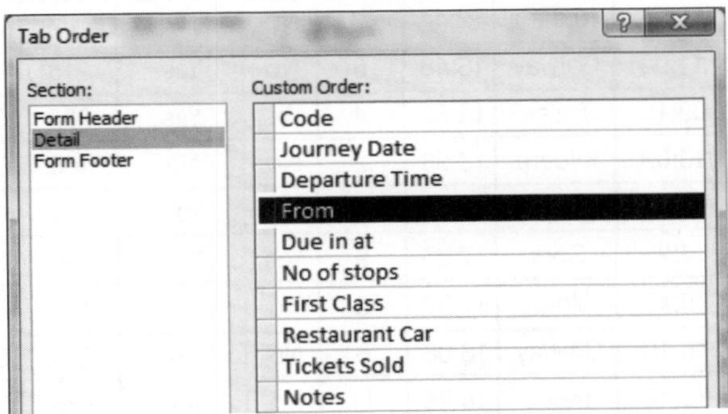

Figure 5.14: Adjusting the tab order

3. Drag the *From* field until it is fourth in the tab order list, as shown in Figure 5.14. Click *OK*.
4. If necessary, adjust the remaining fields in your tab order so that it matches the list displayed in Figure 5.14.

5. Click the *Form View* button. Test the tab order by tabbing through the text boxes using the *Tab* key. The cursor should move to the *From* text box after the *Departure Time* text box.

6. Save the *National Railways Train Schedule* Form.

ENTER DATA

Task 4: Open the *National Railways Train Schedule* Form in Form view. Click the *New Record* button and enter all the records shown in Table 5.5.

The records stored in the *Train Schedule* Table will be in ascending order of *Code*, which is the primary key field, regardless of the order in which they are entered in the Form. If you enter some of the records displayed in Table 5.5, close the Form and then open it again later on, the records will not be displayed in the order they were entered. They will be in ascending alphabetical order of *Code*. This makes it quite difficult to complete the data entry. If possible, enter all the records in one session.

As all journey dates are the same, you can speed up the data entry by using the *CTRL + 2* key combination to copy data from the previous record.

Code	Journey Date	Departure Time	From	Due in at	No of Stops	First Class	Restaurant Car	Tickets Sold	Notes
CD001	25/08/2014	07:05	Cork	09:46	3	Yes	Yes	275	Running late
KD001	25/08/2014	09:07	Kildare	09:59	2	No	No	282	Running late
KD002	25/08/2014	09:24	Kildare	10:01	2	No	No	225	On Time
GD001	25/08/2014	07:45	Galway	10:26	4	Yes	Yes	298	On Time
CD002	25/08/2014	08:00	Cork	11:06	9	Yes	Yes	193	Running late
CD003	25/08/2014	09:05	Cork	12:27	7	No	No	270	On Time
KD003	25/08/2014	11:55	Kildare	12:44	2	No	No	187	On Time
GD002	25/08/2014	11:00	Galway	13:48	6	No	Yes	216	Delayed
TD001	25/08/2014	09:15	Tralee	13:55	4	Yes	Yes	282	On Time
KD004	25/08/2014	13:06	Kildare	13:58	2	No	No	105	Cancelled
WD001	25/08/2014	13:15	Westport	17:17	10	Yes	Yes	155	On Time
CD004	25/08/2014	14:25	Cork	17:26	9	Yes	Yes	180	On Time
KD005	25/08/2014	16:45	Kildare	17:37	2	No	No	196	Running late
GD003	25/08/2014	15:10	Galway	18:08	6	No	Yes	203	On Time
TD002	25/08/2014	13:48	Tralee	18:25	11	No	Yes	276	On Time
KD006	25/08/2014	18:30	Kildare	19:22	2	No	No	280	Delayed
CD005	25/08/2014	17:30	Cork	20:16	3	Yes	No	270	Running late
GD004	25/08/2014	18:08	Galway	21:22	4	Yes	Yes	295	On Time
WD002	25/08/2014	18:00	Westport	22:01	10	No	No	301	On Time
TD003	25/08/2014	17:47	Tralee	22:41	11	No	Yes	320	Delayed

Table 5.5

LEARN HOW TO CREATE QUERY CONDITIONS IN DATE/TIME FIELDS

In the Riverside Rugby Club database, we used logical operators to create Query conditions for Number fields. For example, the condition *Between 5 and 8* in the *No of Tackles* field found records of players who made between 5 and 8 tackles inclusive. Logical operators can also be used to create conditions in Date/Time fields. Examples of using logical operators with time values are shown in Table 5.6.

Logical Expression	Effect
Between #10:00:00# and #12:00:00#	Finds all times between 10:00 and 12:00 inclusive
>=#10:00:00# and <=#12:00:00#	Finds all times between 10:00 and 12:00 inclusive
>#10:00:00# and <#12:00:00#	Finds all times from 10:01 to 11:59
>=#10:00:00# and <#12:00:00#	Finds all times from 10:00 to 11:59
>#10:00:00# and <=#12:00:00#	Finds all times from 10:01 to 12:00

Table 5.6

Access adds the # symbol to times used in a logical expression. It also adds seconds to the time value. When you type *>10:00 and <12:00* and press Enter, Access edits the logical expression and displays it as *>#10:00:00# and <#12:00:00#*.

Examples of logical operators used with Date fields are shown in Table 5.7.

Logical Expression	Effect
Between #23/01/2014# and #26/01/2014#	Finds 23/01/2014, 24/01/2014, 25/01/2014 and 26/01/2014
>=#23/01/2014# and <=#26/01/2014#	Finds 23/01/2014, 24/01/2014, 25/01/2014 and 26/01/2014
>#23/01/2014# and <#26/01/2014#	Finds 24/01/2014 and 25/01/2014
>=#23/01/2014# and <#26/01/2014#	Finds 23/01/2014, 24/01/2014 and 25/01/2014
>#23/01/2014# and <=#26/01/2014#	Finds 24/01/2014, 25/01/2014 and 26/01/2014
>=#01/01/2014# and <=#31/12/2014#	Finds all dates in 2014
>=#01/11/2014# and <=#30/11/2014#	Finds all dates in November 2014

Table 5.7

Access adds the # symbol to dates used in a logical expression. When you type *>23/01/2014 and <26/01/2014* and press Enter, Access edits the logical expression and displays it as *>#23/01/2014# and <#26/01/2014#*.

When creating conditions that refer to dates or times, it is better not to type the # symbols, as Access will put them in for you.

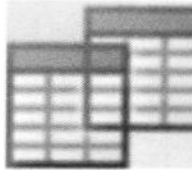

CREATE QUERIES

Create a separate Query for each of the tasks described in Table 5.8. Save each Query using the name provided.

	Purpose of Query	Sort Order	Query Name	Records Found
Task 5	Find records of trains departing from Cork	–	Trains from Cork	5
Task 6	Find records of trains departing from 18:00 onwards	Ascending order of Departure Time	Trains departing from 18:00 onwards	3
Task 7	Find records of trains departing from Cork between 08:00 and 17:30 inclusive	–	Trains leaving Cork between 08:00 and 17:30 inclusive	4
Task 8	Find records of trains departing after 11:00 and before 18:00	Ascending order of Departure Time	Trains departing after 11:00 and before 18:00	9
Task 9	Find records of trains that are running late	–	Trains that are running late	5
Task 10	Find records of trains that haven't been cancelled	Ascending order of Notes field	Trains that haven't been cancelled	19
Task 11	Find records of trains where the number of tickets sold was greater than or equal to 180 and less than 270	Descending order of Tickets Sold	Trains with up to 10% profit	7
Task 12	Find records of trains from Kildare where the number of tickets sold was less than 200	Descending order of Tickets Sold	Kildare promotional campaign	3
Task 13	Find records of trains from Cork where the number of tickets sold was less than 250	Descending order of Tickets Sold	Cork promotional campaign	2

Table 5.8

LEARN ABOUT ACCESS REPORTS

Each object in an Access database has a specific function. To date, we have looked at Tables, Queries and Forms. The main function of each of these database objects is summarised in Table 5.9.

Database Object	Primary Function
Table	Stores data in rows of records. Each record is divided into fields.
Form	Provides a user-friendly means of entering data. Data entered in the Form is transferred to the Table record by record.
Query	Allows us to search for specific records in the Table.

Table 5.9

The Table is the central and most important object in the database. A Form is used to input data in the Table. A Query is used to find specific data in the Table. While you can look at or print out the data in a Table or Query, both of these objects have limited formatting options. This often makes it difficult to interpret the data in a Table or Query. The specific purpose of a Report is to produce printouts from the database that are easy to understand and that are in a professional format. Even if you have never used a database before, you will be able to understand the information in a well-produced report.

FUNCTIONS OF A REPORT

1. Apply Formatting to Data

The main function of a Report is to take the data from a Table or Query and apply formatting to it so that it can be easily understood. This is particularly important when the reader of the Report is not a database expert. A well-designed report will read just like a Word document.

Central Station Arrivals Information

25/08/2014

20 trains expected

All trains are currently running to schedule

From	Expected Arrival	Number of stops	First Class	Restaurant Car	Tickets Sold	Notes
Cork	09:46	3	Yes	Yes	275	On Time
Kildare	09:59	2	No	No	282	Running 10 mins late
Kildare	10:01	2	No	No	225	On Time
Galway	10:26	4	Yes	Yes	298	On Time
Cork	11:06	9	Yes	Yes	193	Running 20 mins late
Cork	12:27	7	No	No	270	Running 5 mins late

Figure 5.15: An extract from a Report detailing expected train arrivals

Figure 5.15 is an example of a Report. It displays expected train arrivals. The formatting options available in Access allow the database designer to make Reports informative and easy to read.

Once the Report has been created and designed, you can open the Report in Access at any time and view the data in it. Reports are dynamic and will automatically adjust to include new records as they are entered in the database. If the Report is sorted in a particular order, the new records will be inserted in the correct sequence.

One of the advantages of printed reports is that they are portable. Carrying a printout of a Report in your bag is much easier than hauling your laptop around. You can print out multiple copies of a Report and hand them out to colleagues or clients. Reports can be used by all sorts of people, as you don't need to have an understanding of Microsoft Access to understand what's in a Report.

2. Sort Records into Different Orders

The second function of a Report is to sort records into different orders. The records stored in a Table will be in ascending order of the primary key field. You will often want to view the records in a different order. Records can be quickly sorted into a different order using a Report. Although records can also be sorted in a Table Query, Reports have more powerful sorting options.

Figure 5.16 displays the sorting options in the Report Wizard. Each Report can be sorted by up to four fields. Sorting using the Report Wizard is much easier than sorting records in a Table or Query.

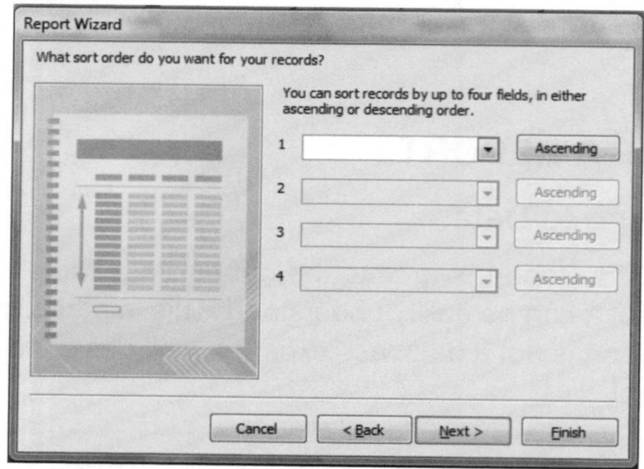

Figure 5.16: Sorting options in the Report Wizard

3. Perform Calculations

The third function of a Report is to perform calculations on the records displayed in the Report. For example, a Report function could be used to calculate the total or average of numbers in a Number or Currency field.

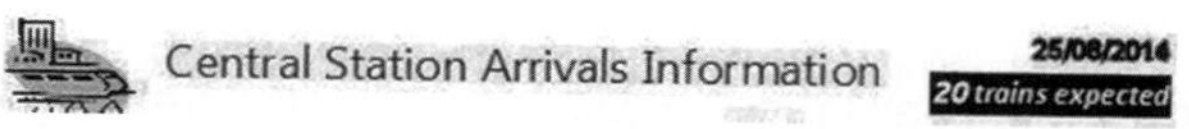

Figure 5.17: An example of a Report function used to count the number of trains

In Figure 5.17, the Count function has been used to determine that 20 trains are expected. The great feature of Report functions is that they are dynamic. As trains arrive in Central Station and this is recorded in the database, the Count function will update automatically.

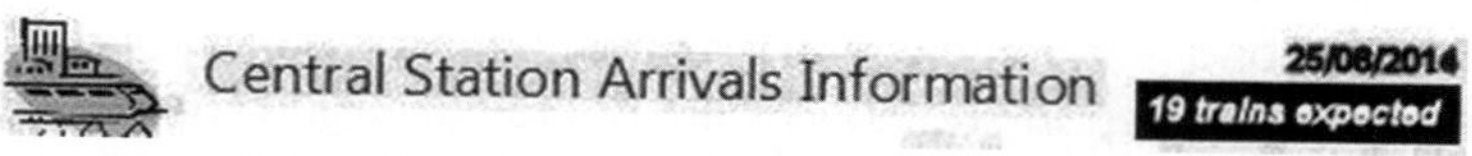

Figure 5.18: The Count function updates automatically

Figure 5.18 displays the Report function having entered data relating to the arrival of a train. Once this information has been entered in the database, the Report function updates automatically. It now calculates that 19 trains are expected.

PRODUCING A REPORT FROM A TABLE

Figure 5.19 demonstrates some of the features available in Reports.

- A title can be displayed at the top of the Report. The Report title indicates to the reader what type of information is contained in the Report.
- You don't have to display all the fields in your Report. In Figure 5.19, the *Code*, *Journey Date* and *Departure Time* fields have been omitted.
- Records can be sorted into different orders. In Figure 5.19, the records are sorted in ascending order of the *Due in at* field.
- The column headings, which contain the field names from the Table, can be edited to make them more descriptive. In Figure 5.19, *Due in at* has been changed to *Expected Arrival.*
- Text can be wrapped within the column headings. This allows more columns of data to be displayed in the Report.
- Graphics and company logos can be included. In Figure 5.19, a train image appears to the left of the Report title.

Table

Code	Journey Date	Departure	From	Due	No of stops	First Class	Restaurant	Tickets Sold	Notes
CD001	25/08/2014	07:05	Cork	09:46	3	☑	☑	275	On Time
CD002	25/08/2014	08:00	Cork	11:06	9	☑	☑	193	Running late
CD003	25/08/2014	09:05	Cork	12:27	7	☐	☐	270	Running late
CD004	25/08/2014	14:25	Cork	17:26	9	☑	☑	180	On Time
CD005	25/08/2014	17:30	Cork	20:16	3	☑	☐	270	Running late
GD001	25/08/2014	07:45	Galway	10:26	4	☑	☑	298	On Time
GD002	25/08/2014	11:00	Galway	13:48	6	☐	☑	216	Delayed

A Table has limited formatting options, so it can be difficult to read and interpret data in a Table

The formatting, sorting and calculation features of a Report make it easier to interpret the data

Report

Central Station Arrivals Information

25/08/2014

20 trains expected

Departure Time	From	Expected Arrival	Notes
07:05	Cork	09:46	On Time
09:07	Kildare	09:59	Running 5 mins late
09:24	Kildare	10:01	On Time
07:45	Galway	10:26	On Time
08:00	Cork	11:06	Running 20 mins late
09:05	Cork	12:27	On Time
11:55	Kildare	12:44	On Time
11:00	Galway	13:48	Delayed

Figure 5.19: An extract from a Report produced from the Table, detailing train arrivals

- Report functions perform calculations on the data displayed in the Report. In Figure 5.19, a function is used to display the date. A second function counts the number of records and displays the message *20 trains expected*. As trains arrive, this number will automatically decrease.

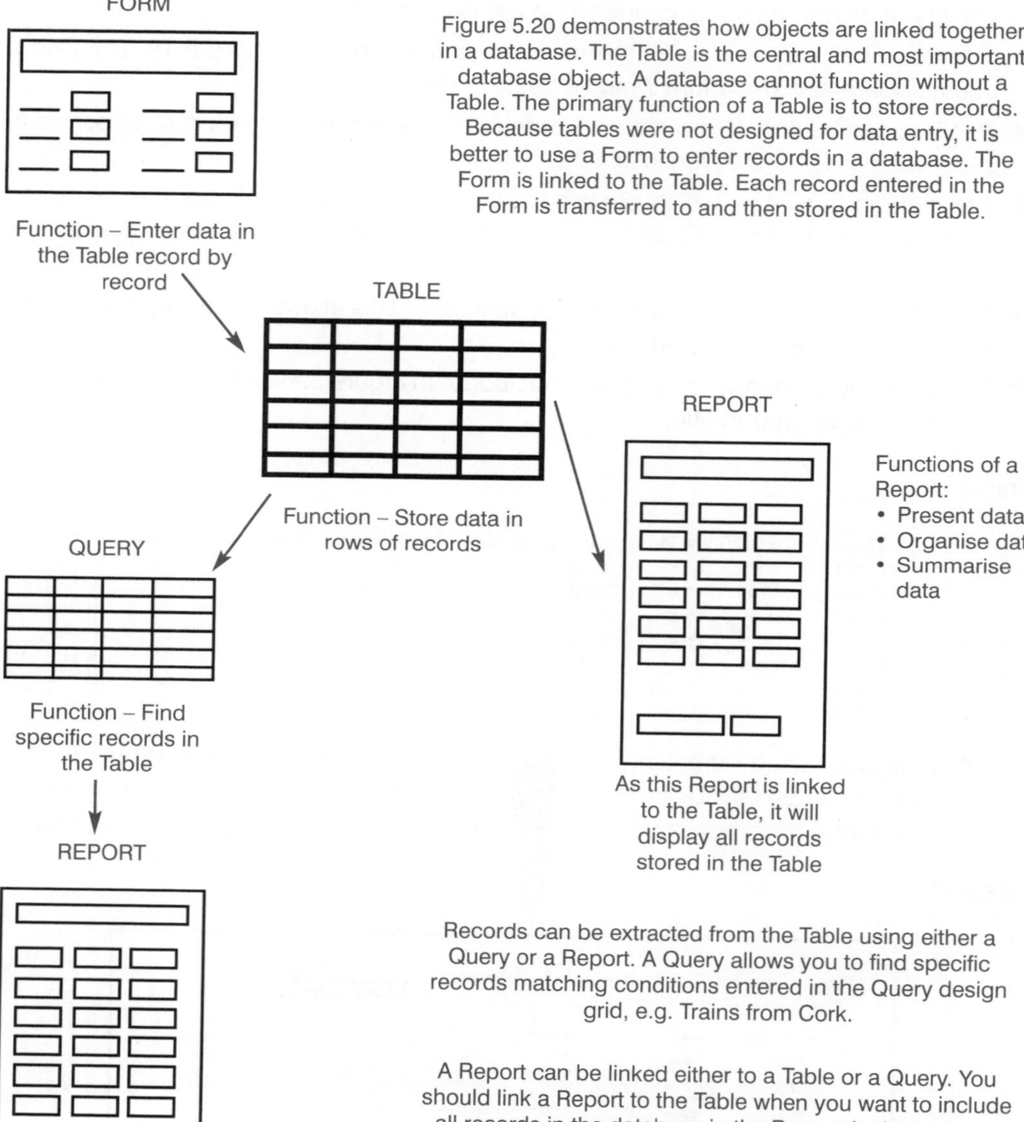

FORM
Function – Enter data in the Table record by record
TABLE
Function – Store data in rows of records
QUERY
Function – Find specific records in the Table
REPORT
As this Report is linked to a Query, it will only display the records found by the Query
REPORT
As this Report is linked to the Table, it will display all records stored in the Table
Functions of a Report:
• Present data
• Organise data
• Summarise data

Figure 5.20 demonstrates how objects are linked together in a database. The Table is the central and most important database object. A database cannot function without a Table. The primary function of a Table is to store records. Because tables were not designed for data entry, it is better to use a Form to enter records in a database. The Form is linked to the Table. Each record entered in the Form is transferred to and then stored in the Table.

Records can be extracted from the Table using either a Query or a Report. A Query allows you to find specific records matching conditions entered in the Query design grid, e.g. Trains from Cork.

A Report can be linked either to a Table or a Query. You should link a Report to the Table when you want to include all records in the database in the Report. In the National Railways database, a Report detailing all trains and their arrival times would be linked to the *Train Schedule* Table. You should link a Report to a Query when you only want to include a limited number of records in the Report. For example, a Report detailing trains from Cork would be linked to a Query.

Figure 5.20: How objects work together in a database

VIEWING REPORTS IN ACCESS

A Report can be viewed in four different ways.

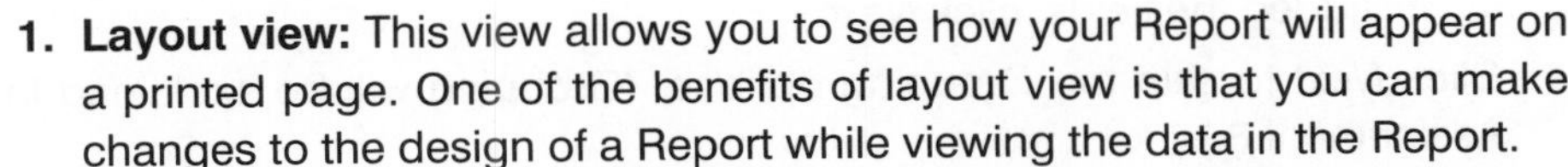

1. **Layout view:** This view allows you to see how your Report will appear on a printed page. One of the benefits of layout view is that you can make changes to the design of a Report while viewing the data in the Report.

2. **Design view:** This is the most technical view of a Report. In design view, you won't see any data. Instead you will see the labels and text boxes that represent the fields in the Report together with the label box for the Report title. Design view also shows the different sections of an Access Report: the Report header, page header, detail section and page footer. Design view is useful for fine tuning a Report.

3. **Report view:** You can't make changes to your Report when you are viewing it in Report view. This view displays how your Report will appear when printed. Unlike print preview, Report view doesn't divide your Report into pages, so it is useful for previewing long reports.

4. **Print preview:** This view allows you to check how your Report will appear on a printed page before you print it out. Print preview divides your Report into pages and puts page numbers at the bottom of each page. This is useful with long reports, as print preview will tell you exactly how many pages will be required to print the Report. You can't make changes to a Report when you are viewing it in print preview.

WORKED EXAMPLE: CREATE A REPORT

1. Select the *Train Schedule* Table in the Navigation Pane.

2. In the Create section of the Ribbon, click the *Report Wizard* button. The Report Wizard links the Report to the *Train Schedule* Table (Figure 5.21).

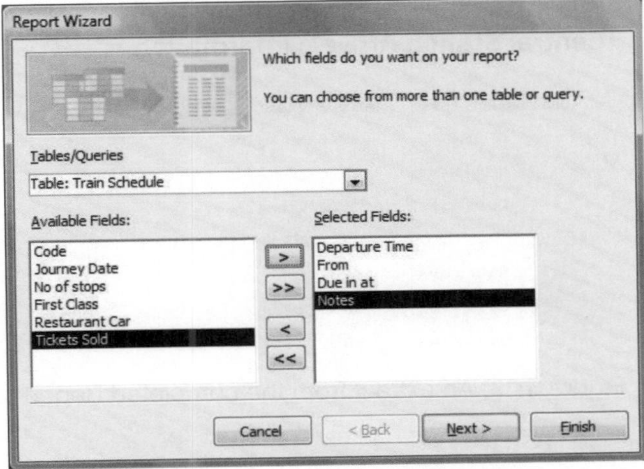

Figure 5.21: Adding fields to a Report

3. Add the *Departure Time*, *From*, *Due in at* and *Notes* fields to the Report, as shown in Figure 5.21. Each field is added to the Report by selecting it in the *Available Fields* box and then clicking the single right arrow. When you have added the fields, click *Next*.
4. Click *Next* to skip the Grouping options. (Grouping will be explained in detail in Assignment 8.)

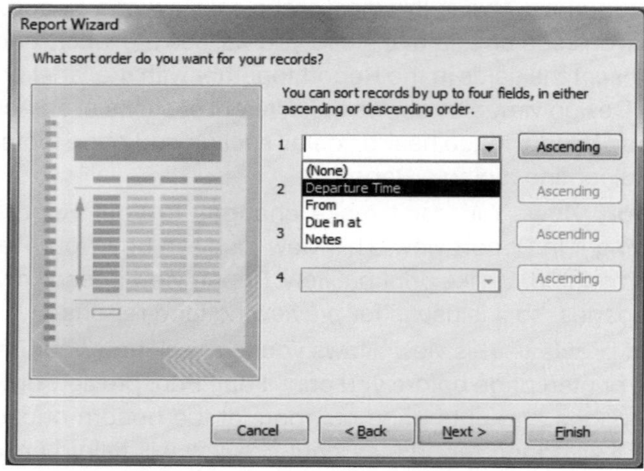

Figure 5.22: Sorting records using the Report Wizard

5. Select the *Departure Time* field as the first-level sort order of the Report, as shown in Figure 5.22. Records in the Report will be in ascending order of Departure Time. Click *Next*.
6. Click *Next* again to accept *Tabular* as the Report layout and *Portrait* as the page orientation.
7. Enter *Central Station Arrivals Information* as the Report title. Click *Finish*.

Central Station Arrivals Information

Departure Time	From	Due in at	Notes
07:05	Cork	09:46	Running late
07:45	Galway	10:26	On Time
08:00	Cork	11:06	Running late
09:05	Cork	12:27	On Time
09:07	Kildare	09:59	Running late
09:15	Tralee	13:55	On Time
09:24	Kildare	10:01	On Time

Figure 5.23: An extract from the completed Report

An extract from the completed Report is displayed in Figure 5.23. Access aligns Date/Time fields to the right by default, while aligning Text fields to the left. This gives the Report an unbalanced appearance.

FINE TUNE THE REPORT

Making design changes in a Report is best done in layout view.

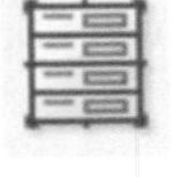

1. View the *Central Station Arrivals Report* in layout view. Select all label boxes in the page header and all text boxes in the Detail section. *(Holding down the CTRL button while clicking with the mouse allows you to select multiple Report controls.)*

2. In the Arrange section of the Ribbon, click the *Tabular* button. This organises the selected controls into Tabular Layout, making it easier to resize and move label and text boxes.

3. Select the *Departure Time* column by clicking the *07:05* value. Centre data in the *Departure Time* column and the *Departure Time* label using the *Center* button, as shown in Figure 5.24.

4. Select the *Due in at* column by clicking the *09:46* value. Centre the data in this column.

5. Centre the *Due in at* label.

6. Adjust column widths so that the data is evenly spaced across the page, as shown in Figure 5.24. Increase the width of the *Notes* text box control if necessary.

Central Station Arrivals Information

Departure Time	From	Due in at	Notes
07:05	Cork	09:46	Running late
07:45	Galway	10:26	On Time
08:00	Cork	11:06	Running late
09:05	Cork	12:27	On Time

Figure 5.24: Columns widths have been adjusted

In layout view, the dotted line along the edge of the Report indicates the edge of the printed area of the page.

7. Apply the *Trek* theme to the Report. In the Design section of the Ribbon, select *Trek* from the list of themes.

In Access 2007, applying a style to a Report is completed during the Report Wizard.

8. In the Report header, select the label box containing the Report title. Increase the width of the label box so that it spans the entire Report (Figure 5.25).

9. Centre the Report title, as shown in Figure 5.25.

10. Save the changes to your Report.

11. Preview the completed Report. It should look something like Figure 5.25, which is an extract from the Report.

Central Station Arrivals Information

Departure Time	From	Due in at	Notes
07:05	Cork	09:46	On Time
07:45	Galway	10:26	On Time
08:00	Cork	11:06	Running late
09:05	Cork	12:27	Running late

Figure 5.25: An extract from the completed Report

12. Print the *Central Station Arrivals Information* Report.

LEARN ABOUT THE STRUCTURE OF AN ACCESS REPORT

A standard Access Report is divided into four sections: the Report header, page header, detail section and page footer.

The Report Header

The Report header contains the Report title and may also contain a company logo, address or calculation. It is also common to put introductory text explaining the nature of the Report in the Report header.

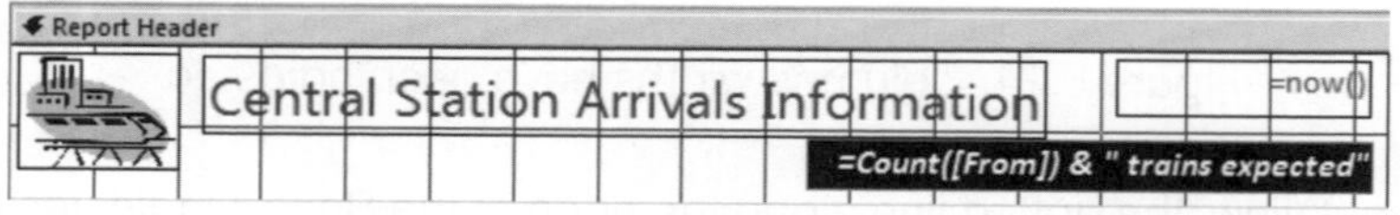

Figure 5.26

In Figure 5.26, the Report header contains a company logo, the Report title, the *Now* function, which displays today's date, and the *Count* function, which counts the number of records in the Report. (Report functions will be explained in detail in Assignment 8.)

The Page Header

The page header displays the column headings in your Report. By default, Access uses the field names as the column headings. These can be edited if required. In Reports created with the Report Wizard, a horizontal line appears immediately above and below the label boxes in the page header.

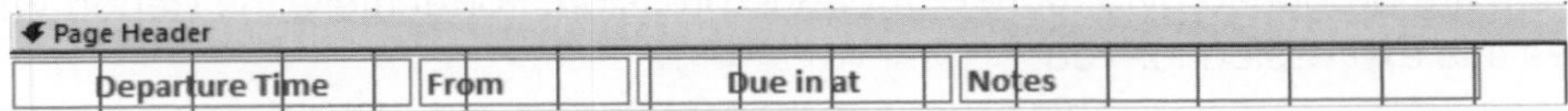

Figure 5.27

In Figure 5.27, the page header contains label boxes for the *Departure Time*, *From*, *Due in at* and *Notes* fields. These will appear as column headings above the records in the Report.

The Detail Section

The detail section is the most important section of an Access Report. The detail section produces the records in the Report. Each time you add a field to a Report using the Wizard, a corresponding text box is added to the detail section. In Figure 5.28, the detail section contains text boxes for the *Departure Time*, *From*, *Due in at* and *Notes* fields. These fields were added to the Report using the Report Wizard. The number of records produced by the detail section depends on the record source of the Report, which can be a Table or a Query.

Each text box links to a specific field in the Table or Query that the Report is linked to

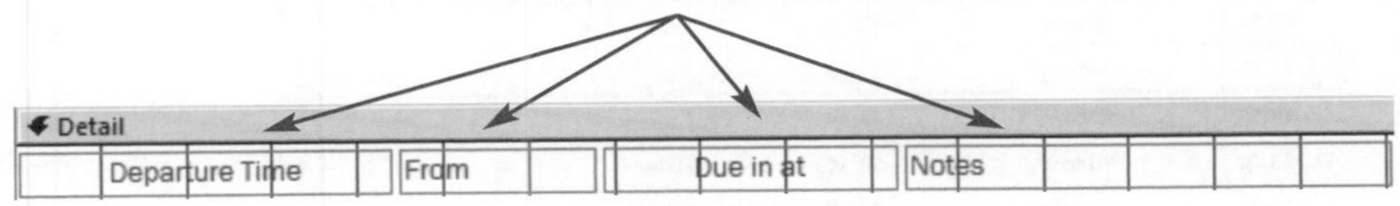

Figure 5.28: Detail section of an Access Report

Never edit the field name in a text box in the detail section, as this will break the link to the corresponding field in the Table.

Record Source	Train Schedule

When the Report in Figure 5.28 is linked to the *Train Schedule* Table, the text boxes in the detail section will display data from the *Departure Time*, *From*, *Due in at* and *Notes* fields for each record in the Table. The resulting Report will display all of the records in the database – a total of 20 records.

Record Source	Restaurant Car

When the Report is linked to a Query, the text boxes in the detail section will only display data for each record found by the Query. When the Report in Figure 5.28 is linked to a Query that finds records of trains with a restaurant car, the detail section displays 11 records.

The Page Footer

Data contained in the page footer appears at the bottom of each page in the Report. By default, Access puts the date and the page number in the page footer.

`=Now()`

The date is produced by the *=Now()* expression. This gets the date from the computer's clock and displays it at the bottom of the page. The page numbers are produced by a more complex expression. Fortunately, the Report Wizard creates this expression for you.

`"Page " & [Page] & " of " & [Pages]`

This produces the text *Page 1 of 1*. If there is more than one page in your Report, it will produce the text *Page 1 of 2* or *Page 1 of 3*, and so on. In a multiple-page Report, the text will adjust as you scroll through the Report. For example, in a three-page report, the text on page 2 would be *Page 2 of 3*.

Figure 5.29 demonstrates where the Report header, page header, detail section and page footer appear in an Access Report.

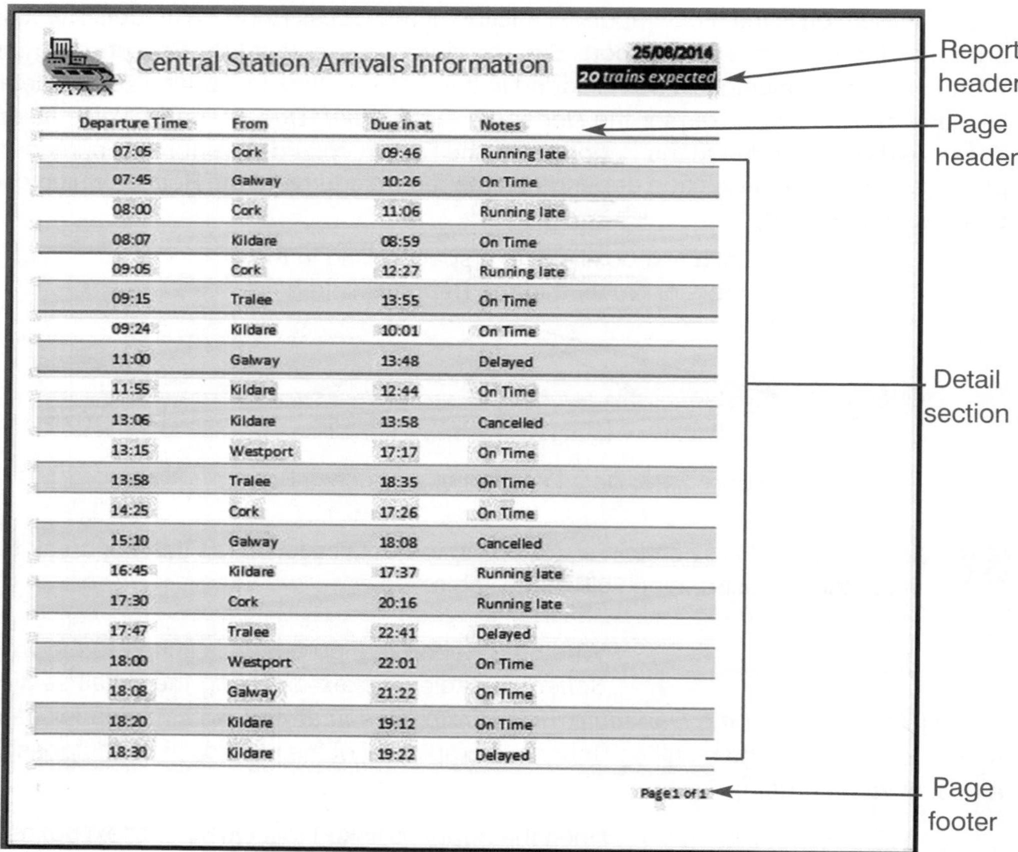

Central Station Arrivals Information

25/08/2014

20 trains expected

Departure Time	From	Due in at	Notes
07:05	Cork	09:46	Running late
07:45	Galway	10:26	On Time
08:00	Cork	11:06	Running late
08:07	Kildare	08:59	On Time
09:05	Cork	12:27	Running late
09:15	Tralee	13:55	On Time
09:24	Kildare	10:01	On Time
11:00	Galway	13:48	Delayed
11:55	Kildare	12:44	On Time
13:06	Kildare	13:58	Cancelled
13:15	Westport	17:17	On Time
13:58	Tralee	18:35	On Time
14:25	Cork	17:26	On Time
15:10	Galway	18:08	Cancelled
16:45	Kildare	17:37	Running late
17:30	Cork	20:16	Running late
17:47	Tralee	22:41	Delayed
18:00	Westport	22:01	On Time
18:08	Galway	21:22	On Time
18:20	Kildare	19:12	On Time
18:30	Kildare	19:22	Delayed

Page 1 of 1

Figure 5.29: Sections of a standard Access Report

LEARN HOW TO LINK A REPORT TO A QUERY

Each time you create an Access Report, you have the option of linking the Report to an existing Table or Query. If you want to display all records in your Report, e.g. a complete list of trains, you should link the Report to the Table. In cases where you only want to display specific records in the Report, e.g. trains with a first-class carriage, you should firstly create a Query to find the records you require and then link the Report to that Query. In the following worked example, we will create a Report that displays information relating to trains with a first-class carriage.

WORKED EXAMPLE: CREATE A REPORT LINKED TO A QUERY

1. Create a new Query to find records of trains with a first-class carriage. Save the Query as *Trains with first class carriage*.
2. Select the *Trains with first class carriage* Query in the Navigation Pane.

3. In the Create section of the Ribbon, click the *Report Wizard* button. The Report is automatically linked to the *Trains with first class carriage* Query, as shown in Figure 5.30.

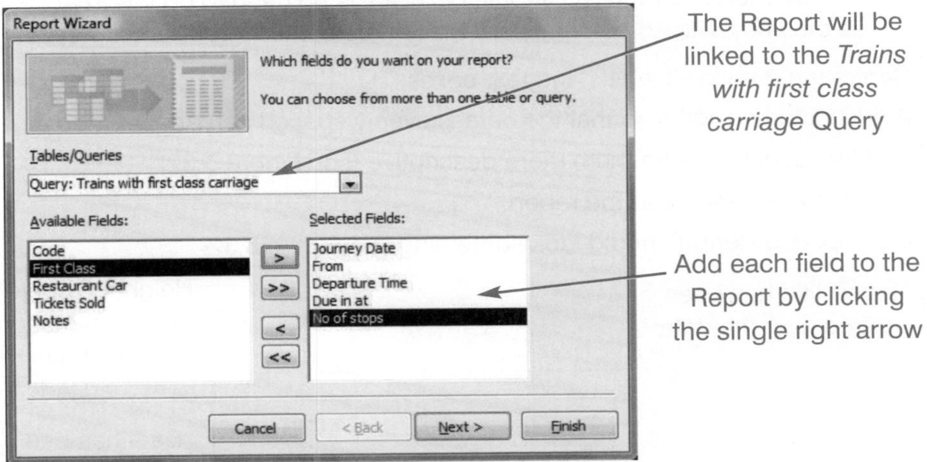

Figure 5.30: Adding fields to a Report with the Report Wizard

4. Add the *Journey Date*, *From*, *Departure Time*, *Due in at* and *No of Stops* fields to the Report, as shown in Figure 5.30. Click *Next*.
5. Click *Next* to skip the Grouping options.
6. Sort the Report in ascending order of *Due in at*. Click *Next*.
7. Click *Next* to accept tabular as the layout and portrait as the page orientation.
8. Enter *First Class Trains* as the Report title.
9. To preview the Report, click *Finish*. The completed Report is displayed in Figure 5.31.

First Class Trains

Due in at	Journey Date	From	Departure Time	No of stops
09:46	25/08/2014	Cork	07:05	3
10:26	25/08/2014	Galway	07:45	4
11:06	25/08/2014	Cork	08:00	9
13:55	25/08/2014	Tralee	09:15	4
17:17	25/08/2014	Westport	13:15	10
17:26	25/08/2014	Cork	14:25	9
20:16	25/08/2014	Cork	17:30	3
21:22	25/08/2014	Galway	18:08	4

Figure 5.31: Initial Report produced by the Report Wizard

The Report Wizard has positioned the *Due in at* field first in the Report, as the records are in ascending order of this field.

Some adjustments need to be made to the Report displayed in Figure 5.31 to make it presentable. Make the following changes to the Report in layout view.

It is much easier to adjust column widths when the labels and text boxes are grouped together in a layout. In layout view, select all labels and text boxes except for the Report title. Right click the selected controls and select Layout from the pop-up menu. Now select Tabulator. There is no need to do this in Access 2007, as the 2007 Wizard automatically places the controls in a Tabular layout.

- Centre the data in all labels and text boxes.
- Adjust column widths so that the data is evenly spaced across the Report.
- Edit the labels to make them more descriptive (see Figure 5.32).
- Apply the *Trek* theme to the report.

The completed Report should look something like Figure 5.32.

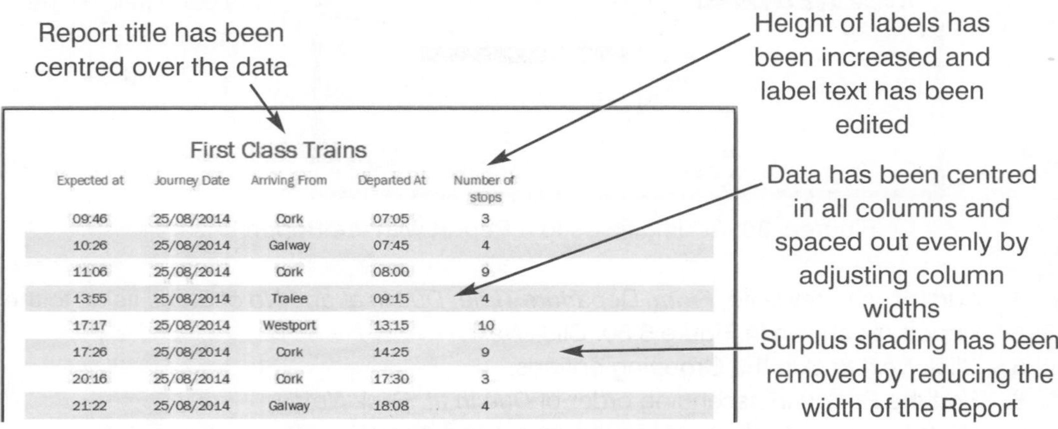
Report title has been centred over the data
Height of labels has been increased and label text has been edited
Data has been centred in all columns and spaced out evenly by adjusting column widths
Surplus shading has been removed by reducing the width of the Report

First Class Trains

Expected at	Journey Date	Arriving From	Departed At	Number of stops
09:46	25/08/2014	Cork	07:05	3
10:26	25/08/2014	Galway	07:45	4
11:06	25/08/2014	Cork	08:00	9
13:55	25/08/2014	Tralee	09:15	4
17:17	25/08/2014	Westport	13:15	10
17:26	25/08/2014	Cork	14:25	9
20:16	25/08/2014	Cork	17:30	3
21:22	25/08/2014	Galway	18:08	4

Figure 5.32: The completed *First Class Trains* Report

10. Save the *First Class Trains* Report.

CREATE REPORTS

The Report Wizard automatically links a new Report to the Table or Query currently selected in the Navigation Pane. Before you click the *Report Wizard* button, ensure that the correct database object is selected in the Navigation Pane.

Task 14: Display early trains from Cork.

- Create a Query to find records of trains from Cork departing before 12:00 a.m. Save the Query as *Cork trains departing before 12:00am.*
- Using the Report Wizard, create a Report linked to this Query.
- Include the *Journey Date*, *Departure Time*, *Due in at* and *Notes* fields in the Report.
- Sort the Report in ascending order of the *Departure Time* field.
- Apply the *Trek* style to the Report.
- The Report title is *Early Trains from Cork.*
- Format the Report so that it appears like Figure 5.33.

Early Trains from Cork

Departure Time	Journey Date	Due in at	Notes
07:05	25/08/2014	09:46	On Time
08:00	25/08/2014	11:06	Running late
09:05	25/08/2014	12:27	Running late

Figure 5.33: Formatted Report from Task 14

Task 15: Display express trains.

- Create a Query to find records of train journeys with less than four stops. Save the Query as *Journeys with less than 4 stops.*
- Using the Report Wizard, create a Report linked to this Query.
- Include all fields except for *First Class* and *Restaurant Car* in the Report.

If you are displaying a lot of fields in a Report, add all the fields and then remove the fields you don't want to display in the Report instead of adding each field individually. Fields can be removed from a Report by clicking the single left-pointing arrow in the Report Wizard.

- Sort the Report in descending order of the *No of Stops* field.
- Display the Report in landscape orientation.
- Apply the *Trek* style to the Report.
- The Report title is *Express Trains.*
- Format the Report so that it appears like Figure 5.34.

Express Trains

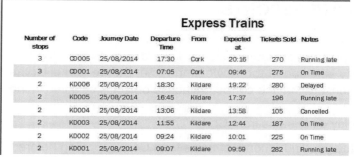

Number of stops	Code	Journey Date	Departure Time	From	Expected at	Tickets Sold	Notes
3	CD005	25/08/2014	17:30	Cork	20:16	270	Running late
3	CD001	25/08/2014	07:05	Cork	09:46	275	On Time
2	KD006	25/08/2014	18:30	Kildare	19:22	280	Delayed
2	KD005	25/08/2014	16:45	Kildare	17:37	196	Running late
2	KD004	25/08/2014	13:06	Kildare	13:58	105	Cancelled
2	KD003	25/08/2014	11:55	Kildare	12:44	187	On Time
2	KD002	25/08/2014	09:24	Kildare	10:01	225	On Time
2	KD001	25/08/2014	09:07	Kildare	09:59	282	Running late

Figure 5.34: Formatted Report from Task 15

- Print the *Express Trains* Report.

Task 16: Display trains with a restaurant car.

If you want the Report to display "Yes" or "No" instead of a check box, open the *Train Schedule* Table in design view and change the *Display Control* property of the *First Class* field from check box to text box before creating the Report. This can be found in the Lookup section of the field properties.

Trains with Dining Facilities

From	Journey Date	Departure Time	No of stops	First Class
Cork	25/08/2014	14:25	9	☑
Cork	25/08/2014	08:00	9	☑
Cork	25/08/2014	07:05	3	☑
Galway	25/08/2014	18:08	4	☑
Galway	25/08/2014	15:10	6	☐
Galway	25/08/2014	11:00	6	☐
Galway	25/08/2014	07:45	4	☑
Tralee	25/08/2014	17:47	11	☐
Tralee	25/08/2014	13:48	11	☐
Tralee	25/08/2014	09:15	4	☑
Westport	25/08/2014	13:15	10	☑

Figure 5.35: Formatted Report from Task 16

- Create a Query to find records of trains with a restaurant car. Save the Query as *Restaurant car.*
- Using the Report Wizard, create a Report linked to this Query.
- Include the *Journey Date*, *From*, *Departure Time*, *No of Stops* and *First Class* fields in the Report.
- Sort the Report in ascending order of the *From* field.

- Apply the *Trek* style to the Report.
- The Report title is *Trains with Dining Facilities.*
- Format the Report so that it appears like Figure 5.35.

To centre the check box, remove it from the layout, then resize the border surrounding the check box.

- Print the *Trains with Dining Facilities* Report.

FIND AND EDIT RECORDS

Task 17: Open the *National Railways Train Schedule* Form. Use the *Find* and *New Record* buttons to make the following changes.

1. The 09:05 train from Cork is running late. Enter this information in the *Notes* field.
2. The 15:10 train from Galway has been cancelled. Enter this information in the *Notes* field.
3. The departure time for the 13:48 from Tralee was incorrectly recorded. The correct departure time is 13:58 and the train is due to arrive at 18:35.
4. The 18:00 from Westport has a first-class carriage and a restaurant car.

Verify that train *CD003*, the 09:05 from Cork due in at 12:32: **Completed (√)**

- Is recorded as running five minutes late in the *Early Trains from Cork* Report. ☐
- Is now found by the *Trains that are running late* Query. ☐

Verify that train *GD003*, the 15:10 from Galway due in at 18:08: **Completed (√)**

- Is no longer found by the *Trains that haven't been cancelled* Query. ☐

ADD NEW RECORDS

Another train from Kildare has been added to cope with demand. Using the *National Railways Train Schedule* Form, enter the details shown in Table 5.10.

Code	Journey Date	Departure Time	From	Due in at	No of Stops	First Class	Restaurant Car	Tickets Sold	Notes
KD007	25/08/2014	18:40	Kildare	19:12	2	No	No	225	On Time

Table 5.10

Verify that train *KD007*, the 18:40 from Kildare due in at 19:12:

Completed (√)

- Is displayed in the *Express Trains* Report. ☐
- Is found by the *Trains departing from 18:00 onwards* Query. ☐

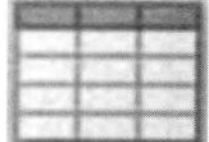

ADD A NEW FIELD TO THE TABLE

1. Add a new field named *Duration (Hours)* to the *Train Schedule* Table, using an appropriate data type and field size (see Table 5.11).

2. Open the *National Railways Train Schedule* Form in design view.
3. Add the *Duration (Hours)* field to the *National Railways Train Schedule* Form using the *Add Existing Fields* button.
4. Position the *Duration (Hours)* controls below the Tickets Sold field.
5. Set the alignment of the *Duration (Hours)* text box to centre.

6. Using the *National Railways Train Schedule* Form, enter the *Duration (Hours)* data displayed in the shaded cells in Table 5.11.

Press the *Page Down* button on the keyboard to quickly advance to the next record.

Code	From	Departure Time	Duration (Hours)
CD001	Cork	07:05	
CD002	Cork	08:00	
CD003	Cork	09:05	
CD004	Cork	14:25	
CD005	Cork	17:30	
GD001	Galway	07:45	
GD002	Galway	11:00	
GD003	Galway	15:10	
GD004	Galway	18:08	
KD001	Kildare	09:07	
KD002	Kildare	09:24	
KD003	Kildare	11:55	
KD004	Kildare	13:06	
KD005	Kildare	16:45	
KD006	Kildare	18:30	
KD007	Kildare	18:40	
TD001	Tralee	09:15	
TD002	Tralee	13:58	
TD003	Tralee	17:47	
WD001	Westport	13:15	
WD002	Westport	18:00	

Table 5.11

ADD THE NEW FIELD TO EXISTING REPORTS

1. Open the *Central Station Arrivals Information* Report in layout view.
2. Click the *Add Existing Fields* button to view the field list.

3. Drag the *Duration (Hours)* field from the field list and drop in the Report to the right of the *Notes* field.
4. If necessary, reduce the width of the *Notes* controls so the *Duration (Hours)* controls fit on the page.

5. Centre data in the *Duration (Hours)* label and text box controls.
6. Increase the width of the label in the Report header so that it spans the full width of the Report.

Central Station Arrivals Information

Departure Time	From	Due in at	Notes	Duration (Hours)
07:05	Cork	09:46	On Time	2.7
07:45	Galway	10:26	On Time	2.7
08:00	Cork	11:06	Running 20 mins late	3.1

Figure 5.36: The *Duration (Hours)* field has been added to the Report

The Report, with the new field added, should look something like Figure 5.36, which is an extract from the completed Report.

ADD THE NEW FIELD TO THE *FIRST CLASS TRAINS* REPORT

Adding the new *Duration (Hours)* field to the *First Class Trains* Report is a little more complex, as this Report is linked to a Query named *Trains with first class carriage*.

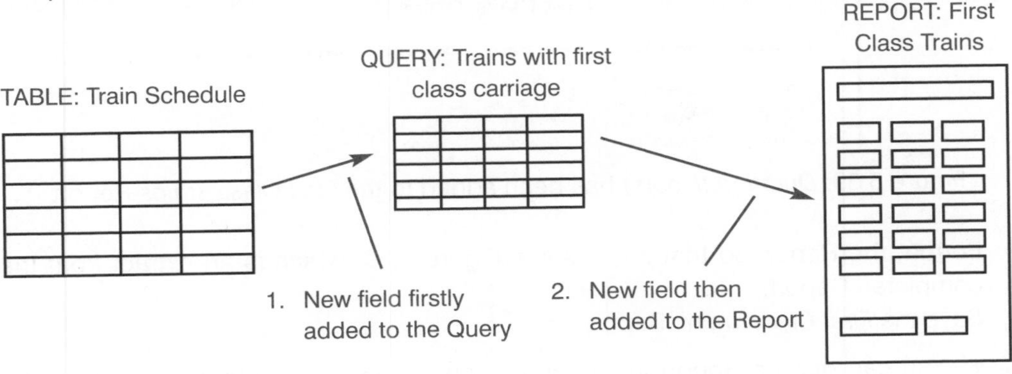

Figure 5.37: Adding the *Duration (Hours)* field to the *First Class Trains* Report

From Figure 5.37, it can be seen that the *First Class Trains* Report is linked to the *Trains with a first class carriage* Query, which in turn is linked to the *Train Schedule* Table. The new Field will not be picked up by the Report unless it is added to the query.

1. Open the *Trains with first class carriage* Query in design view.

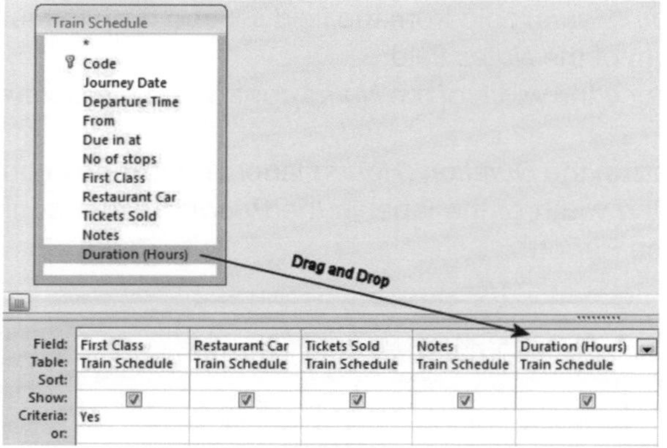

Figure 5.38: Adding the *Duration (Hours)* field to the Query design grid

2. Add the *Duration (Hours)* field to the Query design grid by dragging from the field list and dropping to the right of the *Notes* field (Figure 5.38).
3. Save and close the *Trains with first class carriage* Query.

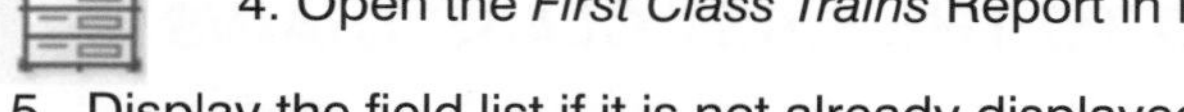

4. Open the *First Class Trains* Report in layout view.
5. Display the field list if it is not already displayed.
6. Drag the *Duration (Hours)* field and drop to the right of the *No of Stops* field.

First Class Trains

Expected at	Journey Date	Arriving From	Departed At	Number of stops	Duration (Hours)
09:46	25/08/2014	Cork	07:05	3	2.7
10:26	25/08/2014	Galway	07:45	4	2.7
11:06	25/08/2014	Cork	08:00	9	3.1

Figure 5.39: *Duration (Hours)* has been added to the *First Class Trains* Report

7. Format the Report so that it looks like Figure 5.39, which is an extract from the completed Report.
8. Save the *First Class Trains* Report.

You can open a Report in layout, design or Report view by right clicking the Report name in the Navigation Pane. To open a Report in layout view or design view, simply select the required view in the pop-up menu. Double clicking the Report name in the Navigation Pane or selecting *Open* from the pop-up menu opens the Report in Report view.

ADD THE NEW FIELD TO REMAINING REPORTS

1. Add the *Duration (Hours)* field to each of the following Reports, ensuring that the *Duration (Hours)* field is first added to the appropriate Query.
   - *Early Trains from Cork*
   - *Express Trains*
   - *Trains with Dining Facilities*
2. View each Report in layout view. Add the *Duration (Hours)* field using the field list.
3. Centre data in the *Duration (Hours)* controls in each Report.
4. Adjust each Report title so that it spans the full width of the Report.

CREATE QUERIES

Create a separate Query for each of the tasks described in Table 5.12. Save each Query using the name provided.

	Purpose of Query	Sort Order	Query Name	Records Found
Task 18	Finds records of train journeys with a duration of more than 2 hours	Descending order of Duration (Hours)	Journeys over 2 hours	14
Task 19	Finds records of train journeys with a duration of less than 1 hour	Ascending order of Duration (Hours)	Journeys under 1 hour	7

Table 5.12

DEFINE DATABASE STRUCTURE

Task 20: Complete the database structure form (Table 5.13) with data types and field sizes for all fields in the *Train Schedule* Table.

For a detailed explanation of how to complete a database structure form, refer to pages 52–3 in Assignment 3.

Ensure that the field sizes of Text fields specified in design view of the *Train Schedule* Table match those specified in the database structure form.

Task 21: Using Access Help, search for information on field sizes. Write a short report summarising information relating to the range of values and storage requirements for the Byte, Integer, Long Integer and Single field sizes.

Field Name	Data Type	Field Size
Code		
Journey Date		
Departure Time		
From		
Due in at		
No of Stops		
First Class		
Restaurant Car		
Tickets Sold		
Notes		
Duration (Hours)		

Table 5.13

REVIEW YOUR WORK

Use the checklist below to verify that you have completed all the tasks in the National Railways database.

		Completed (√)
Table:	• Train Schedule	☐
Form:	• National Railways Train Schedule	☐
Queries:	• Cork promotional campaign	☐
	• Cork trains departing before 12:00am	☐
	• Journeys over 2 hours	☐
	• Journeys under 1 hour	☐
	• Journeys with less than 4 stops	☐
	• Kildare promotional campaign	☐
	• Restaurant car	☐
	• Trains departing after 11:00 and before 18:00	☐
	• Trains departing from 18:00 onwards	☐
	• Trains from Cork	☐
	• Trains leaving Cork between 08:00 and 17:30 inclusive	☐

Completed (√)

- Trains that are running late ☐
- Trains that haven't been cancelled ☐
- Trains with first class carriage ☐
- Trains with up to 10% profit ☐

Reports:

- Central Station Arrivals Information ☐
- Early Trains from Cork ☐
- Express Trains ☐
- First Class Trains ☐
- Trains with Dining Facilities ☐

Others:

- Database structure form ☐

ASSIGNMENT SUMMARY

Basic Concepts	
Index	Created in the Table to speed up searches on a particular field. Indexes slow down updates. Access automatically creates an index on the primary key field. Indexes only improve the performance of Queries in very large databases.
Field Size of a Number	The field size of a number in the Table determines the range of numbers that can be entered in that field. The field sizes you will encounter in this book are Byte, Integer, Long Integer and Single. The Single field size is used to store numbers with up to seven decimal places. Byte, Integer and Long Integer are used to store whole numbers of varying sizes.
Layout	A group of controls in a Form or Report that can be treated as a separate unit for the purpose of formatting and positioning. In a Stacked layout, Form controls are arranged in columns, with a single record displayed on the Form. In a Tabular layout, controls are arranged in a single row, with multiple records displayed on the Form. Stacked layouts are generally used in Forms, while Tabular layouts are used in Reports.

Combo Box	A drop-down list in an Access Form from which the database user can select an item, which in turn is entered in a specific field in the Table. Combo boxes eliminate spelling errors and make data entry easier because they reduce the amount of typing required. By setting the *Limit to List* property to *Yes*, the database designer can restrict data entry to items listed in the combo box.
Report	A database object that is used to format and present data. Reports are portable, as they can be printed out. You don't have to have knowledge of databases to understand the information in a Report. Reports are regularly used in business to help people make informed decisions. Records in a report can be sorted into different orders and report functions can perform summary calculations on the records in the Report. A Report can be linked to either a Table or a Query. In a database with a single Table, a Report linked to the Table will display all the records in the database. A Report linked to a Query will only display the specific records found by that Query.

Potential Pitfalls

- Records in the Table will be stored in ascending order of the primary key field, regardless of the order in which they are entered in the Form. When a code is used for the primary key field, the sequence of data entry may not match the sequence of records in the Table. For example, codes entered as KD001, CD001, KD002, GD001 and CD002 in the Form will be stored as CD001, CD002, GD001, KD001 and KD002 in the Table.
- If you store numbers with decimals in a field whose field size is either Byte, Integer or Long Integer, all numbers entered in that field will be rounded to zero places of decimals. For example, 15.43 will be stored as 15 and 27.85 will be stored as 28.
- When creating a combo box using the Wizard, always drag the field you are working with from the field list. If you don't do this, the combo box will be unbound, meaning that data selected in the combo box will not be transferred to the Table.
- The data entry operator will be able to enter items that are not listed in the combo box unless you set the *Limit to List* property to *Yes*.
- If you don't adjust the tab order after creating a combo box, the Form may 'jump' to a new record unexpectedly as you tab from text box to text box.
- It is difficult to adjust column widths in a Report unless the labels and text boxes are grouped together in a Tabular layout. This does not apply to Access 2007.

- When a Query is selected in the Navigation Pane, a new Report created using the Report Wizard will be automatically linked to that Query. If the Table or any Form or Report is selected in the Navigation Pane, the new Report will be automatically linked to the Table. Before creating a new Report, ensure that the correct database object is selected in the Navigation Pane.
- When a Report is linked to a Query, any new field added to the Table cannot be included in the Report until that field is also added to the Query.

Log on to www.gillmacmillan.ie to download review questions for Assignment 5.

6 Night Vision Database

SCENARIO

Siobhan O'Sullivan works in the local video rentals store. She is new to the job and when customers ask her questions such as 'What comedies do you have on DVD?', she has to go searching for the answer. As new DVD and Blu-ray films are purchased by the store, they are entered in a ledger. Finding all films in a particular category necessitates scanning through the ledger from beginning to end, which is proving to be very time consuming. In Assignment 6 you will create a database to store data relating to DVD and Blu-ray films available for rent. The Queries and Reports in the database will help Siobhan answer her customers' questions quickly and efficiently.

By completing this assignment, you will learn how to:

- Create a list box in a Form.
- Add a company logo to a Form.
- Combine Query conditions using the *AND* logical operator.
- Combine Query conditions using the *OR* logical operator.
- Display the top 10 and top 20 records found by a Query.
- Create labels with the Label Wizard.
- View and edit a Query in SQL view.
- Create Reports in a format suitable for emailing.

CREATE THE DATABASE AND SET UP THE TABLE

Task 1: Create a new database named *Night Vision.*

Task 2: Create a new Table and save the Table as *Films in Stock.*

- Using the data displayed in Table 6.1, create fields with appropriate data types in the *Films in Stock* Table.

Code	Title	Date Released	Rating	Running Time	Genre	Starring	Director	Format	Price per Night
DVD001	Angels and Demons	24/11/2009	12	150	Action/ Adventure	Tom Hanks	Ron Howard	DVD	€5.85

Table 6.1

- Set the *Code* field as the primary key. Set the field size of this field to an exact number, as all codes have the same number of characters.
- Set the format of the *Date Released* field to Long Date.
- Set the data type of the *Rating* field to Text to accommodate PG and U.
- Set the field sizes of the *Rating, Genre* and *Format* fields to exactly match the data (refer to Table 6.4 on page 117).
- Select appropriate data types and field sizes for all other fields in the Table.
- Set the format of the *Price per Night* field to Euro.
- Set up separate indexes on the *Rating* field and the *Genre* field.
- Do not enter data in the Table at this point.

- Save the *Films in Stock* Table.

An index in a field that is not the primary key must allow duplicates.

CREATE THE FORM

Task 3: Using the Form Wizard, create a Form including all fields from the *Films in Stock* Table. Information relating to the design of the Form is displayed in Table 6.2.

Form Layout	Columnar
Form Title	Night Vision Rentals

Table 6.2

In design view, adjust the width of the Form so that it takes up the full width of the PC screen.

Use layout view to make the following changes to the Form.

- Apply the *Civic* theme to the Form.
- Resize and position text boxes similar to Figure 6.1.

You will have to remove the Form controls from the existing layout to be able to move and resize text boxes independently of each other.

- Edit the *Title* label so that it reads *Title of Film.*
- Set the alignment of the *Running Time* and *Price per Night* text boxes to centre.

Use design view to make the following changes to the Form.

- Create separate combo boxes for the *Rating* and *Genre* fields using the information displayed in Table 6.3.

For a detailed explanation of how to create a combo box, refer to pages 78–81 in Assignment 5.

When creating a combo box, always ensure that you drag the appropriate field from the field list. If you forget to do this, your combo box will be unbound.

Rating (Combo Box)	Genre (Combo Box)
18	Action/Adventure
15	Children's
12A	Comedy
12	Drama
PG	Sci-Fi
U	Thriller

Table 6.3

- Set the *Limit to List* property for both the *Rating* and *Genre* combo boxes to *Yes*. Set the *Allow Value List Edits* property to *No* for both combo boxes.

Left
- Align label and text box controls in each *column* using the *Align Left* button.

Top
- Align label and text box controls in each *row* using the *Align Top* button.

- The completed Form should look something like Figure 6.1.

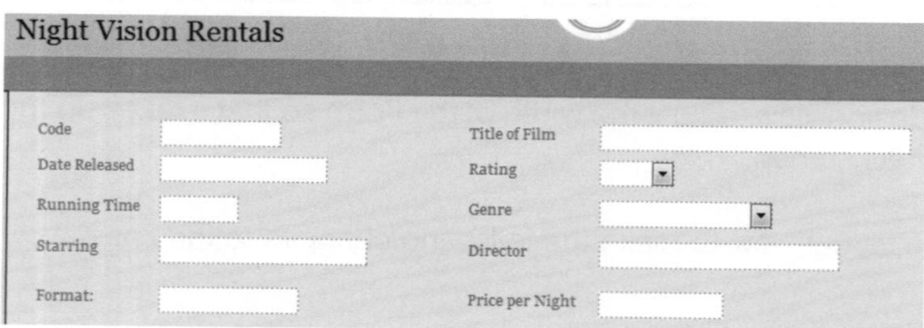

Figure 6.1: The completed *Night Vision Rentals* Form

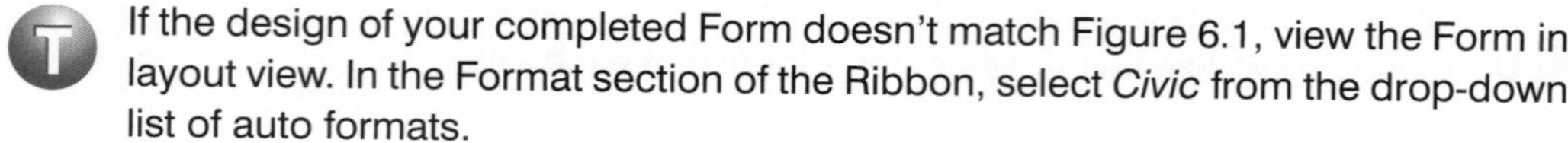
If the design of your completed Form doesn't match Figure 6.1, view the Form in layout view. In the Format section of the Ribbon, select *Civic* from the drop-down list of auto formats.

- Save the *Night Vision Rentals* Form.

WORKED EXAMPLE: FORMAT THE FORM TITLE

1. Open the *Night Vision Rentals* Form in design view.
2. In the Form header, select the label box containing the text *Night Vision Rentals*.
3. Apply a font style and size similar to Figure 6.2.

4. Increase the width of the label box so that the text doesn't wrap.
5. Increase the height of the Form header. Point at the top of the Detail bar. When the mouse pointer changes to a vertical double arrow, drag downwards, as shown in Figure 6.2, to make space below the title.

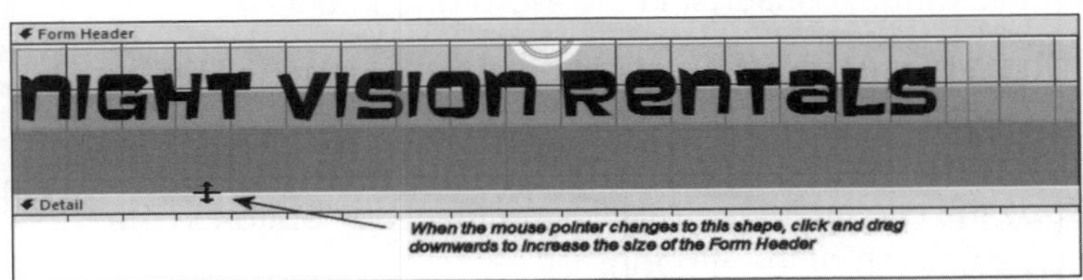

Figure 6.2: Increasing the size of the Form header

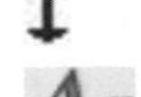

6. Increase the height of the label box so that the text is fully visible.

7. In the Design section of the Ribbon, click the *Label* button.
8. Click in the Form header immediately below the *Night Vision Rentals* label. Type the following text: *Your vision is our mission*
9. Select the new label box and apply a font style and font size similar to Figure 6.3.

10. Set the font colour of the new label box to black.

11. Resize the label box to fit the text.

Figure 6.3

12. Position the new label box as shown in Figure 6.3. Adjust the height of the Form header to fit the two label boxes.
13. Save the *Night Vision Rentals* Form.

WORKED EXAMPLE: ADD A LOGO TO THE FORM

1. Start Microsoft Word. A new blank document automatically opens.
2. Click the *Clip Art* button in the Insert section of the Ribbon.

3. In the Clip Art Pane, type *camera* in the *Search for:* box, as shown in Figure 6.4. Click the *Go* button.

Figure 6.4

4. Scroll through the clip art images until you find Figure 6.5 or a similar image. Click the image to insert it in the Word document.

Figure 6.5

You will find a bigger selection of images by clicking the *Clip art on Office Online* link at the bottom of the Clip Art Pane.

5. Copy the clip art image by clicking the *Copy* button in the Home section of the Ribbon.

6. In design view of the *Night Vision Rentals* Form, click anywhere in a blank area of the Form header.

7. Click the *Paste* button in the Home section of the Ribbon.

8. Resize the image by pointing at its bottom right-hand corner and then dragging upwards and leftwards with the mouse. Part of the image will be cut off when you do this.

9. If the property sheet is not displayed, right click the image and select *Properties* from the pop-up menu.
10. In the Format section of the property sheet, change the *Size Mode* property from *Clip* to *Zoom*.
11. Change the Border Style property to *Transparent*.
12. Position the clip art image to the right of the text, as shown in Figure 6.6.

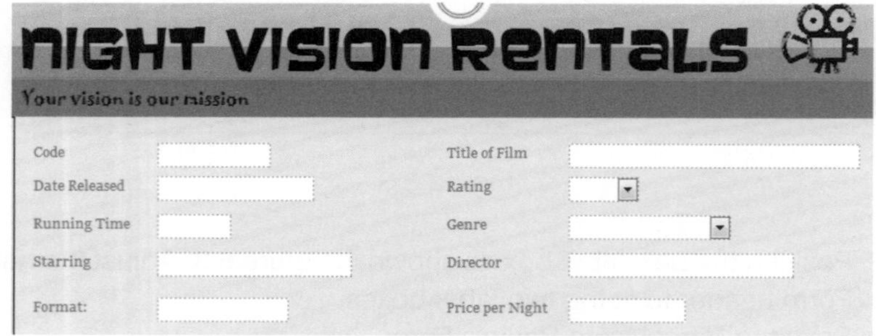

Figure 6.6: The completed *Night Vision* Form

13. The completed Form should look something like Figure 6.6.
14. Save the *Night Vision Rentals* Form.

LEARN HOW TO CREATE A LIST BOX

In the National Railways database, we created a combo box to record the city that each train was originating from. A combo box is a drop-down list from which the data entry operator can select an item, making data entry faster and more accurate. A list box is similar to a combo box in that it is a list from which items can be selected and it is used for data entry. One minor difference is that all the items in the list are visible in a list box, whereas in a combo box the items only become visible once the list is expanded.

Figure 6.7: Items in a combo box list are not visible until the list is expanded

Figure 6.7 shows a combo box for the Format field. The formats listed in the combo box (*Blu-ray* and *DVD*) do not become visible until the data entry operator clicks the down arrow in the combo box.

Figure 6.8

Figure 6.8 shows a list box for the same field. In a list box, all items are visible without having to click a down arrow. List boxes are useful where there is a very limited number of items that can be entered in a particular field. In Figure 6.8, as there are only two possible formats, a list box is suitable for the *Format* field. Combo boxes are more suitable where there is a longer list of potential data entry items.

Figure 6.9 displays a combo box from the Aer Lingus website, which customers use to select their country of origin. As this list is quite long, a list box would not be suitable because it would take up too much space on the Form. Combo boxes are much more suitable for long lists, as the list is only visible while the data entry operator is selecting an item from the combo box. Once the item has been selected, the combo box reverts back to its original size.

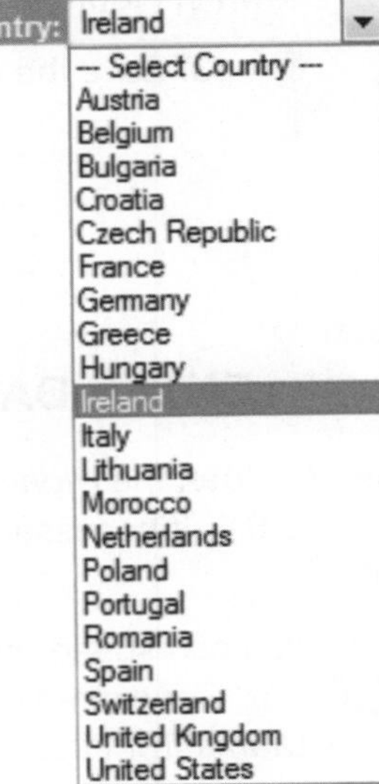

Figure 6.9

1. Open the *Night Vision Rentals* Form in design view.
2. Delete the controls for the *Format* field.
3. In the Design section of the Ribbon, click the *List Box* button.
4. If the field list is not already displayed, click the *Add Existing Fields* button. Drag the *Format* field from the field list and drop in the detail section of the Form, immediately below the *Starring* controls.

Add Existing Fields

5. In the List Box Wizard dialog box, select *I will type in the values that I want*. Click *Next*.
6. Type the list shown in Figure 6.10. Click *Next.*
7. Ensure that the value selected from the list box is stored in the *Format* field. Click *Next.*
8. Type *Format* as the label for the list box.
9. Click *Finish*.

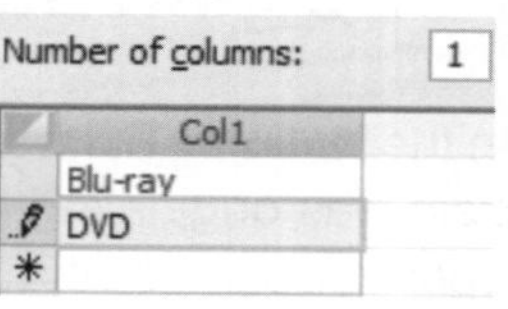

Figure 6.10

10. In layout view, adjust the size of the list box so that it fits the items in the list, as shown in Figure 6.11.

Figure 6.11: The size of the list box has been adjusted to fit the items in the list

11. Align the *Format* controls as shown in Figure 6.11.
12. Set the tab order of the Form so that it matches the list shown in Figure 6.12.

13. Save the *Night Vision Rentals* Form.

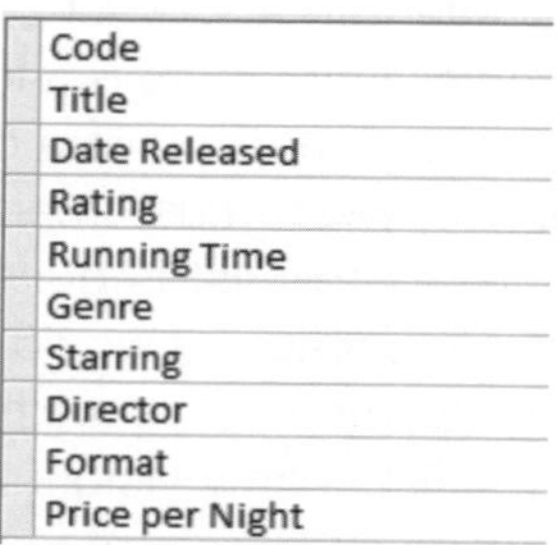

Figure 6.12: Tab order of the *Night Vision Rentals* Form

ENTER DATA

Task 4: Open the *Night Vision Rentals* Form in Form view. Enter all the records shown in Table 6.4. If necessary, use layout view to increase the width of text boxes to fit the data.

You can speed up your data entry by typing the first letter of an item in a combo box. For example, when the cursor is in the *Genre* combo box, typing *D* selects *Drama* from the list.

Code	Title	Date Released	Rating	Running Time	Genre	Starring	Director	Format	Price per Night
BLR001	Kung Fu Panda	09/11/2008	PG	59	Children's	Jack Black	Mark Osborne	Blu-ray	€5.35
BLR002	X-Men Origins: Wolverine	15/09/2009	12	107	Action/Adventure	Hugh Jackman	Gavin Hood	Blu-ray	€5.85
BLR003	Shaun of the Dead	09/04/2004	18	99	Comedy	Dylan Moran	Edgar Wright	Blu-ray	€5.00
BLR004	27 Dresses	29/04/2008	12	107	Drama	Katherine Heigl	Anne Fletcher	Blu-ray	€5.00
BLR005	The Hangover	20/07/2009	15	99	Comedy	Bradley Cooper	Todd Phillips	Blu-ray	€5.85
BLR006	Bagdad Cafe	24/07/2001	12	95	Drama	Jack Palance	Percy Adlon	Blu-ray	€5.00
BLR007	Hitman	11/03/2008	18	93	Action/Adventure	Timothy Olyphant	Xavier Gens	Blu-ray	€5.35
BLR008	10 Things I Hate About You	24/04/2006	15	97	Comedy	Julia Stiles	Gil Junger	Blu-ray	€5.35
BLR009	Laws of Attraction	30/04/2004	12	90	Comedy	Pierce Brosnan	Peter Howitt	Blu-ray	€5.00
BLR010	Evan Almighty	03/08/2007	PG	95	Comedy	Steve Carell	Tom Shadyac	Blu-ray	€5.35
DVD001	Angels and Demons	24/11/2009	12	150	Action/Adventure	Tom Hanks	Ron Howard	DVD	€5.85
DVD002	In Bruges	15/06/2008	18	107	Comedy	Colin Farrell	Martin McDonagh	DVD	€5.85
DVD003	Blood Diamond	08/12/2006	15	143	Drama	Leonardo DiCaprio	Edward Zwick	DVD	€5.35
DVD004	Hannah Montana: The Movie	18/08/2009	U	92	Children's	Miley Cyrus	Peter Chelsom	DVD	€5.85
DVD005	Hancock	25/11/2008	12	92	Comedy	Will Smith	Peter Berg	DVD	€5.35
DVD006	Fast and Furious	21/09/2009	12	107	Action/Adventure	Vin Diesel	Justin Lin	DVD	€5.85
DVD007	Alien vs Predator: Requiem	25/12/2007	18	100	Sci-Fi	John Ortiz	Colin Strause	DVD	€5.35
DVD008	Failure to Launch	27/06/2006	12	97	Comedy	Mathew McConaughey	Tom Dey	DVD	€5.00
DVD009	Gran Torino	06/09/2009	15	114	Thriller	Clint Eastwood	Clint Eastwood	DVD	€5.85
DVD010	Fight Club	06/06/2000	18	139	Drama	Edward Norton	David Fincher	DVD	€5.00
DVD011	Pirates of the Caribbean 3	21/11/2007	12	168	Action/Adventure	Johnny Depp	Gore Verbinski	DVD	€5.35

Table 6.4

LEARN HOW TO CREATE QUERIES WITH MULTIPLE CONDITIONS

So far, we have created Queries with one or two conditions. In the Riverside Rugby Club database, we created a Query to find records of players with a rating of 7 or less (one condition). In the National Railways database, we created a Query to find records of trains from Cork leaving before 12:00 a.m. (two conditions).

To find more specific information, more conditions can be added to a Query, as shown in Table 6.5.

1 Condition	• Rating=12	Finds 9 records
2 Conditions	• Rating=12 • Genre=Action/Adventure	Finds 4 records
3 Conditions	• Rating=12 • Genre=Action/Adventure • Format=DVD	Finds 3 records

Table 6.5

Table 6.5 demonstrates the effect of adding conditions to a Query. In general, adding more conditions to a Query results in the Query finding fewer records. This is because the search becomes more specific each time you add a condition. When there are two or more conditions in a Query, the conditions can be joined using either the *AND* logical operator or the *OR* logical operator. Whether you join conditions with *AND* or *OR* greatly affects how many records the Query will find.

JOINING CONDITIONS USING *AND*

When this method is used, the conditions are linked.

Field:	Genre	Format	Starring	Director
Table:	Films in Stock	Films in Stock	Films in Stock	Films in Stock
Sort:				
Show:	☑	☑	☑	☑
Criteria:	"Comedy"	"DVD"		
or:				

Figure 6.13: Two conditions joined with the *AND* logical operator

Using the conditions displayed in Figure 6.13, the Query searches for comedies available on DVD format, finding three records. When conditions are joined with *AND*, a Query will only find records which satisfy *all* the conditions.

JOINING CONDITIONS USING *OR*

When this method is used, the conditions are independent of each other.

Field:	Genre	Format	Starring	Director
Table:	Films in Stock	Films in Stock	Films in Stock	Films in Stock
Sort:				
Show:	☑	☑	☑	☑
Criteria:	"Comedy"			
or:		"DVD"		

Figure 6.14: Two conditions joined with the *OR* logical operator

Using the conditions displayed in Figure 6.14, the Query searches for films that either have a format of DVD *or* are comedies, finding 16 records. When conditions are joined with *OR*, a Query will find records which satisfy *at least one* of the conditions. From this example, it can be seen that whether you choose *AND* or *OR* to join conditions in a Query greatly affects how many records the Query will find. In general, a Query will find more records when conditions are joined with *OR*. Table 6.6 summarises the effects of using *AND* or *OR* in a Query.

Conditions	Conditions Joined With	Number of Records Found
Format="DVD" Genre="Comedy"	AND	3
Format="DVD" Genre="Comedy"	OR	16

Table 6.6: Effects of using *AND* or *OR* logical operators to join Query conditions

AND LOGICAL OPERATOR

Conditions are linked and are entered in different fields. When creating the Query, *all conditions must be in the Criteria line*. There is no need to type the word "*AND*". When Access sees more than one condition on the Criteria line, it interprets these conditions as being joined with the *AND* logical operator. The conditions displayed in Figure 6.15 would be interpreted by Access as "Comedies on DVD format".

Field:	Genre	Format	Starring	Director
Table:	Films in Stock	Films in Stock	Films in Stock	Films in Stock
Sort:				
Show:	☑	☑	☑	☑
Criteria:	"Comedy"	"DVD"		
or:				

Figure 6.15: Two conditions joined with the *AND* logical operator

Using the conditions displayed in Figure 6.15, the Query finds three records: In Bruges, Hancock and Failure to Launch.

AND conditions can be used on as many fields as you want. The more conditions you add to the Query, the more refined the search becomes, causing the Query to find fewer records. The conditions displayed in Figure 6.16 would be interpreted as "Comedies rated 12 on DVD format".

Field:	Rating	Genre	Format	Starring	Director
Table:	Films in Stock	Films in Stock	Films in Stock	Films in Stock	Films in Stock
Sort:					
Show:	☑	☑	☑	☑	☑
Criteria:	"12"	"Comedy"	"DVD"		
or:					

Figure 6.16: Three conditions joined with the *AND* logical operator

Using the conditions in Figure 6.16, the Query finds two records: Hancock and Failure to Launch.

OR CONDITION (SINGLE FIELD)

Conditions are independent of each other and are entered in the same field. When creating the Query, the conditions are joined with the *OR* logical operator. The conditions in Figure 6.17 would be interpreted by Access as "Films whose genre is *either* Drama *or* Action/Adventure". When conditions are joined using this method, each record found by the Query can only satisfy one of the listed conditions. Using the conditions in Figure 6.17, the Query finds nine records.

Field:	Genre	Format	Starring	Director	Price per Night
Table:	Films in Stock	Films in Stock	Films in Stock	Films in Stock	Films in Stock
Sort:					
Show:	☑	☑	☑	☑	☑
Criteria:	"Drama" Or "Action/Adventure"				
or:					

Figure 6.17: Two conditions in the same field joined with the *OR* logical operator

A second method of joining conditions with *OR* is to use the "or:" line in the Query design grid. If you use this method, there is no need to type the word "*or*".

Field:	Genre	Format	Starring	Director	Price per Night
Table:	Films in Stock	Films in Stock	Films in Stock	Films in Stock	Films in Stock
Sort:					
Show:	☑	☑	☑	☑	☑
Criteria:	"Drama"				
or:	"Action/Adventure"				

Figure 6.18: Alternative method of joining conditions with *OR*

In Figure 6.18, the *Action/Adventure* condition has been entered in the "or:" line of the Query design grid. Access will interpret the conditions in Figure 6.18 as "Films whose genre is *either* Drama *or* Action/Adventure".

You can continue adding *OR* conditions to the Query design grid using additional lines below the "or:" line.

Never join conditions in the same field with the *AND* logical operator. The condition ***"Drama" and "Action/Adventure"*** does not make sense logically, as a film can't be both a Drama and an Action/Adventure film at the same time.

OR CONDITION (MULTIPLE FIELDS)

Conditions are independent of each other and are entered in different fields. (Note: Conditions are not on the same line.) The second condition is entered in the "or:" line (see Figure 6.19). With this type of Query, there is no need to type *OR* to join the conditions. The conditions displayed in Figure 6.19 would be interpreted by Access as "Films whose rating is PG *or* whose genre is Children's". When conditions are joined using this method, the Query will find records that satisfy one or more of the listed conditions.

Field:	Rating	Genre	Format	Starring
Table:	Films in Stock	Films in Stock	Films in Stock	Films in Stock
Sort:				
Show:	☑	☑	☑	☑
Criteria:	"PG"			
or:		"Children's"		

Figure 6.19: Two conditions in different fields joined with the *OR* logical operator

Using the conditions in Figure 6.19, the Query finds three records: Hannah Montana: The Movie (*Children's rated U*), Kung Fu Panda (*Children's rated PG*) and Evan Almighty (*Comedy rated PG*).

A MIXTURE OF *OR* AND *AND*

Conditions are linked and are entered in different fields. The conditions displayed in Figure 6.20 would be interpreted by Access as "Films rated 12 that are *either* comedies *or* dramas".

Field:	Rating	Genre	Format	Starring
Table:	Films in Stock	Films in Stock	Films in Stock	Films in Stock
Sort:				
Show:	☑	☑	☑	☑
Criteria:	"12"	"Comedy" Or "Drama"		
or:				

Figure 6.20: Conditions are joined using a combination of *AND* and *OR* logical operators

This Query finds five records: Hancock (*Comedy rated 12*), Failure to Launch (*Comedy rated 12*), 27 Dresses (*Drama rated 12*), Bagdad Cafe (*Drama rated 12*) and Laws of Attraction (*Comedy rated 12*).

When entering text as a Query condition, there is no need to type the inverted commas. Access does this for you.

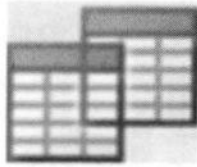

CREATE QUERIES

Create a separate Query for each of the tasks described in Table 6.7. Save each Query using the name provided.

Never join conditions in the same field using the *AND* logical operator. However, it is OK to use *AND* in conjunction with the *Between* logical operator, e.g. Between #01/01/2009# and #31/12/2009#.

	Purpose of Query	Sort Order	Query Name	Records Found
Task 5	Find records of Sci-Fi, Thriller and Action/Adventure films	Ascending order of Genre	High octane	7
Task 6	Find records of films rated U, PG or 12	Descending order of Rating	Suitable for children	12
Task 7	Find records of comedies rated 15 or 18	Ascending order of Title	Adult comedies	4
Task 8	Find records of films rated PG or 12 except for children's films	Ascending order of Title	Family night in	10
Task 9	Find records of Action/Adventure films released in 2009	Descending order of Date Released	Action 2009	3
Task 10	Find records of Comedies and Dramas, rated 12 or PG, available in Blu-ray format	Ascending order of Title	Family Blu-ray titles	4
Task 11	Find records of Children's and Comedy films rated PG or 12 whose running time is under 100 minutes and which are available in Blu-ray format	Ascending order of Title	Short and sweet	3
Task 12	Find records of Blu-ray films with a running time greater than 100 minutes, except for those rated 18	Ascending order of Title	Suitable for adolescents	2
Task 13	Find records of comedies except for those released in 2008	Ascending order of Date Released	Comedies except for 2008	6

Table 6.7

In Task 13, use *Not Between.*

CREATE REPORTS

For a detailed explanation of Access Reports, refer to pages 86–91 in Assignment 5.

Task 14: Display a complete list of titles.

- Create a Report linked to the *Films in Stock* Table, including the *Title, Date Released, Rating* and *Genre* fields.
- Sort the Report in descending order of *Date Released*.
- Apply the *Concourse* theme to the Report.
- The Report title is *Complete List of Titles.*

If hash symbols are displayed in your Report, it means that the column isn't wide enough to display the data. This often happens with Date/Time fields. Increase the width of the text box in layout view until the hash symbols disappear.

############

WORKED EXAMPLE: ADD A LOGO TO A REPORT

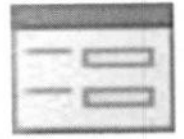

1. Open the *Night Vision Rentals* Form in design view.

2. Select the movie camera clip art image in the Form header. Click the *Copy* button in the Home section of the Ribbon. Close the *Night Vision Rentals* Form.

3. View the *Complete List of Titles* Report in design view.
4. Right click in a blank area of the Report header and select *Paste* from the pop-up menu.
5. Position the clip art image so that it appears like Figure 6.21, which is an extract from the completed Report.

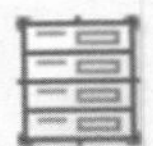

6. In layout view, move the *Date Released* controls so that they are positioned as in Figure 6.21.
7. Adjust column widths and align data, as shown in Figure 6.21.

Complete List of Titles

Title	Rating	Genre	Date Released
Angels and Demons	12	Action/Adventure	24 November 2009
Fast and Furious	12	Action/Adventure	21 September 2009
X-Men Origins: Wolverine	12	Action/Adventure	15 September 2009
Gran Torino	15	Thriller	06 September 2009

Figure 6.21: Extract from the completed Report for Task 14

8. Save the *Complete List of Titles* Report.

Because this Report was sorted by the *Date Released* field, by default this field appears first in the Report.

Task 15: Display Blu-ray titles.

- Create a Query to find Blu-ray films. Save the Query as *Blu-ray.*
- Create a Report linked to the *Blu-ray* Query, including the *Title, Date Released, Rating* and *Genre* fields.

Select the *Blu-ray* Query in the Navigation Pane before creating the Report.

- Sort the Report in descending order of *Date Released*.
- Apply the *Concourse* theme to the Report.
- The Report title is *Blu-Ray Titles.*
- Add the movie camera clip art image to the Report header.
- Adjust column widths and align data, as shown in Figure 6.22.
- Move the *Date Released* controls to the right of the *Genre* controls.
- An extract from the completed Report is displayed in Figure 6.22.

Blu-ray Titles

Title	Rating	Genre	Date Released
X-Men Origins: Wolverine	12	Action/Adventure	15 September 2009
The Hangover	15	Comedy	20 July 2009
Kung Fu Panda	PG	Children's	09 November 2008
27 Dresses	12	Drama	29 April 2008

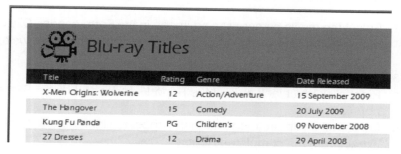

Figure 6.22: Extract from the completed Report for Task 15

You can view the Query that a Report is linked to by following these steps.

1. In design view, ensure that the entire Report is selected by clicking the square in the top left-hand corner of the Report window. When the entire Report is selected, a black dot will appear inside the square (Figure 6.23).
2. Display the Property Sheet.
3. Click the [...] button in the *Record Source* property.
4. To return to Report design, close the Query.

Figure 6.23

Task 16: Display DVD titles.

- Create a Query to find DVD films. Save the Query as *DVD.*
- Create a Report linked to the *DVD* Query, including the *Title, Date Released, Rating* and *Genre* fields.
- Sort the Report in descending order of *Date Released*.
- Apply the *Concourse* theme to the Report.
- The Report title is *DVD Titles.*
- Add the movie camera clip art image to the Report header.
- Adjust column widths and align data, as shown in Figure 6.24.
- Move the *Date Released* controls to the right of the *Genre* controls.
- An extract from the completed Report is displayed in Figure 6.24.

DVD Titles

Title	Rating	Genre	Date Released
Angels and Demons	12	Action/Adventure	24 November 2009
Fast and Furious	12	Action/Adventure	21 September 2009
Gran Torino	15	Thriller	06 September 2009
Hannah Montana: The Movie	U	Children's	18 August 2009

Figure 6.24: Extract from the completed Report for Task 16

Task 17: Display DVD rentals rated 15 or 18.

Adult DVDs

Title	Rating	Genre	Price per Night
Fight Club	18	Drama	€5.00
Alien vs Predator: Requiem	18	Sci-Fi	€5.35
In Bruges	18	Comedy	€5.85
Gran Torino	15	Thriller	€5.85
Blood Diamond	15	Drama	€5.35

Figure 6.25: Completed Report from Task 17

- Create a Query to find DVDs rated 15 or 18. Save the Query as *DVDs rated 15 or 18.*
- Create a Report linked to this Query, including the *Title, Genre, Rating* and *Price per Night* fields.
- Sort the Report in descending order of *Rating*.

- Apply the *Concourse* theme to the Report.
- The Report title is *Adult DVDs.*
- Add the movie camera clip art image to the Report header.
- Adjust column widths and align data, as shown in Figure 6.25.
- The completed Report should look something like Figure 6.25.

LEARN ABOUT LABELS

A label is a removable and adhesive sticker. Labels are commonly used when creating price and bar code tags for products in a shop. Once printed, the labels can be affixed to the products. In large-scale mail merge applications, where names and addresses in a database are combined with a standard letter to produce personalised letters for thousands of people, labels are used to automate the process of letter addressing. Many companies, such as Reader's Digest, base their entire business around this process.

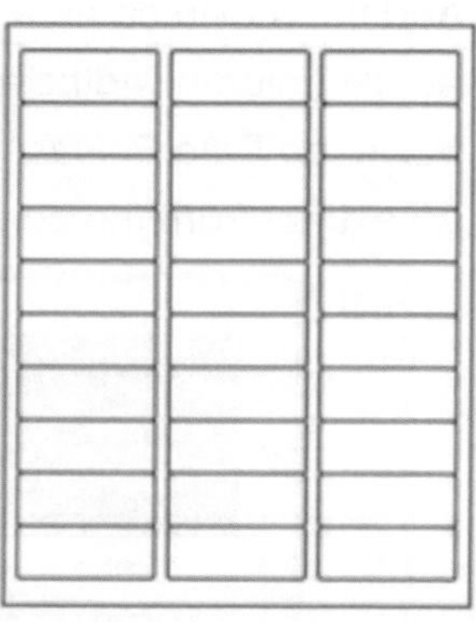

Figure 6.26: Blank labels

When you purchase a box of labels, each individual label sheet will have rows of blank labels, like Figure 6.26. Each set of labels has a unique product number which tells Access the physical dimensions of individual labels.

Access has a special Label Wizard designed to guide you through the process of creating and formatting labels.

WORKED EXAMPLE: CREATE PRODUCT LABELS

1. Select the *Films in Stock* Table in the Navigation Pane.

2. Click the *Labels* button in the Create section of the Ribbon.
3. Select the label size. Each set of labels has a product number that tells Access the physical dimensions of individual labels as well as the positioning of individual labels on each sheet. When printing on actual labels, it is important that you select the product number corresponding to the labels you are using. The product number will be printed on the box the labels came in as well as on each individual page of labels. In this exercise, it doesn't really matter which product number we use, as the labels will be printed on an A4 page.

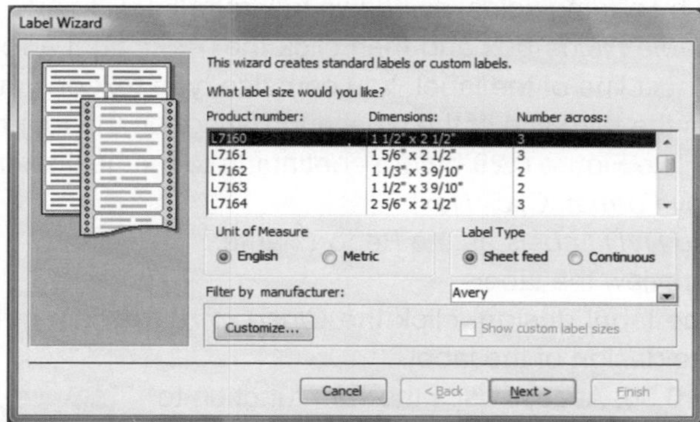

Figure 6.27: Selecting a label product number

4. Select Product Number *L7160*, as shown in Figure 6.27. Click *Next*.

You won't see *L7160* in the list of product numbers if the unit of measure is set to metric.

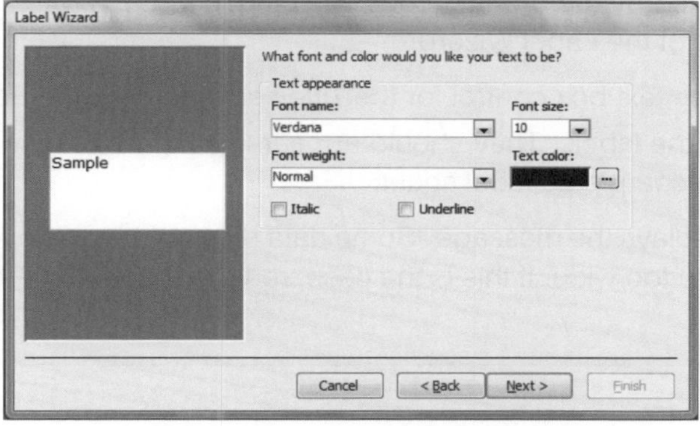

Figure 6.28: Formatting label text

5. Select *Verdana* as the font name, a font size of *10* and a font weight of *Normal*, as shown in Figure 6.28. Click *Next*.

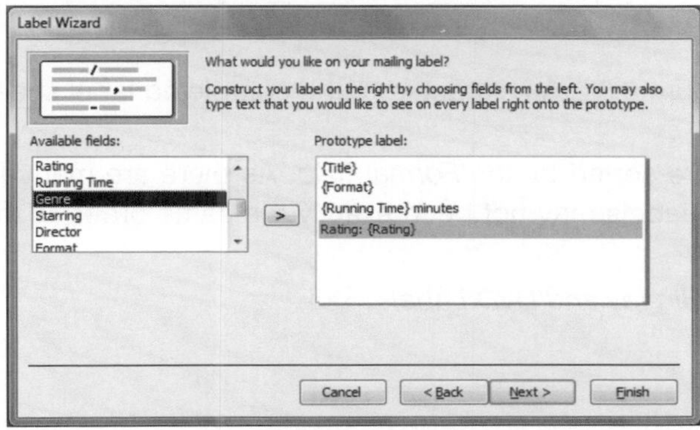

Figure 6.29: Adding fields and text to a label

6. Set up the label by adding fields, as shown in Figure 6.29. To add a field, select the field in the *Available Fields* box and then click the > right arrow. Press *Enter* to move on to the next line of the label. You can also type text on your label. Type the word *minutes* on the third line of the label and *Rating:* on the fourth line. Check that your label looks like Figure 6.29 before continuing to the next step. Click *Next*.
7. Sort the labels by *Format*. Click *Next*.
8. Enter *Blu-ray and DVD Labels* as the Report name.
9. Click *Finish* to preview the labels.

10. To see the label design, click the *Close Print Preview* button. Figure 6.30 shows the design of the label.

In Figure 6.30, Access uses the *Trim* function to remove unnecessary space. The & symbol is used to join field names and text in an expression.

The expression *="Rating:" & [Rating]* produces the text *Rating: 12*, *Rating: 15*, etc. The physical size of the label in Figure 6.30 is determined by the product code selected in the first step of the Label Wizard.

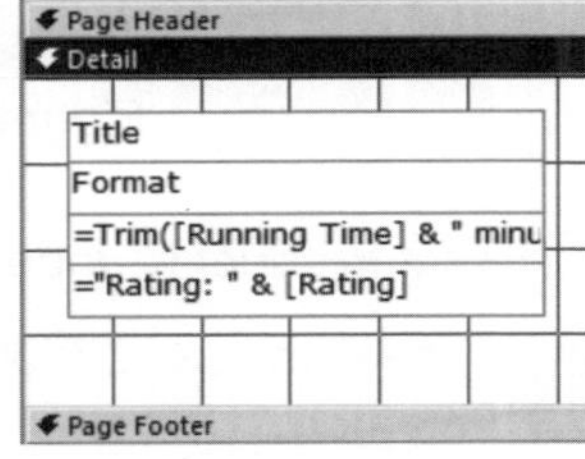

Figure 6.30: Label design

11. Select the text box control for the *Title* field and click the *Bold* button.

12. Preview the labels. They should appear like Figure 6.31, which is an extract from the completed label sheet.

If Access displays the message "Some data may not be displayed", it means that the labels are too wide. If this is the case, reduce the width of the label in design view.

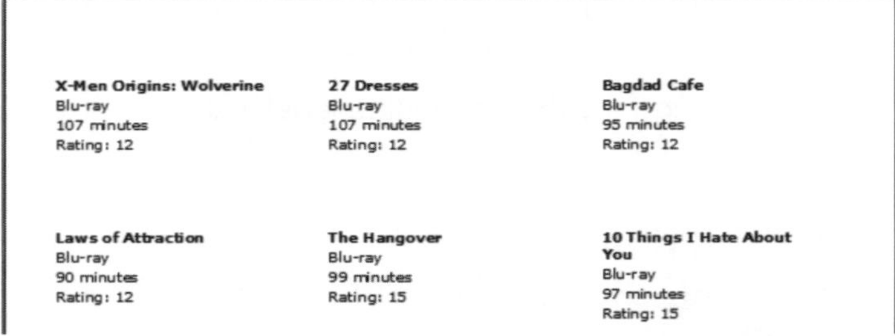

Figure 6.31: An extract from the completed label sheet

The labels are sorted by the *Format* field. As there are many films of the same format, your labels may not be in exactly the same order as those displayed in Figure 6.31.

13. Save *Blu-ray and DVD Labels*.

WORKED EXAMPLE: CREATE PRODUCT LABELS FOR SPECIFIC RECORDS

To create labels for specific records, simply select the appropriate Query in the Navigation Pane before running the Label Wizard.

1. Select the *Blu-ray* Query in the Navigation Pane.

2. Create new labels with the Label Wizard, using *L7160* as the code.
3. Select *Verdana* as the font, a font size of *14* and a font weight of *Bold*.
4. Add the *Format* field together with descriptive text to the label so that it looks like Figure 6.32.
5. Enter *Special Offer Labels* as the Report name.

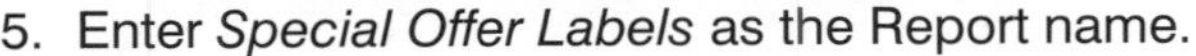

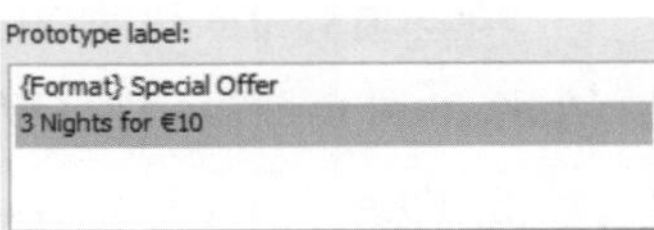

Figure 6.32: Label set-up

6. View the labels in design view.
7. Select the text box containing the *Format* field. Change the font size to 12 and remove the bold formatting.
8. Preview the labels. They should appear like Figure 6.33, which is an extract from the completed label sheet.

Blu-ray Special Offer **3 Nights for €10**	Blu-ray Special Offer **3 Nights for €10**	Blu-ray Special Offer **3 Nights for €10**

Figure 6.33: An extract from the completed label sheet

9. Save the *Special Offer Labels* Report.

There should be 10 labels in total.

Database terminology is a little bit ambiguous here. A label created with the Label Wizard should not be confused with a label control, which is used to display text in a Form or Report.

FIND AND EDIT RECORDS

Task 18: Open the *Night Vision Rentals* Form in Form view. Use the *Find*, *Delete Record* and *New Record* buttons to make the following changes.

1. The running time for Kung Fu Panda is 95 minutes.
2. Evan Almighty is on DVD and not Blu-ray, as recorded. The correct code for this film is DVD012.

3. Verify that Evan Almighty:

Completed (√)

- Is now displayed in the *DVD Titles* Report. ☐
- Is no longer displayed in the *Blu-Ray Titles* Report. ☐

Access will not update the Reports until you advance the Form to the next record by pressing the *Tab* key. Alternatively, click the *Refresh All* button in the Home section of the Ribbon.

4. Verify that the *Special Offer Labels* Report now contains nine labels.

5. Due to a fall in rentals, Fight Club is to be withdrawn. Delete this record.

6. Verify that DVD010, Fight Club:

Completed (√)

- Is no longer displayed in the *DVD Titles* Report. ☐
- Is no longer displayed in the *Adult DVDs* Report. ☐

7. Add the films displayed in Table 6.8 to the database, using appropriate codes.

Code	Title	Date Released	Rating	Running Time	Genre	Starring	Director	Format	Price per Night
	After Earth	31/05/2013	12A	100	Sci-Fi	Will Smith	M. Shyamalan	Blu-ray	€5.85
	World War Z	21/06/2013	15A	116	Thriller	Brad Pitt	Marc Forster	Blu-ray	€5.85
	Star Trek Into Darkness	16/05/2013	12A	132	Sci-Fi	Chris Pine	J.J. Abrams	Blu-ray	€5.85
	Man of Steel	14/06/2013	12A	143	Thriller	Christopher Meloni	Zack Snyder	DVD	€5.85

Table 6.8

You will need to add 15A to the Rating combo box.

8. Verify that Man of Steel is displayed in the following reports:

Completed (√)

- *Complete List of Titles* ☐
- *DVD Titles* ☐
- *Blu-ray and DVD Labels* ☐

9. Verify that After Earth, World War Z and Star Trek Into Darkness are displayed in the *Blu-Ray Titles* Report.
10. Verify that the *Special Offer Labels* Report now includes 12 labels.

ADD A NEW FIELD TO THE TABLE

1. Add a new field named *Chart Position* to the *Films in Stock* Table, using an appropriate data type and field size (see Table 6.9).

2. Open the *Night Vision Rentals* Form in design view.
3. Add the *Chart Position* field to the *Night Vision Rentals* Form, positioning the new field below the *Price per Night* field.
4. Set the alignment of the *Chart Position* text box to centre.

5. Save the *Night Vision Rentals* Form.

6. Using the *Night Vision Rentals* Form, enter the *Chart Position* data displayed in the shaded cells in Table 6.9.

Press the *Page Down* button on the keyboard to quickly advance to the next record.

Code	Title	Chart Position
BLR001	Kung Fu Panda	13
BLR002	X-Men Origins: Wolverine	1
BLR003	Shaun of the Dead	17
BLR004	27 Dresses	7
BLR005	The Hangover	5
BLR006	Bagdad Cafe	21
BLR007	Hitman	19
BLR008	10 Things I Hate About You	15
BLR009	Laws of Attraction	20
	After Earth	3
	World War Z	6
	Star Trek Into Darkness	8
DVD001	Angels and Demons	2
DVD002	In Bruges	4
DVD003	Blood Diamond	10
DVD004	Hannah Montana: The Movie	22
DVD005	Hancock	9
DVD006	Fast and Furious	14
DVD007	Alien vs Predator: Requiem	12
DVD008	Failure to Launch	23
DVD009	Gran Torino	11
DVD011	Pirates of the Caribbean 3	18
DVD012	Evan Almighty	22
	Man of Steel	16

Table 6.9

CREATE REPORTS

Task 19: Display the Night Vision Top 20.

1. Create a new Query that finds records of films whose chart position is between 1 and 20 inclusive. Save the Query as *Top 20.*
2. Create a Report linked to the *Top 20* Query, including the *Chart Position, Title, Rating, Starring* and *Director* fields.
3. Sort the Report in ascending order of *Chart Position*.
4. Apply the *Concourse* theme to the Report.
5. The Report title is *Night Vision Top 20.*
6. Add the clip art image to the Report header.
7. Adjust column widths and align data, as shown in Figure 6.34.
8. The completed Report should look something like Figure 6.34, which is an extract from the Report.

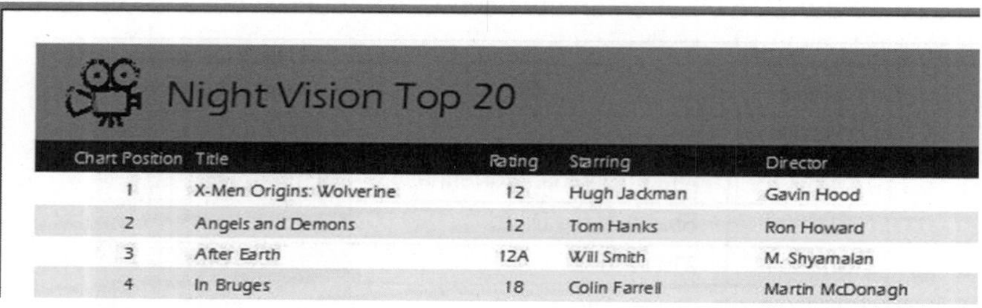

Night Vision Top 20

Chart Position	Title	Rating	Starring	Director
1	X-Men Origins: Wolverine	12	Hugh Jackman	Gavin Hood
2	Angels and Demons	12	Tom Hanks	Ron Howard
3	After Earth	12A	Will Smith	M. Shyamalan
4	In Bruges	18	Colin Farrell	Martin McDonagh

Figure 6.34: Completed Report from Task 19

WORKED EXAMPLE: CREATE THE BLU-RAY TOP 10 CHART

Part 1: Create the Query

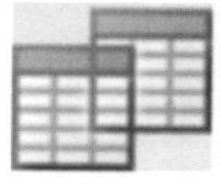

1. Create a new Query to find films of Blu-ray format. (This is separate to the existing Blu-ray Query.)
2. Sort the Query in ascending order of *Chart Position*.

3. Run the Query. Twelve records are displayed.

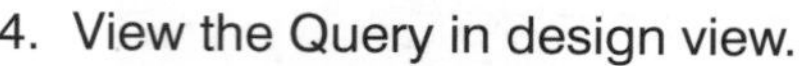

4. View the Query in design view.

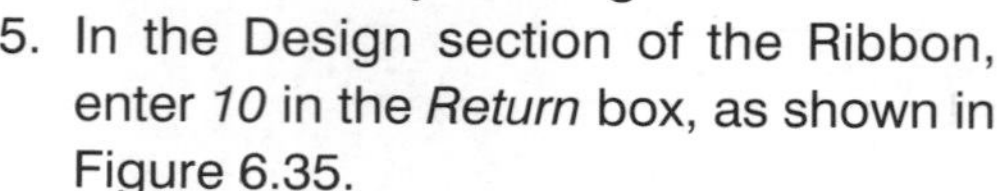

5. In the Design section of the Ribbon, enter *10* in the *Return* box, as shown in Figure 6.35.

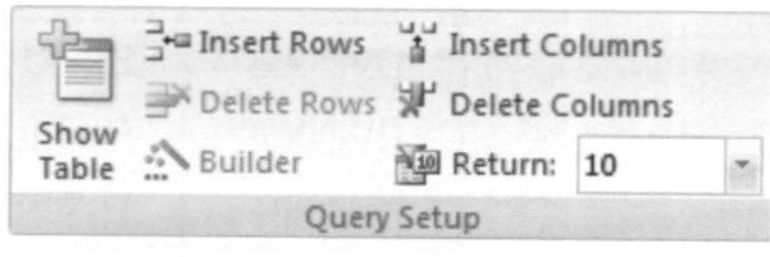

Figure 6.35: Displaying the top 10 records

Using the Return drop-down list, you can specify the number of records to be displayed by the Query. There are six options: display the top 5, 25 or 100 records found by the Query, display the top 5% or 25% of the records found by the Query or display all records found by the Query. Even though displaying the top 10 records isn't an option in the list, you can still type *10* in the Return box. You will have to delete a zero, as Access assumes you are typing *100*.

6. Run the Query. Only the top 10 records are displayed. Laws of Attraction and Bagdad Cafe, which are 20th and 21st in the chart, respectively, are not displayed.
7. Save the Query as *Blu-ray top 10*.

Part 2: Create the Report

1. Create a Report linked to the *Blu-ray top 10* Query, including the *Chart Position, Title, Rating, Starring* and *Director* fields.
2. Sort the Report in ascending order of *Chart Position*.
3. Apply the *Concourse* theme to the Report.
4. The Report title is *Blu-Ray Top 10.*
5. Add the clip art image to the Report header.
6. Adjust column widths and align data, as shown in Figure 6.36.
7. The completed Report should look something like Figure 6.36, which is an extract from the Report.

Night Vision Top 20

Chart Position	Title	Rating	Starring	Director
1	X-Men Origins: Wolverine	12	Hugh Jackman	Gavin Hood
2	Angels and Demons	12	Tom Hanks	Ron Howard
3	State of Play	12	Russell Crowe	Kevin MacDonald
4	In Bruges	18	Colin Farrell	Martin McDonagh
5	The Hangover	15	Bradley Cooper	Todd Phillips
6	Terminator Salvation	12A	Christian Bale	McG

Figure 6.36: An extract from the *Blu-Ray Top 10* Report

PORTABLE DOCUMENT FORMAT (PDF)

The PDF format was developed to allow the sharing of files across all types of devices regardless of operating system. This idea has become more important in recent years, as most people are now using more than one device (e.g. PCs, laptops, tablets and smartphones) to store and process their files across multiple locations. In Microsoft Access, any Table, Query, Form or Report can be exported to a PDF file, which can then be emailed as an attachment. This PDF file can be read by any device even if Microsoft Access is not loaded on that device. The PDF format preserves the look and feel of the document. This means that anyone opening a PDF of an Access Report, for example, will see the Report exactly as you created it, even if they don't have Microsoft Access on their device. All that is required to view PDF documents is an up-to-date version of Adobe Reader, which can be downloaded for free from the Adobe website.

WORKED EXAMPLE: OUTPUT A REPORT TO A FORMAT SUITABLE FOR EMAIL

Before completing this worked example, ensure that you have an up-to-date version of Adobe Reader on your PC, laptop or device. Adobe Reader is a free download available on the Adobe website (www.adobe.com).

1. Open the *Night Vision Top 20* Report.
2. In the *External Data* section of the Ribbon, click the *PDF or XPS* button.
3. Ensure that the *Save As Type* is PDF and then click *Publish*. Access saves the Report in PDF format. The document opens automatically in Adobe Reader (Figure 6.37). It can be emailed as an attachment and can be read by any PC, laptop or device with an up-to-date version of Adobe Reader.

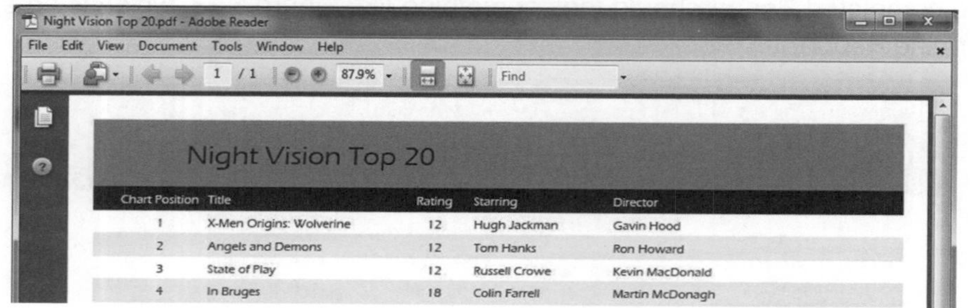

Chart Position	Title	Rating	Starring	Director
1	X-Men Origins: Wolverine	12	Hugh Jackman	Gavin Hood
2	Angels and Demons	12	Tom Hanks	Ron Howard
3	State of Play	12	Russell Crowe	Kevin MacDonald
4	In Bruges	18	Colin Farrell	Martin McDonagh

Figure 6.37: An Access Report that has been converted to a PDF document

4. Close the Export PDF Wizard. There is no need to save the steps.
5. This document can be attached.

An Access Report can be converted to a PDF document and attached to an email in a single step by clicking the *E-mail* button in the *External Data* section of the Ribbon. However, when this method is used, the PDF document is not saved as a file on your computer and will not be available for future use.

WORKED EXAMPLE: ADD A NEW FIELD TO A REPORT

A Report can be linked to a Table or a Query. When a Report is linked to the Table, adding a new field to the Report is straightforward. Once the new field has been set up in the Table, it will appear in the Report's field list. The new field is added to the Report by dragging it from the field list and dropping it in the detail section. When a Report is linked to a Query, adding a new field to the Report is a little more complex.

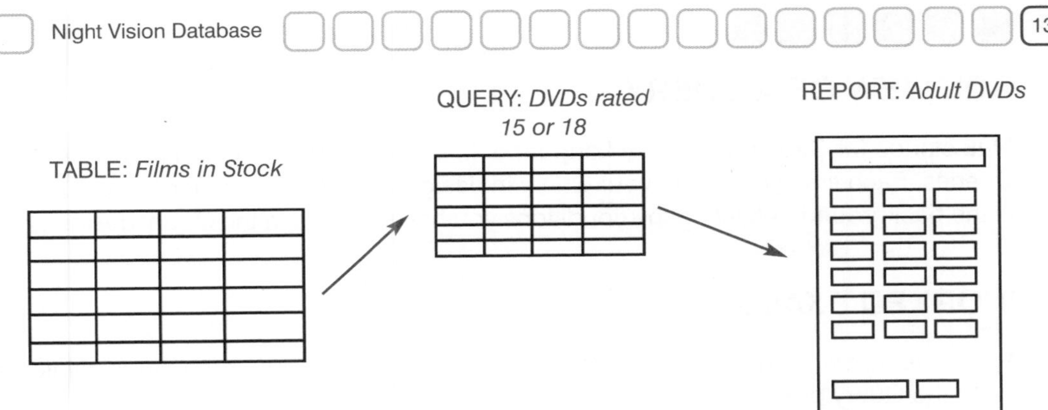

Figure 6.38: Adding the *Chart Position* field to the *Adult DVDs* Report

Figure 6.38 is a diagram of the *Adult DVDs* Report. This Report is linked to the *DVDs rated 15 or 18* Query. Even though the new *Chart Position* field has been added to the *Films in Stock* Table, the new field will not appear in the field list of the *Adult DVDs* Report until it is added to the *DVDs rated 15 or 18* Query.

In Access 2010, it is much easier to add a new field to a Report when the labels and text boxes in the page header and detail section are grouped together in a Tabular layout.

1. Open the *DVDs rated 15 or 18* Query in design view.
2. Add the *Chart Position* field to the Query design grid.
3. Save and close the *DVDs rated 15 or 18* Query.
4. Open the *Adult DVDs* Report in layout view.
5. Display the field list.
6. Drag the *Chart Position* field from the field list and drop to the left of the *Title* field.
7. Set the alignment of the *Chart Position* label and text box controls to Centre.

Group & Sort

8. Sort the records in descending order of *Chart Position*.
9. The completed Report should look something like Figure 6.39.

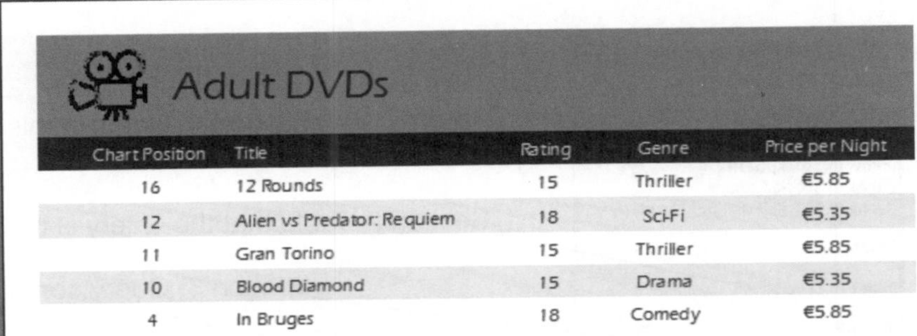

Adult DVDs

Chart Position	Title	Rating	Genre	Price per Night
16	12 Rounds	15	Thriller	€5.85
12	Alien vs Predator: Requiem	18	SciFi	€5.35
11	Gran Torino	15	Thriller	€5.85
10	Blood Diamond	15	Drama	€5.35
4	In Bruges	18	Comedy	€5.85

Figure 6.39: The *Chart Position* field has been added to the Report

SQL VIEW OF A QUERY

SQL stands for Structured Query Language. It is the programming language used by Queries. Each time you set up your Query in design view, Access generates SQL code in the background, reflecting the conditions you have entered in the Query design grid.

WORKED EXAMPLE

1. Create a new Query. Add the *Title*, *Rating*, *Genre*, *Format* and *Price per Night* fields to the Query design grid.
2. Enter the conditions displayed in Figure 6.40.

Field:	Title	Rating	Genre	Format	Price per Night
Table:	Films in Stock	Films in Stock	Films in Stock	Films in Stock	Films in Stock
Sort:					
Show:	☑	☑	☑	☑	☑
Criteria:		"12"	"comedy" Or "drama"		
or:					

Figure 6.40: Query conditions displayed in design view

3. Save the Query as *Comedies and Dramas rated 12*.
4. Display the SQL code corresponding to these conditions by selecting *SQL View* from the View drop-down menu (Figure 6.41).
5. Access displays the SQL code powering the Query (Figure 6.42).

Figure 6.41

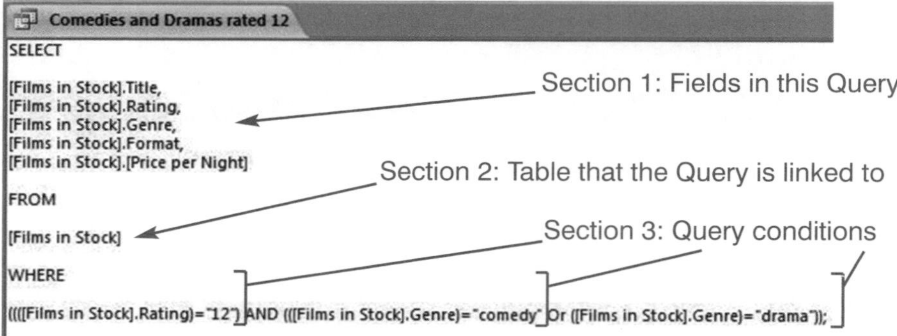

Figure 6.42: SQL code representing conditions entered in the Rating and Genre fields

The SQL code in Figure 6.42 is relatively easy to understand.

- **Section 1** is the structure of the Query, reflecting the fields that were added to the Query design grid. It specifies that data from the *Title*, *Rating*, *Genre*, *Format* and *Price per Night* fields will be displayed when the Query is run.
- **Section 2** specifies that the Query will search for records in the *Films in Stock* Table.
- **Section 3** corresponds to the conditions entered in the Query Design Grid. Conditions in the Genre field are joined with the logical operator *OR*, as it is impossible for a film to have two genres. The *Rating* condition and *Genre* condition are joined with the logical operator *AND*. This means that the Query will only find records where either of the following sets of conditions are satisfied:
  (i) *Rating* = "12" and *Genre* = "Comedy"
  (ii) *Rating* = "12" and *Genre* = "Drama"

6. Run the Query. Five records are displayed.
7. View the Query in SQL view. In the SQL code, change the value in the *Rating* condition from "12" to "15".
8. Run the Query again. It now finds three records.
9. Change the condition for the *Rating* field back to "12". Verify that the Query runs correctly and then save the Query.

Task 20: Using Access Help, search for articles on database forms. Write a brief report outlining the use of Forms in a database.

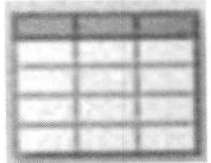

DEFINE DATABASE STRUCTURE

Task 21: Complete the database structure form (Table 6.10) with data types and field sizes for all fields in the *Films in Stock* Table.

Field Name	Data Type	Field Size
Code		
Title		
Date Released		
Rating		
Running Time		
Genre		
Starring		
Director		
Format		
Price per Night		
Chart Position		

Table 6.10

Ensure that the field sizes of Text fields specified in design view of the *Films in Stock* Table match those specified in the database structure form.

REVIEW YOUR WORK

Use the checklist below to verify that you have completed all the tasks in the Night Vision database.

		Completed (√)
Table:	• Films in Stock	☐
Form:	• Night Vision Rentals	☐
Queries:	• Action 2009	☐
	• Adult comedies	☐
	• Blu-ray	☐
	• Blu-ray top 10	☐
	• Comedies and dramas rated 12	☐
	• Comedies except for 2008	☐
	• DVD	☐
	• DVDs rated 15 or 18	☐
	• Family Blu-ray titles	☐
	• Family night in	☐
	• High octane	☐
	• Short and sweet	☐
	• Suitable for adolescents	☐
	• Suitable for children	☐
	• Top 20	☐
Reports:	• Adult DVDs	☐
	• Blu-ray and DVD Labels	☐
	• Blu-Ray Titles	☐
	• Blu-Ray Top 10	☐
	• Complete List of Titles	☐
	• DVD Titles	☐
	• Night Vision Top 20	☐
	• Special Offer Labels	☐
Other:	• Database structure form	☐

ASSIGNMENT SUMMARY

Basic Concepts	
***AND* Logical Operator**	When conditions are entered in the same line of the Query design grid, Access joins the conditions using the *AND* logical operator. Only records satisfying *all* of the conditions will be found by the Query.
***OR* Logical Operator – Single Field**	When multiple conditions are entered in a single field, they are joined using the *OR* logical operator. For example, the expression "12" or "PG" or "U" consists of three conditions joined with *OR*. Access will return records where any one of these conditions is satisfied. It is logically impossible for more than one condition to be satisfied, as each film can only have one rating. An alternative method is to enter each condition on a separate line in the Query design grid.
***OR* Logical Operator – Multiple Fields**	To join conditions involving multiple fields with the *OR* logical operator, enter each condition in the appropriate column on a separate line in the Query design grid. Access will find records where at least one condition is satisfied. This is very different to a Query involving conditions joined with *AND*, where only records satisfying all conditions are returned by the Query.
Labels	The Label Wizard is used to print names and addresses, product information or other data on sheets of adhesive labels. Using the Label Wizard, you can produce labels for all the records stored in the Table or for specific records found by a Query. Once printed, individual labels can be removed and affixed to envelopes or products.
List Box	Used in Access Forms. Provides a list in which the data entry operator can select items when entering data in a particular field. Unlike combo boxes, multiple list items are visible in a list box without having to expand the list.
Query Return Option	Using this option, you can specify the number of records to be displayed by a Query. There are six options: display the top 5, 10 or 25 records found by the Query, display the top 5% or 25% or display all records found by the Query.

Potential Pitfalls

- Never join conditions in a single field using the *AND* logical operator. It is OK to use *AND* in conjunction with the *Between* logical operator.
- When displaying dates in a Report, Access displays a series of # symbols when the text box is not wide enough to display the dates. If this is the case, you should increase the width of the text box.
- A combo box or list box in a Form will be unbound if you don't drag the field from the field list when you are creating the "combo or list box".
- When creating Query conditions, it is better not to type inverted commas. Access will put these in for you.
- In cases where there is a long list of potential data entry items for a specific field, it is better to use a combo box, as a list box will take up too much space on the Form. However, you cannot use a combo or list box unless there is a definite limit to the number of possible data entry items. For example, it would be inappropriate to use a combo box for a person's name.

Log on to www.gillmacmillan.ie to download review questions for Assignment 6.

7 Technical Zone Database

SCENARIO

Andrew Burke co-ordinates the technical support service in Technical Zone Learning. As PCs rapidly become obsolete and need to be upgraded regularly, Andrew is finding it very difficult to keep up-to-date lists of PCs by classroom. He also needs to be able to quickly determine which PCs currently need to be upgraded. At the moment, the only way of doing this is to walk around the college checking PCs and making a list of their specifications. In Assignment 7, you will create a database to store data relating to the PCs in Technical Zone Learning. A number of Queries and Reports will allow Andrew to get the information he needs with the click of a button.

By completing this assignment, you will practise the following skills:

- Setting up the Table.
- Designing and creating a Form.
- Creating combo boxes and list boxes.
- Combining Query conditions using *AND* and *OR*.
- Creating Reports.
- Creating labels.

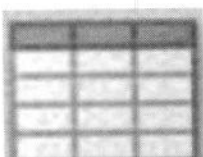

CREATE THE DATABASE AND SET UP THE TABLE

Task 1: Create a new database named *Technical Zone.*
Task 2: Create a new Table and save the Table as *College PCs.*

- Using the data displayed in Table 7.1, create fields with appropriate data types in the *College PCs* Table.

PC Number	Manuf	Model	Processor	Processor Speed GHz	Hard Disk Gb	Ram Gb	Web Cam	Wi-Fi Enabled	Date Purchased	Room No
601001	Compaq	Presario	Core 2 Quad	2.6	640	2	No	No	21/05/10	601

Table 7.1

- Set the *PC Number* field as the primary key, using an appropriate field size.
- Set the format of the *Processor Speed GHz* field to fixed, 1 place of decimals.
- Set the format of the *Date Purchased* field to Medium Date.

- Set the field sizes of the *Manuf*, *Model*, *Processor* and *Room No* fields to exactly match the data (see Table 7.5 on page 144).
- Select appropriate data types and field sizes for all other fields in the Table.
- Set up separate indexes on the *Hard Disk Gb* field and the *Ram Gb* field.
- Do not enter data in the Table at this point.

- Save the *College PCs* Table.

When you select *Single* as the field size of a Number field, it is best to set the decimal places to a fixed number, rather than leaving decimal places set to Auto. Doing this at the Table design stage ensures that the correct number of decimal places will be displayed in Forms, Queries and Reports created later on in the assignment.

CREATE THE FORM

Task 3: Using the Form Wizard, create a Form including all fields from the *College PCs* Table. Information relating to the design of the Form is displayed in Table 7.2.

Form Layout	Columnar
Form Title	Technical Support Zone

Table 7.2

Use layout view to make the following changes to the Form.

- Apply the *Civic* theme to the Form.
- Resize the *PC Number, Model* and *Date Purchased* text boxes similar to Figure 7.2 on page 144.
- Set the alignment of the *PC Number* and *Date Purchased* text boxes to centre.
- Insert a clip art image in the Form header, similar to that in Figure 7.2.
- Format the Form title using a style similar to Figure 7.2.
- Insert the email address and extension number in the Form header using a label box. Display this text in italics.

Hold down the *Shift* key and press *Enter* when going onto a new line in the label box.

Use design view to make the following changes to the Form.

- Create separate combo boxes for the *Processor*, *Processor Speed GHz* and *Hard Disk Gb* fields using the information displayed in Table 7.3.

Processor (Combo Box)	Processor Speed GHz (Combo Box)	Hard Disk Gb (Combo Box)
Athlon 64 X2	3.1	4096
Core 2 Quad	3.0	3072
Core i7	2.8	2048
Core i9	2.6	1024
Phenom II	2.5	640
Phenom II X4	2.3	500

Table 7.3

- Set the *Limit to List* property of all combo boxes to *Yes*.
- Set the *Allow Value List Edits* property of all combo boxes to *No*.
- Set the alignment of the combo boxes to centre.
- Create separate list boxes for the *Manuf*, *RAM* and *Room No* fields using the information displayed in Table 7.4.

Manuf (List Box)	RAM Gb (List Box)	Room No (List Box)
Compaq	8	601
Dell	4	601a
Sony	2	

Table 7.4

If your list box has vertical scroll bars, you should increase the height of the list box until the scroll bars disappear.

- Edit the *Manuf* label so that it reads *Manufacturer.*
- Edit the *Room No* label so that it reads *Room Number.*
- Set the tab order of the Form so that it matches the list shown in Figure 7.1.
- Position Form controls as shown in Figure 7.2.

To move and resize controls independently, they must be removed from the existing layout.

The completed Form should look something like Figure 7.2.

PC Number
Manuf
Model
Processor
Processor Speed GHz
Hard Disk Gb
Ram Gb
Web Cam
Wi-Fi Enabled
Date Purchased
Room No

Figure 7.1: Tab order of the *Technical Support Zone* Form

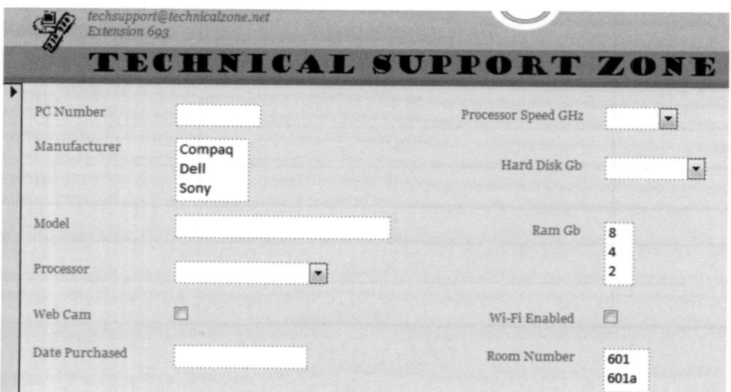

Figure 7.2: Completed *Technical Support Zone* Form

ENTER DATA

Task 4: Using the *Technical Support Zone* Form, enter all the records displayed in Table 7.5.

If necessary, adjust the width of text boxes, using layout view, as you enter the data.

PC Number	Manuf	Model	Processor	Processor Speed GHz	Hard Disk Gb	Ram Gb	Web Cam	Wi-Fi Enabled	Date Purchased	Room No
601001	Compaq	Presario	Core 2 Quad	2.6	640	2	No	No	21/05/10	601
601002	Sony	Vaio	Athlon 64 X2	2.8	500	2	No	No	14/09/08	601
601003	Dell	Optiplex	Phenom II	2.3	1024	4	No	Yes	24/01/08	601
601004	Dell	Precision	Core i9	3.1	4096	8	Yes	Yes	14/09/10	601
601005	Sony	Vaio	Phenom II X4	3.0	2048	4	No	Yes	21/10/09	601
601006	Sony	Vaio	Phenom II X4	3.0	3072	8	Yes	Yes	15/01/10	601
601007	Dell	Vostro	Core 2 Quad	2.8	1024	2	Yes	Yes	24/01/08	601
601008	Dell	Precision	Core i7	3.0	3072	8	Yes	Yes	03/01/10	601
601009	Dell	Vostro	Athlon 64 X2	2.3	500	2	No	No	24/01/08	601
601010	Compaq	Pavilion	Phenom II	2.6	2048	4	Yes	No	18/02/09	601
601011	Sony	Vaio	Phenom II X4	3.0	3072	8	Yes	Yes	21/10/10	601a
601012	Compaq	Presario	Core i9	3.1	4096	8	Yes	Yes	21/05/10	601a
601013	Dell	Precision	Core i7	2.8	2048	4	Yes	No	21/05/09	601a
601014	Dell	Vostro	Core i9	3.1	4096	8	Yes	Yes	10/05/10	601a
601015	Sony	Vaio	Phenom II X4	2.3	1024	2	Yes	No	10/05/10	601a
601016	Dell	Optiplex	Core 2 Quad	2.6	2048	4	Yes	No	24/01/08	601a
601017	Compaq	Presario	Athlon 64 X2	2.5	1024	2	No	Yes	18/02/09	601a
601018	Dell	Precision	Core 2 Quad	2.3	640	2	No	Yes	21/10/08	601a
601019	Dell	Optiplex	Core i7	2.8	3072	4	No	Yes	24/01/08	601a
601020	Compaq	Pavilion	Phenom II X4	3.0	4096	8	Yes	Yes	21/05/10	601a

Table 7.5

Task 5: Table 7.6 is the database structure form for the *College PCs* Table. Complete the database structure form by recording the field names, data types and field sizes for all fields in the *College PCs* Table.

Field Name	Data Type	Field Size
PC Number		
Manuf		
Model		
Processor		
Processor Speed GHz		
Hard Disk Gb		
RAM Gb		
Web Cam		
Wi-Fi Enabled		
Date Purchased		
Room No		

Table 7.6

Ensure that the field sizes of Text fields specified in design view of the *College PCs* Table match those specified in the database structure form.

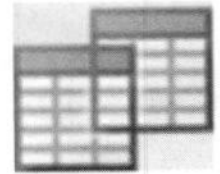

CREATE QUERIES

Create a separate Query for each of the tasks described in Table 7.7. Save each Query using the name provided.

For a detailed explanation of how to join multiple conditions in a Query, refer to pages 118–21 in Assignment 6.

	Purpose of Query	Sort Order	Query Name	Records Found
Task 6	Find records of PCs in room 601	Ascending order of Manuf field	PCs in room 601	10
Task 7	Find records of PCs purchased in 2010	Descending order of Date Purchased	PCs purchased in 2010	9
Task 8	Find records of PCs except for those purchased in May 2010	Ascending order of Date Purchased	Except for PCs purchased in May 2010	15
Task 9	Find records of PCs except for those with a Phenom II X4 processor	Ascending order of Processor	Except for Phenom II X4	15

Table 7.7

	Purpose of Query	Sort Order	Query Name	Records Found
Task 10	Find records of PCs with Core 2 Quad, Core i7 or Core i9 processors	Ascending order of Processor	Intel PCs	10
Task 11	Find records of PCs with Core i7 or Core i9 processors in room 601a	Ascending order of Processor	Room 601a i7s and i9s	4
Task 12	Find records of PCs that either have a web cam or are Wi-Fi enabled	Ascending order of Model	Web cam or Wi-Fi	17
Task 13	Find records of PCs with either a processor speed of 2.5 GHz or less or that have 2 Gb of RAM	Ascending order of Date Purchased	PCs for upgrade	8
Task 14	Find records of PCs with Core i7 or Core i9 processors that have both web cam and Wi-Fi capabilities	Ascending order of Processor	Video conferencing PCs	4
Task 15	Find the top 25% of PCs by hard disk size	Descending order of Hard Disk Gb	Hard disks – top 25%	6
Task 16	Find the top 5% of PCs by processor speed	Descending order of Processor Speed GHz	Processors – top 5%	3

Table 7.7 (continued)

CREATE REPORTS

Select the Table or appropriate Query in the Navigation Pane before starting the Report Wizard.

Task 17: Display a complete list of PCs.

- Create a Report linked to the *College PCs* Table.
- Include the *PC Number, Manuf, Model, Processor, Processor Speed GHz, Hard Disk Gb* and *RAM Gb* fields in the Report.
- Sort the Report in ascending order of the *PC Number* field.
- Apply the *Concourse* style to the Report.
- The Report title is *Technical Zone PCs.*

Use layout view to make the following changes to the Report.

- Centre the data in the *PC Number, Processor Speed GHz, Hard Disk Gb* and *RAM Gb* controls.

- Copy the clip art image from the *Technical Support Zone* Form and paste it in the Report header, as shown in Figure 7.3.
- Edit the labels in the page header so that they appear like Figure 7.3. You will need to remove all controls from the existing layout to do this.
- The completed Report should look something like Figure 7.3, which is an extract from the Report.

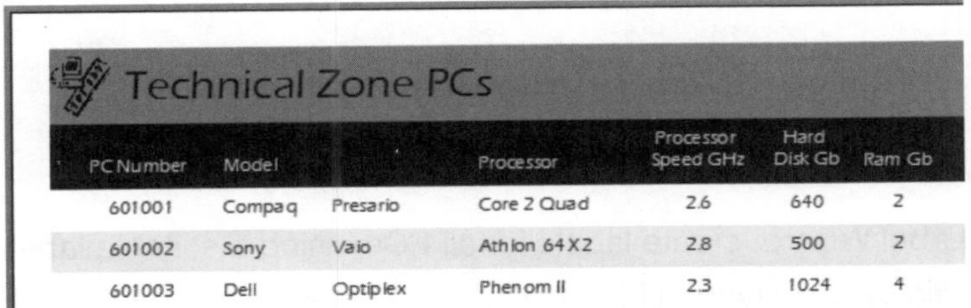

Technical Zone PCs

PC Number	Model		Processor	Processor Speed GHz	Hard Disk Gb	Ram Gb
601001	Compaq	Presario	Core 2 Quad	2.6	640	2
601002	Sony	Vaio	Athlon 64X2	2.8	500	2
601003	Dell	Optiplex	Phenom II	2.3	1024	4

Figure 7.3: Extract from the Report created in Task 17

- Export the *Technical Zone PCs* Report to a PDF document.

Task 18: Display a list of PCs in room 601.

- Create a Report linked to the *PCs in room 601* Query.
- Include the *Manuf, Model, Processor, Processor Speed GHz, Hard Disk Gb, RAM Gb, Web Cam* and *Wi-Fi Enabled* fields in the Report.
- Sort the Report in ascending order of the *Manuf* field.
- Apply the *Concourse* style to the Report.
- The Report title is *Room 601.*

Use layout view to make the following changes to the Report.

- Centre the data in the *Processor Speed GHz, Hard Disk Gb* and *RAM Gb* controls.
- Position the check box controls centrally beneath their respective labels.

Check box controls can't be centred using the *Center* button. Adjust the width of the box containing the check box control instead.

- Copy the clip art image from the *Technical Support Zone* Form and paste it in the Report header.
- Edit the labels in the page header so that they appear like Figure 7.4.
- The completed Report should look something like Figure 7.4, which is an extract from the Report.

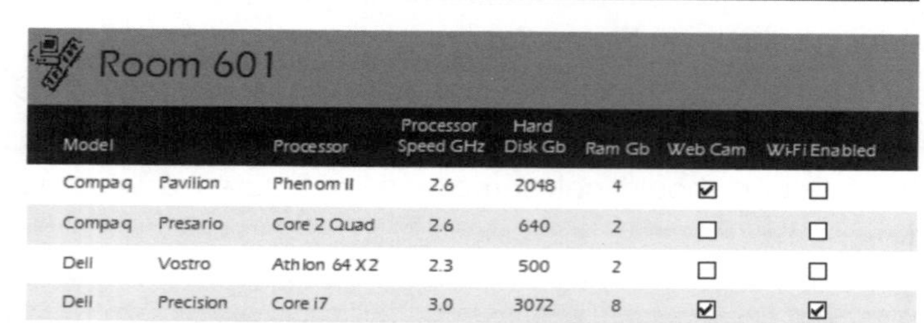

Room 601

Model		Processor	Processor Speed GHz	Hard Disk Gb	Ram Gb	Web Cam	Wi-Fi Enabled
Compaq	Pavilion	Phenom II	2.6	2048	4	☑	☐
Compaq	Presario	Core 2 Quad	2.6	640	2	☐	☐
Dell	Vostro	Athlon 64 X2	2.3	500	2	☐	☐
Dell	Precision	Core i7	3.0	3072	8	☑	☑

Figure 7.4: Extract from the Report created in Task 18

Task 19: Create PC labels.

- Using the Label Wizard, create labels for all PCs, using a suitable label code.
- Include the fields displayed in Figure 7.5 in the labels.
- Include the text “PC”, “GHz”, “Purchased” and “Location: Room” in the labels, as shown in Figure 7.5.
- Sort the Labels in ascending order of *PC Number.*
- The name of the Report is *PC Labels.*
- Format the *PC Number* in bold print.
- Figure 7.5 is a sample of the completed labels.

PC 601001 2.6 GHz Core 2 Quad Purchased: 21/05/2010 Location: Room 601	**PC 601002** 2.8 GHz Athlon 64 X2 Purchased: 14/09/2008 Location: Room 601	**PC 601003** 2.3 GHz Phenom II Purchased: 24/01/2008 Location: Room 601

Figure 7.5: Extract from the labels created in Task 19

If Access displays the message “Some data may not be displayed” when you preview the labels, you need to reduce the width of the label in design view.

Task 20: Create *Video Conferencing Labels.*

- Using the Label Wizard, create labels linked to the *Video conferencing PCs* Query, using the layout shown in Figure 7.6.

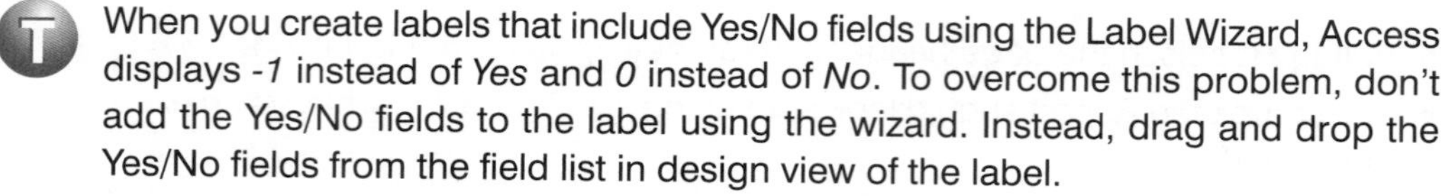

When you create labels that include Yes/No fields using the Label Wizard, Access displays *-1* instead of *Yes* and *0* instead of *No*. To overcome this problem, don’t add the Yes/No fields to the label using the wizard. Instead, drag and drop the Yes/No fields from the field list in design view of the label.

- The name of the Report is *Video Conferencing Labels.*
- Display the text *Video Conferencing PC* in bold print.
- Figure 7.6 is a sample of the completed labels. There should be four labels in total.

Video Conferencing PC	Video Conferencing PC	Video Conferencing PC
Web Cam ☑	Web Cam ☑	Web Cam ☑
Wi-Fi Enabled ☑	Wi-Fi Enabled ☑	Wi-Fi Enabled ☑

Figure 7.6: Extract from the labels created in Task 20

FIND AND EDIT RECORDS

Task 21: Open the *Technical Support Zone* Form. Use the *Find*, *Delete Record* and *New Record* buttons to make the following changes.

1. PC 601010, the Compaq Pavilion, doesn't have a web cam.
2. The processor speed of PC 601015, the Sony Vaio, is 2.8 GHz and not 2.3 GHz, as recorded. The hard disk size was also incorrectly recorded and should be 4096.
3. PC 601019, the Dell Optiplex, has a web cam.
4. Verify that PC 601010: **Completed (√)**
   - Is no longer found by the *Web cam or Wi-Fi* Query. ☐
5. Verify that PC 601015: **Completed (√)**
   - Is now found by the *Hard disks – top 25%* Query. ☐
6. Verify that PC 601019: **Completed (√)**
   - Is now found by the *Video conferencing PCs* Query. ☐
   - Is now included in the *Video Conferencing Labels* (the number of labels will have increased by one to five). ☐
7. PC 601001, the Compaq Presario, is to be scrapped. Delete this record, using the *Technical Support Zone* Form.
8. Verify that PC 601001: **Completed (√)**
   - Is no longer displayed in the *Technical Zone PCs* Report. ☐
   - Is no longer displayed in the *Room 601* Report. ☐
   - Is no longer displayed in the *PC Labels* Report. ☐
   - Is no longer found by the *PCs for upgrade* Query. ☐

Two new PCs have been purchased by the college and must be entered in the database. The PCs are manufactured by Packard Bell and eMachines. As these manufacturers are not listed in the list box, it must be updated.

1. Open the *Technical Support Zone Form* in design view.
2. View the properties of the *Manuf* list box.
3. Scroll down through the list of properties until you find the *Row Source* property.
4. Add *Packard Bell* and *eMachines* to the row source, as shown in Figure 7.7. If necessary, increase the width of the property sheet so that you can see the complete row source list.

Items in the row source list are enclosed in double quotes and are separated using semi-colons.

Row Source	"Compaq";"Dell";"Sony";"Packard Bell";"eMachines"

Figure 7.7: Packard Bell and eMachines have been added to the row source

If you prefer to edit the combo box list in Form view, first view the Form in design view and change the *Allow Value List Edits* property of the *Manuf* control to *Yes*. In Form view, display the combo box list by clicking the down arrow. A bulleted list icon appears immediately below the last item in the list. Click this icon and then add *Packard Bell* and *eMachines* to the combo box list using the *Edit List Items* dialog box. Don't forget to change the *Allow Value List Edits* property to *No* when you have finished!

5. View the Form in layout view. Increase the size of the list box to accommodate the new list items.

A list box should be big enough to display all list items without a vertical scroll bar.

6. View the Form in Form view. The edited list box should look something like Figure 7.8.

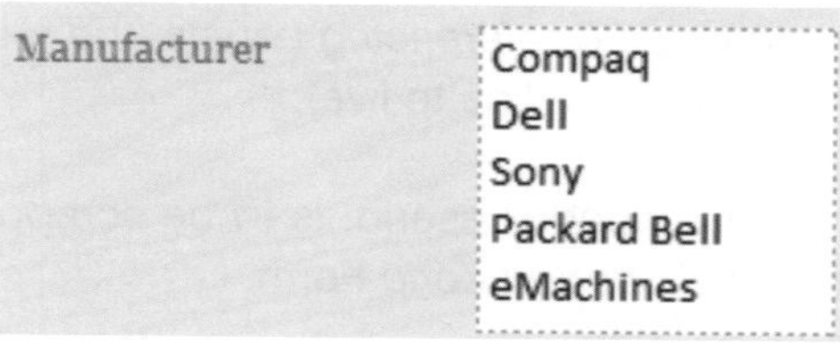

Figure 7.8

7. In design view of the Form, edit the row source of the *Processor* combo box to include the Atom N270, as shown in Figure 7.9.

Row Source	"Athlon 64 X2";"Core 2 Quad";"Core i7";"Core i9";"Phenom II";"Phenom II X4";"Atom N270"

Figure 7.9: Atom N270 has been added to the row source

8. View the Form in Form view. Display the *Processor* combo box list. It should now include the Atom N270, as shown in Figure 7.10.
9. Using the *Technical Support Zone* Form, add the records displayed in Table 7.8 to the database, using appropriate codes.

You will need to adjust the field size of the *Manuf* field.

Athlon 64 X2
Core 2 Quad
Core i7
Core i9
Phenom II
Phenom II X4
Atom N270

Figure 7.10

PC Number	Manuf	Model	Processor	Processor Speed GHz	Hard Disk Gb	Ram Gb	Web Cam	Wi-Fi Enabled	Date Purchased	Room No
	Packard Bell	iMedia	Phenom II X4	2.8	4096	8	Yes	Yes	07/01/15	601
	eMachines	EZ1600	Atom N270	2.3	500	2	Yes	Yes	07/01/15	601a

Table 7.8

10. Verify that the Packard Bell iMedia and the eMachines EZ1600 are displayed in the following reports:

Completed (√)

- *Technical Zone PCs* ☐
- *PC Labels* ☐

EDIT SQL CODE

Task 22

1. View the *PCs in Room 601* Query in SQL view.
2. Edit the SQL code so that the Query finds PCs in room 601a.
3. Run the Query and verify that it finds 11 records of PCs in room 601a.
4. Close the Query without saving it.

Task 23

1. View the *PCs purchased in 2010* Query in SQL view.
2. Edit the SQL code so that the Query finds records of PCs purchased from the beginning of July 2010 to the end of December 2010.
3. Run the Query and verify that it finds two records.
4. Close the Query without saving it.

Task 24

1. View the *Except for Phenom II X4* Query in SQL view.
2. Edit the SQL code so that the Query excludes *Core i7* instead of *Phenom II X4*.
3. Run the Query and verify that it finds 18 records.
4. Close the Query without saving it.

ADD A NEW FIELD TO THE TABLE

1. Add a new field named *Processor Type* to the *College PCs* Table using an appropriate data type and field size (see Table 7.9).

2. Open the *Technical Support Zone* Form in design view.

3. Create a combo box for the *Processor Type* field, including *AMD* and *Intel* in the combo box list.
4. Delete the label for the new combo box and position the combo box to the left of the *Processor* combo box, as shown in Figure 7.11.

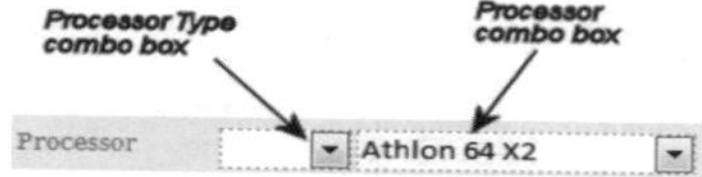

Figure 7.11: Position of the new combo box

5. Adjust the tab order of the Form so that the new *Processor Type* field is immediately before the *Processor* field in the tab order list.

6. Save the *Technical Support Zone* Form.

7. Using the *Technical Support Zone* Form, enter the *Processor Type* data displayed in the shaded cells in Table 7.9.

Press the *Page Down* key to quickly advance to the next record.

PC Number	Manuf	Model	Processor Type
601002	Sony	Vaio	AMD
601003	Dell	Optiplex	AMD
601004	Dell	Precision	Intel
601005	Sony	Vaio	AMD
601006	Sony	Vaio	AMD
601007	Dell	Vostro	Intel
601008	Dell	Precision	Intel
601009	Dell	Vostro	AMD
601010	Compaq	Pavilion	AMD
601011	Sony	Vaio	AMD
601012	Compaq	Presario	Intel
601013	Dell	Precision	Intel
601014	Dell	Vostro	Intel

Table 7.9

PC Number	Manuf	Model	Processor Type
601015	Sony	Vaio	AMD
601016	Dell	Optiplex	Intel
601017	Compaq	Presario	AMD
601018	Dell	Precision	Intel
601019	Dell	Optiplex	Intel
601020	Compaq	Pavilion	AMD
	Packard Bell	iMedia	AMD
	eMachines	EZ1600	Intel

Table 7.9 (continued)

Task 25: Add the *Processor Type* field to existing Reports.

1. Open the *Technical Zone PCs* Report in layout view.
2. Add the *Processor Type* field to the Report and position to the left of the *Processor* field, as shown in Figure 7.12.

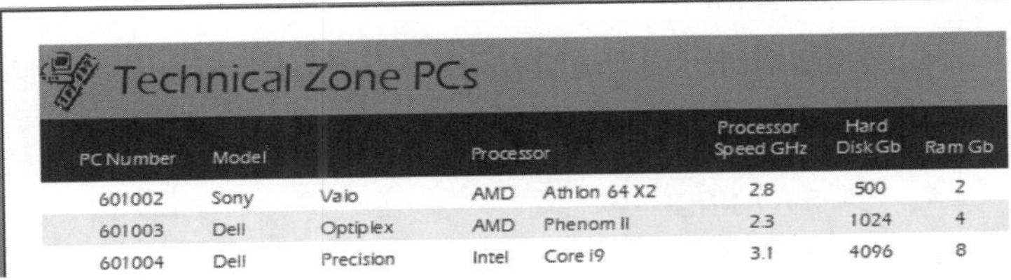

Technical Zone PCs

PC Number	Model		Processor		Processor Speed GHz	Hard Disk Gb	Ram Gb
601002	Sony	Vaio	AMD	Athlon 64 X2	2.8	500	2
601003	Dell	Optiplex	AMD	Phenom II	2.3	1024	4
601004	Dell	Precision	Intel	Core i9	3.1	4096	8

Figure 7.12: The *Processor Type* field has been added to the Report

3. Delete the *Processor Type* label and move the *Processor* label so that it appears like Figure 7.12.

4. Save the *Technical Zone PCs* Report.
5. Add the *Processor Type* field to the *Room 601* Report in the same way. The edited *Room 601* Report should appear like Figure 7.13.

You will have to add the *Processor Type* field to the *PCs in room 601* Query first.

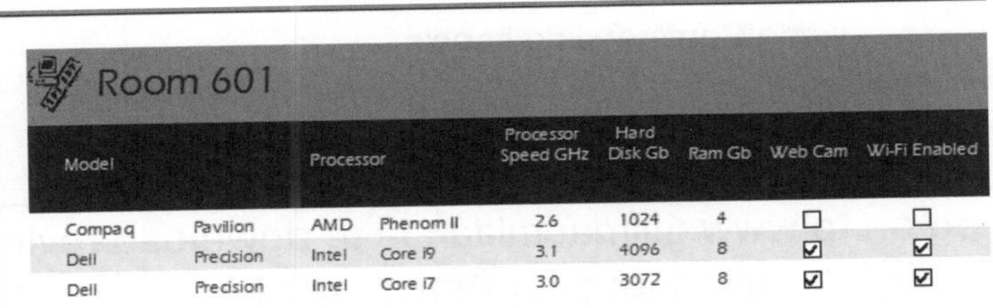

Room 601

Model		Processor		Processor Speed GHz	Hard Disk Gb	Ram Gb	Web Cam	Wi-Fi Enabled
Compaq	Pavilion	AMD	Phenom II	2.6	1024	4	☐	☐
Dell	Precision	Intel	Core i9	3.1	4096	8	☑	☑
Dell	Precision	Intel	Core i7	3.0	3072	8	☑	☑

Figure 7.13: The *Processor Type* field has been added to the *Room 601* Report

6. Save the *Room 601* Report.

Task 26: Using Access Help, search for articles on SQL. Write a brief report explaining what SQL is. Give an example of an SQL statement, explaining the function of the Select, From and Where clauses.

REVIEW YOUR WORK

Use the checklist below to verify that you have completed all the tasks in the Technical Zone database.

		Completed (√)
Table:	• College PCs	☐
Form:	• Technical Support Zone	☐
Queries:	• Except for PCs purchased in May 2010	☐
	• Except for Phenom II X4	☐
	• Hard disks – top 25%	☐
	• Intel PCs	☐
	• PCs for upgrade	☐
	• PCs in room 601	☐
	• PCs purchased in 2010	☐
	• Processors – top 5%	☐
	• Room 601a i7s and i9s	☐
	• Video conferencing PCs	☐
	• Web cam or Wi-Fi	☐
Reports:	• PC Labels	☐
	• Room 601	☐
	• Technical Zone PCs	☐
	• Video Conferencing Labels	☐
Other:	• Database structure form	☐

Log on to www.gillmacmillan.ie to download review questions for Assignment 7.

SECTION 2 REVIEW

Database

A database is used to store, organise and retrieve data. A database can be paper based, e.g. the telephone directory, or computerised, e.g. the iTunes database of artists and songs. Computerised databases are much more efficient than paper-based databases, as specific records can be found instantly and can be quickly sorted into different orders. An Access database consists of four main objects: Tables, Queries, Forms and Reports. Each object carries out a specific function.

The Table

The Table is the most important object in a database. It is responsible for storing data. A database cannot function without a Table. A Table is divided into columns and rows. The columns are called fields. The rows are called records.

The Table – Important Concepts

Number Type

The Number type of a field, which is set up in Table design, affects three factors:

1. The range of values that can be stored in that field.
2. Whether numbers with decimal places can be stored in that field.
3. Storage space, in bytes, required for each field entry.

The number types used in this book are summarised in Table 7.10.

Number Type	Description	Max No. of Decimals	Storage Size per Field Entry
Byte	Stores whole numbers from 0 to 255	None	1 byte
Integer	Stores whole numbers from –32,768 to +32,767	None	2 bytes
Long Integer	Stores whole numbers from –2,147,483,648 to +2,147,483,648	None	4 bytes
Single	Stores numbers with decimals	7	4 bytes

Table 7.10

Tables – Potential Pitfalls

- Records in the Table will be stored in ascending order of the primary key field, regardless of the order in which they have been entered in the Form. When a code is used for the primary key field, the sequence of data entry may not match the sequence of records stored in the Table. For example, codes entered as KD001, CD001, KD002, GD001 and CD002 in the Form will be stored as CD001, CD002, GD001, KD001 and KD002 in the Table.

- Once a particular field has been identified as the primary key, Access will not allow you to duplicate values in that field.
- Access will not allow you to enter letters or symbols in a field whose data type is Number.
- When the field size of a Number field is set to Byte, Integer or Long Integer, any numbers entered with decimals will be either rounded up or rounded down. When storing numbers with decimals, the field size should be set to Single.

Queries

The function of a Query is to search for records in the Table. Conditions entered in the Query design grid give specific instructions on exactly which records to search for. A Query searches through the Table, record by record. Any records that satisfy the Query condition(s) are copied into a separate datasheet, which is then displayed on the screen.

Queries – Important Concepts

AND

When conditions are joined using the *AND* logical operator, the Query will only find records that satisfy all the conditions. Access joins the conditions using the *AND* logical operator when the conditions are entered in the same line of the Query design grid. There is no need to type *AND*. Conditions joined with *AND* are typed in the Criteria line of the Query design grid. The conditions displayed in Figure 7.14 are joined with the *AND* logical operator. These conditions can be interpreted as "Comedies rated 12 that are available on DVD format".

Field:	Rating	Genre	Format	Starring	Director
Table:	Films in Stock	Films in Stock	Films in Stock	Films in Stock	Films in Stock
Sort:					
Show:	☑	☑	☑	☑	☑
Criteria:	"12"	"Comedy"	"DVD"		
or:					

Figure 7.14: Three conditions joined with the *AND* logical operator

As *AND* is also used with the *Between* logical operator, it is important to be clear about the difference between using *AND* to join conditions and using *AND* with *Between*. *Between* is used to find numbers that fall within an upper and lower limit. In Figure 7.15, *Between* is used as a logical operator to find players who made between 5 and 8 tackles inclusive.

Field:	Player Name	Position	No of Tackles	No of Passes
Table:	Players	Players	Players	Players
Sort:				
Show:	☑	☑	☑	☑
Criteria:			Between 5 And 8	
or:				

Figure 7.15

In Figure 7.15, *AND* is used with *Between* to create a logical expression. It is OK to type *AND* in this situation. However, you should never type *AND* when joining conditions in the same field.

Field:	Title	Date Released	Rating
Table:	Films in Stock	Films in Stock	Films in Stock
Sort:			
Show:	☑	☑	☑
Criteria:			PG and U
or:			

Figure 7.16: Incorrect use of the *AND* logical operator

In Figure 7.16, conditions are incorrectly joined with the *AND* logical operator. Logically, it is impossible for a film to have two ratings. When this Query is run, it will not find any records.

To summarise, don't type *AND* when joining conditions in the same field. Simply position all the conditions in the Criteria line. It is OK to type *AND* when using the *Between* logical operator.

OR

The *OR* logical operator can be used to join conditions in a single field or in multiple fields. When *OR* is used in a single field, the Query will find records that satisfy one of the listed conditions. When *OR* is used in multiple fields, the Query will find records that satisfy *at least one* of the listed conditions.

OR – Single Field

There are two methods of joining conditions in the same field with the *OR* logical operator.

Method 1: Join the conditions by typing *OR*

Field:	Genre	Format	Starring	Director	Price per Night
Table:	Films in Stock	Films in Stock	Films in Stock	Films in Stock	Films in Stock
Sort:					
Show:	☑	☑	☑	☑	☑
Criteria:	"Drama" Or "Action/Adventure"				
or:					

Figure 7.17: Two conditions in the same field joined with the *OR* logical operator

Using the conditions in Figure 7.17, Access will find records of films whose genre is *either* Drama *or* Action/Adventure.

Method 2: Use the *or:* line in the Query design grid

Field:	Genre	Format	Starring	Director	Price per Night
Table:	Films in Stock	Films in Stock	Films in Stock	Films in Stock	Films in Stock
Sort:					
Show:	☑	☑	☑	☑	☑
Criteria:	"Drama"				
or:	"Action/Adventure"				

Figure 7.18: Alternative method of using *OR* in a Query

Using the conditions in Figure 7.18, Access will also find records of films whose genre is *either* Drama *or* Action/Adventure.

OR – Multiple Fields

The *OR* logical operator can also be used to join conditions in multiple fields. The *or:* line of the Query design grid is used for this purpose.

Field:	Rating	Genre	Format	Starring
Table:	Films in Stock	Films in Stock	Films in Stock	Films in Stock
Sort:				
Show:	☑	☑	☑	☑
Criteria:	"PG"			
or:		"Children's"		

Figure 7.19: Two conditions in different fields joined with the *OR* logical operator

Using the conditions in Figure 7.19, Access will find records of films whose rating is *PG* *or* whose genre is *Children's*.

Combining *AND* with *OR*

The *AND* and *OR* logical operators can be used together in a Query.

Field:	Rating	Genre	Format	Starring
Table:	Films in Stock	Films in Stock	Films in Stock	Films in Stock
Sort:				
Show:	☑	☑	☑	☑
Criteria:	"12"	"Comedy" Or "Drama"		
or:				

Figure 7.20: Conditions are joined using a combination of *AND* and *OR* logical operators

Using the conditions in Figure 7.20, Access will find records of films rated 12 that are *either* comedies *or* dramas. The *Rating* and *Genre* conditions are joined with *AND*. The conditions in the *Genre* field are joined with *OR*.

Summary of Query Logical Operators

Logical Operator	Meaning
<	Less than
<=	Less than or equal to
=	Equal to
<>	Not equal to
Not	Can be used as an alternative to <>. *Not 5* and *<>5* achieve the same result in a Query.
>	Greater than
>=	Greater than or equal to
Between	Finds numbers ranging from a lower to an upper limit
AND	Joins conditions in different fields. When conditions are joined with *AND*, the Query will only find records where *all* of the conditions are satisfied. When joining conditions in multiple fields, there is no need to type *AND*. Simply position all the conditions in the same row of the Query design grid.
OR	When *OR* is used to join conditions in a single field, the Query will find records that satisfy *one* of the listed conditions. When *OR* is used to join conditions in multiple fields, the Query will find records that satisfy *at least one* of the listed conditions.

Table 7.11

Queries – Potential Pitfalls

- When referring to a date or a time in a Query condition, each date or time must be enclosed in # symbols. It is better not to type the # symbol, as incorrect positioning will cause an error in the condition. Simply type the date or time as normal. When you press *Enter*, Access will insert the # symbols in the correct position.
- Never join conditions in the same field with the *AND* logical operator. If you do this, the Query will not find any records.
- A single spelling error at the data entry stage will often result in multiple Queries not finding all the relevant records.
- If there is a spelling error in a Query condition, it is most likely that the Query will not find any records.
- Even if your condition is correct, the Query will not find any records if you have entered the condition in the wrong field.
- Data is entered in a Yes/No field by ticking or not ticking a check box. However, you must enter *Yes* as a Query condition to find all records where the check box was ticked. Type *No* as a Query condition to find all records where the check box wasn't ticked.

- When creating a Query condition for a Currency field, never type the euro (€) sign.
- When creating Query conditions, it is better not to type inverted commas. Access will put these in for you.

Forms

The main function of a Form is to facilitate data entry. The Form is linked to the Table. Data entered in the Form filters down to and is stored in the Table. A Form can also be used to find records, edit records and delete records. When you do this, you are essentially using the Form as an interface to the Table. It is more efficient to use a Form for data entry and record editing, as Forms are much easier to work with than Tables.

Combo Box

A drop-down list from which the data entry operator can select an item instead of typing it (Figure 7.21).

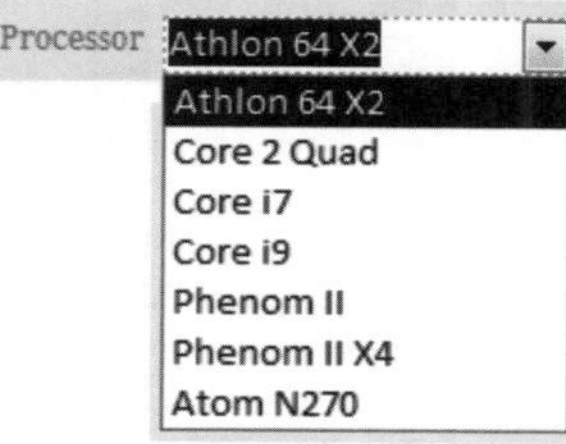

Figure 7.21

The advantages of using a combo box in a Form are as follows:

1. Spelling errors in that field are eliminated.
2. Data entry is faster and easier.
3. Data entry can be restricted to items in the combo box list by setting the *Limit to List* property to *Yes*.

List Box

Similar to a combo box, except that all the items in the list are permanently visible (Figure 7.22).

Format | Blu-ray
DVD

Figure 7.22

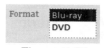

With a list box, the data entry operator doesn't need to click a down arrow to see the items in the list. List boxes are suitable for fields where there is a small number of data entry options. Figure 7.22 is the list box that was used to enter data in the *Format* field of the *Night Vision* database. Films are available in two formats: Blu-ray and DVD.

Clip Art

Using clip art in Microsoft Word, you can add a logo to your Access Form. Simply copy the clip art image from Word and paste it into design view of your Form. To fully display the clip art image, the *Size Mode* property must be set to *Zoom*. It is also best to set the *Border* property of the clip art image to *Transparent*.

Forms – Potential Pitfalls

- When creating a combo or list box using the wizard, always drag the field you are working with from the field list. If you don't do this, the combo or list box will be unbound, meaning that data selected in the combo or list box will not be transferred to the Table.

- The database user will be able to enter items that are not listed in the combo box unless you set the *Limit to List* property to *Yes*.
- If you don't adjust the tab order, after creating a combo box, the Form may "jump" to a new record unexpectedly as you tab from text box to text box.
- In cases where there is a long list of potential data entry items for a specific field, it is better to use a combo box because a list box will take up too much space on the Form. However, you cannot use a combo box or list box unless there is a definite limit to the number of possible data entry items.

Reports

The main functions of a Report are to format, sort and summarise data stored in a database. Reports are often printed out. You don't need to have knowledge of databases or of Microsoft Access to understand and interpret the information displayed in a printed Report. Many businesspeople use Reports to assist them in decision making. A Report can be linked to a Table or a Query. In a database with a single Table, a Report linked to the Table will display all the records in the database. A Report linked to a Query will only display the specific records found by that Query.

Report Views

There are four ways of viewing an Access Report.

1. **Layout view:** Allows you to make minor design adjustments to your Report while viewing the data.
2. **Design view:** Used for making major design changes or fine tuning a Report. In design view, the data is not visible.
3. **Report view:** Displays a preview of your Report without dividing the data into pages. This is useful when previewing lengthy reports.
4. **Print preview:** Displays the Report exactly as it will appear on a printed page, including margins and page numbers.

Report Sections

A standard Access Report is divided into four sections.

1. **Report header:** This appears at the top of the first page of the Report. It is generally used to display the Report title. A company logo and address or a paragraph of introduction can also be included in the Report header.
2. **Page header:** Appears immediately below the Report header on page 1 of the Report and at the top of all other pages when the Report spans multiple pages. The page header contains the column headings, which by default are the field names. Each field name in the page header is contained in a label box. These can be edited to make them more descriptive, if necessary.

3. **Detail:** This is the main section of a Report. It displays the records in the Report and appears immediately below the page header. The detail section adjusts to accommodate the number of records in the Table or Query to which the Report is linked.
4. **Page footer:** Appears at the bottom of each page in the Report. The page footer normally contains the page number and the date. These are inserted automatically by the Report Wizard.

Adding New Fields

When new fields are created in the Table, they can be added to a Report by dragging the field from the field list and dropping in the detail section. This is best done in layout view. This is straightforward when the Report is linked to the Table. When a Report is linked to a Query, you must first add the new field to the Query. The field will not appear in the Report's field list unless you do this.

Label Wizard

A special type of Report used to print data on sticky labels, which are generally used when printing names and addresses or product data. In a mail merge application, labels with addresses can be affixed to envelopes. In retail applications, labels can be used to affix bar codes or prices to individual products. Link your labels to the Table or to a specific Query by selecting the Table or appropriate Query in the Navigation Pane before starting the Label Wizard.

Reports – Potential Pitfalls

- When a Report is sorted using the Report Wizard, the sorted field will always appear first in the Report. If you don't want this to happen, sort the Report in design or layout view after it has been created.
- If you want the Report to display "Yes" or "No" instead of a check box, change the Lookup of the Yes/No field from check box to text box in design view of the Table before creating the Report.
- If you are displaying a check box in a Report, it cannot be centred under a heading using the *Center* button. Instead, resize the border surrounding the check box control.
- A label created with the Label Wizard is not the same as a label control, which is used to display text (usually a title or a field name) in a Form or Report.
- If a Query is currently selected in the Navigation Pane, a Report created using the Report Wizard will be automatically linked to that Query. If the Table or any Form or Report is selected in the Navigation Pane, the Report will be automatically linked to the Table. Before you start the Report Wizard, ensure that the correct database object is selected in the Navigation Pane.
- When a Report is linked to a Query, any new field added to the Table cannot be included in the Report until that field is also added to the Query.

- When displaying dates in a Report, Access displays a series of # symbols when the column is not wide enough to display the dates.
- It is difficult to adjust column widths in an Access 2010 Report unless you first add the labels and text boxes in the page header and detail section to a Tabular layout.

TOOLBAR BUTTONS INTRODUCED IN SECTION 2

	**Select:** Used to select all the controls in a Form or Report layout. It appears in the top left-hand corner of the detail section when a Form is viewed in either layout or design view. When a Report is viewed in either layout or design view, the select symbol appears in the top left-hand corner of the page header.
	**Combo Box button:** Used to create a combo box in a Form. Click the *Combo Box* button and then drag the appropriate field from the field list, dropping the field in the detail section of the Form. The Combo Box Wizard will guide you through the process of creating a combo box as long as the Control Wizard is turned on.
	**Control Wizard button:** When the Control Wizard is turned on, a wizard will assist you each time you create a combo box or list box.
	**Tab Order button:** Click this button to change the order in which the cursor moves through the text box controls in the Form as you press the *Tab* key on the keyboard. The Tab Order button is available in layout and design view. Report view is useful for previewing lengthy reports.
	**Report View button:** Click this button to view your Report in Report view. This is similar to print preview, except that the Report is not divided into pages. Margins and page numbers are not displayed when a Report is viewed in Report view. Report view is useful for previewing lengthy reports.
	**Print Preview button:** Click this button to preview your Report before printing it. Unlike Report view, print preview divides a Report into pages as well as displaying margins and page numbers.
	**Add Field button:** When creating a Report with the Report Wizard, click this button to add a field to a Report.
	**Report Wizard button:** In the Create section of the Ribbon, click this button to start the Report Wizard.
	**Adjust Height:** Used to adjust the height of sections in a Form or Report. It is only available in design view.

	**Label button:** Used to insert text in a Form or Report. Click the *Label* button and draw a box. Text is then typed inside the box. Labels are used in Forms and Reports to display titles and field names.
	Font Color button: Used to change the colour of text in a label or text box control. Click the down arrow to see a palette of available colours.
	**Clip Art button:** In Microsoft Word, click this button to search for and insert a clip art image, which can then be copied to an Access Form or Report.
	**Diagonal resize:** Used to simultaneously adjust the width and height of a Form or Report control. The diagonal resize symbol is displayed when you point at the corner of a selected label or text box.
	**Properties button:** Displays the properties of a selected item, such as a label or text box, when in design or layout view of a Form or Report. You can also view the properties of the entire Form or Report or of a specific section, such as the detail section.
	**List Box button:** Used to create a list box in a Form. Click the *List Box* button, then drag the appropriate field from the field list and drop in the detail section of the Form. The List Box Wizard will guide you through the process of creating a list box as long as the Control Wizard is turned on.
	**Labels button:** Located in the Create section of the Ribbon, click this button to start the Label Wizard, which guides you through the process of creating labels.

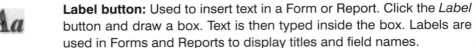

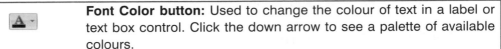

SECTION 3

Advanced Database Assignments

Assignment 8: Southside Motor Tests Database

Assignment 9: Southern Estate Agents Database

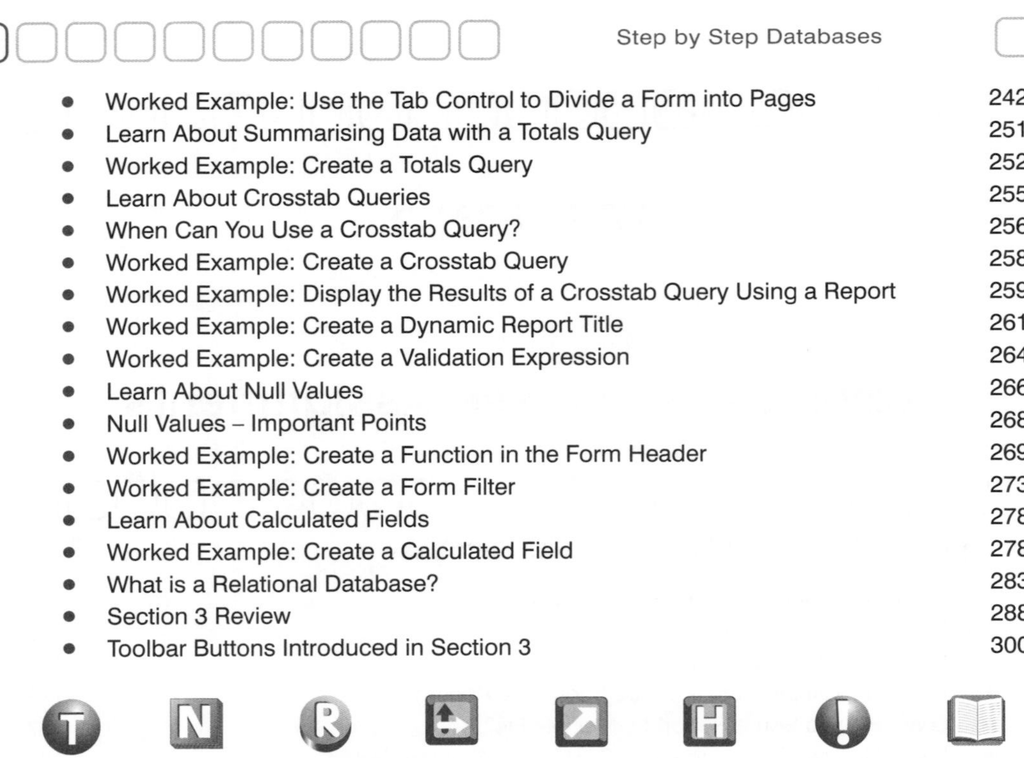

Tip
Note
Rule
Cross-reference
Shortcut
Hint
Important Point
Theory Section

8 Southside Motor Tests Database

SCENARIO

Southside Motor Tests provides a vehicle testing service for motorists in the south side of Dublin. Due to the high volume of tests, the staff are unable to keep up with the huge amount of administration work. In Assignment 8 you will create a database to store data relating to clients and their vehicles. Using the database, you will streamline correspondence with clients with mail merge and produce a range of Queries and Reports to support the staff of Southside Motor Tests.

By completing this assignment, you will learn how to:

- Use the Autonumber data type.
- Use the Attachment data type.
- Display a digital photo in a Form.
- Create a Parameter Query.
- Use a wildcard in a Query.
- Use the *Not* logical operator in a Query.
- Join negative conditions in a Query.
- Merge a database with a Word document.
- Sort a Report by multiple fields.
- Change the sort order of an existing Report.
- Perform calculations in a Report.
- Create a grouped Report.
- Create a Pivot Query.
- Create a Pivot Chart.

DOWNLOAD PHOTOS

To complete this assignment, you will need to download photos from the Gill & Macmillan website. To download the photos, follow these steps.

1. Log on to www.gillmacmillan.ie.
2. Click the 'Education' link.
3. Search for *Step by Step Databases* using the search box in the top right-hand corner of the web page.
4. In the search results, select *Step by Step Databases 3rd Edition*.
5. Click either the *Lecturer Resources* or the *Student Resources* link.
6. Click the link to download the photos.

 LEARN ABOUT THE AUTONUMBER DATA TYPE

Commercial databases commonly store records of transactions, such as purchases or sales. It is very important that each record can be identified by a unique transaction number. Generating unique transaction numbers manually is time consuming and error prone. To overcome this problem, Access has a special Autonumber data type that allocates a unique number to each record in the Table. Numbers are generated in sequence. The first record will be allocated the number *1*, the second record will be allocated the number *2* and so on.

The Autonumber data type is particularly useful where there is a high volume of transactions. It is generally used in conjunction with the primary key field. In the Southside Motor Tests database, we will use the Autonumber data type to allocate a unique test number to each record stored in the Table.

Once a field's data type has been set to Autonumber, no data entry is required in that field. The data entry happens automatically. Data stored in an Autonumber field requires 4 bytes of storage per record.

 LEARN ABOUT THE ATTACHMENT DATA TYPE 

The Attachment data type is used to store a file created in another application in an Access database. Using the Attachment data type, you can store pictures, sound files, Word documents and Excel spreadsheets in an Access database. Attaching a specific file to a record is similar to the way that you would attach a file to an email message.

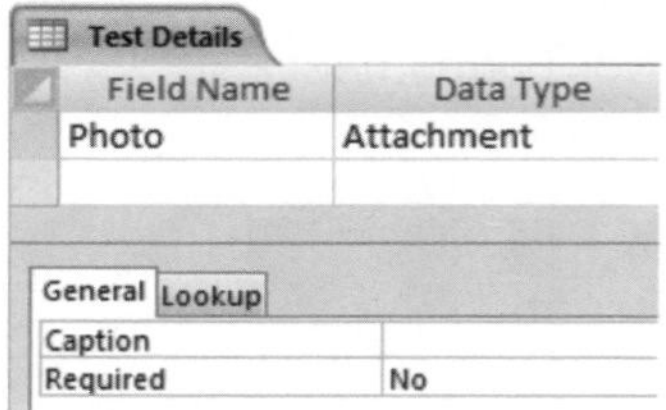

Figure 8.1: Setting up an Attachment field in the Table

Creating an Attachment field in the Table is straightforward. Simply set the data type of the field to Attachment, as shown in Figure 8.1. Data stored in an Attachment field requires 4 bytes of storage per record.

In the Southside Motor Tests database, we will use the Attachment data type to store a digital photo for each record in the Table.

 LEARN ABOUT DEFAULT VALUES

A default value is where a value specified by the database designer is entered automatically in a particular field each time a new record is created in the database. Default values are useful when the same value occurs frequently in a field. For example, in this assignment, *Co. Dublin* will be entered in the *Address3* field for all records, as all the clients live in Co. Dublin.

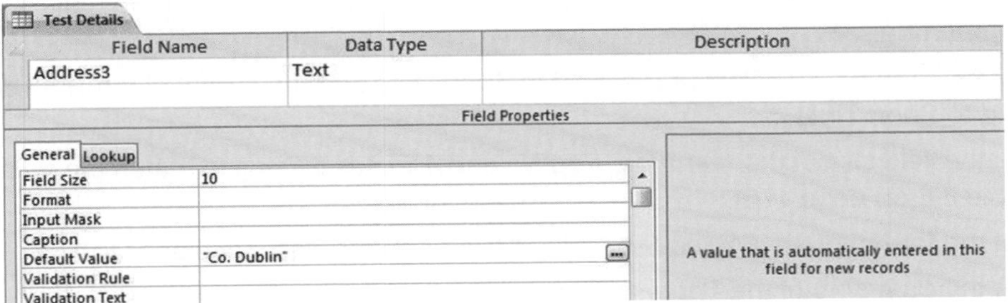

Figure 8.2: The default value for the *Address3* field has been set to Co. Dublin

To reduce the amount of data entry, *Co. Dublin* can be specified as the default value of the *Address3* field when creating the Table, as shown in Figure 8.2.

CREATE THE DATABASE AND SET UP THE TABLE

Task 1: Create a new database named *Southside Motor Tests.*
Task 2: Create a new Table and save the Table as *Test Details.*

- Using the data displayed in Table 8.1, create fields with appropriate data types in the *Test Details* Table.

Test Number	1
Date of Test	03/06/14
Time of Test	9:00
Test Type	Full
Reg No	09DL679
Make	Opel
Model	Astra
Engine Size	1.6
Firstname	Paul
Surname	Jenkins
Address1	25 The Avenue
Address2	Deansgrange
Address3	Co. Dublin
Cost	€68.00
Photo	

Table 8.1

- Set the *Test Number* field as the primary key. Set the data type for this field to Autonumber.
- Set the format of the *Date of Test* field to Short Date and the format of the *Time of Test* field to Short Time.
- Set the field size of the *Test Type, Reg No* and *Address 3* fields to match the data (see Table 8.6 on page 175).
- Set the format of the *Engine Size* field to fixed and the decimal places to 1.
- Set the data type of the *Photo* field to Attachment.
- Set the default value of the *Address3* field to *Co. Dublin*.
- Set up separate indexes on the *Test Type* field and the *Make* field.

- Save the *Test Details* Table.

CREATE THE FORM

Task 3: Using the Form Wizard, create a Form including all fields from the *Test Details* Table. Information relating to the design of the Form is displayed in Table 8.2.

Form Layout	Columnar
Form Title	Southside Motor Tests Bookings

Table 8.2

Use design view to make the following changes to the Form.

- Apply the *Paper* theme to the Form.
- Create separate combo boxes for the *Time of Test, Engine Size, Make* and *Cost* fields using the information displayed in Table 8.3.
- Set the *Limit to List* property of all combo boxes to *Yes*.
- Set the *Allow Value List Edits* property of all combo boxes to *No*.
- Create a list box for the *Test Type* field using the information displayed in Table 8.4.

Time of Test (Combo Box)	Engine Size (Combo Box)	Make (Combo Box)	Cost (Combo Box)
9:00	1.0	Ford	68
9:30	1.1	Honda	47
10:00	1.2	Nissan	
10:30	1.3	Opel	
11:00	1.4	Toyota	
11:30	1.5		
12:00	1.6		
12:30	1.8		
14:00	2.0		
14:30	2.2		
15:00	2.5		
15:30	2.8		
16:00	3.0		
16:30			
17:00			

Table 8.3

Test Type (List Box)
Full
Retest

Table 8.4

- Set the tab order of the Form so that it matches the list shown in Figure 8.3.

- Save the *Southside Motor Tests Bookings* Form.

Use layout view to make the following changes to the Form.

- Position and resize text boxes similar to Figure 8.4.
- Edit the *Reg No* label so that it reads *Registration Number.*
- Delete the *Surname* label. Edit the *Firstname* label so that it reads *Client.*
- Position the *Firstname* and *Surname* text box controls next to the *Client* label, as shown in Figure 8.4.

Test Number
Date of Test
Time of Test
Test Type
Reg No
Make
Model
Engine Size
Firstname
Surname
Address1
Address2
Address3
Cost
Photo

Figure 8.3: Tab order of the *Southside Motor Tests Bookings* Form

- Edit the *Address1* label so that it reads *Address.*
- Delete the *Address2* and *Address3* label controls.
- Delete the *Photo* label.
- Delete the *Model* label.
- Position the *Model* text box control next to the *Make* combo box control, as shown in Figure 8.4.
- Edit the *Make* label so that it reads *Make and Model.*
- Centre data in the *Test Number*, *Date of Test*, *Time of Test*, *Reg No*, *Engine Size* and *Cost* text box controls.
- Align labels and text box controls in columns using the *Align Left* button.
- Format the Form title using a font similar to that in Figure 8.4.
- Insert the address in the Form header using a label box. Display this text in *italics*, using a font colour of *white*.
- Set the Tab Stop property of the *Test Number* text box control to *No*.

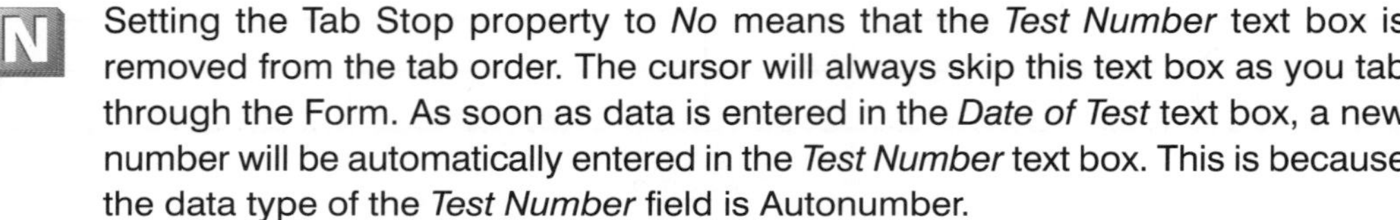

Setting the Tab Stop property to *No* means that the *Test Number* text box is removed from the tab order. The cursor will always skip this text box as you tab through the Form. As soon as data is entered in the *Date of Test* text box, a new number will be automatically entered in the *Test Number* text box. This is because the data type of the *Test Number* field is Autonumber.

- Save the *Southside Motor Tests Bookings* Form.

- The completed Form should look something like Figure 8.4

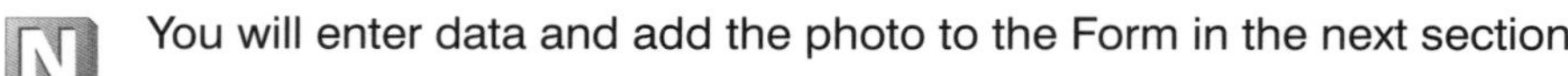

You will enter data and add the photo to the Form in the next section.

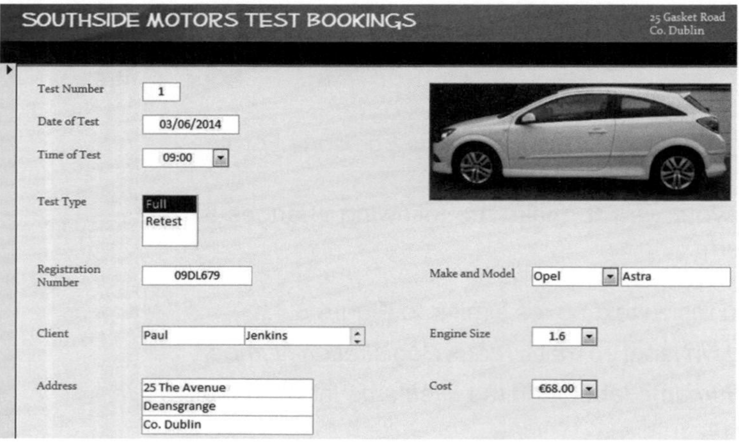

Figure 8.4: The completed *Southside Motor Tests Bookings* Form

WORKED EXAMPLE: ADD A DIGITAL PHOTO TO A RECORD

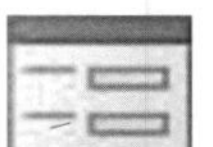

1. Open the *Southside Motor Tests Bookings* Form in Form view.
2. Enter the record for Paul Jenkins, displayed in Table 8.5.

Test Number	1
Date of Test	03/06/2014
Time of Test	9:00
Test Type	Full
Reg No	09DL679
Make	Opel
Model	Astra
Engine Size	1.6
Firstname	Paul
Surname	Jenkins
Address1	25 The Avenue
Address2	Deansgrange
Address3	Co. Dublin
Cost	€68.00

Table 8.5

3. Double click the Photo attachment control, as shown in Figure 8.5.

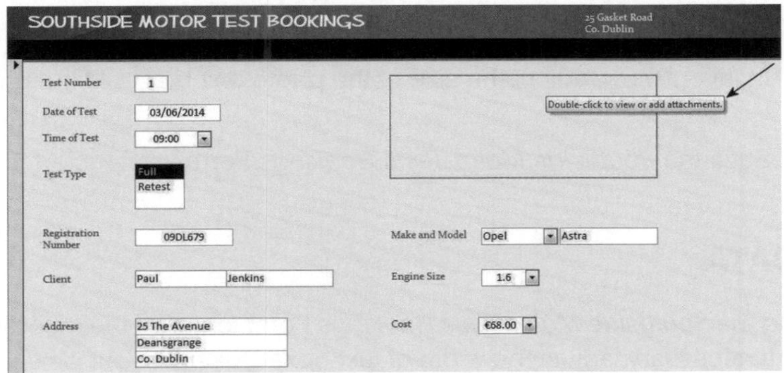

Figure 8.5: To add a photo, double click the Photo attachment control

4. In the *Attachments* dialog box, click the *Add* button.
5. In the *Choose File* dialog box, select the folder containing the downloaded car images and then select the *astra09.jpg* file, as shown in Figure 8.6.

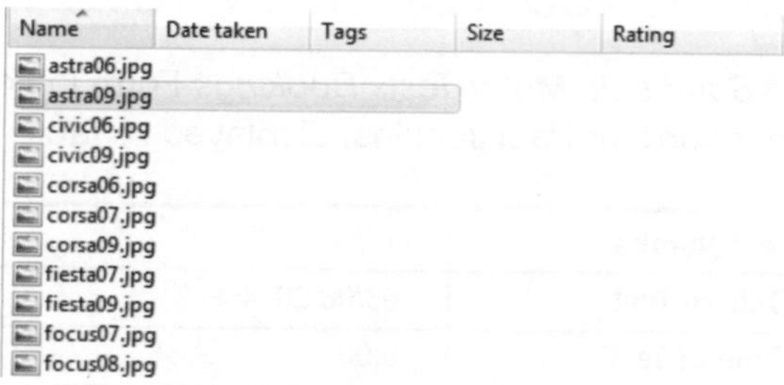

Figure 8.6: The astra09.jpg file has been selected

6. Click the *Open* button. The astra09.jpg file is added to the Attachments list (Figure 8.7).

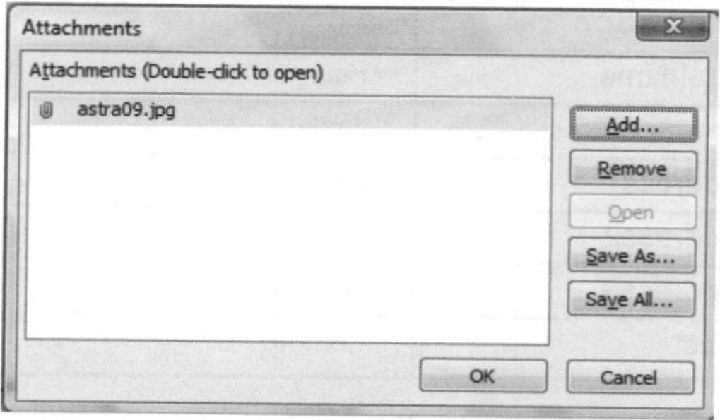

Figure 8.7: The astra09.jpg file has been added to the Attachments list

7. Click *OK* to display the picture in the Form.

8. In layout view, adjust the size of the photo text box to fit the photo.

9. Save the *Southside Motor Tests Bookings* Form.

ENTER DATA

Task 4: Using the *Southside Motor Tests Bookings* Form, enter all the records displayed in Table 8.6. If necessary, adjust the width of text boxes, using layout view, as you enter the data.

Use the *CTRL + 2* key combination to copy the Date of Test from the previous record.

Test No.	Date of Test	Time of Test	Test Type	Reg No	Make	Model	Engine Size	First Name	Surname	Address1	Address2	Address3	Cost	Photo
2	03/06/14	10:30	Full	06D201	Honda	Civic	1.3	Keith	Morgan	54 Woodley Park	Blackrock	Co. Dublin	€68.00	civic06.jpg
3	03/06/14	11:00	Full	07KE3398	Toyota	Prius	1.6	Andrew	Mooney	2 Prospect Drive	Blackrock	Co. Dublin	€68.00	prius07.jpg
4	03/06/14	12:30	Retest	06D4071	Opel	Corsa	1.0	Jennifer	Butler	71 Seapark Court	Shankill	Co. Dublin	€47.00	corsa06a.jpg
5	03/06/14	14:00	Retest	07D1556	Ford	Fiesta	1.3	Maeve	O Shea	76 Forest Gardens	Killiney	Co. Dublin	€47.00	fiesta07.jpg
6	03/06/14	15:00	Full	07WW692	Nissan	Primera	1.8	Liam	Dolan	68 Elmbrook Crescent	Dun Laoghaire	Co. Dublin	€68.00	primera07.jpg
7	03/06/14	15:30	Retest	09D51223	Opel	Corsa	1.1	Thomas	Fennessey	12 Old Mill Road	Dun Laoghaire	Co. Dublin	€47.00	corsa09.jpg
8	03/06/14	16:30	Full	07D44981	Ford	Ka	1.3	Joe	Murphy	84 The Moorings	Blackrock	Co. Dublin	€68.00	ka07.jpg
9	03/06/14	17:00	Full	08LH8002	Nissan	Micra	1.0	Wojtek	Adamski	2 Avondale Villas	Shankill	Co. Dublin	€68.00	micra08.jpg
10	04/06/14	9:00	Full	09D10648	Ford	Mondeo	1.6	Martin	Brennan	15 Greenfort Drive	Deansgrange	Co. Dublin	€68.00	mondeo09.jpg
11	04/06/14	10:00	Retest	09LD2096	Ford	Focus	1.6	Hugh	Watson	10 Meadow Gardens	Blackrock	Co. Dublin	€47.00	focus09.jpg
12	04/06/14	10:30	Full	09WW480	Honda	Civic	1.8	Eoin	McCluskey	23 Parkvale Road	Blackrock	Co. Dublin	€68.00	civic09.jpg
13	04/06/14	11:00	Full	08D2948	Toyota	Landcruiser	3.0	Stephen	McCarthy	34 Riverwood Court	Shankill	Co. Dublin	€68.00	cruiser08.jpg
14	04/06/14	12:00	Full	07D639	Nissan	Micra	1.3	Rose	Corcoran	23 Beechhill Road	Deansgrange	Co. Dublin	€68.00	micra07.jpg
15	04/06/14	14:00	Retest	06D36192	Opel	Corsa	1.3	Colette	Burke	27 Abbeywood Road	Killiney	Co. Dublin	€47.00	corsa06b.jpg
16	04/06/14	14:30	Full	08LD8087	Ford	Mondeo	1.6	Suresh	Keertipati	12 Beechwood Road	Dun Laoghaire	Co. Dublin	€68.00	mondeo08.jpg
17	04/06/14	15:00	Full	06WX1227	Opel	Astra	1.4	Noleen	Higgins	20 Longwood Close	Shankill	Co. Dublin	€68.00	astra06.jpg
18	04/06/14	15:30	Full	07D14933	Ford	Focus	1.4	John	O Connell	1 Elm Tree Road	Blackrock	Co. Dublin	€68.00	focus07.jpg
19	04/06/14	16:00	Retest	07KE6791	Toyota	Yaris	1.0	Richard	Doherty	19 Larkhill Park	Dun Laoghaire	Co. Dublin	€47.00	yaris07.jpg
20	04/06/14	16:30	Full	08DL2018	Nissan	Qashqai	2.0	Lisa	Burke	8 Clifden Road	Killiney	Co. Dublin	€68.00	qashqai08.jpg
21	05/06/14	09:30	Retest	10LD1095	Ford	Fiesta	1.3	Martin	Nolan	52 Old Crescent Road	Blackrock	Co. Dublin	€47.00	fiesta10.jpg
22	05/06/14	10:30	Full	10DL22011	Ford	Focus	1.6	Deirdre	Brennan	22 Grove Road	Killiney	Co. Dublin	€68.00	focus10.jpg

Table 8.6

ADD NEW FIELDS TO THE TABLE

1. Add four new fields named *Odometer*, *Test Result, Notes* and *Paid* to the *Test Details* Table, using appropriate data types and field sizes (see Table 8.7).

2. Set the field size of the *Test Result* field to match the data.
3. Open the *Southside Motor Test Bookings* Form in design view.
4. Add the *Odometer* field to the Form, positioning the new field below the *Engine Size* combo box (Figure 8.8). Set the alignment of this text box control to centre.
5. Create a combo box for the *Test Result* field, including *Pass, Fail* and *Fail Advisory* in the combo box list. Position the new combo box below the *Cost* combo box, as shown in Figure 8.8.
6. Add the *Notes* field to the Form, positioning the new field below the *Test Result* combo box (Figure 8.8). Adjust the width and height of the *Notes* text box control so that text can wrap inside the text box.
7. Add the *Paid* field to the Form, positioning the new field below the *Notes* field. Position the label to the left of the check box, as shown in Figure 8.8.
8. Move the *Test Type* label and list box controls to their new position, as shown in Figure 8.8.

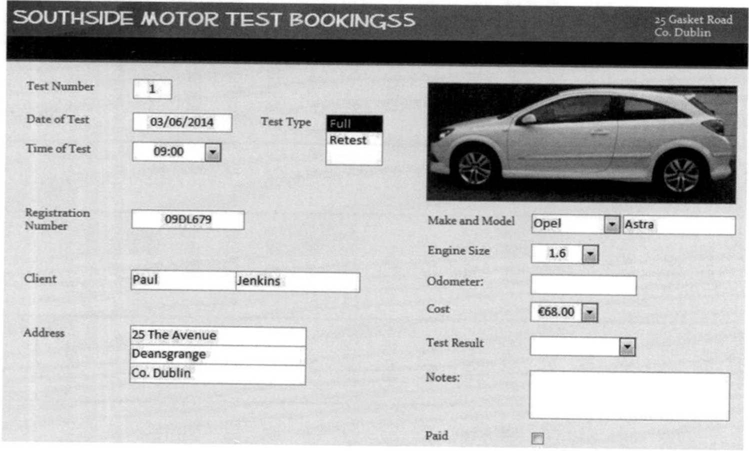

Figure 8.8: Four new fields have been added to the Form

9. Set the tab order as follows: *Test Number, Date of Test, Time of Test, Test Type, Reg No, Make, Model, Engine Size, Firstname, Surname, Address1, Address2, Address3, Odometer, Cost, Test Result, Notes, Paid, Photo.*

10. Save the *Southside Motor Tests* Form.

11. Using the *Southside Motor Tests* Form, enter the *Odometer, Test Result, Notes* and *Paid* data displayed in the shaded cells in Table 8.7.

Client First Name	Client Surname	Odometer	Test Result	Notes	Paid
Paul	Jenkins	22759	Fail	Rear left brake light faulty	Yes
Keith	Morgan	35007	Fail Advisory	Replace side lamp bulb	No
Andrew	Mooney	15418	Pass		Yes
Jennifer	Butler	63544	Pass		Yes
Maeve	O Shea	25510	Fail Advisory	Excessive exhaust emissions	No
Liam	Dolan	32019	Pass		No
Thomas	Fennessey	12045	Pass		Yes
Joe	Murphy	45289	Pass		No
Wojtek	Adamski	27996	Fail	Front left full beam not working	Yes
Martin	Brennan	7015	Pass		No
Hugh	Watson	4537	Pass		No
Eoin	McCluskey	21868	Fail Advisory	Realign headlights	Yes
Stephen	McCarthy	38899	Pass		Yes
Rose	Corcoran	60002	Pass		Yes
Colette	Burke	65633	Pass		No
Suresh	Keertipati	25913	Fail	Rear left indicator faulty	No
Noleen	Higgins	76818	Pass		No
John	O Connell	33675	Pass		Yes
Richard	Doherty	28099	Pass		Yes
Lisa	Burke	19438	Fail	Tyre tread not within specified limits	No
Martin	Nolan	4395	Pass		Yes
Deirdre	Brennan	25602	Fail	Replace shock absorbers	No

Table 8.7

LEARN HOW TO SORT A REPORT BY MULTIPLE FIELDS

To date we have sorted Reports using a single field. The Report Wizard in Access allows you to sort by up to four fields. The actual number of fields that you can sort by depends on the data stored in the Table.

Consider the data in Table 8.8, which is an extract from the records in the *Test Details* Table. To be able to sort by two fields, data must be repeated in at least one field. In Table 8.8, data is repeated in the *Date of Test*, *Test Type* and *Make* fields. When creating a multiple-level sort, it is usually best to start with the field where most repetitions occur. In Table 8.8, this is the *Date of Test* field.

Test Number	Date of Test	Time of Test	Test Type	Reg No	Make
1	03/06/14	9:00	Full	09DL679	Opel
2	03/06/14	10:30	Full	06D201	Honda
3	03/06/14	11:00	Full	07KE3398	Toyota
4	03/06/14	12:30	Retest	06D4071	Opel
5	03/06/14	14:00	Retest	07D1556	Ford
6	03/06/14	15:00	Full	07WW692	Nissan
7	03/06/14	15:30	Retest	09D51223	Opel
8	03/06/14	16:30	Full	07D44981	Ford
9	03/06/14	17:00	Full	08LH8002	Nissan
10	04/06/14	9:00	Full	09D10648	Ford

Table 8.8

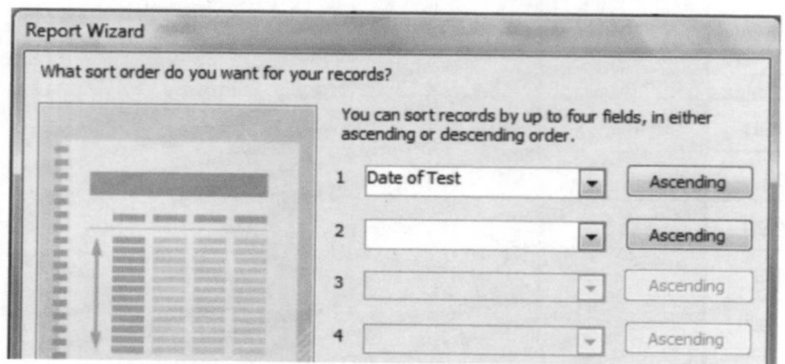

Figure 8.9: First-level sort

In Figure 8.9, the *Date of Test* field has been specified as the first-level sort. A second-level sort can be added using any of the remaining fields. However, a third-level sort will only be possible if data is repeated in the second-level sort. In Table 8.8, data is repeated in the *Test Type* and *Make* fields. Again, the field with the most repetitions is generally used for the second-level sort. This is the *Test Type* field.

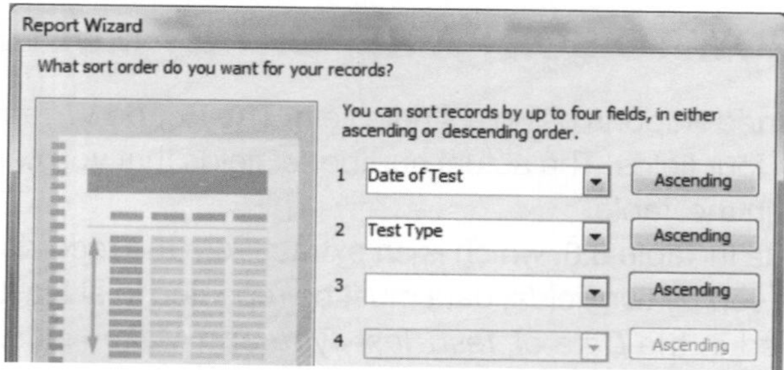

Figure 8.10: A second-level sort has been added

In Figure 8.10, the *Test Type* field has been specified as the second-level sort in the Report Wizard dialog box. Because the sort order is Ascending, *Full* tests will be displayed before *Retests*.

Test Schedule

Date of Test	Test Type	Make	Model	Time of Test	Registration	Owner	
03/06/2014	Full	Honda	Civic	10:30	06D201	Keith	Morgan
03/06/2014	Full	Toyota	Prius	11:00	07KE3398	Andrew	Mooney
03/06/	Full	Nissan	Primera	15:00	07WW692	Liam	Dolan
03/06/2014	Full	Ford	Ka	16:30	07D44981	Joe	Murphy
03/06/2014	Full	Nissan	Micra	17:00	08LH8002	Wojtek	Adamski
03/06/2014	Full	Opel	Astra	09:00	09DL679	Paul	Jenkins
03/06/	Retest	Opel	Corsa	12:30	06D4071	Jennifer	Butler
03/06/	Retest	Ford	Fiesta	14:00	07D1556	Maeve	O Shea
03/06/2014	Retest	Opel	Corsa	15:30	09D51223	Thomas	Fennessey
04/06/	Full	Toyota	Landcruise	11:30	08D2948	Stephen	McCarthy
04/06/	Full	Ford	Mondeo	09:00	09D10648	Martin	Brennan

Figure 8.11: Records are sorted first by *Date of Test* and then by *Test Type*

In Figure 8.11, the records are sorted first by *Date of Test* and then by *Test Type*. For each *Date of Test*, records are then sorted in ascending order of *Test Type*. This sort occurs twice in Figure 8.11 – first in ascending order of *Test Type* for tests completed on 03/06/2014 and second in ascending order of *Test Type* for the tests completed on 04/06/2014. As data is repeated in the *Test Type* field, it is possible to add a third-level sort to the Report.

In Figure 8.12, a third-level sort in ascending order of the *Make* field has been added to the Report. For each *Test Type*, records are sorted in ascending order of *Make (Ford, Honda, Nissan, Opel, Toyota)*. This sort occurs twice for cars tested on 03/06/2014 – first in ascending order of *Make* for the full tests and second in ascending order of *Make* for the retests. The sort is repeated for cars tested on 04/06/2014. As data is repeated in the *Make* field, a fourth-level sort can be added to the Report.

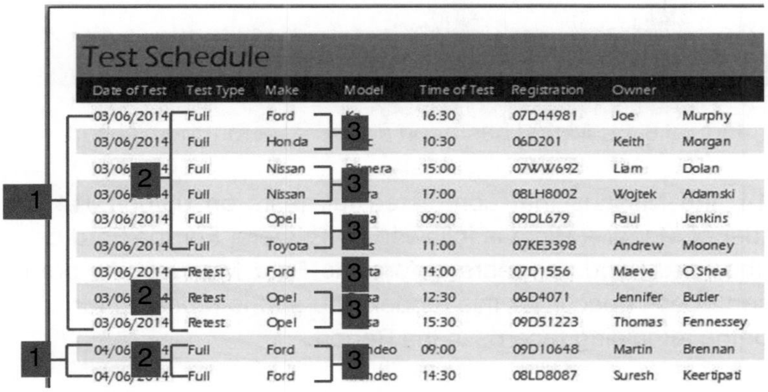

Test Schedule

Date of Test	Test Type	Make	Model	Time of Test	Registration	Owner	
03/06/2014	Full	Ford		16:30	07D44981	Joe	Murphy
03/06/2014	Full	Honda	c	10:30	06D201	Keith	Morgan
03/06	Full	Nissan	mera	15:00	07WW692	Liam	Dolan
03/06	Full	Nissan	a	17:00	08LH8002	Wojtek	Adamski
03/06/2014	Full	Opel	a	09:00	09DL679	Paul	Jenkins
03/06/2014	Full	Toyota	s	11:00	07KE3398	Andrew	Mooney
03/06/2014	Retest	Ford	ta	14:00	07D1556	Maeve	O Shea
03/06	Retest	Opel	sa	12:30	06D4071	Jennifer	Butler
03/06/2014	Retest	Opel	sa	15:30	09D51223	Thomas	Fennessey
04/06	Full	Ford	deo	09:00	09D10648	Martin	Brennan
04/06	Full	Ford	ndeo	14:30	08LD8087	Suresh	Keertipati

Figure 8.12: *Make* has been added as the third-level sort

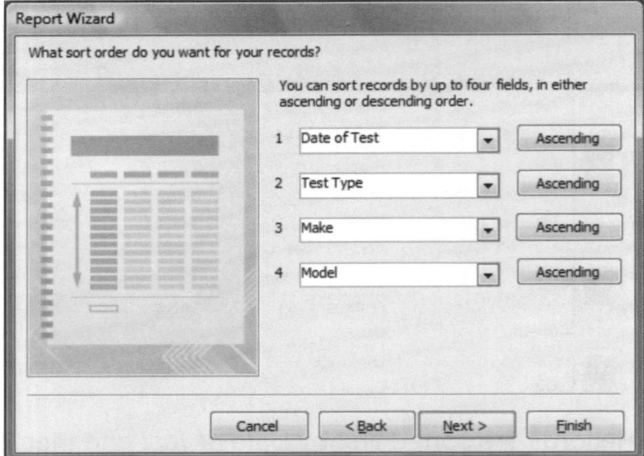

Figure 8.13: A fourth-level sort has been added

In Figure 8.13, the *Model* field has been specified as the fourth-level sort in the Report Wizard dialog box. Where *Makes* are repeated, records will be listed in ascending order of *Model*.

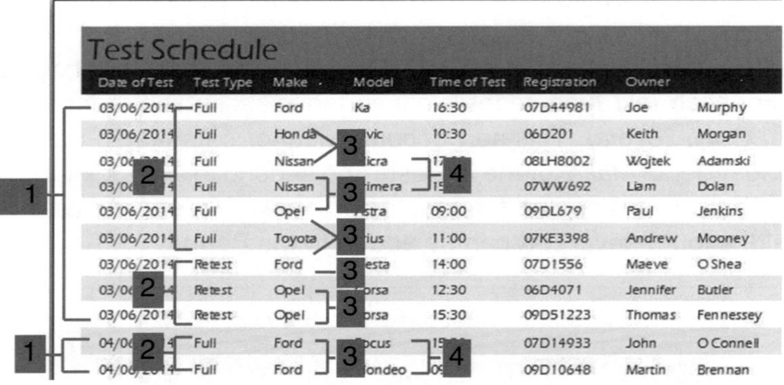

Figure 8.14: *Model* has been added as a fourth-level sort

In Figure 8.14, the Nissans that completed full tests on 03/06/2014 are listed in ascending order of *Model* – Micra is followed by Primera. For the Ford cars tested on 04/06/2014, the Ford Focus appears before the Ford Mondeo. As both Opels are Corsas, the sort doesn't occur for this model. The sort is repeated for cars tested on 04/06/2014 for the remaining records in the Report.

CREATE REPORTS

Task 5: Display the Test Schedule.

- Create a Report linked to the *Test Details* Table.
- Include the *Date of Test, Test Type, Make, Time of Test, Model, Reg No, Firstname* and *Surname* fields in the Report.
- Sort the Report using the following sorting levels:
  1. Ascending order of *Date of Test.*
  2. Ascending order of *Test Type.*
  3. Ascending order of *Make.*
  4. Ascending order of *Model.*
- Apply the *Concourse* style to the Report.
- The Report title is *Test Schedule.*
- Adjust column widths and set alignments so that the data appears like Figure 8.14.
- Edit the text in the *Reg No* label so that it reads *Registration.*
- Adjust the page header so that the headings wrap, as shown in Figure 8.14.
- Delete the *Surname* label. Edit the *Firstname* label so that it reads *Owner.*

Remove all label and text box controls from the layout so that you can delete the Surname label.

Task 6: Display vehicles in ascending order of Make.

- Create a Report linked to the *Test Details* Table.
- Include the *Make, Model, Odometer, Reg No* and *Test Result* fields in the Report.
- Sort the Report in ascending order of the *Make* field.
- Apply the *Concourse* style to the Report.
- The Report title is *Vehicle List by Make.*
- Edit the *Reg No* label so that it reads *Registration.*

LEARN HOW TO CHANGE THE SORT ORDER OF AN EXISTING REPORT

To date we have used the Report Wizard to sort our reports. The sort order of an existing Report can be changed using the Group & Sort facility. This is best done in layout view, as you will instantly see the effect of changing the sort order.

When a Report is in layout view, clicking the *Group & Sort* button displays the Group, Sort, and Total Pane (Figure 8.15).

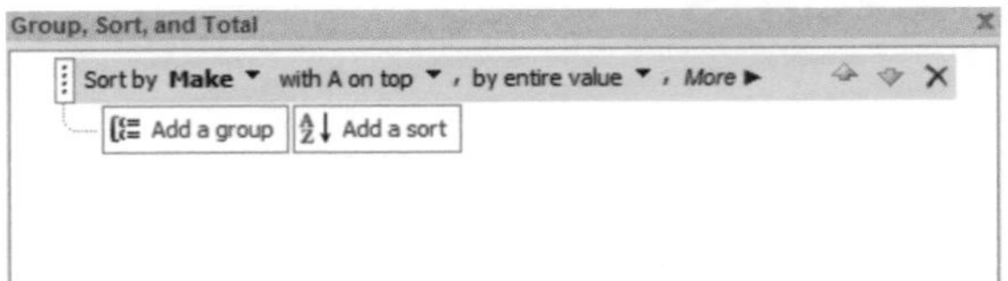

Figure 8.15: The Group, Sort, and Total Pane

The Group, Sort, and Total Pane displays the existing sort order of a Report. In Figure 8.15, the Report has been sorted in ascending order (with A on top) of the *Make* field. The Group, Sort, and Total Pane allows you to change the sort order of a Report using a variety of options (see Table 8.9).

Sort Option	Effect
with A on top with Z on top	Sorts Text fields in ascending or descending order.
from smallest to largest from largest to smallest	Sorts Number, Autonumber and Currency fields in ascending or descending order.
from oldest to newest from newest to oldest	Sorts Date/Time fields in ascending or descending order.
from selected to cleared from cleared to selected	Sorts Yes/No fields with selected check boxes first or with non-selected check boxes first.
Add a sort	Adds an extra sorting level to a Report. It is possible to sort a Report by an additional field as long as data is repeated in the previously sorted field.
Add a group	Groups a Report by the selected field (grouped reports will be explained later on in this assignment).
X	Removes sorting for the selected Report field.
	Changes the sort order of a Report by moving the selected field up a sort level. This only works when a Report is sorted by two or more fields.
	Changes the sort order of a Report by moving the selected field down a sort level. This only works when a Report is sorted by two or more fields.

Table 8.9

WORKED EXAMPLE: CHANGE THE SORT ORDER OF AN EXISTING REPORT

1. Open the *Vehicle List by Make* Report in layout view.

2. In the Format section of the Ribbon, click the *Group & Sort* button. The Group, Sort, and Total Pane shown in Figure 8.16 details the existing sort order of the *Vehicle List by Make* Report. Records are sorted in ascending order (with A on top) of the *Make* field.

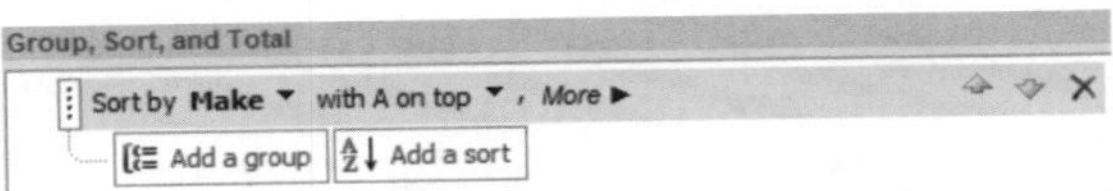

Figure 8.16: Group, Sort, and Total Pane

3. Expand the sort order drop-down list. Change the sort order to descending by selecting *with Z on top*. Because we are viewing the Report in layout view, the effects of changing the sort order are instantly seen on the screen (Figure 8.17).

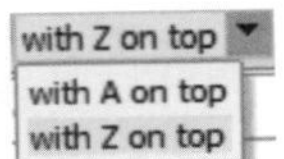

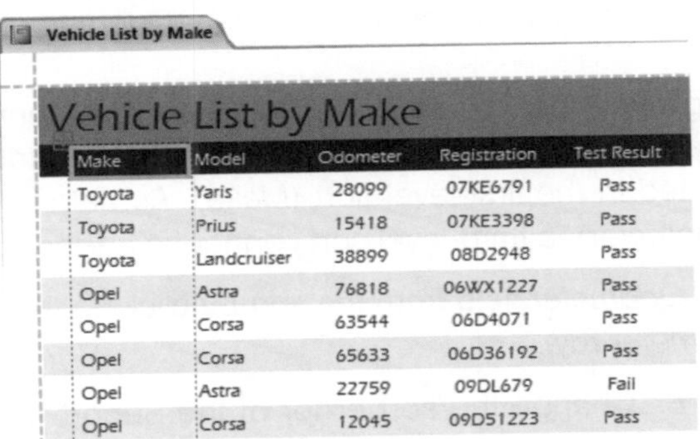

Vehicle List by Make

Make	Model	Odometer	Registration	Test Result
Toyota	Yaris	28099	07KE6791	Pass
Toyota	Prius	15418	07KE3398	Pass
Toyota	Landcruiser	38899	08D2948	Pass
Opel	Astra	76818	06WX1227	Pass
Opel	Corsa	63544	06D4071	Pass
Opel	Corsa	65633	06D36192	Pass
Opel	Astra	22759	09DL679	Fail
Opel	Corsa	12045	09D51223	Pass

Figure 8.17: Layout view of the Report with the sort order changed to descending order of *Make*

A second-level sort can be added by clicking the *Add a sort* button. Remember that you can only add a second-level sort if items are repeated in the first-level sort. As Toyota and Opel are repeated in Figure 8.17, it is possible to add a second-level sort to this Report.

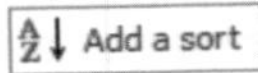

4. Click the *Add a sort* button. Select *Odometer* from the list of fields. Select *From largest to smallest* as the sort order, as shown in Figure 8.18.

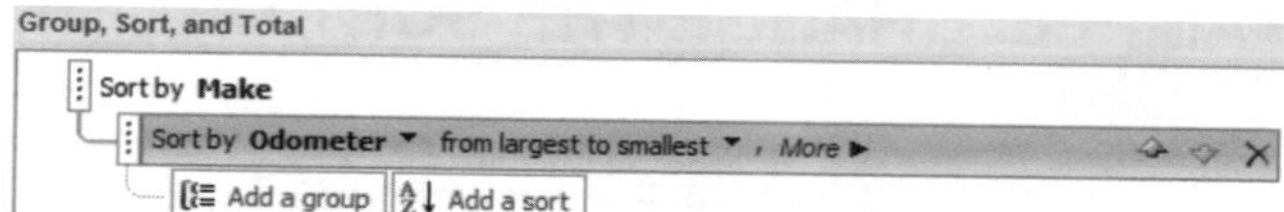

Figure 8.18: *Odometer* has been added as a second-level sort

Figure 8.18 displays the Group, Sort, and Total Pane having added the *Odometer* field as the second-level sort. As the Report is in layout view, the results of adjusting the sort are seen instantly, as shown in Figure 8.19.

Vehicle List by Make

Vehicle List by Make

Make	Model	Odometer	Registration	Test Result
Toyota	Landcruiser	38899	08D2948	Pass
Toyota	Yaris	28099	07KE6791	Pass
Toyota	Prius	15418	07KE3398	Pass
Opel	Astra	76818	06WX1227	Pass
Opel	Corsa	65633	06D36192	Pass
Opel	Corsa	63544	06D4071	Pass
Opel	Astra	22759	09DL679	Fail
Opel	Corsa	12045	09D51223	Pass

Figure 8.19: Records are in descending order of *Odometer* for each *Make*

The number of sorting levels that can be added to a Report depends on the number of fields in which data is repeated. In Figure 8.19 it was possible to add a second-level sort, as data is repeated in the first-level sort (*Make*). As data is not repeated in the second-level sort (*Odometer*), a third-level sort cannot be added to this Report.

5. Remove the *Odometer* field from the sort by clicking the *Delete* button in the *Sort by Odometer* row.

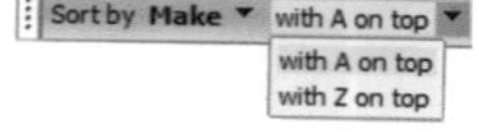

6. Change the sort order of the Report to ascending order of *Make*.

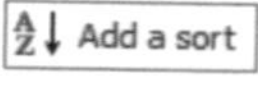

7. Add the *Test Result* field to the sort. Select *with Z on top* as the sort order.

In Figure 8.20 Ford cars appear at the top of the page, as the records are sorted first in ascending order of *Make*. Records of Ford cars are in descending order of *Test Result*, as this is the second-level sort. As items are repeated in the *Test Result* field, a third-level sort can be added to the Report.

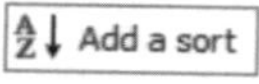

8. Add the *Odometer* field to the sort. Select *from largest to smallest* as the sort order.

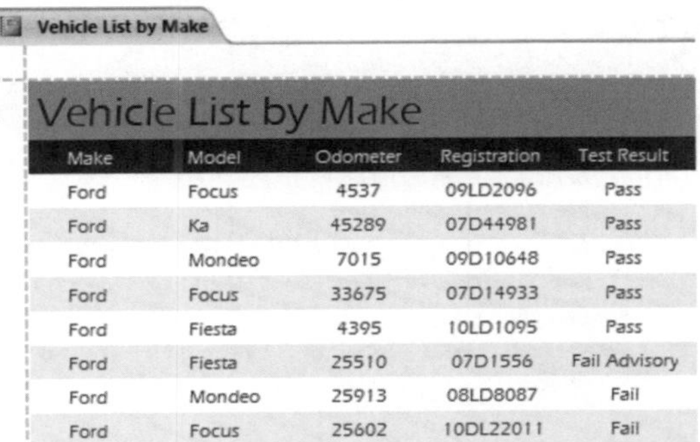

Vehicle List by Make

Make	Model	Odometer	Registration	Test Result
Ford	Focus	4537	09LD2096	Pass
Ford	Ka	45289	07D44981	Pass
Ford	Mondeo	7015	09D10648	Pass
Ford	Focus	33675	07D14933	Pass
Ford	Fiesta	4395	10LD1095	Pass
Ford	Fiesta	25510	07D1556	Fail Advisory
Ford	Mondeo	25913	08LD8087	Fail
Ford	Focus	25602	10DL22011	Fail

Figure 8.20: Records are sorted in ascending order of *Make* and then in descending order of *Test Result*

9. Rearrange the order of fields in the Report so that they appear like Figure 8.21.

Vehicle List by Make

Make	Model	Test Result	Odometer	Registration
Ford	Ka	Pass	45289	07D44981
Ford	Focus	Pass	33675	07D14933
Ford	Mondeo	Pass	7015	09D10648
Ford	Focus	Pass	4537	09LD2096
Ford	Fiesta	Pass	4395	10LD1095
Ford	Fiesta	Fail Advisory	25510	07D1556
Ford	Mondeo	Fail	25913	08LD8087
Ford	Focus	Fail	25602	10DL22011

Figure 8.21: Records are sorted in ascending order of *Make*, then in descending order of *Test Result* and then in descending order of *Odometer*

The results of the sort are seen in Figure 8.21. The Ford cars that passed are listed in descending order of the *Odometer* field. Ford cars that failed are also listed in descending order of the *Odometer* field. As only one Ford car has a test result of fail advisory, it is not possible to sort records in this category.

When a Report is sorted by more than one field, the sequence of fields in the sort can be adjusted using the *Move up* and *Move down* buttons.

10. Select *Test Result* in the Group, Sort, and Total Pane. Click the *Move up* button.
11. Change the sort order of Test Result to *with A on top*.
12. Move the *Test Result* field so that it appears first in the Report, as shown in Figure 8.22.
13. Preview the Report.

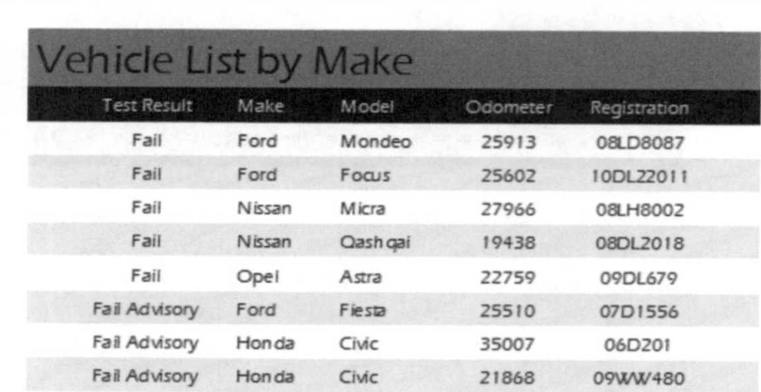

Vehicle List by Make

Test Result	Make	Model	Odometer	Registration
Fail	Ford	Mondeo	25913	08LD8087
Fail	Ford	Focus	25602	10DL22011
Fail	Nissan	Micra	27966	08LH8002
Fail	Nissan	Qashqai	19438	08DL2018
Fail	Opel	Astra	22759	09DL679
Fail Advisory	Ford	Fiesta	25510	07D1556
Fail Advisory	Honda	Civic	35007	06D201
Fail Advisory	Honda	Civic	21868	09WW480

Figure 8.22: Records are sorted in ascending order of *Test Result*, ascending order of *Make* and descending order of *Odometer*

Figure 8.22, which is an extract from the completed Report, shows the results of moving the *Test Result* field up a level in the sort order. The records in Figure 8.22 are now sorted first in ascending of *Test Result*, then in ascending order of *Make* and finally in descending order of *Odometer*.

14. Save the *Vehicle List by Make* Report.

You can also change the sort order of a Report using design view. Although the *Group & Sort* button is a different design to the one that appears in layout view, the steps are the same. One disadvantage of sorting a Report in design view is that you will have to preview the Report to see the effect of the new sort order.

LEARN ABOUT MAIL MERGE

Mail merge is a powerful feature where data stored in a database Table or Query can be combined with a document created in a word processing application to produce multiple personalised letters or documents. The profitability of many companies depends on the efficiency of mail merge. Reader's Digest was one of the first companies to recognise the potential of mail merge. Their database stores the names and addresses of the entire population of Great Britain and Ireland – over 65 million records! Using this database, Reader's Digest creates Queries to find potential customers for new products, such as books and DVDs. The mail merge feature allows Reader's Digest to produce thousands of personalised letters offering the products for sale. The various responses of the recipients of the letters are recorded in the database. A person may:

1. Not respond.
2. Enter the free prize draw without buying the product.
3. Buy the product.

Whatever response the customer makes, it is recorded in the database. Customers who don't respond will not be picked up by future promotional mailing Queries. Customers who either enter the prize draw or buy the product will be indentified by Queries and will receive more promotional offers in the future.

Many companies now use mail merge as a means of promoting and selling products. Due to the growth of e-commerce on the Internet, promotional mail merges are also done by email. This is much cheaper, as companies can complete a mail merge without having to purchase paper, envelopes and postage stamps. Most of the bills and statements you receive through the post are created using mail merge, e.g. your electricity bill, phone bill and bank statement. Many banks now give you the option of receiving your bank statements by email instead of surface mail.

Using Microsoft Word and Microsoft Access, you can create a mail merge application on your PC. A document created in Word is combined with an Access Table or Query to produce a personalised document for each record stored in the Table or in a specific Query.

Steps in Creating a Mail Merge

Each mail merge is created in four distinct steps.

1. **Create the main document:** This is the document, created in Word, that will be sent to people whose details are stored in the database. The main document is usually a letter or email.
2. **Create the data source:** The data source can be either a Table or a Query in an Access database. The data source stores names, addresses and any other data that will be referred to in the main document.
3. **Insert merge fields:** Merge fields connect the main document to the data source. Each merge field is a field from the Table or Query. Individual merge fields are inserted into the Word document.
4. **Merge the main document with the data source:** A separate personalised document is produced for each record in the data source. This document can be sent via email or surface mail. If the data source contains 20 records, then 20 documents will be produced. If the data source contains 1,000 records, then 1,000 documents will be produced.

Figure 8.23 demonstrates the mail merge process in practice. The main document is a letter. The data source is the *Test Details* Table. The *Firstname, Surname, Address1, Address2, Address3, Test Number, Reg No, Date of Test, Time of Test* and *Cost* fields have been inserted in the main document. These are the merge fields.

When the main document in Figure 8.23 is merged with the data source, multiple personalised letters are produced. In the example, five letters are produced, as there are five records in the *Test Details* Table. Each letter is personalised. In the first letter, the salutation is *Dear Paul*. In the second letter, the salutation is *Dear Keith*, and so on.

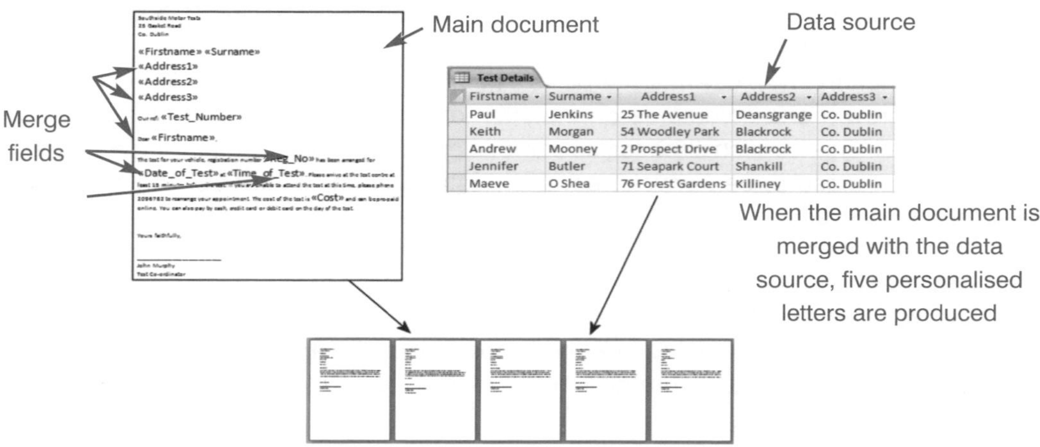

Figure 8.23: In a mail merge, a word processing document is combined with a database to produce multiple personalised documents

WORKED EXAMPLE: CREATE A MAIL MERGE

1. Start Microsoft Word.
2. Create a new document and type the letter displayed below.

N The missing information will be filled in later on in the mail merge process.

Southside Motor Tests
25 Gasket Road
Co. Dublin

Our ref:

Dear ,
The test for your vehicle, registration number has been arranged for at. Please arrive at the test centre at least 15 minutes before the test. If you are unable to attend the test at this time, please phone 2096782 to rearrange your appointment. The cost of the test is euro and can be pre-paid online. You can also pay by cash, credit card or debit card on the day of the test.

Yours faithfully,

____

John Murphy
Test Co-ordinator

3. Save this document as *Test Notification.*

4. In the Mailings section of the Ribbon, click *the Start Mail Merge* button. Select *Letters* from the drop-down list. This sets up *Test Notification* as the main document.

5. Click the *Select Recipients* button. Select *Use Existing List*.

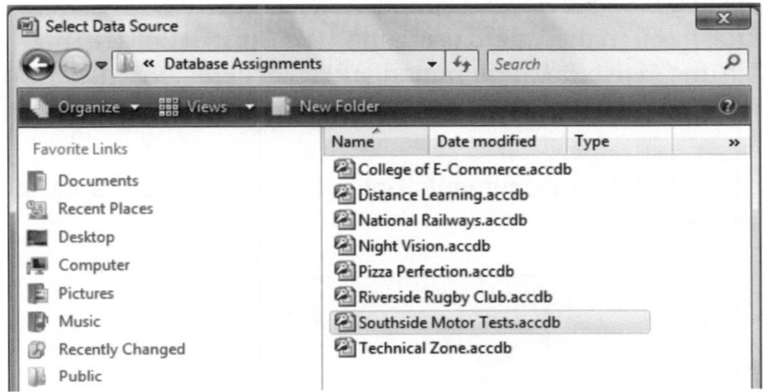

Figure 8.24: Selecting Southside Motor Tests as the data source

6. In the Select Data Source dialog box, navigate to the folder containing the Southside Motor Tests database (Figure 8.24). Select the Southside Motor Tests database and then click *Open*. As there are no Queries in the database at this point, Access uses the *Test Details* Table as the data source.
7. In the *Test Notification* document, position the cursor after the word *Dublin* and press *Enter*.

Southside Motor Tests
25 Gasket Road
Co. Dublin

«Firstname» «Surname»
«Address1»
«Address2»
«Address3»

Our ref: «Test_Number»

Dear «Firstname»,

Figure 8.25

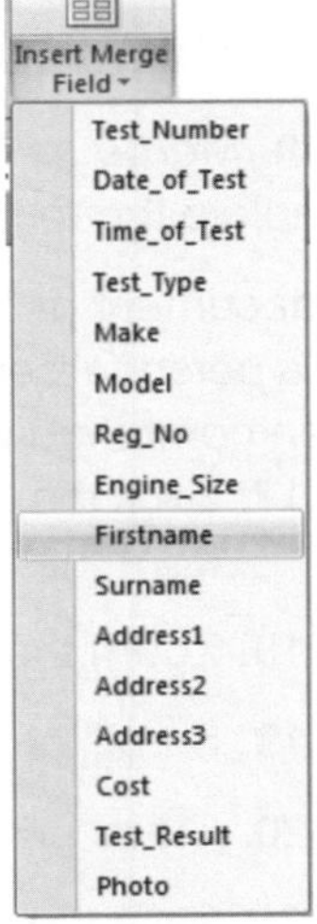

Figure 8.26

8. In the Mailings section of the Ribbon, display the Insert Merge Field drop-down list (Figure 8.26) using the *Insert Merge Field* button.
9. Select *Firstname* from the list of fields, as shown in Figure 8.26.
10. Press the space bar on the keyboard and then select *Surname*, using the Insert Merge Field drop-down list.
11. Insert the *Address1, Address2, Address3, Test Number* and *Firstname* fields, as shown in Figure 8.25.
12. Insert the *Reg No, Date of Test, Time of Test* and *Cost* fields, as shown in Figure 8.27. Make sure that you insert a space to the left and right of each merge field.

The test for your vehicle, registration number **«Reg_No»** has been arranged for **«Date_of_Test»** at **«Time_of_Test»**. Please arrive at the test centre at least 15 minutes before the test. If you are unable to attend the test at this time, please phone 2096782 to rearrange your appointment. The cost of the test is **«Cost»** Euro and can be pre-paid online. You can also pay by cash, credit card or debit card on the day of the test.

Figure 8.27

13. Click the *Preview Results* button.
14. Scroll through the letters using the *Next Record* button.

15. Click the *Finish & Merge* button and select *Edit Individual Documents* from the drop-down list.

If you select the Print Documents options, this will waste a lot of paper, as 22 letters will be printed.

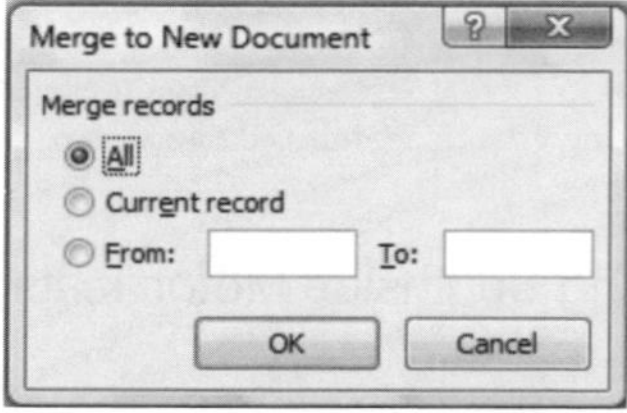

Figure 8.28

16. In the *Merge to New Document* dialog box, select *All* (Figure 8.28). Click *OK* to complete the merge.

A new document named *Letters1* is created. This document contains 22 pages. Each page is a personalised letter where data from one of the records in the *Test Details* Table has been combined with the letter created in Word.

17. Click the *Office* button (or the File tab in Office 2010) and select *Print Preview* from the list of Print options.

18. Zoom the document to 100%.
19. Scroll through the letters using the *Next Page* button. Next Page
20. Close print preview.

21. Save the merged document as *Test Notification Letters*.

For a detailed explanation of how to create labels, refer to pages 126–9 in Assignment 6.

Task 7: Create address labels.

- Open the Southside Motor Tests database if it is not already open.
- Create address labels for each of the test notification letters.
- Design the labels so that they appear like Figure 8.29.
- Sort the labels in ascending order of *Surname.*
- Enter *Test Notification Labels* as the Report name.

Wojtek Adamski
2 Avondale Villas
Shankill
Co. Dublin

Figure 8.29

Task 8: Create a Query to find records of clients whose test result is *Fail*. Save the Query as *Failed tests.*

As this Query will be used in a mail merge, you will need to omit the *Photo* field from the Query design grid. Word will not connect to a Query that includes an Attachment field.

Task 9: Create a mail merge for clients who failed the test.

1. Create a new document in Microsoft Word.
2. Type the letter displayed below. Some text is missing and will be added later on in the mail merge process.

Southside Motor Tests
25 Gasket Road
Co. Dublin

Our ref:

Dear ,
Your , registration number , did not pass its last test on and is now due for a retest. Please phone us on 2096782 to arrange a time for your retest.

Yours faithfully,

____
John Murphy
Test Co-ordinator

3. Save the letter as *Fail Notification.*

4. In the Mailings section of the Ribbon, click the *Start Mail Merge* button. Set up the *Fail Notification* document as a Letter.
5. Using the *Select Recipients* button, link the *Fail Notification* document to the *Failed tests* Query.

Select Recipients

6. Using the *Insert Merge Field* button, add fields to the document so that it appears like Figure 8.30.

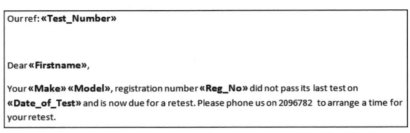

Our ref: **«Test_Number»**

Dear **«Firstname»**,

Your **«Make» «Model»**, registration number **«Reg_No»** did not pass its last test on **«Date_of_Test»** and is now due for a retest. Please phone us on 2096782 to arrange a time for your retest.

Figure 8.30: Merge fields have been added to the *Fail Notification* document

7. Click the *Finish & Merge* button and select *Edit Individual Documents* from the drop-down list. Click *OK* to merge to a new document.

8. Preview the letters. There should be five letters in total.
9. Save the merged document as *Fail Notification Letters.*

LEARN ABOUT REPORT FUNCTIONS

Many of the advantages of computerised databases are based on the power of the reporting facility. The sort order of records can be instantly changed in a Report simply by clicking a button. Reports can be formatted and printed so that the reader of the Report can understand the content even though they may have no knowledge of databases. Another major advantage of reports is the ability to perform calculations on the records displayed in the Report. These calculations are carried out using Report functions.

There are many Report functions available in Access, each of which is designed for a specific calculation. In the *Southside Motor Tests* assignment, we will learn about the functions listed in Table 8.10.

Function	Effect	Data Types
Sum	Adds values in a Report field	• Number • Currency • Autonumber
Avg	Calculates the average of values in a Report field	
Count	Counts the number of times data occurs in a Report field	• Text • Date/Time • Number • Currency • Autonumber • Yes/No

Table 8.10

Function	Effect	Data Types
Max	Displays the highest number in a particular Report field	• Text • Date/Time • Number • Currency • Autonumber
Min	Displays the lowest number in a particular Report field	

Table 8.10 (continued)

The Sum, Avg, Max and Min functions can be used with Number, Currency and Autonumber fields. In addition to Number, Currency and Autonumber fields, the Count, Max and Min functions can also be used with Text and Date/Time fields.

SYNTAX OF REPORT FUNCTIONS

Report functions refer to field names. The field name referred to by the Report function must be enclosed in square brackets, which are in turn enclosed in circular brackets. All Report functions start with the equals sign.

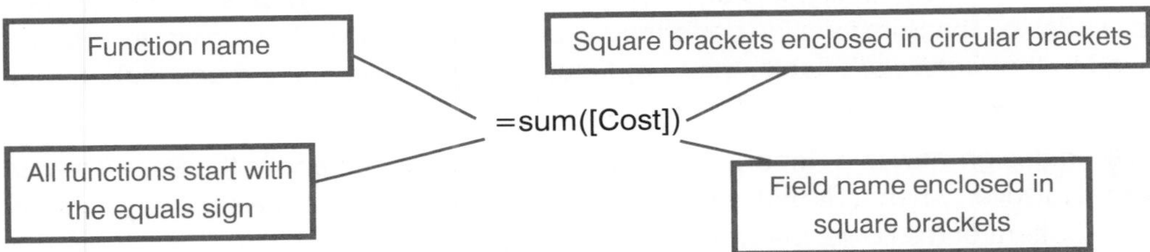

Report functions are most commonly created in the Report footer, but can also be created in the Report header, Detail and Group footer. As the name suggests, the Report footer appears at the end of the Report, after the last record. The Report footer only appears once in a Report. In a single-page Report, the Report footer will be on page 1, as shown in Figure 8.31.

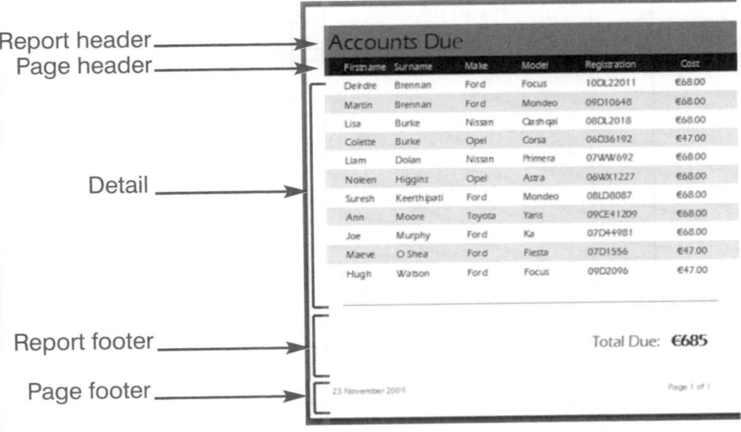

Accounts Due

Firstname	Surname	Make	Model	Registration	Cost
Deirdre	Brennan	Ford	Focus	10DL22011	€68.00
Martin	Brennan	Ford	Mondeo	09D10648	€68.00
Lisa	Burke	Nissan	Qashqai	08DL2018	€68.00
Colette	Burke	Opel	Corsa	06D36192	€47.00
Liam	Dolan	Nissan	Primera	07WW692	€68.00
Noleen	Higgins	Opel	Astra	06WX1227	€68.00
Suresh	Keerthipati	Ford	Mondeo	08LD8087	€68.00
Ann	Moore	Toyota	Yaris	09CE41209	€68.00
Joe	Murphy	Ford	Ka	07D44981	€68.00
Maeve	O Shea	Ford	Fiesta	07D1556	€47.00
Hugh	Watson	Ford	Focus	09D2096	€47.00

Total Due: **€685**

23 November 2009 Page 1 of 1

Figure 8.31: Position of the Report footer in a single-page Report

The Report in Figure 8.31 is linked to a Query. The Query finds records of clients who have not paid for their test (a total of 11 records). Figure 8.32 shows the corresponding design view of the Report displayed in Figure 8.31.

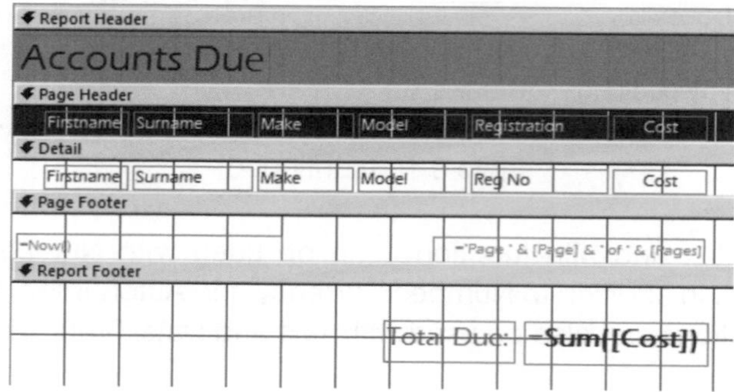

Figure 8.32: Design view of the Report displayed in Figure 8.31

In Figure 8.32, the Sum function in the Report footer calculates the total due of €685 for the records displayed in the Report. It is important to note that since the *Accounts Due* Report is linked to a Query, it is displaying only 11 of the 22 records stored in the *Test Details* Table. The Sum function performs its calculation on these 11 records. In a Report linked to the *Test Details* Table, the Sum function would calculate a much higher total, as the total would be based on 22 records.

N In design view of a Report, the page footer is positioned above the Report footer. However, when a Report is previewed, the page footer is always displayed at the bottom of the page, below the Report footer.

Figure 8.33 illustrates the positions of the various Report sections in a multiple-page Report.

Page 1 of Report

Report header

Page header

Detail

Page footer

Page 2 of Report

Page header

Detail

Page footer

Page 3 of Report

Page header

Detail

Report footer

Page footer

Figure 8.33: How Report sections are positioned in a multiple-page Report

It is important to understand how the Report sections are positioned in a multiple-page Report.

- The Report header appears at the top of the first page in the Report. It displays the Report title. Introductory text and graphics can also be displayed in the Report header. The Report header only appears once in a multiple-page Report.
- The page header appears at the top of each page, except for page 1, where it is immediately below the Report header. The page header displays the column headings, which Access generates using the field names.
- The detail section appears immediately below the page header in each page of the Report. The detail section displays the records in the Report. The size of the detail section adjusts according to the number of records displayed in the Report. The more records are in the Report, the bigger the detail section will be.
- The Report footer appears on the last page of the Report, immediately below the last record displayed in the detail section. It is used primarily for calculations, which are performed by Report functions. Summary text can also be displayed in the Report footer. The Report footer appears once in a multiple-page Report.
- The page footer appears at the bottom of every page in the Report. It displays the date and the page numbers.

ab| Report functions are best created in design view, using the *Text Box* button. The text box is created in the Report footer (Figure 8.34).

Report Footer
Text17: Unbound

Figure 8.34: A text box in the Report footer

In Figure 8.34, a text box has been created in the Report footer. The text box is unbound. This means that it is not linked to any field in the Table. Each time you create a text box, Access inserts a label to the left of the text box. In Figure 8.34, this label contains the text "Text 17:". When creating a function, the function is typed in the text box, replacing the text *Unbound*.

Total Due: =Sum([Cost])

Figure: 8.35: The Sum function

In Figure 8.35, a Sum function to add values in the *Cost* field has been created in the unbound text box. The label text has been edited. When the Report is previewed, the result of the calculation is displayed (Figure 8.36).

The Report in Figure 8.36 displays records of clients who have not paid for their test. The sum function calculates the total amount due by adding up all the values in the *Cost* field.

Report functions are dynamic and update as data is added to the database. Ticking the *Paid* check box for Keith Morgan's record in the *Southside Motor Tests Bookings* Form results in the total due changing from €685 to €617, as shown in Figure 8.37. The total has reduced by €68, which is the cost of a full test.

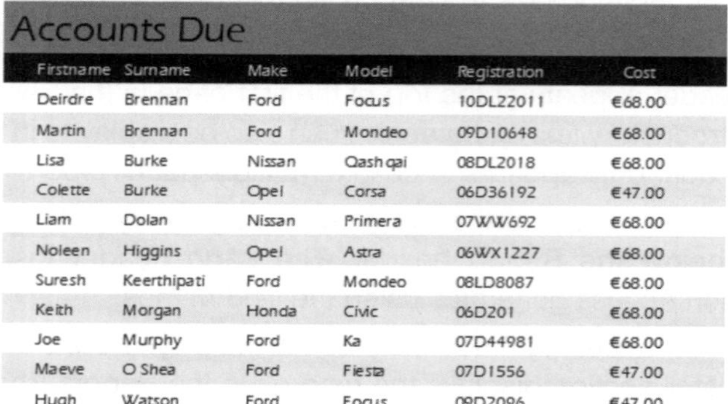

Accounts Due

Firstname	Surname	Make	Model	Registration	Cost
Deirdre	Brennan	Ford	Focus	10DL22011	€68.00
Martin	Brennan	Ford	Mondeo	09D10648	€68.00
Lisa	Burke	Nissan	Qashqai	08DL2018	€68.00
Colette	Burke	Opel	Corsa	06D36192	€47.00
Liam	Dolan	Nissan	Primera	07WW692	€68.00
Noleen	Higgins	Opel	Astra	06WX1227	€68.00
Suresh	Keerthipati	Ford	Mondeo	08LD8087	€68.00
Keith	Morgan	Honda	Civic	06D201	€68.00
Joe	Murphy	Ford	Ka	07D44981	€68.00
Maeve	O Shea	Ford	Fiesta	07D1556	€47.00
Hugh	Watson	Ford	Focus	09D2096	€47.00

Total Due: **€685**

Figure 8.36: Using the Sum function in a Report

Accounts Due

Firstname	Surname	Make	Model	Registration	Cost
Deirdre	Brennan	Ford	Focus	10DL22011	€68.00
Martin	Brennan	Ford	Mondeo	09D10648	€68.00
Lisa	Burke	Nissan	Qashqai	08DL2018	€68.00
Colette	Burke	Opel	Corsa	06D36192	€47.00
Liam	Dolan	Nissan	Primera	07WW692	€68.00
Noleen	Higgins	Opel	Astra	06WX1227	€68.00
Suresh	Keerthipati	Ford	Mondeo	08LD8087	€68.00
Joe	Murphy	Ford	Ka	07D44981	€68.00
Maeve	O Shea	Ford	Fiesta	07D1556	€47.00
Hugh	Watson	Ford	Focus	09D2096	€47.00

Total Due: **€617**

Figure 8.37: The function has automatically recalculated

The process by which the Sum function updates depends on the fact that objects in a database are linked. The update of the total due calculated by the Sum function involves four distinct stages, as follows.

1. Form

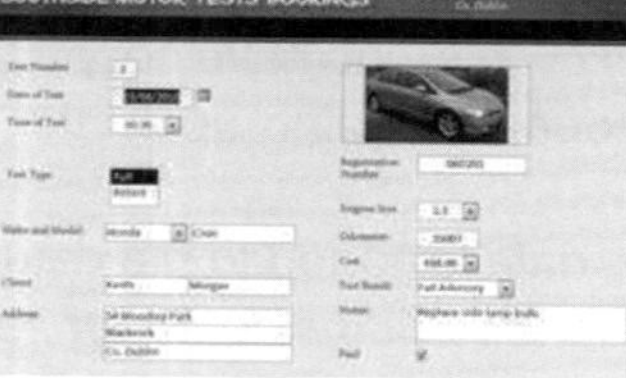

Figure 8.38: The Paid check box is ticked for Keith Morgan's record in the *Southside Motor Tests Bookings* Form

2. Table

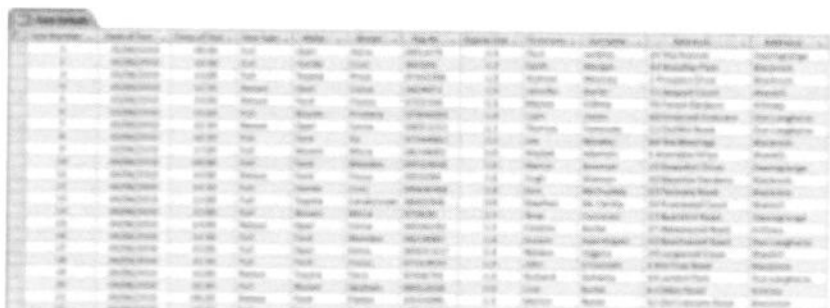

Figure 8.39: This in turn updates Keith Morgan's record in the *Test Details* Table

3. Query

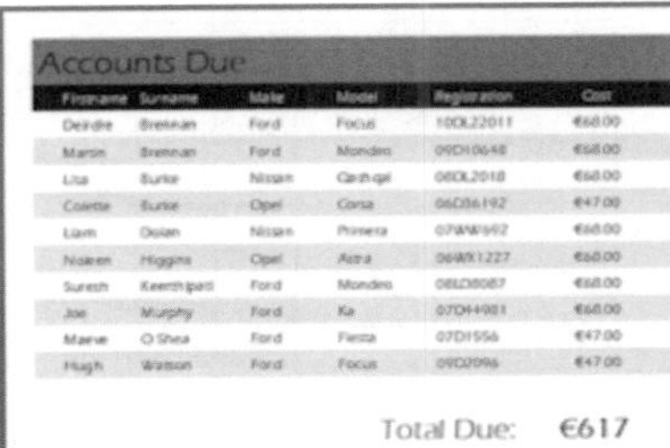

Not paid

Firstname	Surname	Make	Model	Reg No	Cost
Maeve	O Shea	Ford	Fiesta	07D1556	€47.00
Liam	Dolan	Nissan	Primera	07WW692	€68.00
Joe	Murphy	Ford	Ka	07D44981	€68.00
Martin	Brennan	Ford	Mondeo	09D10648	€68.00
Hugh	Watson	Ford	Focus	09D2096	€47.00
Colette	Burke	Opel	Corsa	06D36192	€47.00
Suresh	Keerthipati	Ford	Mondeo	08LD8087	€68.00
Noleen	Higgins	Opel	Astra	06WX1227	€68.00
Lisa	Burke	Nissan	Qashqai	08DL2018	€68.00
Deirdre	Brennan	Ford	Focus	10DL22011	€68.00

Figure 8.40: The *Not paid* Q no longer finds Keith Morgan's record

4. Report

Accounts Due

Firstname	Surname	Make	Model	Registration	Cost
Deirdre	Brennan	Ford	Focus	10DL22011	€68.00
Martin	Brennan	Ford	Mondeo	09D10648	€68.00
Lisa	Burke	Nissan	Qashqai	08DL2018	€68.00
Colette	Burke	Opel	Corsa	06D36192	€47.00
Liam	Dolan	Nissan	Primera	07WW692	€68.00
Noleen	Higgins	Opel	Astra	06WX1227	€68.00
Suresh	Keerthipati	Ford	Mondeo	08LD8087	€68.00
Joe	Murphy	Ford	Ka	07D44981	€68.00
Maeve	O Shea	Ford	Fiesta	07D1556	€47.00
Hugh	Watson	Ford	Focus	09D2096	€47.00

Total Due: €617

Figure 8.41: The *Accounts Due* Report, which is linked to the *Not paid* Query, no longer displays Keith Morgan's record. It is now displaying 10 records. The Sum function that calculates the total due updates to €617, as it is no longer including the €68 previously owed by Keith Morgan.

WORKED EXAMPLE: CREATE A REPORT FUNCTION

1. Create a Query to find records of clients who have not paid for their test. Save the Query as *Not paid.*
2. Create a Report linked to the *Not paid* Query.
3. Include the *Firstname, Surname, Make, Model, Reg No* and *Cost* fields in the Report.
4. Sort the Report in ascending order of the *Surname* field.
5. Apply the *Concourse* theme to the Report.
6. The Report title is *Accounts Due.*
7. Edit the text in the *Reg No* label so that it reads *Registration.*
8. Adjust column widths and set alignments so that the data appears like Figure 8.37.
9. View the *Accounts Due* Report in design view.
   In the National Railways database, we saw that a standard Access Report is divided into four sections: the Report header, page header, detail section and page footer. To perform calculations in a Report, a fifth section – the Report footer – must be added to the Report.
10. Create the Report footer as shown in Figure 8.42.

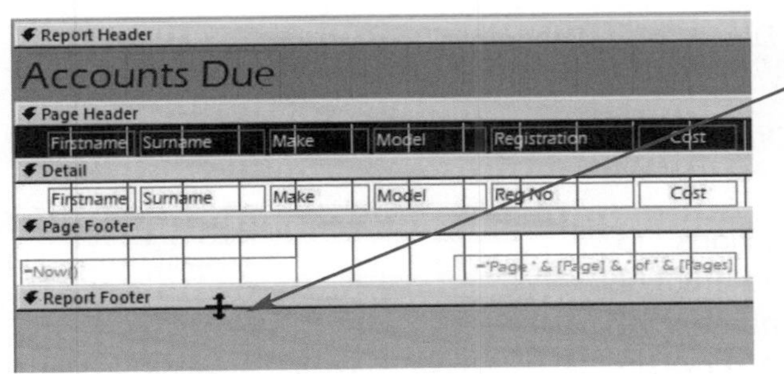

Point at the bottom of the Report footer bar. When the mouse pointer changes to a double-headed vertical arrow, create the Report footer by dragging downwards.

Figure 8.42

11. Click the *Text Box* button in the Design section of the Ribbon.
12. Create a text box in the Report footer by dragging with the mouse, as shown in Figure 8.43.

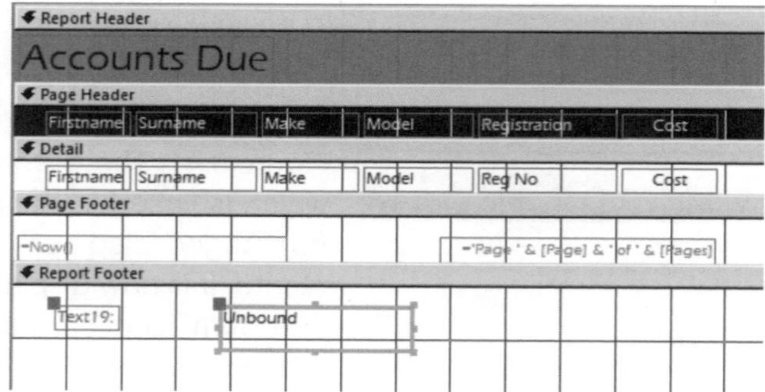

Figure 8.43: Creating a text box in the Report footer

13. Enter the Sum function in the text box. Enter descriptive text in the label box, as shown in Figure 8.44.

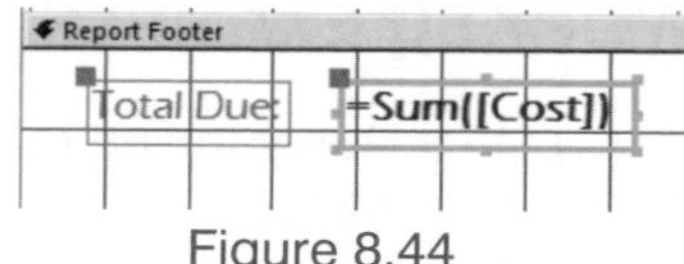

Figure 8.44

14. Increase the font size of the label and text box to 14. Display the Sum function in bold print. Adjust the size of the label and text box to fit the text and the result of the function, respectively.

15. Display the properties of the text box. Set the *Format* property to *Currency* and *Decimal Places* to *0*.
16. Preview the Report. The total due is €685.

17. Save the *Accounts Due* Report.

18. Close the *Accounts Due* Report and open the *Southside Motor Tests Bookings* Form in Form view.

19. Find Keith Morgan's record and then tick the *Paid* check box for Keith's record. Close the Form.

20. Open the *Accounts Due* Report. The total due has updated to €617.

21. View the *Accounts Due* Report in design view.

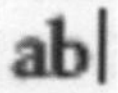

22. Create Report functions to calculate the average amount due and the total number of overdue accounts, as shown in Figure 8.45.

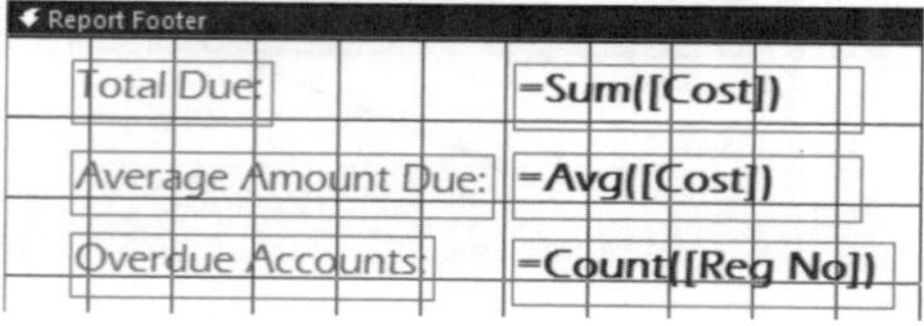

Figure 8.45: Avg and Count functions have been added to the Report footer

You can quickly create new functions by copying the existing Sum function. Select the text box containing the Sum function. Copy the text box using the *CTRL + C* keyboard combination. Now press *CTRL + V* to paste the text box. Edit the copy of the function so that it calculates the average.

23. Change the *Decimal Places* property of the Avg text box to *2*.
24. Change the *Format* property of the Count text box to *Fixed* and the *Decimal Places* property to *0*.

25. Save the *Accounts Due* Report.

26. Preview the Report. The average amount due is €61.70. There are 10 overdue accounts.
27. Close the *Accounts Due* Report.
28. Open the *Southside Motor Tests Bookings* Form in Form view. Enter the record displayed in Table 8.11.

Test Number	23
Date of Test	05/06/14
Time of Test	11:00
Test Type	Full
Reg No	09CE41209
Make	Toyota
Model	Yaris
Engine Size	1.6
Firstname	Ann
Surname	Moore
Address1	12 Deerpark Heights
Address2	Blackrock
Address3	Co. Dublin
Odometer	12553
Cost	€68.00
Test Result	Fail Advisory
Notes	Replace brake light
Paid	No
Photo	yaris09.jpg

Table 8.11

29. Close the *Southside Motor Tests Bookings* Form and open the *Accounts Due* Report. The total due has updated to €685. The average amount due is now €62.27 and there are 11 overdue accounts.

It is also possible to insert functions in the Report header and the detail section. We will see this in Assignment 9.

You can quickly create a function using the *Totals* drop-down list in layout view. Simply select the text box for which you want to create a function and then select the required function from the *Totals* drop-down list. Although this is a quick and easy method of creating a function, you have no control over the positioning of the function and Access doesn't attach a label to the function.

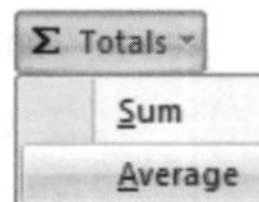

COMMON REPORT FUNCTION ERRORS

1. Incorrect Spelling of Field Name

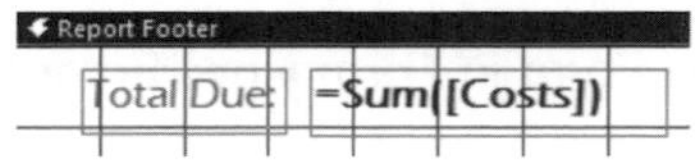

Figure 8.46: Field name is incorrect – it should be "Cost"

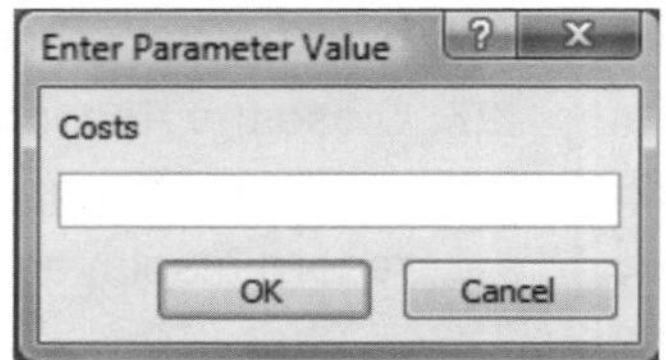

Figure 8.47

In Figure 8.46, the field name has been typed incorrectly. The correct spelling is *Cost*. When the Report is previewed, Access displays an Enter Parameter Value dialog box (Figure 8.47) with the incorrectly referenced field displayed in the box. Clicking *OK* will display the Report but the total due won't be displayed.

Always display the field list (Figure 8.49) before you create your function. The field list is a list of fields in the Table or Query that the Report is linked to. To display the field list, click the *Add Existing Fields* button in the Design section of the Ribbon. Once you have completed your function, check that you have typed the field name using exactly the same spelling as that in the field list.

In Figure 8.48, the function is correct because the field name is typed exactly as it appears in the field list (Figure 8.49).

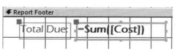

Report Footer
Total Due =Sum([Cost])

Figure 8.48: Correct spelling of field name

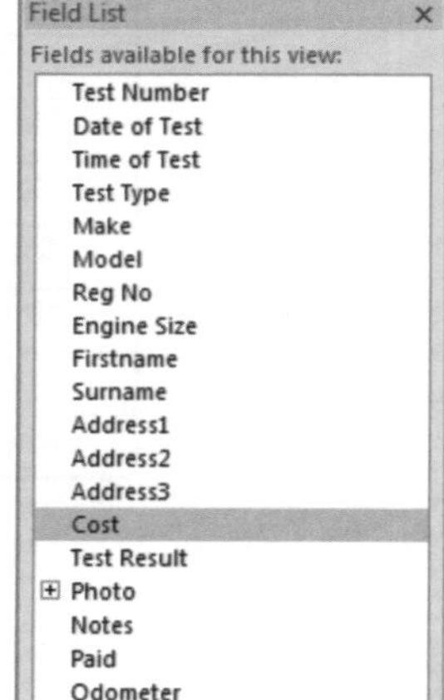

Figure 8.49: The field list

2. Brackets Mixed Up

In a Report function, the square brackets must always be inside the curved brackets. It is easy to make a mistake here.

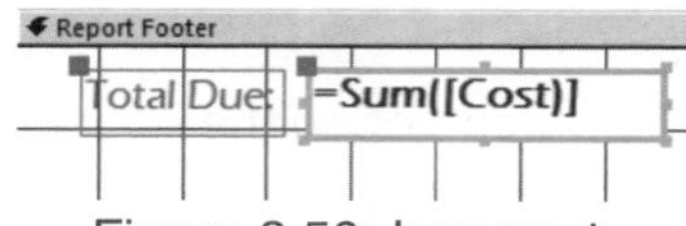

Figure 8.50: Incorrect positioning of closing brackets

In Figure 8.50, the function is incorrect because the curved bracket was closed before the square bracket. When the Report is previewed, Access will display the error message shown in Figure 8.51.

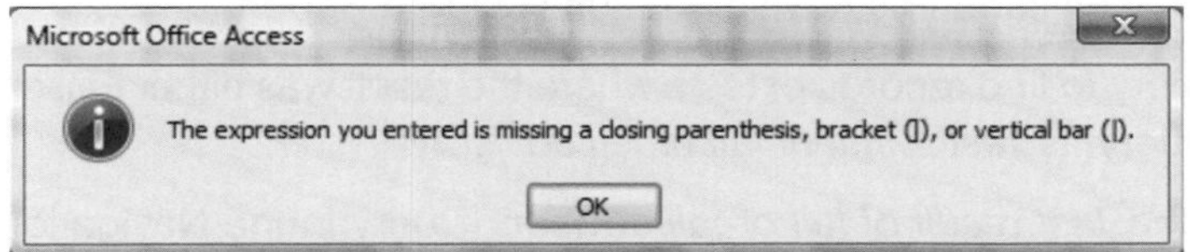

Figure 8.51: Error message displayed when function brackets are positioned incorrectly

3. Missing Brackets

You must include all the brackets in the function. In Figure 8.52, the round brackets have been omitted.

As soon as you click outside the text box, Access will display the error message shown in Figure 8.53.

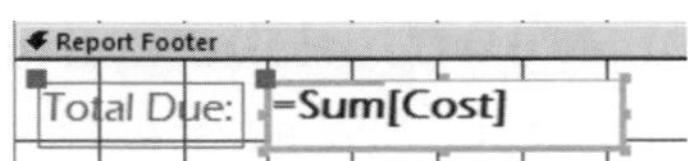

Figure 8.52: Round brackets have been omitted from the function

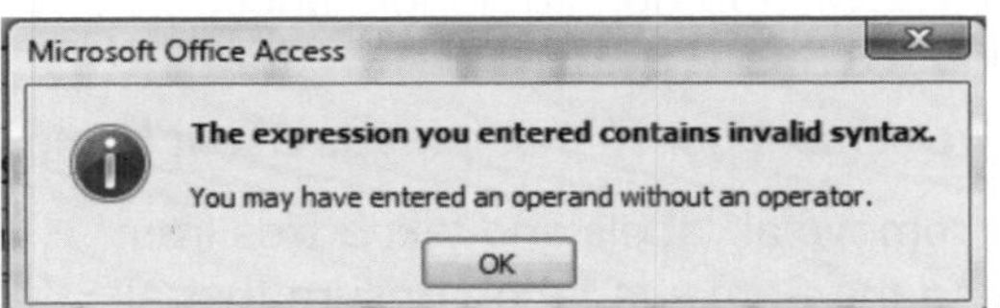

Figure 8.53: Error message displayed when round brackets are omitted from a function

4. Function in Page Footer

Functions must be created in the Report footer. The page footer is not designed to accommodate Report functions.

In Figure 8.54, even though the function is correct, it has been incorrectly positioned in the page footer. Access will display the error message shown in Figure 8.55 when this Report is previewed.

Figure 8.54: Function incorrectly created in the page footer

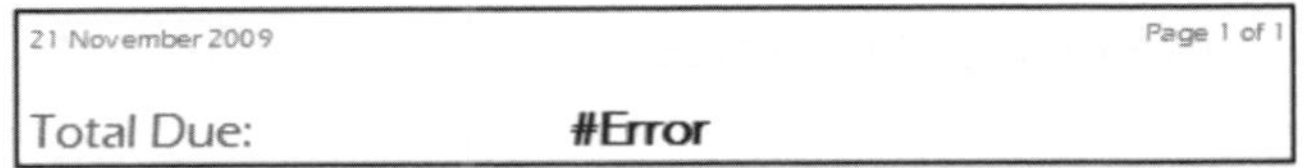

Figure 8.55: This error results from incorrectly creating the function in the page footer

CREATE REPORTS

Task 10: Display Fail and Fail Advisory results using a Report.

- Create a Query to find records of tests where the result was either Fail or Fail Advisory. Save the Query as *Test result of fail or fail advisory.*

Select the *Test result of fail or fail advisory* Query in the Navigation Pane before starting the Report Wizard.

- Produce a Report linked to this Query. Include the *Firstname, Surname, Test Result, Date of Test, Make, Model* and *Test Type* fields in the Report.
- Sort the Report in ascending order of *Test Result.*
- Apply the *Concourse* style to the Report.
- The Report title is *List of Failed Tests.*
- Adjust column widths and set alignments so that the Report appears like Figure 8.56.
- Calculate the number of failed tests using an appropriate Report function. Format the result of the function as shown in Figure 8.56.
- Delete the *Surname* label. Edit the *Firstname* label so that it reads *Client Name.*

In Access 2007, you will have to remove all labels and text boxes from the existing layout before deleting the *Surname* label. Ensure that all other formatting is complete before removing the labels and text boxes from the layout.

List of Failed Tests

Client Name		Test Result	Date of Test	Make	Model	Test Type
Deirdre	Brennan	Fail	05/06/2014	Ford	Focus	Full
Lisa	Burke	Fail	04/06/2014	Nissan	Qashqai	Full
Suresh	Keertipati	Fail	04/06/2014	Ford	Mondeo	Full
Wojtek	Adamski	Fail	03/06/2014	Nissan	Micra	Full
Paul	Jenkins	Fail	03/06/2014	Opel	Astra	Full
Ann	Moore	Fail Advisory	05/06/2014	Toyota	Yaris	Full
Eoin	McCluskey	Fail Advisory	04/06/2014	Honda	Civic	Full
Maeve	O Shea	Fail Advisory	03/06/2014	Ford	Fiesta	Retest
Keith	Morgan	Fail Advisory	03/06/2014	Honda	Civic	Full

Number of Failed Tests: **9**

Figure 8.56: Completed Report for Task 10

- Export the *List of Failed Tests Report* to a PDF document.

LEARN HOW TO DISPLAY SPECIFIC FIELDS IN A QUERY

When there are a lot of fields in the Table, it is sometimes difficult to interpret the results of a Query, as all the fields will not fit on a single screen. You will have to scroll to the right to see the remaining fields. As you scroll, the fields on the left disappear. To make it easier to interpret the results of a Query, you can specify which fields you want to display, using the *Show* row of the Query design grid (Figure 8.57).

Field:	Test Number	Date of Test	Time of Test	Test Type	Make	Model	Reg No	Engine Size
Table:	Test Details	Test Details	Test Details	Test Details	Test Details	Test Details	Test Details	Test Details
Sort:								
Show:	☑	☑	☐	☑	☑	☑	☐	☐
Criteria:				"Full"				

Figure 8.57

The Query in Figure 8.57 will find records where the Test Type is *Full*. By default, a Query will display all fields unless you specify otherwise. To remove a particular field from the Query, simply uncheck that field's check box. In Figure 8.57, the *Time of Test, Reg No* and *Engine Size* fields will not be displayed when the Query is run.

LEARN HOW TO JOIN NEGATIVE CONDITIONS IN A QUERY

In the Night Vision database, we learned how to join multiple conditions in a Query. Conditions can be joined using either the *AND* or the *OR* logical operator.

AND Conditions

Field:	Test Type	Engine Size	Test Result
Table:	Test Details	Test Details	Test Details
Sort:			
Show:	☑	☑	☑
Criteria:	"Full"	1.6	"Pass"
or:			

Figure 8.58: Conditions are joined with the *AND* logical operator

Figure 8.58 is an example of joining conditions using the *AND* logical operator. Because all three conditions are in the *Criteria:* line, Access joins the conditions with *AND*. Only records that satisfy *all* of the conditions are found by the Query. Using the conditions displayed in Figure 8.58, the Query will find records of *cars with 1.6 litre engines that passed the full test* – a total of two records (the 07 Toyota Prius and the 09 Ford Mondeo). When joining conditions like this, there is no need to type *AND*.

Converting these conditions to negative conditions is straightforward. Simply type <> immediately before each condition, as shown in Figure 8.59.

Field:	Test Type	Engine Size	Test Result
Table:	Test Details	Test Details	Test Details
Sort:			
Show:	☑	☑	☑
Criteria:	<>"Full"	<>1.6	<>"Pass"
or:			

Figure 8.59: Negative conditions joined with the *AND* logical operator

Using the conditions displayed in Figure 8.59, the Query finds records of cars that didn't complete a full test *and* that don't have a 1.6 litre engine *and* that didn't pass the test (one record in total – the 07 Ford Fiesta).

To see how this Query works, it is best to take it one condition at a time.

Condition 1: Test Type <>Full

Using this condition, the Query finds records of cars that didn't complete a full test (a total of seven records).

Condition 2: Engine Size <>1.6

By the time it gets to the second condition, the Query is searching through seven records, as it has already eliminated records of cars that completed a full test. Of the seven remaining records, six cars don't have a 1.6 litre engine.

Condition 3: Test Result <>Pass

The Query is now searching through six records, as it has eliminated records of cars that didn't complete a full test and which don't have a 1.6 litre engine. Of these six records, one car doesn't have a test result of Pass (Maeve O Shea's 1.3 litre Ford Fiesta).

The end result is that the Query finds one record of a car that didn't complete the full test, doesn't have a 1.6 litre engine and didn't achieve a pass.

OR Conditions

Field:	Make	Model	Reg No
Table:	Test Details	Test Details	Test Details
Sort:			
Show:	☑	☑	☑
Criteria:	"Ford" Or "Honda" Or "Nissan"		
or:			

Figure 8.60: *OR* is used to join positive conditions in the same field

Figure 8.60 is an example of joining conditions using the *OR* logical operator. Because all three conditions are in the *Make* field, joining them with *AND* doesn't make sense logically. A car can only be made by one company. This is why the conditions are joined with *OR*. Records that satisfy any one of these three conditions are found by the Query. It is not possible for a record to satisfy more than one condition. Using the conditions displayed in Figure 8.60, the Query will find records of *cars made by either Ford, Honda or Nissan* – a total of 14 records.

Converting these conditions to negative conditions is not straightforward. When joining negative conditions in the same field, the *AND* logical operator must be used instead of *OR*.

Field:	Make	Model	Reg No
Table:	Test Details	Test Details	Test Details
Sort:			
Show:	☑	☑	☑
Criteria:	<>"Ford" And <>"Honda" And <>"Nissan"		
or:			

Figure 8.61: *AND* is used to join negative conditions in the same field

Using the conditions displayed in Figure 8.61, the Query finds records of cars that are not made by Ford *and* are not made by Honda *and* are not made by Nissan (a total of nine records). Unlike the positive version of these conditions, the Query will only find records where all three of the conditions are satisfied.

If you join negative conditions using *OR*, as shown in Figure 8.62, the conditions cancel each other out.

Field:	Make	Model	Reg No
Table:	Test Details	Test Details	Test Details
Sort:			
Show:	☑	☑	☑
Criteria:	<>"Ford" Or <>"Honda" Or <>"Nissan"		
or:			

Figure 8.62: Negative conditions incorrectly joined with *OR*

The conditions displayed in Figure 8.62 have no effect. Using these conditions, the Query will find all 23 of the records stored in the *Test Details* Table. To understand the reason for this, it is best to take it one condition at a time.

Condition 1: <>Ford

Using this condition, the Query finds 15 records, including two records of Honda cars and four records of Nissan cars.

Condition 2: <>Honda

Using this condition, the Query finds 21 records, including eight records of Ford cars and four records of Nissan cars.

<>Ford Or <>Honda

When the two conditions are joined with *OR*, the eight Ford cars found by the *<>Honda* condition cancel out the Ford cars excluded by the *<>Ford* condition. Similarly, the two Honda cars found by the *<>Ford* condition cancel out the Honda cars excluded by the *<>Honda* condition. The result is that the conditions have no effect and the Query finds all 23 of the records stored in the Table.

Condition 3: <>Nissan

Adding the *<>Nissan* condition has no effect, as this condition has also been incorrectly joined with the *OR* logical operator in Figure 8.62.

An error frequently made by students is to omit < > in the second and subsequent conditions. Although the condition *<>"Ford" or "Honda"* looks like it will search for cars that are made by neither Ford nor Honda, it will actually

search for cars that are not made by Ford or <u>are</u> made by Honda – a total of 15 records. Adding ***or "Honda"*** to the condition has no effect, as the first condition *<>"Ford"* already finds the two Honda cars. The correct way to join these two negative conditions is *<>"Ford" and <>"Honda".*

CREATE QUERIES

- Create a separate Query for each of the tasks described in Table 8.12.
- Sort each Query using the sort order specified.
- Use the *Show* row of the Query design grid to specify the fields displayed by the Query.

	Purpose of Query	Sort Order	Fields Displayed in Query	Query Name	Records Found
Task 11	Find records of cars except for those manufactured by Nissan and Toyota	Ascending order of Make	Date of Test, Reg No, Make, Model, Engine Size, Odometer, Test Result	Except Nissan and Toyota	15
Task 12	Find records of cars that are not manufactured by Ford and do not have 1.0 litre engines	Descending order of Engine Size	Date of Test, Reg No, Make, Model, Engine Size, Odometer, Test Result	Except Ford 1 litre	12

Table 8.12

LEARN ABOUT WILDCARD QUERIES

A wildcard Query enables you to search for records using a partial search condition. Wildcard Queries are used in the following situations.

- Searching for data that matches a pattern. This technique is commonly used with fields that store codes. For example, in a field storing car registration numbers, a wildcard Query could search for all registration numbers containing the letters *WX*.
- Searching for records when you don't have all the necessary information, e.g. when you know a customer's name begins with the letter *M* but you don't have any other information.

In a wildcard Query, the data that is missing is replaced with the wildcard symbol (*). There are three scenarios in which wildcards can be used.

Data Is Missing at the End

For example, we are searching for a particular customer whose first name begins with *M*. We don't have any other information. The Query condition is made up of two sections, as shown in Table 8.13.

What we know (beginning of the name)	*What we don't know (end of the name)*
M	*****

Table 8.13

The wildcard (*) represents the data that is missing. The Query condition is *M**. It is entered in the *Firstname* column in the Query design grid, as shown in Figure 8.63. When you type *M** and press *Enter*, Access encloses the search condition in double quotes and inserts the word *Like*.

Field:	Customer ID	Firstname	Surname
Table:	Customers	Customers	Customers
Sort:			
Show:	☑	☑	☑
Criteria:		Like "M*"	
or:			

Figure 8.63: Wildcard Query condition

The complete condition is ***Like "M*"***, which finds Martin, Michael, Michelle, Misha, Mohammad, Morgan, Muriel, etc.

Although you can type the complete condition shown in Figure 8.63, it is better to type *M**, press *Enter* and let Access fill in the rest of the condition for you.

Data Is Missing at the Beginning

For example, we are searching for a particular customer whose first name ends with *d*. We don't have any other information. The Query condition is made up of two sections, as shown in Table 8.14.

What we don't know (beginning of the name)	*What we know (end of the name)*
*****	**d**

Table 8.14

The wildcard (*) represents the data that is missing. The Query condition is **d*. It is entered in the *Firstname* column in the Query design grid, as shown in Figure 8.64. When you press *Enter*, Access changes ***d** to **Like "*d"**.

Field:	Customer ID	Firstname	Surname
Table:	Customers	Customers	Customers
Sort:			
Show:	☑	☑	☑
Criteria:		Like "*d"	
or:			

Figure 8.64

In Figure 8.64, *Like "*d"* finds Brigid, David, Dzevad, Gerard, Richard, etc.

Use of uppercase or lowercase letters does not affect the results of a Query. *M** finds the same records as *m**. Similarly, **d* finds the same records as **D*.

Data Is Missing at the Beginning and the End

For example, we are searching for car registrations that include the letters *LH*. The Query condition is made up of three sections, as shown in Table 8.15.

What we don't know (beginning of registration)	*What we know*	*What we don't know (end of registration)*
*****	**LH**	*****

Table 8.15

Two wildcard (*) symbols are required. The first wildcard represents the data that is missing at the beginning of the registration. The second wildcard represents the data that is missing at the end of the registration. The Query condition is **LH**, which is entered in the Query design grid as shown in Figure 8.65. When you press *Enter*, Access changes ***LH*** to ***Like "*LH*"***.

Field:	Reg Number	Make	Model
Table:	Cars	Cars	Cars
Sort:			
Show:	☑	☑	☑
Criteria:	Like "*LH*"		
or:			

Figure 8.65

In Figure 8.65, *Like "*LH*"* finds 11LH61255, 10LH9077, 13LH22980, 14LH1301, etc.

CREATE WILDCARD QUERIES

	Purpose of Query	Sort Order	Fields Displayed in Query	Query Name	Records Found
Task 13	Find records of cars registered in 2008	Ascending order of Reg No	Test Type, Reg No, Make, Model, Engine Size, Odometer, Test Result	2008 cars	4
Task 14	Find records of cars registered in Kildare	Ascending order of Reg No	Reg No, Make, Model, Engine Size, Firstname, Surname	Kildare registrations	2
Task 15	Find records of customers whose surname ends with Y	Ascending order of Surname	Firstname, Surname, Address1, Address2, Address3, Cost, Paid	Surname ends with Y	6

Table 8.16

Create a separate Query for each of the tasks described in Table 8.16. Sort each Query using the sort order specified in Table 8.16. Use the *Show* row of the Query design grid to specify the fields displayed by each Query. Save each Query using the name provided.

LEARN ABOUT NEGATIVE WILDCARD QUERIES

Single Negative Wildcard Condition

Using the condition in Figure 8.66, the Query finds all cars except for those registered in Kildare. The *Not* logical operator is combined with *Like* in this situation.

Field:	Make	Model	Reg No
Table:	Test Details	Test Details	Test Details
Sort:			Ascending
Show:	☑	☑	☑
Criteria:			Not Like "*KE*"
or:			

Figure 8.66

In Figure 8.66, the condition ***Not Like "*KE*"*** finds records of cars except for those registered in Kildare (a total of 21 records). As this is quite a complex condition, it is easy to make a mistake if you try to type the complete condition in one step. It is recommended that you create this condition in two steps.

Step 1: Create a positive condition.

- Type **KE**.
- Press *Enter.*
- Access changes the condition to *Like "*KE*".*

Step 2: Edit the condition created in Step 1.

- Complete your negative wildcard condition by typing *Not* at the beginning of the condition, giving *Not Like "*KE*".*

Breaking down a negative wildcard condition into two steps greatly reduces the chance of an error in the condition.

Multiple Negative Wildcard Conditions in Different Fields

Joining multiple negative wildcard conditions is relatively straightforward.

Field:	Reg No	Address1	Address2
Table:	Test Details	Test Details	Test Details
Sort:			
Show:	☑	☑	☑
Criteria:	Not Like "*KE*"	Not Like "*Road"	
or:			

Figure 8.67: Negative wildcard conditions joined with the *AND* logical operator

Using the conditions displayed in Figure 8.67, the Query finds records of cars that are not registered in Kildare where the registered address doesn't end with the word "Road" (a total of 12 records). Because the conditions are in the same line of the Query design grid, Access joins the conditions using the *AND* logical operator.

Multiple Negative Wildcard Conditions in a Single Field

Joining multiple negative wildcard conditions in a single field requires the *AND* logical operator. However, this time you must type "And".

Field:	Reg No	Address1	Address2
Table:	Test Details	Test Details	Test Details
Sort:			
Show:	☑	☑	☑
Criteria:	Not Like "*KE*" And Not Like "*LD*" And Not Like "*LH*"		
or:			

Figure 8.68: Negative wildcard conditions in a single field joined with *AND*

Using the conditions displayed in Figure 8.68, the Query finds records of cars that are not registered in Kildare *and* are not registered in Longford *and* are not registered in Louth (a total of 17 records). Because the conditions are negative, they must be joined with *AND*.

Multiple negative conditions in a single field must be joined with *AND*. Using *OR* will result in the Query finding all records in the Table, as the conditions will cancel each other out.

As negative wildcard Queries involving multiple conditions in a single field are quite complex, it is best to build up these Queries one condition at a time. Run the Query with one condition. When you are satisfied that this condition works correctly, go back to design view and add the next condition. Continue adding and testing conditions one at a time until the Query is complete.

Combining Positive and Negative Wildcard Conditions

Sometimes a wildcard Query may give unexpected results. Consider the Query condition in Figure 8.69. At first glance, it would appear that this condition will find records of Dublin registered cars.

Field:	Reg No	Engine Size
Table:	Test Details	Test Details
Sort:		
Show:	☑	☑
Criteria:	Like "*D*"	
or:		

Figure 8.69: Wildcard search for the letter D in the *Reg No* field

However, when the Query is run, it also finds Donegal and Longford registrations. This is because the *DL* of the Donegal registrations includes the letter *D*, as does the Longford registration of *LD*. Two additional conditions are required to exclude the Donegal and Longford registrations, as shown in Figure 8.70.

Field:	Reg No	Engine Size
Table:	Test Details	Test Details
Sort:		
Show:	☑	☑
Criteria:	Like "*D*" And Not Like "*DL*" And Not Like "*LD*"	
or:		

Figure 8.70: Wildcard search for registrations including the letter D but excluding LD and DL

Using the conditions displayed in Figure 8.70, the Query finds records of cars that are registered in Dublin *and* are not registered in Donegal *and* are not registered in Longford (a total of 10 records).

The negative version of this Query, i.e. which finds all cars except for those registered in Dublin, is quite complex.

Field:	Model	Reg No
Table:	Test Details	Test Details
Sort:		
Show:	☑	☑
Criteria:		Not Like "*D*"
or:		

Figure 8.71

The Query condition in Figure 8.71 finds seven records. It excludes the 10 Dublin registrations. However, it also excludes the three Donegal registrations and the three Longford registrations, as both Donegal and Longford registrations include the letter *D*. Two additional conditions are required to ensure that the Donegal and Longford registrations are found by the Query (Figure 8.72).

Field:	Model	Reg No
Table:	Test Details	Test Details
Sort:		
Show:	☑	☑
Criteria:		Not Like "*D*" Or Like "*DL*" Or Like "*LD*"
or:		

Figure 8.72

The additional conditions in Figure 8.72 ensure that the Query finds all the cars registered outside of Dublin, including those registered in Donegal and Longford (a total of 13 records). As the additional conditions in Figure 8.72 are positive conditions, they must be joined to the first condition using the *OR* logical operator.

POTENTIAL PROBLEMS WITH WILDCARDS

Many students have problems understanding when to use a wildcard and when not to use a wildcard. You should only use a wildcard in a Query when part of the search term is missing. Don't use a wildcard in any other circumstances. Some important points relating to wildcards are listed below.

1. Don't use a wildcard when you have all the information you need to create a Query condition. For example, when searching for records of Opel Corsas, the Query condition is "*Corsa*" and not "**Corsa**".

Field:	Make	Model
Table:	Test Details	Test Details
Sort:		
Show:	☑	☑
Criteria:		Like "*Corsa*"
or:		

Figure 8.73: Incorrect use of wildcard

Field:	Make	Model
Table:	Test Details	Test Details
Sort:		
Show:	☑	☑
Criteria:		"Corsa"
or:		

Figure 8.74: Correct Query condition

Figure 8.74 displays the correct Query condition required to search for records of Opel Corsas. Figure 8.73 is incorrect due to the unnecessary use of the wildcard (*). Although "**Corsa**" works and finds the correct number of records, there is no need to use the wildcard, as we have all the information needed to create the Query condition. Using wildcards unnecessarily will affect your overall understanding of the correct use of Query conditions.

2. Don't get confused between <> and *Not Like*. <> doesn't work with wildcard Queries.

Field:	Model	Reg No
Table:	Test Details	Test Details
Sort:		
Show:	☑	☑
Criteria:		<>"*KE*"
or:		

Figure 8.75: Incorrect Query condition

Field:	Model	Reg No
Table:	Test Details	Test Details
Sort:		
Show:	☑	☑
Criteria:		Not Like "*KE*"
or:		

Figure 8.76: Correct Query condition

The condition <> ***"*KE*"*** in Figure 8.75 doesn't have any effect. When the Query is run, it finds all 23 records, including records of cars registered in Kildare. Negative wildcard Queries require the *Not* logical operator. The correct search condition is *Not Like "*KE*"* (Figure 8.76).

CREATE WILDCARD QUERIES

Create a separate Query for each of the tasks described in Table 8.17.

- Sort each Query using the sort order specified.
- Use the *Show* row of the Query design grid to specify the fields displayed by each Query.
- Save each Query using the name provided.

	Purpose of Query	Sort Order	Fields in Query	Query Name	Records Found
Task 16	Find records of cars whose owner's surname doesn't begin with O	Ascending order of Surname	Firstname, Surname, Address1, Address2, Address3, Cost, Paid	Surname does not begin with O	21
Task 17	Find records of Dublin registered cars	Ascending order of Reg No	Make, Model, Reg No, Engine Size, Firstname, Surname	Dublin registered cars	10
Task 18	Find records of cars except for those registered in Dublin, Kildare and Longford	Ascending order of Reg No	Reg No, Make, Model, Engine Size, Firstname, Surname	Excluding Dublin Kildare and Longford	8
Task 19	Find records of cars that were not registered in Longford where the owner's address does not end with the words Road, Court or Drive	Ascending order of Address1	Reg No, Make, Model, Firstname, Surname, Address1, Address2, Address3	Address search excluding Longford	9
Task 20	Find records of cars where the registration does not end with 1, 2 or 3	Ascending order of Reg No	Reg No, Make, Model, Engine Size, Firstname, Surname	Registration does not end with 1 2 or 3	13

Table 8.17

The records found by the Query in Task 18 should include the two Donegal cars.

FIND, EDIT AND ADD RECORDS

Task 21: Open the *Southside Motor Tests Bookings* Form. Use the *Find*, *Delete Record* and *New Record* buttons to make the following changes.

When searching for records, Access needs to match the search term exactly. Searching for *Joe Murphy* will not find any records. Either select the *Firstname* text box control and search for *Joe* or select the *Surname* text box control and search for *Murphy*.

1. Joe Murphy's test result is Fail.
2. Hugh Watson's car registration is 09C2096.
3. Stephen Mc Carthy's test time has been changed to 11:30.
4. Martin Brennan's address is 15 Greenfort Close.
5. Verify that Joe Murphy's record:

Completed (√)

- Is now found by the *Failed tests* Query. ☐
- Is now displayed in the *List of Failed Tests* Report. ☐

6. Verify that Martin Brennan's record: **Completed (√)**
   - Is now found by the *Address search excluding Longford* Query. ☐

7. Add the record displayed in Table 8.18 to the database, making the following changes to the *Southside Motor Tests Bookings* Form.
   - Edit the *Make* combo box to include *Smart* in the list. ☐
   - Add *0.6* to the *Engine Size* combo box. ☐

Edit the *Row Source* property of each combo box.

Test Number	24
Date of Test	05/06/14
Time of Test	11:30
Test Type	Retest
Reg No	10C8871
Make	Smart
Model	City-Coupe
Engine Size	0.6
Firstname	Lucasz
Surname	Orlinski
Address1	28 The Rise
Address2	Dun Laoghaire
Address3	Co. Dublin
Odometer	41998
Cost	€47.00
Test Result	Pass
Notes	
Paid	Yes
Photo	smart10.jpg

Table 8.18

8. Verify that the Smart car is found by the following Query. **Completed (√)**
   - *Except Ford and 1 litre* ☐
9. Verify that the Smart car is displayed by the following Report.
   - *Test Schedule* ☐

CREATE QUERIES

Create a separate Query for each of the tasks described in Table 8.19.

- Sort each Query using the sort order specified.
- Use the *Show* row of the Query design grid to specify the fields displayed by each Query.
- Save each Query using the name provided.

	Purpose of Query	Sort Order	Fields in Query	Query Name	Records Found
Task 22	Find records of cars registered in Cork	Ascending order of Reg No	Make, Model, Reg No, Engine Size, Firstname, Surname	Cork registered cars	2
Task 23	Find records of cars registered in Clare	–	Make, Model, Reg No, Engine Size, Firstname, Surname	Clare registered cars	1

Table 8.19

LEARN ABOUT PARAMETER QUERIES

Up to now we have created Queries by typing specific conditions in the Query design grid.

Field:	Make	Model	Reg No
Table:	Test Details	Test Details	Test Details
Sort:			
Show:	☑	☑	☑
Criteria:	"Ford"		
or:			

Figure 8.77: A Query to find Ford cars

When the Query displayed in Figure 8.77 is run, it finds records of Ford cars. The problem with this Query is that were we to search for other manufacturers, a separate Query would be required for each manufacturer.

Field:	Make	Model	Reg No
Table:	Test Details	Test Details	Test Details
Sort:			
Show:	☑	☑	☑
Criteria:	"Honda"		
or:			

Figure 8.78: A Query to find Honda cars

In Figure 8.78, a second Query has been created to find Honda cars. To find all of the car manufacturers using this method, six separate Queries would be required. The conditions displayed in Figures 8.77 and 8.78 are static – they never change. A dynamic condition can be created using a Parameter Query. Dynamic conditions allow us to prompt the database user for input. This means that we could search for all six car manufacturers using a single Query.

Field:	Make	Model	Reg No
Table:	Test Details	Test Details	Test Details
Sort:			
Show:	☑	☑	☑
Criteria:	[Enter make of car]		
or:			

Figure 8.79: A Parameter Query uses a dynamic condition

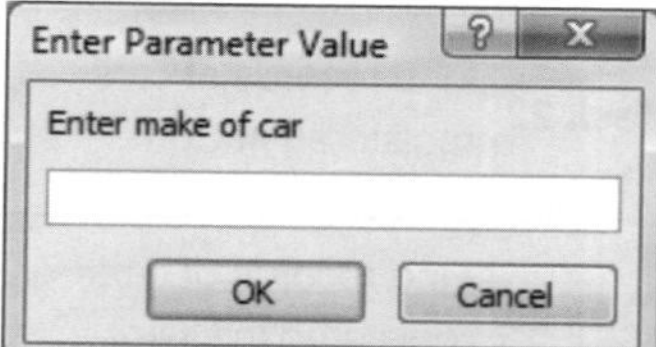

Figure 8.80: Dialog box displayed when the Parameter Query in Figure 8.79 is run

Figure 8.79 is a Parameter Query because the condition is enclosed in square brackets. Because of the square brackets, Access doesn't treat it as a standard Query condition. Instead, it displays the text enclosed in the brackets as a message in an *Enter Parameter Value* dialog box (Figure 8.80) when the Query is run.

Any make of car can be entered in the dialog box displayed in Figure 8.80. Having used the Query to find Ford cars, we could run it again and enter Honda in the dialog box to find Honda cars. Instead of creating six separate Queries to find Ford, Honda, Nissan, Opel, Smart and Toyota cars, all the car manufacturers can now be found using a single Parameter Query.

Parameter Queries work very well when data is repeated in a particular field. In the Southside Motor Tests database, a Parameter Query could be used to find records of cars according to engine size (1.0, 1.3, 1.4, 1.6, 1.8, 2.0, 3.0). A second Parameter Query could be created to find records of cars based on the *Address2* field (Blackrock, Deansgrange, Dun Laoghaire, Killiney, Shankill).

Parameter Queries are also useful when searching for a specific record.

Field:	Firstname	Surname	Address1	Address2	Address3
Table:	Test Details	Test Details	Test Details	Test Details	Test Details
Sort:				Ascending	
Show:	☑	☑	☑	☑	☑
Criteria:	[Enter first name]	[Enter surname]			
or:					

Figure 8.81: A Parameter Query that will prompt the database user to enter a specific name

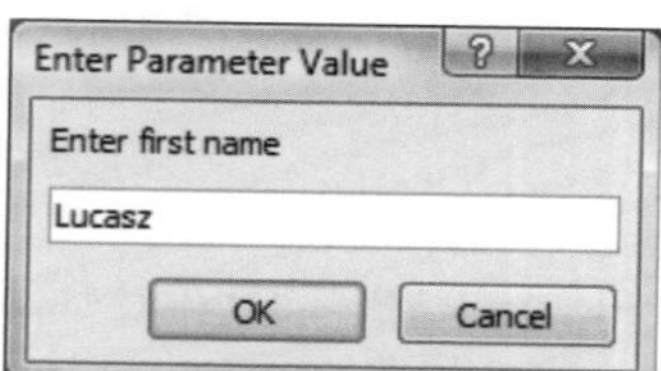

Figure 8.82

The Query displayed in Figure 8.81 has two parameter conditions. When the Query is run, the dialog boxes will be displayed in sequence. As the *[Enter first name]* parameter is displayed first in the Query design grid, the database user is first prompted to enter the first name of the person they are searching for (Figure 8.82).

In Figure 8.82, *Lucasz* has been entered as the first

name. The database user is now prompted by a second dialog box (Figure 8.83), corresponding to the *[Enter surname]* condition in Figure 8.81.

In Figure 8.83, the database user has entered *Orlinski* as the surname. Once the database user clicks *OK*, the Query will search for the record where the Firstname is *Lucasz* and the Surname is *Orlinski*.

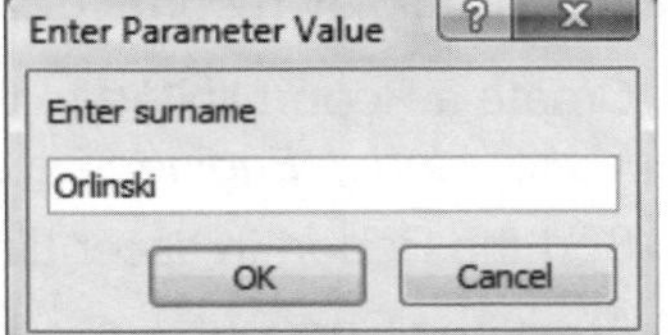

Figure 8.83

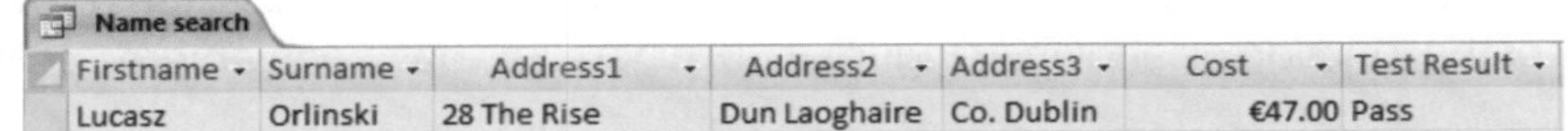
Name search

Firstname	Surname	Address1	Address2	Address3	Cost	Test Result
Lucasz	Orlinski	28 The Rise	Dun Laoghaire	Co. Dublin	€47.00	Pass

Figure 8.84: Single record found by the parameter conditions in Figure 8.81

The Query finds Lucasz Orlinski's record, which is displayed in Figure 8.84.

CREATE PARAMETER QUERIES

Create a separate Query for each of the tasks described in Table 8.20. Save each Query using the name provided. Test each Query by running it a number of times, entering a different value in the *Enter Parameter Value* dialog box on each occasion.

	Purpose of Query	Sort Order	Fields in Query	Query Name	Records Found
Task 24	Prompt the database user with the message *Enter client location* and then display records corresponding to the location entered, e.g. Blackrock, Deansgrange	Ascending order of Date of Test	Date of Test, Firstname, Surname, Address1, Address2, Address3, Test Result	Find clients by location	Blackrock ....8 Deansgrange ....3 Dun Laoghaire ..5 Killiney ....4 Shankill..............4
Task 25	Prompt the database user with the message *Enter test result* and then display records corresponding to the test result entered, e.g. Pass, Fail or Fail Advisory	Ascending order of Test Type	Date of Test, Test Type, Reg No, Make, Model, Engine Size, Firstname, Surname, Test Result	Records by test result	Pass..................14 Fail.....................6 Fail Advisory 4
Task 26	Prompt the database user with the message *Enter first name* followed by the message *Enter surname*. Display the record corresponding to the first name and surname entered.	–	Firstname, Surname, Address1, Address2, Address3, Paid	Name search	1

Table 8.20

Task 27: Display records of vehicles matching the result entered.

- Create a Report linked to the *Records by test result* Query. Include the *Date of Test, Make, Model, Engine Size* and *Test Result* fields in the Report.
- Sort the Report in ascending order of *Date of Test*.
- Apply the *Concourse* style to the Report.
- The Report title is *Analysis of Test Results*.
- Calculate the number of vehicles using an appropriate Report function. Format the result of the function as shown in Figure 8.85, where *Fail* has been entered as the test result.

Analysis of Test Results

Date of Test	Make	Model	Engine Size	Test Result
03/06/2014	Nissan	Micra	1.0	Fail
03/06/2014	Ford	Ka	1.3	Fail
03/06/2014	Opel	Astra	1.6	Fail
04/06/2014	Nissan	Qashqai	2.0	Fail
04/06/2014	Ford	Mondeo	1.6	Fail
05/06/2014	Ford	Focus	1.6	Fail

Number of Vehicles: **6**

Figure 8.85: Completed Report for Task 27

LEARN ABOUT GROUPED REPORTS

Grouping is an advanced form of sorting. In a grouped Report, records are in ascending or descending order of the grouped field. However, each value in the grouped field is only displayed once.

Test Schedule by Make

Make	Model	Engine Size	Registration	Date of Test	Test Result
Ford					
	Fiesta	1.3	10LD1095	05/06/2014	Pass
	Fiesta	1.3	07D1556	03/06/2014	Fail Advisory
	Focus	1.6	09C2096	04/06/2014	Pass
	Focus	1.6	10DL22011	05/06/2014	Fail
	Focus	1.4	07D14933	04/06/2014	Pass
	Ka	1.3	07D44981	03/06/2014	Fail
	Mondeo	1.6	09D10648	04/06/2014	Pass
	Mondeo	1.6	08LD8087	04/06/2014	Fail
Honda					
	Civic	1.3	06D201	03/06/2014	Fail Advisory
	Civic	1.8	09WW480	04/06/2014	Fail Advisory
Nissan					
	Micra	1.3	07D639	04/06/2014	Pass
	Micra	1.0	08LH8002	03/06/2014	Fail
	Primera	1.8	07WW692	03/06/2014	Pass
	Qashqai	2.0	08DL2018	04/06/2014	Fail

Figure 8.86: An extract from a Report grouped by the *Make* field

The Report in Figure 8.86 is grouped by the *Make* field. Each *Make* is listed once. Records associated with a particular *Make* are listed below the relevant heading. One of the advantages of grouping a Report is the ability to perform calculations on the records in individual groups. For example, in Figure 8.86, we could use the Count function to calculate the total number of Fords, Hondas and Nissans.

Test Schedule by Make

Make	Model	Engine Size	Registration	Date of Test	Test Result
Ford					
	Fiesta	1.3	10LD1095	05/06/2014	Pass
	Fiesta	1.3	07D1556	03/06/2014	Fail Advisory
	Focus	1.6	09C2096	04/06/2014	Pass
	Focus	1.6	10DL22011	05/06/2014	Fail
	Focus	1.4	07D14933	04/06/2014	Pass
	Ka	1.3	07D44981	03/06/2014	Fail
	Mondeo	1.6	09D10648	04/06/2014	Pass
	Mondeo	1.6	08LD8087	04/06/2014	Fail
	Total:	8			
Honda					
	Civic	1.3	06D201	03/06/2014	Fail Advisory
	Civic	1.8	09WW480	04/06/2014	Fail Advisory
	Total:	2			
Nissan					
	Micra	1.3	07D639	04/06/2014	Pass
	Micra	1.0	08LH8002	03/06/2014	Fail
	Primera	1.8	07WW692	03/06/2014	Pass
	Qashqai	2.0	08DL2018	04/06/2014	Fail
	Total:	4			

Figure 8.87: The Count function calculates the number of records in each group

In Figure 8.87, the Count function is used to calculate the number of records in each group. The function is created in the *Group* footer. There are eight Fords, two Hondas and four Nissans. The ability to perform calculations on individual groups of records is the main advantage of grouped Reports. It is not possible to do this in a sorted Report.

Calculations can also be added to the Report footer in a grouped Report. The calculations performed by functions created in the Report footer will be applied to *all* the records in the Report. Calculations in the Report footer are displayed immediately after the last record in the Report (Figure 8.88).

Toyota					
	Landcruiser	3.0	08KE2948	04/06/2010	Pass
	Prius	1.6	07KE3398	03/06/2010	Pass
	Yaris	1.0	07KE6791	04/06/2010	Pass
	Yaris	1.6	09CE41209	05/06/2010	Fail Advisory
Total: 4					
Overall Total: 24					

Figure 8.88: A Count function in the Report footer calculates that there are 24 records overall

Figure 8.88 shows the last group in the Report. The total for Toyota is four. This has been calculated by a Count function positioned in the *Group* footer. The overall total of 24 applies to all of the records in the Report and has been calculated by a Count function positioned in the Report footer.

WHEN CAN YOU CREATE A GROUPED REPORT?

You can create a grouped Report as long as data is repeated in at least one field in the Table. In the *Test Details* table, data is repeated in the *Date of Test, Test Type, Make, Model, Engine Size, Address2* and *Test Result* fields. We could create separate grouped reports using each of these fields. The number of groups displayed in the Report depends on the number of values occurring in the grouped field. For example, a Report grouped on the *Test Type* field would contain two groups: Full and Retest. A Report grouped on the *Test Result* field would contain three groups: Fail, Fail Advisory and Pass.

SECTIONS OF A GROUPED REPORT

To date we have seen that an Access Report consists of up to five separate sections:

1. Report header
2. Page header
3. Detail
4. Page footer
5. Report footer

A grouped Report has two additional sections – the group header and the group footer. These appear immediately before and after the detail, as follows:

1. Report header
2. Page header
3. ***Group header***
4. Detail
5. ***Group footer***
6. Page footer
7. Report footer

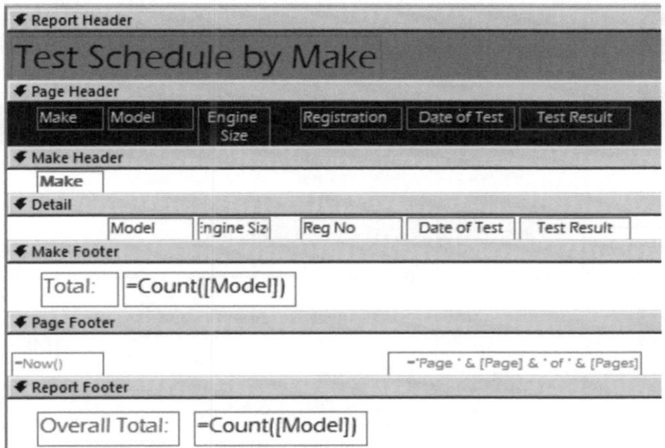

Figure 8.89: A grouped Report has two extra sections

Figure 8.89 shows the *Test Schedule by Make* Report in design view. As this Report has been grouped by the *Make* field, there are two additional sections – the *Make* header and the *Make* footer. Data in the *Make* header and footer will appear once for each value in the *Make* field. The *Make* header contains a label, which produces the headings Ford, Honda, Nissan, Opel, Smart and Toyota. The Count function in the *Make* footer calculates six different totals, one for each of the different car manufacturers. The Count function in the Report footer counts *all* the records displayed in the Report.

Figure 8.90 demonstrates how the sections of a grouped Report are positioned on the page.

- The Report header and page header appear at the top of the page, as normal.
- The Report in Figure 8.90 is grouped by *Make*. As there are six individual makes, this Report is divided into six groups. Each *Make* is listed once – Ford, Honda, Nissan, Opel, Smart and Toyota. This text is in the *Make* header.
- Each *Make* is then followed by its own detail section. The detail section occurs six times in Figure 8.90, once for each group.
- Each of the six detail sections is followed by the *Make* footer. This contains a Count function, which calculates the number of records in each respective group.
- The Report footer appears once after the last record in the Report. The Count function in the Report footer applies to *all* the records in the Report.
- The page footer appears at the bottom of the page. It displays the date and the page number.

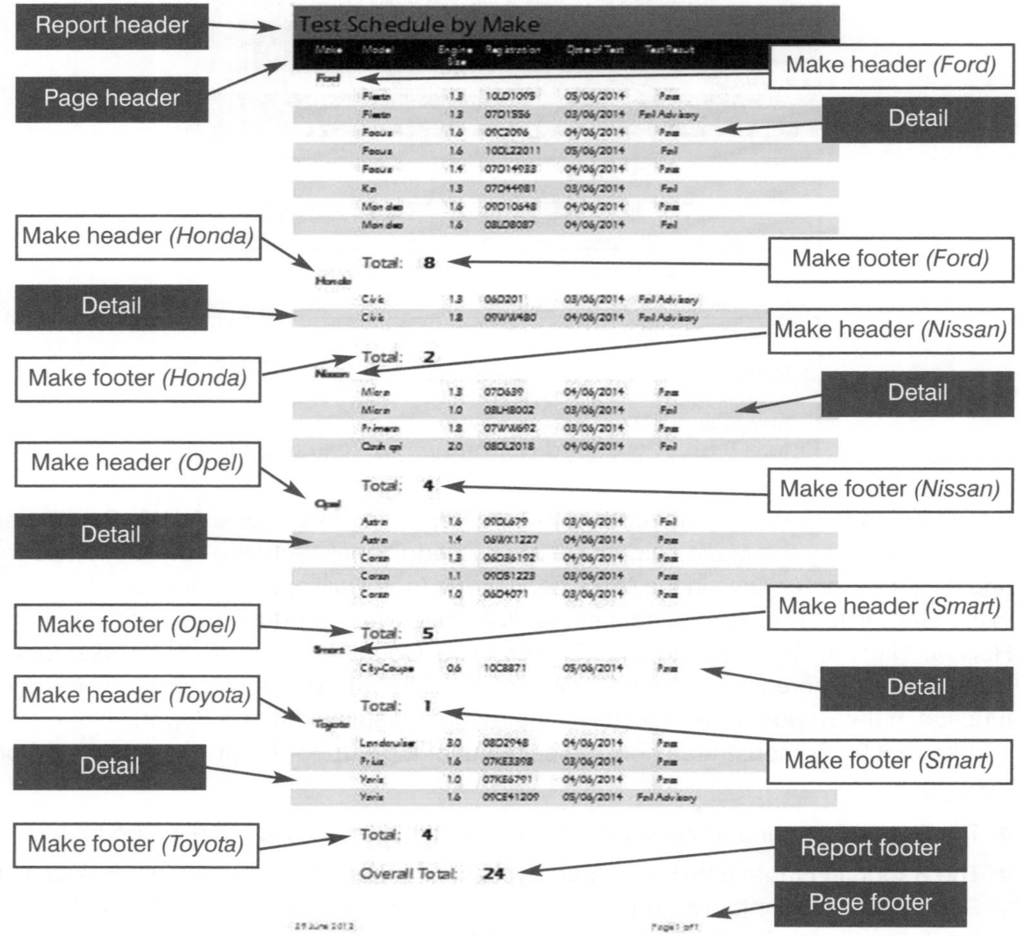

Figure 8.90: Sections of a grouped Report

WORKED EXAMPLE: CREATE A GROUPED REPORT

1. Using the Report Wizard, create a new Report, linked to the *Test Details* Table.
2. Add the *Make, Model, Engine Size, Reg No, Date of Test* and *Test Result* fields to the Report.
3. Group the Report by the *Make* field.

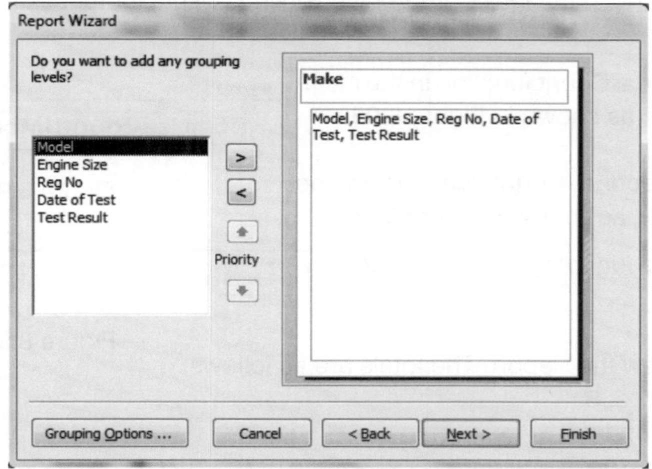

Figure 8.91: The Report will be grouped by the *Make* field

Select *Make* in the list of fields on the left and then click the single right arrow. The *Make* field is displayed in bold print above the other fields in the Report, as shown in Figure 8.91. This indicates that the Report will be grouped by the *Make* field.

4. Sort the records in ascending order of *Model*. This means that the records in each group will be in alphabetical order of *Model*. In the example, the Fords will be listed as Fiesta, Focus, Ka and Mondeo.
5. Select *Stepped* as the layout and *Portrait* as the orientation.
6. Apply the *Concourse* style to the Report.
7. The Report title is *Test Schedule by Make.*
8. View the Report in layout view. Adjust the width of the text boxes so that the Report appears like Figure 8.87 on page 219.
9. Edit the *Reg No* label so that it reads *Registration.*
10. Adjust the *Engine Size* label so that it wraps across two lines.

11. View the Report in design view.

12. Click the *Group & Sort* button. The Group, Sort, and Total Pane is displayed (Figure 8.92).

13. Click the *More* button to display all the settings of the *Make* group. The *Make* group is currently listed as "without a footer section".

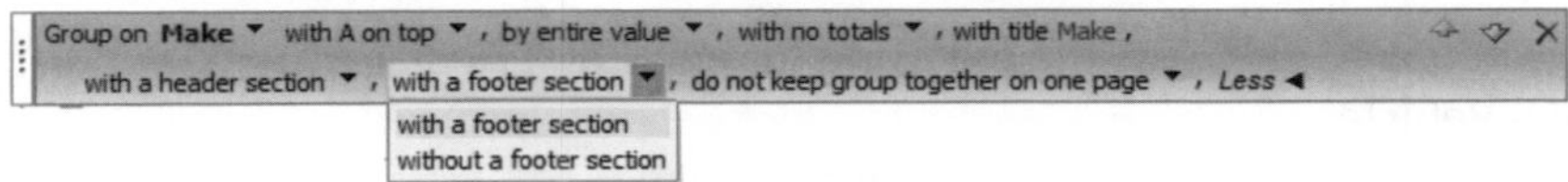

Figure 8.92: Adding a *Make* footer to the Report

Add a group footer to the *Make* group by selecting "with a footer section", as shown in Figure 8.92.

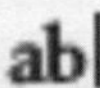

14. Create a Count function in the *Make* footer, as shown in Figure 8.93.

Figure 8.93

15. Create a second Count function in the Report footer, as shown in Figure 8.94.

Copy the function from the *Make* footer.

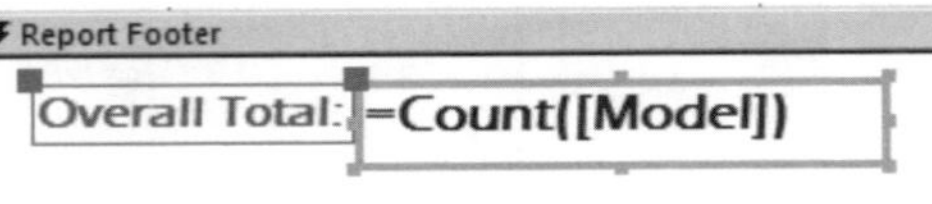

Figure 8.94

16. Preview the Report. The totals are as follows:
    - Ford: 8
    - Honda: 2
    - Nissan: 4
    - Opel: 5
    - Smart: 1
    - Toyota: 4
    - The overall total is 24

17. Save the *Test Schedule by Make* Report.

CREATE GROUPED REPORTS

Task 28: Display test result statistics.

- Create a Report linked to the *Test Details* Table.
- Include the *Test Result, Make, Model, Odometer, Engine Size* and *Reg No* fields in the Report.
- Group the Report by *Test Result.*
- Sort the Report using the following sorting levels:
  1. Ascending order of *Make.*
  2. Ascending order of *Model.*
  3. Descending order of *Odometer.*
- Apply the *Concourse* style to the Report.
- The Report title is *Test Results Statistics.*
- Edit the *Reg No* label so that it reads *Registration.*
- In the *Test Result* header, increase the font size of the *Test Result* text box to 12.
- Add functions to calculate the following for each *Test Result:*
  1. Total Vehicles.
  2. Average Kilometres (use the *Odometer* field).
  3. Max Kilometres.
  4. Min Kilometres.

- Format the *Average Kilometres* text box so that the result is displayed with 0 decimals.
- Sample output from this Report is displayed in Figure 8.95.

Test Result Statistics

Test Result	Make	Model	Odometer	Engine Size	Registration
Fail					
	Ford	Focus	25602	1.6	10DL22011
	Ford	Ka	45289	1.3	07D44981
	Ford	Mondeo	25913	1.6	08LD8087
	Nissan	Micra	27966	1.0	08LH8002
	Nissan	Qashqai	19438	2.0	08DL2018
	Opel	Astra	22759	1.6	09DL679

Total Vehicles: **6**

Average Kilometres: **27833**

Max Kilometres: **45289**

Min Kilometres: **19438**

Figure 8.95: Sample output from the *Test Result Statistics* Report (Task 28)

- Export the *Test Results Statistics* Report to a PDF document.

Task 29: Display test result statistics by date.

- Create a Report linked to the *Test Details* Table.
- Include the *Date of Test, Test Result, Test Type, Make, Model, Odometer, Engine Size* and *Reg No* fields in the Report.
- Group the Report using the following grouping levels:
  1. Date of Test.
  2. Test Result.

Grouping Options ...

Select **Date of Test by Month**. Click the *Grouping Options* button and change the grouping level of the *Date of Test* field from *Month* to *Day*, as shown in Figure 8.96. Click *OK*.

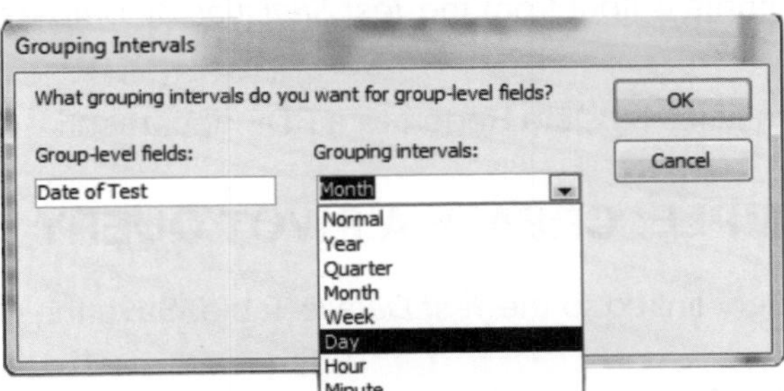

Figure 8.96: Changing the grouping interval of the *Date of Test* field

- Sort the Report using the following sorting levels:
  1. Ascending order of *Test Type.*
  2. Ascending order of *Make.*
  3. Ascending order of *Model.*
  4. Descending order of *Odometer.*
- Apply the *Concourse* style to the Report.
- The Report title is *Test Statistics by Date.*
- Edit the *Date of Test by Day* label so that it reads *Date of Test.*
- Edit the *Reg No* label so that it reads *Registration.*
- In the *Date of Test* header, increase the font size of the *Date of Test* text box to 12.
- Add functions to calculate the following for each *Date of Test:*
  1. Total Vehicles.
  2. Average Kilometres.
- Format the *Average Kilometres* text box so that the result is displayed with 0 decimals.
- Ensure that individual groups are not split across two pages.
- Sample output from this Report is displayed in Figure 8.97.

Test Statistics by Date

Date of Test	Test Result	Test Type	Make	Model	Odometer	Engine Size	Registration
03 June 2014							
	Fail						
		Full	Ford	Ka	45289	1.3	07D44981
		Full	Nissan	Micra	27966	1.0	08LH8002
		Full	Opel	Astra	22759	1.6	09DL679
	Fail Advisory						
		Full	Honda	Civic	35007	1.3	06D201
		Retest	Ford	Fiesta	25510	1.3	07D1556
	Pass						
		Full	Nissan	Primera	32019	1.8	07WW692
		Full	Toyota	Prius	15418	1.6	07KE3398
		Retest	Opel	Corsa	63544	1.0	06D4071
		Retest	Opel	Corsa	12045	1.1	09D51223

Total Vehicles: **9**

Average Kilometers: **31062**

Figure 8.97: Sample output from the *Test Statistics by Date* Report (Task 29)

- Export the Test Statistics by Date Report to a PDF document.

WORKED EXAMPLE: CREATE A PIVOT QUERY

1. Create a new Query linked to the *Test Details* Table. Save the Query as *Test Result Analysis by Make*.
2. Add all fields to the Query design grid.
3. In the Home section of the Ribbon, select *PivotTable View* from the View drop-down menu (Figure 8.98).

4. Drag the *Make* field from the PivotTable Field List and drop on the text "*Drop Row Fields Here*".
5. Drag the *Test Type* field and drop on the text "*Drop Column Fields Here*" (Figure 8.99).

Figure 8.98

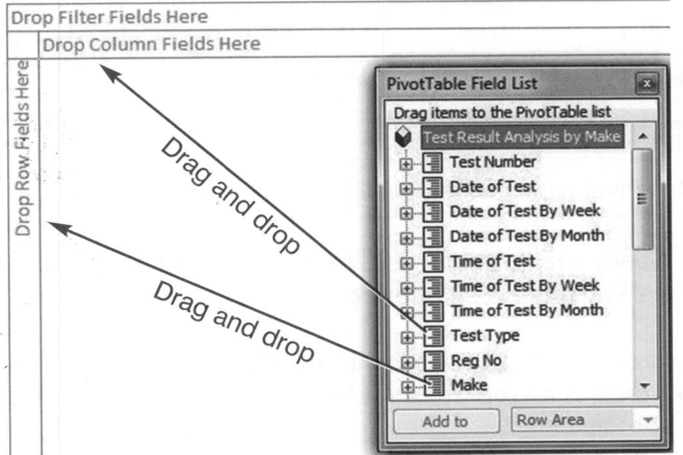

Figure 8.99: Using the PivotTable Field List to build a PivotTable Query

6. Drag the *Test Result* field from the PivotTable Field List and drop on the text "*Drop Totals or Detail Fields Here*". Access builds the pivot table shown in Figure 8.100.

The pivot table in Figure 8.100 breaks down the *Test Results* for each *Make* of car by *Test Type*. For example, there were three retests for Ford cars, which resulted in one test result of fail advisory and two passes.

7. Right click on the first *Test Result* column heading in the PivotTable Grid. Select *AutoCalc* and then *Count* from the pop-up menu. Access calculates the number of full tests and retests by *Make*, as shown in Figure 8.101, which is an extract from the PivotTable Query.

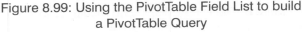

Drop Filter Fields Here

	Test Type		
	Full	Retest	Grand Total
Make	Test Result	Test Result	No Totals
Ford	Fail	Fail Advisory	
	Pass	Pass	
	Fail	Pass	
	Pass		
	Fail		
Honda	Fail Advisory		
	Fail Advisory		
Nissan	Pass		
	Fail		
	Pass		
	Fail		
Opel	Fail	Pass	
	Pass	Pass	
		Pass	
Smart			
Toyota	Pass		
	Pass		
	Fail Ac		
Grand Total			

Figure 8.100:

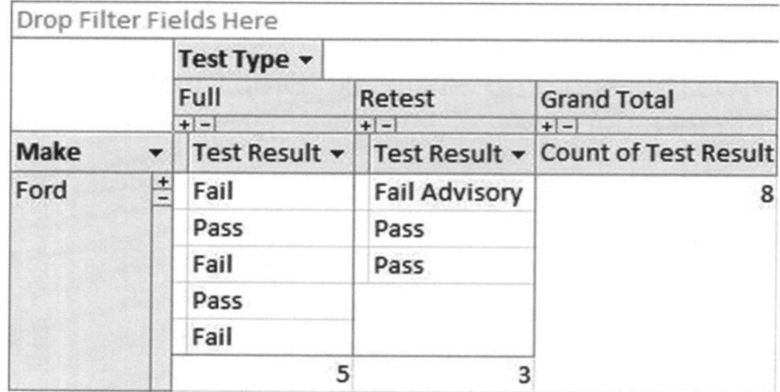

Drop Filter Fields Here

	Test Type		
	Full	Retest	Grand Total
Make	Test Result	Test Result	Count of Test Result
Ford	Fail	Fail Advisory	8
	Pass	Pass	
	Fail	Pass	
	Pass		
	Fail		
	5	3	

Figure 8.101: Pivot table including a Count function

In Figure 8.101, we can now clearly see that eight Ford cars were tested. Five of these cars had full tests and the remaining three were retested.

8. Drag the *Date of Test* field from the PivotTable Field List and drop on the text "*Drop Filter Fields Here*". Access creates a drop-down list for the *Date of Test* field, which can be used to focus on specific dates.
9. Click the *Date of Test* drop-down arrow and untick the *05/06/2014* check box. Click *OK*. The updated pivot table (Figure 8.102) is now displaying results of six Ford cars. It is excluding the two Fords that were tested on 05/06/2014.

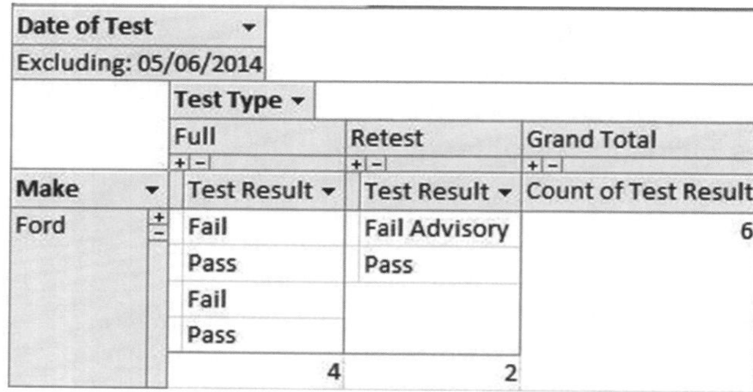

Date of Test
Excluding: 05/06/2014

	Test Type		
	Full	Retest	Grand Total
Make	Test Result	Test Result	Count of Test Result
Ford	Fail	Fail Advisory	6
	Pass	Pass	
	Fail		
	Pass		
	4	2	

Figure 8.102: Date of Test has been added as a filter field

10. In the Home section of the Ribbon, select *PivotChart View* from the View drop-down menu. Using the data displayed in the pivot table in Figure 8.102, Access builds the chart shown in Figure 8.103.

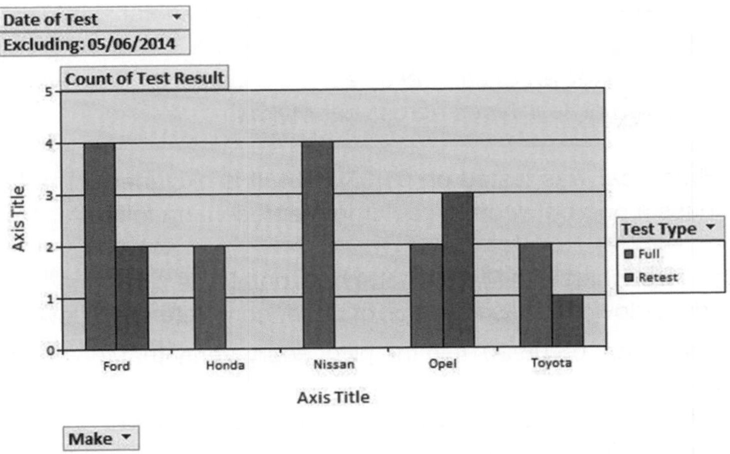

Figure 8.103: A pivot chart is built from data stored in the pivot table

Viewing data in PivotChart View makes it easier to compare values. A PivotChart is a powerful analysis tool allowing detailed analysis.

11. Right click the vertical axis title and select *Properties* from the pop-up menu. Select the Format tab and change the caption to *Number of Tests*.
12. Delete the caption for the horizontal axis.
13. Display the properties of the Chart Workspace by right clicking anywhere in the white space surrounding the plot area. Click the *Add Title* button in the Properties sheet. Right click the text *Chart Workspace Title*. Select the Format tab in the Properties sheet and enter *Test Result Analysis by Make* as the caption.
14. In the Design section of the Ribbon, click the *Switch Row/Column* button. The pivot chart now appears like Figure 8.104.

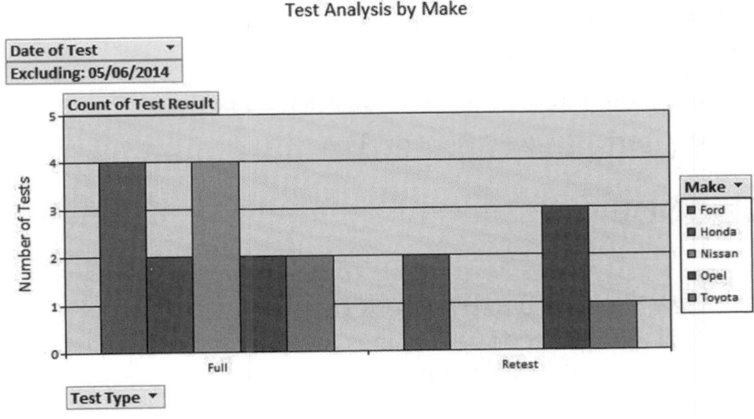

Figure 8.104: Pivot chart with titles and axis labels. Rows and columns have been switched

In Figure 8.104, test types are now displayed on the horizontal axis. This allows us to view the same data from a different perspective. In Figure 8.103, the pivot chart allows us to analyse the breakdown of car *Makes* across a particular *Test Type.* Figure 8.104 shows the breakdown of *Test Types* across car *Makes*.

N As the Smart car was tested on 05/06/2014, it is excluded from the pivot chart. This causes a gap between the columns representing full tests.

15. Display the pivot chart with *Make* on the horizontal axis.
16. Using the drop-down menus in the pivot chart, complete the following tasks:
    - Include data from 05/06/2014 in the pivot chart. Verify that the chart has updated as follows:
      The number of full tests for Ford cars has increased to five.
      The number of full tests for Toyota cars has increased to three.
      An extra column has been added for Smart.
      Untick the check boxes for Honda, Smart and Nissan. Verify that the pivot chart is now displaying data relating to Ford, Opel and Toyota only.
17. Save the *Test Result Analysis by Make* Query.

Task 30: Create a PivotTable Query setting up the PivotTable Grid as follows:

- Add *Address2* as the row field.
- Add *Date of Test* as the column field.
- Add *Cost* as the detail field.
- Calculate the total cost by *Address2* and by *Date of Test.*
- Add *Make* as the Filter field.
- Remove Ford from the results. Verify that the Grand Total for 03/06/2014 has decreased from €549 to €434.
- Display Ford in the results and view the pivot table in PivotChart view.
- Change the vertical axis title to *Revenue Generated*.
- Remove the horizontal axis title.
- Add a chart title, entering the text *Revenue Analysis by Area*.
- Save the Query as *Revenue Analysis by Area.*

EDIT SQL CODE

Task 31

SQL

1. View the *Kildare Registrations* Query in SQL view.
2. Edit the SQL code so that the Query finds Donegal registered cars only.
3. Run the Query and verify that it finds three records of cars registered in Donegal.
4. Close the Query without saving it.

Task 32

SQL

1. View the *Surname does not begin with O* Query in SQL view.
2. Edit the SQL code so that the Query finds records of owners whose surname does not begin with M.
3. Run the Query and verify that it finds 18 records.
4. Close the Query without saving it.

Task 33

SQL

1. View the *Except for Nissan and Honda* Query in SQL view.
2. Edit the SQL code so that the Query also excludes Ford cars.

Copy part of the existing condition.

3. Run the Query and verify that it finds 10 records.
4. Close the Query without saving it.

Task 34: Using the table of contents in Access Help, search for articles on Query Criteria. Write a brief report outlining the use of wildcards in both positive and negative Query conditions.

DEFINE DATABASE STRUCTURE

Task 35: Complete the database structure form (Table 8.21) with data types and field sizes for all fields in the *Test Details* Table.

Field Name	Data Type	Field Size
Test Number		
Date of Test		
Time of Test		
Test Type		
Reg No		
Make		
Model		
Engine Size		
Firstname		

Table 8.21

Field Name	Data Type	Field Size
Surname		
Address1		
Address2		
Address3		
Cost		
Photo		
Odometer		
Test Result		
Notes		
Paid		

Table 8.21 (continued)

Ensure that the field sizes of Text fields specified in design view of the *Test Details* Table match those specified in the database structure form.

REVIEW YOUR WORK

Use the checklist below to verify that you have completed all the tasks in the Southside Motor Tests database.

		Completed (√)
Table:	• Test Details	☐
Form:	• Southside Motor Tests Bookings	☐
Queries:	• 2008 cars	☐
	• Address search excluding Longford	☐
	• Clare registered cars	☐
	• Clients who passed but have not paid	☐
	• Cork registered cars	☐
	• Dublin registered cars	☐
	• Except Ford 1 litre	☐
	• Except Nissan and Toyota	☐
	• Excluding Dublin Kildare and Longford	☐
	• Failed tests	☐

Completed (√)

- Find clients by location ☐
- Kildare registrations ☐
- Name search ☐
- Not paid ☐
- Records by test result ☐
- Revenue analysis by area ☐
- Registration does not end with 1 2 or 3 ☐
- Surname does not begin with O ☐
- Test passes over 40000 kilometres ☐
- Test result analysis by make ☐
- Test result of fail or fail advisory ☐

Reports:

- Accounts Due ☐
- Analysis of Test Results ☐
- List of Failed Tests ☐
- Test Notification Labels ☐
- Test Result Statistics ☐
- Test Schedule ☐
- Test Schedule by Make ☐
- Test Statistics by Date ☐
- Vehicle List by Make ☐

Other:

- Database structure form ☐

ASSIGNMENT SUMMARY

Basic Concepts	
Attachment Data Type	Used to store a picture, sound file, Word document or Excel file in a database. Attaching a file to a record is similar to attaching a file to an email.
Autonumber	A field type where Access automatically allocates a unique number to each record in the Table. It is useful in databases that store records of transactions, particularly when there is a high volume of transactions. A field with an Autonumber data type is usually set as the primary key field.
Default Value	A value that is automatically entered in a specific field in the Table. It is useful when many of the records have the same value in a particular field and can save time by reducing the amount of data entry. In the Southside Motor Tests database, the default value for the *Address3* field was set to *Co. Dublin*, as all the clients live in Co. Dublin.
Grouped Report	Grouping is an advanced form of sorting. Data in a grouped field is displayed in ascending order. However, each grouped value is only displayed once, above the associated records. In terms of Report design, this value is in the group header. Calculations can be performed on individual groups of records by creating functions in the group footer. Calculations can be applied to all the records in a grouped Report by creating functions in the Report footer.
Mail Merge	A process where data stored in an Access Table or Query is combined with a document created in a word processing application to produce a personalised letter or email for each record stored in the Table or for each record found by the Query. There are four steps in the mail merge process: 1. Create the document. 2. Create the data source. 3. Insert merge fields from the data source into the main document. 4. Merge the main document with the data source.
Multiple Sort	An Access Report can be sorted by up to four fields. You can continue adding sorting levels to a Report as long as there are repeated items in the previously sorted field. Sort fields can be specified either in the Report Wizard or by using the *Group & Sort*

	button in layout view. The advantage of sorting a Report in layout view is that the results of the sort are instantly visible. Although a Report can also be sorted in design view, you will have to preview the Report to see the results of the sort.
Negative Query Conditions	<> is used with standard Query conditions. For example, <>*Ford* finds records of cars except for those manufactured by Ford. **Not** is used with wildcard conditions. For example, *Not Like "*CE*"* finds records of cars except for those registered in Clare. To join negative conditions in multiple fields, simply position all the conditions in the criteria line of the Query design grid. Multiple negative conditions in a single field are joined with the *AND* logical operator. If you mistakenly use *OR* to join negative conditions in a single field, the Query will find all the records in the Table, as the conditions will cancel each other out.
Parameter Query	A dynamic Query that prompts the database user for input. Parameter Queries are useful where a limited number of items are repeated in a field. For example, the *Make* field in the Southside Motors database stores either Ford, Honda, Nissan, Opel, Smart or Toyota. Instead of creating six separate Queries (one for each make), all the makes can be found using a single Parameter Query. The Parameter Query will prompt the database user to enter a particular make and then display records for that make. Parameter Queries use square brackets: *[Enter make of car]* is an example of a parameter.
Report Functions	Used to perform calculations on the records displayed in a Report. The most common Report functions are as follows. *SUM* Adds values in a field *AVG* Calculates the average of values in a field *COUNT* Counts the number of times data occurs in a particular field *MAX* Finds the highest value in a field *MIN* Finds the lowest value in a field Fields referred to by Report functions must by enclosed in square brackets, e.g. *=SUM([Cost])* Report functions can be created in the Report footer or in the group footer. Calculations performed by Report functions created in the Report footer appear once at the end of the Report and are based on all the records in the Report. Calculations in the group footer appear a number of times in the Report and are based on each group of records in the Report.

Wildcards	Used to find records in a Query when some of the search data is missing. For example, a wildcard could be used to find records of customers whose surname includes *Mc* or to find PPS numbers including the letter *X*. The star (*) is used as the wildcard symbol and represents the data that is missing. For example: Jack* Finds records of people whose first name is *Jack* *Mc* Finds records of people whose name includes the letters *Mc* *X Finds all PPS numbers ending with *X*

Potential Pitfalls

- If you mistakenly join negative conditions in a single field using the *OR* logical operator, the Query will find all the records in the Table.
- Wildcards should only be used in situations where some of the search data is missing. For example, 10DL* would find Donegal cars registered in 2010. In all other circumstances, wildcards should not be used. When searching for Nissan cars, wildcards are not necessary, as all the search data is available. "**Nissan**" is incorrect. "*Nissan*" is the correct search condition.
- <> doesn't work with negative wildcard Queries. The *Not* logical operator is used instead. *<>"*LD*"* will not find any records. *Not Like "*LD*"* is the correct search condition.
- You can only add another sorting level to a Report when items are repeated in the previously sorted field. In a Report sorted by *Test Number*, where all the test numbers are unique, it is impossible to add a second-level sort.
- When creating Report functions, an incorrectly spelled field name will cause an error. The field name must be typed in the Report function *exactly* as it appears in the field list. Even an extra space will cause an error!
- Report functions don't work when they are created in the page footer. Access will display the *#Error* message when the Report is previewed.
- In a Report function, the square brackets should always be inside the curved brackets. If you mix up the order of brackets, Access will display an error message. If you leave out the round brackets, the result of the function will not be displayed in the Report.
- Grouping a Report doesn't have any meaningful effect unless data is repeated in the grouped field.

Log on to www.gillmacmillan.ie to download review questions for Assignment 8.

9 Southern Estate Agents Database

SCENARIO

Southern Estate Agents, based in south Dublin, is a busy estate agent specialising in the residential market. Customers regularly ring the office asking for details of properties available in specific areas. Due to the antiquated filing system, it takes some time to retrieve the information required by customers. Customers are often put on hold or have to be contacted at a later time once the information has been retrieved. In Assignment 9, you will create a database to keep track of the properties that Southern Estate Agents have for sale. The database will enable the staff of Southern Estate Agents to quickly and efficiently deal with customer enquiries.

By completing this assignment, you will learn how to:

- Check the accuracy of data entry using validation.
- Use the tab control in a Form.
- Create functions in a Form.
- Search for records using a Form filter.
- Create a Totals Query.
- Create a Crosstab Query.
- Use *Is Null* and *Is Not Null* in a Query.
- Create a Crosstab Report.
- Create a calculated field in a Report.
- Create a dynamic Report title.
- Create a relationship between two Tables.
- Display data from two Tables in a Report.

DOWNLOAD PHOTOS

To complete this assignment, you will need to download photos from the Gill & Macmillan website. To download the photos, follow these steps.

1. Log on to www.gillmacmillan.ie.
2. Click the 'Education' link.
3. Search for *Step by Step Databases* using the search box in the top right-hand corner of the web page.
4. In the search results, select *Step by Step Databases 3rd Edition*.
5. Click either the *Lecturer Resources* or the *Student Resources* link.
6. Click the link to download the photos.

CREATE THE DATABASE AND SET UP THE TABLE

Task 1: Create a new database named *Southern Estate Agents.*
Task 2: Create a new Table and save the Table as *Property Details.*

- Using the data displayed in Table 9.1, create fields with appropriate data types in the *Property Details* Table.

Property Number	1
Client First Name	Adam
Client Surname	Delaney
Address1	Beachview House
Address2	Killiney
Address3	Co. Dublin
Client Contact Number	(086) 2889876
Price	€725,000
Property Type	Semi-Detached House
No of Bedrooms	4
Parking	Yes
Alarm	Yes
Description	A substantial four bed semi-detached family residence, situated in a mature development
Highest Offer	
Date Sale Completed	
Photo	

Table 9.1

- The data type of the *Highest Offer* field is Currency. Data will be added to the *Highest Offer* and *Date Sale Completed* fields later on in this assignment.
- Set the *Property Number* field as the primary key.
- Set the data type of the *Photo* field to Attachment.
- Set the *Required* property to *Yes* for all fields except for *Property Number*, *Parking*, *Alarm*, *Highest Offer, Date Sale Completed* and *Photo.*
- Set the default value of the *Address3* field to *Co. Dublin.*

- Set the field size of the *Address2, Address3, Client Contact Number* and *Property Type* fields to exactly match the data in Table 9.5 on page 248.
- Set the *Format* property of the *Price* field to *Currency* and the *Decimal Places* property to *0*.
- Set up separate indexes on the *Address2* field and the *Property Type* field.

- Save the *Property Details* Table.

LEARN ABOUT DATA VALIDATION

Data entry errors can have serious consequences in a database. A single spelling mistake will often cause multiple errors. For example, entering *Kiliney* instead of *Killiney* in the *Address2* field would cause the following errors:

- Any Query that includes *Killiney* as a condition in the *Address2* field will not find the record with the spelling error. The record will also be missing in any Reports linked to Queries searching for *Killiney.*
- In all grouped Reports, the *Killiney* properties will be split into two groups: *Killiney* and *Kiliney.*
- The spelling error will appear in all Reports linked to the *Property Details* Table.

Field Name	Data Type
No of Bedrooms	Number

General | Lookup

Field Size	Byte
Format	
Decimal Places	Auto
Input Mask	
Caption	
Default Value	
Validation Rule	Between 1 And 5
Validation Text	Number of bedrooms must be between 1 and 5 inclusive
Required	Yes
Indexed	No
Smart Tags	
Text Align	General

Figure 9.1: Creating a validation rule for the *No of Bedrooms* field

As you can see, a single spelling mistake at the data entry stage can cause many errors in Queries and Reports. This is why it is so important to check data for accuracy as it is entered in the database. The process whereby data entry is checked is called data validation. By specifying validation rules for specific fields, the number of data entry errors is reduced. The validation rule acts like a bouncer on the door of a nightclub – data that doesn't satisfy a validation rule will not be allowed into the Table. Access will display an error message and you will have to try to enter the data again. Although validation can reduce the number of errors, it cannot trap every error.

Validation is implemented in the Table. Each field can have one validation rule. However, it would be unusual to have a validation rule for every field in the Table. In practice, validation rules are only created for fields where data in the field either falls within defined limits or follows a pattern. For example, we could say the following about data stored in the *No of Bedrooms* field:

- The number can't be negative.
- The number can't be zero.
- The number will be less than or equal to 5 (most residential properties would tend to have five or fewer bedrooms).

We can use this information to create a validation rule for the *No of Bedrooms* field (Figure 9.1).

In Figure 9.1, the validation rule *Between 1 and 5* has been set up for the *No of Bedrooms* field. This means that any numbers less than 1 or greater than 5 will not be allowed into this field. If you attempt to enter a number that breaks the validation rule, Access will not allow the data entry and will display the error message shown in Figure 9.2.

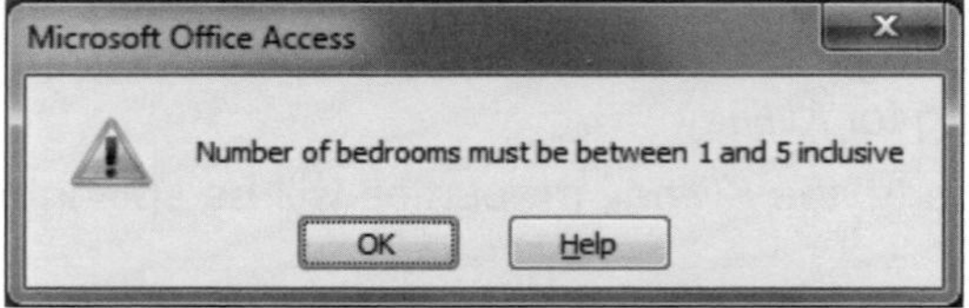

Figure 9.2: Error message displayed when the validation rule in Figure 9.1 is broken

It is not possible to create validation rules for fields with a data type of either Autonumber or Attachment.

EXAMPLES OF VALIDATION RULES

Logical Operator	Validation Rule	Effect on Values Entered in Field
Less than	<100	Must be less than 100
Less than or equal to	<=20	Must be 20 or less
Equal to	=5	The only number allowable is 5 (in practice, it would be unusual to have a use for this type of validation rule)
Not equal to	<>2	The number 2 cannot be entered
Greater than	>50	Must be greater than 50
Greater than or equal to	>=25000	Must be greater than or equal to 25000
Between	Between #01/10/2015# and #31/10/2015#	Must be between 01/10/2015 and 31/10/2015 inclusive
Or	"Region 1" or "Region 2" or "Region 3"	The only values that can be entered are Region 1, Region 2 or Region 3
And, <>	<> "USA" and <> "Canada"	Prevents USA and Canada from being entered

Table 9.2: Logical operators are combined with numbers or text to create validation rules in Number, Currency, Date/Time and Text fields

Creating a validation rule is similar to creating a condition in a Query. Logical operators are used to create validation rules for fields with Number, Currency, Date/Time or Text data types. Examples of validation rules with logical operators are displayed in Table 9.2.

A validation rule in a Currency field should never include the euro symbol.

Data in Text fields can also be validated using wildcards. Examples of validating Text fields using wildcards are shown in Table 9.3.

Validation Rule	Effect on Values Entered in Field
Like Co.*	Data entered in the field must start with "Co.", e.g. Co. Dublin, Co. Wicklow, Co. Wexford
Like *H	All product codes entered must end with "H"

Table 9.3

TESTING A VALIDATION RULE

Each time you create a validation rule in design view of the Table, you should test the rule by entering dummy data in datasheet view of the Table. First, enter data that doesn't break the rule. Verify that this data can be entered in the Table. Press the *Esc* key to cancel the data entry. Now enter data that breaks the validation rule. Verify that Access will not allow this data to be entered and that the correct error message is displayed. Press *Esc* again to cancel the data entry.

Access Tables are not designed to facilitate easy data entry. It is OK to test your validation rules in the Table. Once you have finished testing the validation rules, enter the data using a Form. Each text box in the Form is linked to a specific field in the Table. You will be prevented from entering data in a text box when the data entered breaks the validation rule in the corresponding field in the Table.

WORKED EXAMPLE: CREATE VALIDATION RULES

1. Open the *Property Details* Table in design view.
2. Enter the validation rule and validation text for the *No of Bedrooms* field as shown in Figure 9.3.

3. Save the *Property Details* Table.

4. View the Table in datasheet view.
5. Tab across to the *No of Bedrooms* field.
6. Type *6* in the *No of Bedrooms* field. Press *Enter*. Access displays the error message and will not accept the data entry. Click *OK* and press *Esc* twice to cancel the data entry.

7. View the *Property Details* Table in design view. Enter ***Like "Co.*"*** as a validation rule for the *Address3* field. Enter ***All county names begin with Co.*** as the validation text.

8. Save the *Property Details* Table.

9. View the Table in datasheet view.
10. Tab across to the *Address3* field.
11. Enter *Wicklow* in the *Address3* field. Access will not accept this entry. Click *OK* and press *Esc* twice to cancel the data entry.
12. Enter *Co Wicklow* (i.e. without the full stop). Access won't accept this entry either. Cancel the data entry.
13. Close the *Property Details* Table.

Field Name	Data Type
No of Bedrooms	Number

General | Lookup

Field Size	Byte
Format	
Decimal Places	Auto
Input Mask	
Caption	
Default Value	
Validation Rule	Between 1 And 5
Validation Text	Number of bedrooms must be between 1 and 5 inclusive
Required	Yes
Indexed	No
Smart Tags	
Text Align	General

Figure 9.3: Validation rule and validation text for the *No of Bedrooms* field

WORKED EXAMPLE: USE THE TAB CONTROL TO DIVIDE A FORM INTO PAGES

Because there are a lot of fields in the *Property Details* Table, arranging them all on a Form would make the Form appear cramped, particularly as the *Description* text box control will require a lot of space on the Form. The solution is to use the tab control, which allows us to divide a Form into pages.

1. Create a blank Form using the Create tab in the Ribbon. (Note: Do not use the Form Wizard.) A Form without any fields added is required for the tab control.

2. View the Form in design view.

3. Display the properties of the Form by clicking the *Property Sheet* button in the Design section of the Ribbon. In the *Record Source* property, select *Property Details* from the drop-down list. This links the newly created Form to the *Property Details* Table.

4. Click the *Title* button in the Design section of the Ribbon. Type *Properties For Sale* in the newly created label box.

5. Adjust the width and height of the Form so that it takes up the full screen. Grab the bottom edge of the Form footer and drag upwards so that it is not displayed.

If the Form is too wide, a horizontal scroll bar will be displayed at the bottom of the Form. If the Form is too tall, a vertical scroll bar will be displayed on the right-hand side. Adjust the width and height until the scroll bars disappear.

6. Click the *Tab Control* button in the Design section of the Ribbon. Draw a box in the Detail section (Figure 9.4). Adjust the size of the box so that it occupies the entire detail section.

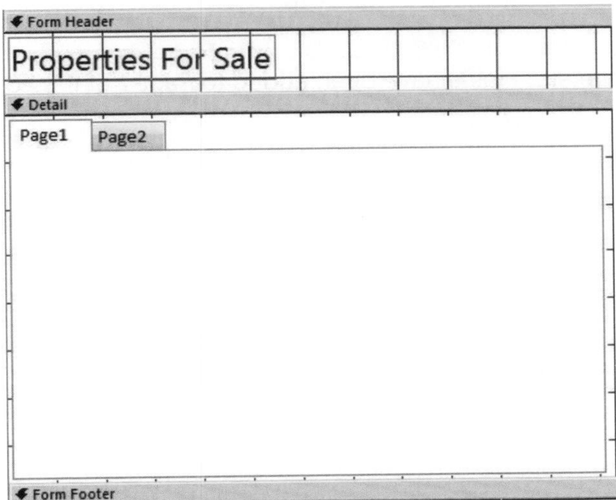

Figure 9.4: The tab control divides the Form into two pages

7. In the Design section of the Ribbon, click the *Add Existing Fields* button. Individual fields are added to the Page 1 section by dragging each field from the field list and then dropping it in *Page1*. Add the fields shown in Figure 9.5 to *Page1* of the Form.

8. Delete the *Client Surname* label and edit the *Client Firstname* label so that it reads *Client*.
9. Add fields to *Page2* of the Form, as shown in Figure 9.6.

Move the check box controls for the *Parking* and *Alarm* fields so that they are displayed on the right-hand side of the label boxes.

10. Save the Form as *Properties For Sale.*

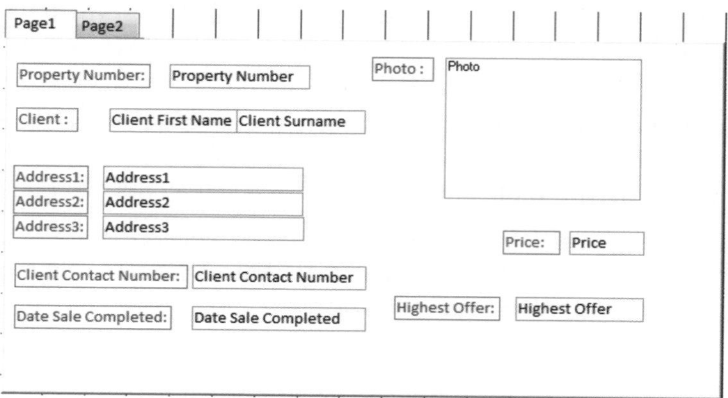

Figure 9.5: Fields have been added to *Page1* of the Form

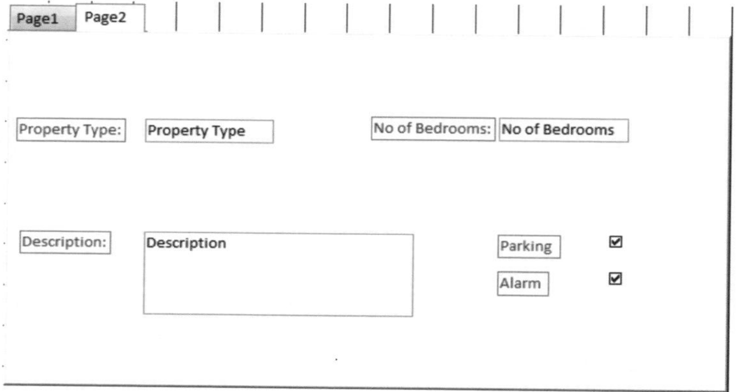

Figure 9.6: Fields have been added to *Page2* of the Form

Task 3: In *Page1*, create a combo box for the *Address3* field. In *Page2*, create combo boxes for the *Property Type* and *No of Bedrooms* fields. The values to be displayed in each combo box are shown in Table 9.4.

Address3 (Combo Box)	Property Type (Combo Box)	No of Bedrooms (Combo Box)
Co. Dublin	Detached House	5
Co. Wicklow	Semi-Detached House	4
	Terraced House	3
	Apartment	2
		1

Table 9.4

- Set the *Limit to List* property of all combo boxes to *Yes*.
- Set the *Allow Value List Edits* property of all combo boxes to *No*.
- In the properties of the *Property Type* combo box, increase the *List Width* property to 3.8 cm (1.5 inches). This ensures that the combo box list is wide enough to display all the property types in the list.
- Set the alignment of the *Property No, Client Contact Number, Date Sale Completed, Price, Highest Offer* and *No of Bedrooms* text box controls to *Center.*

You can select multiple text box controls by holding down the *Shift* key while clicking.

- In *Page1*, delete the *Address2* and *Address3* labels. Edit the *Address1* label so that it reads *Address*.
- Delete the *Photo* label.
- Edit the *Price* label so that it reads *Offers in the region of.*
- Set the *Tab Stop* property of the *Property Number* text box control to *No*. (This prevents the cursor from moving to the *Property Number* text box – it doesn't need to, as it's an Autonumber.)
- Set the *Decimal Places* property to *0* for both the *Price* and *Highest Offer* text boxes.
- In *Page2*, edit the *No of Bedrooms* label so that it reads *Bedrooms.*
- Increase the size of the *Description* text box (see Figure 9.6).
- Click the *Page1* tab. In the property sheet, change the *Name* property from *Page1* to *Sales Details* and select the address book image in the *Picture* property.

If the image does not display correctly, you will need to download a service pack for Office 2007 from the Microsoft website.

- Change the *Name* property of the *Page2* tab to *Property Features*. Select the key image as the *Picture* property.
- Format the *Price* text box using a font size of *14*, a font weight of *bold,* a font colour of *red* and a background colour of *light grey.*
- Format the *Highest Offer* text box using a font size of *14,* a font weight of *bold* and a background colour of *light grey.*
- Increase the height of the *Price* and *Highest Offer* text box controls to accommodate the data.
- Set the *Border Color* property of all label boxes in the *Sales Details* and *Property Features* pages to *#FFFFFF.*

#FFFFFF is the hexadecimal code for white.

- Set the *Border Color* property of all text box controls in the *Sales Details* and *Property Features* pages to *Borders/Gridlines.*
- In the Form header, format the text *Properties for Sale* using a font style of *Berlin Sans FB Demi* and a font size of *36*. Wrap the text in the label box and set the alignment to *Center* so that it appears like Figure 9.7.

- Set the *Back Color* property of the Form header to *Background Light Header.*
- Set up the company name, address and logo in the Form header as shown in Figure 9.7, using appropriate clip art and label boxes. (If you can't find the exact clip art image, a similar one will do.)
- The completed Form should look something like Figure 9.7 and Figure 9.8.

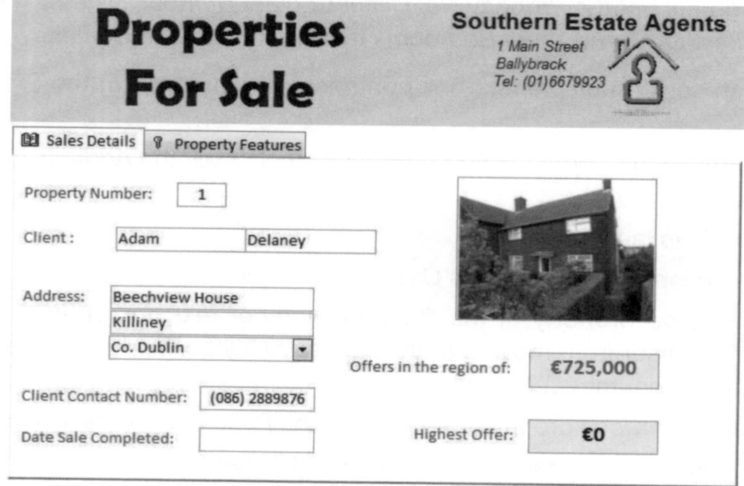

Properties For Sale
Southern Estate Agents
1 Main Street
Ballybrack
Tel: (01)6679923
Sales Details
Property Features
Property Number: 1
Client : Adam Delaney
Address: Beechview House
Killiney
Co. Dublin
Offers in the region of: €725,000
Client Contact Number: (086) 2889876
Date Sale Completed:
Highest Offer: €0

Figure 9.7: Sales Details section of the *Properties for Sale* Form

Properties For Sale
Southern Estate Agents
1 Main Street
Ballybrack
Tel: (01)6679923
Sales Details
Property Features
Property Type: Semi-Detached House
Bedrooms: 4
Description: A substantial four bed semi-detached family residence, situated in a mature development
Parking
Alarm

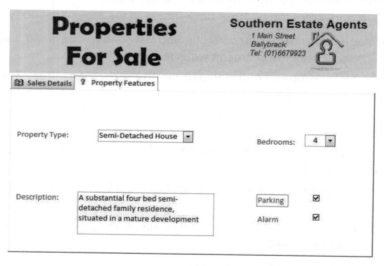

Figure 9.8: Property Features section of the *Properties for Sale* Form

Task 4: In the *Sales Details* page, set the tab order to *Property Number, Client First Name, Client Surname, Address1, Address2, Address3, Client Contact Number, Price, Photo, Highest Offer, Date Sale Completed.*

Fields will not be displayed in the tab order list unless at least one text box is selected before you view the tab order.

Task 5: In the Property Features page, set the tab order to *Property Type, No of Bedrooms, Parking, Alarm, Description*.

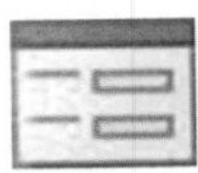

- Save the *Properties For Sale* Form.

ENTER DATA

Task 6: Using the *Properties for Sale* Form, enter all the records displayed in Table 9.5.

- Click the Property Features tab to enter data in the *Property Type*, *No of Bedrooms*, *Parking*, *Alarm* and *Description* fields.
- Data will be entered in the *Highest Offer* and *Date Sale Completed* fields at a later stage.
- Click the *New Record* button to advance the Form to each new record.
- If necessary, adjust the width of text boxes, using layout view, as you enter the data.

For a detailed explanation of how to enter data in an Attachment field, refer to pages 173–4 in Assignment 8.

Property Number	Client First Name	Client Surname	Address1	Address2	Address3	Client Contact Number	Price	Photo	Property Type	No of Bedrooms	Parking	Alarm	Description
1	Adam	Delaney	Beachview House	Killiney	Co. Dublin	(086) 2889876	€725,000	beachview.jpg	Semi-Detached House	4	Yes	Yes	A substantial 4 bed semi-detached family residence, situated in a mature development
2	Joan	Murphy	3 Corbawn Terrace	Shankill	Co. Dublin	(01) 2986017	€425,000	3corbawn.jpg	Semi-Detached House	3	Yes	No	Extensive range of kitchen floor and wall units
3	Pauline	Byrne	23 Seaview Park	Dun Laoghaire	Co. Dublin	(01) 2883011	€475,000	23seaview.jpg	Semi-Detached House	3	Yes	No	A spacious semi-detached 3 bedroom property situated in a quiet cul-de-sac
4	Daniel	Murphy	Rose Lawn	Sandycove	Co. Dublin	(087) 2786581	€495,000	roselawn.jpg	Terraced House	2	No	No	Rare opportunity to purchase this well presented 2 bedroom terraced house retaining many of its original features
5	Peter	Looney	16 Wolverton Grove	Shankill	Co. Dublin	(087) 2685509	€585,000	16wolverton.jpg	Detached House	4	Yes	Yes	No. 16 boasts excellent gardens to front and rear, and a wonderful sunny westerly orientation
6	Carl	O Donnell	4 Martello Road	Dalkey	Co. Dublin	(01) 2785002	€925,000	4martello.jpg	Terraced House	2	No	No	This is an impressive period terraced house of immense character situated in a quiet cul-de-sac

Table 9.5

Property Number	Client First Name	Client Surname	Address1	Address2	Address3	Client Contact Number	Price	Photo	Property Type	No of Bedrooms	Parking	Alarm	Description
7	Fiona	Stapleton	27 Abbey Lane	Dun Laoghaire	Co. Dublin	(085) 2581162	€495,000	27abbey.jpg	Apartment	1	Yes	No	Superbly positioned ground floor 1 bedroom apartment offering superior space and an imaginative design
8	Tadhg	Donovan	12 Bayview Mews	Glasthule	Co. Dublin	(086) 2682297	€590,000	12bayview.jpg	Semi-Detached House	3	Yes	No	A truly delightful modern family home presented with impeccable taste in this much sought after development
9	Jack	Dunne	1 Richmond Close	Killiney	Co. Dublin	(01) 2584029	€499,000	1richmond.jpg	Apartment	2	Yes	No	Spacious modern apartment with parking
10	Ian	McShane	3 Eden Terrace	Monkstown	Co. Dublin	(01) 2789942	€335,000	3eden.jpg House	Terraced	2	No	No	Ideally located brick built, town residence situated in a quiet mews laneway
11	Philip	Donovan	28 Rockford Manor	Bray	Co. Wicklow	(086) 2480002	€379,000	28rockford.jpg	Semi-Detached House	3	Yes	Yes	Situated in a quiet cul-de-sac, the property is within walking distance of Bray Shopping Centre
12	Gerry	O Neill	28 Dorney Road	Dun Laoghaire	Co. Dublin	(086) 2889783	€495,000	28dorney.jpg	Semi-Detached House	3	Yes	No	A most attractive and exclusive residential property
13	Anthony	Murphy	136 O Flynn Park	Bray	Co. Wicklow	(087) 2788850	€455,000	1360flynn.jpg	Semi-Detached House	3	Yes	Yes	A wonderfully presented family home located in this quiet, extremely attractive modern development

Table 9.5 (continued)

Property Number	Client First Name	Client Surname	Address1	Address2	Address3	Client Contact Number	Price	Photo	Property Type	No of Bedrooms	Parking	Alarm	Description
14	Roisin	Murray	122 Plunkett Road	Shankill	Co. Dublin	(01) 2781010	€330,000	122plunkett.jpg	Terraced House	3	No	No	Modern mid-terrace brick fronted townhouse
15	Garreth	Moore	46 Ashlawn Grove	Stillorgan	Co. Dublin	(01) 2786033	€299,000	46ashlawn.jpg	Terraced House	3	Yes	Yes	Conveniently situated within a stroll of shops and all amenities
16	Geraldine	Walsh	38 Seaview Court	Stillorgan	Co. Dublin	(01) 2682912	€249,000	38seaview.jpg	Apartment	2	No	No	No. 38 is a garden level 2 bed apartment within a large modern apartment complex
17	Paul	Mc Carthy	22 Anville Wood	Dun Laoghaire	Co. Dublin	(087) 2281994	€595,000	22anville.jpg	Detached House	5	Yes	Yes	Exceptionally spacious 5 bedroom detached family home
18	Andrew	Collins	101 Westgrove	Glasthule	Co. Dublin	(01) 2283076	€895,000	101westgrove .jpg	Detached House	4	Yes	Yes	Tucked away in this quiet, mature cul-de-sac development lies this spacious family home with a wonderfully sunny southerly rear garden
19	Neil	Conlon	28 Millwood Downs	Bray	Co. Wicklow	(085) 2086789	€465,000	28millwood.jpg	Semi-Detached House	4	Yes	Yes	Superbly renovated 4 bedroom home with sea views
20	Tommy	Dunne	7 Allen Park Road	Dalkey	Co. Dublin	(086) 2282055	€525,000	7allenpark.jpg	Semi-Detached House	3	Yes	Yes	Boasting superb landscaped gardens, this is a most attractive 3 bedroom semi-detached family residence

Table 9.5 (continued)

LEARN ABOUT SUMMARISING DATA WITH A TOTALS QUERY

A Totals Query is a more advanced form of Query. It allows us to do calculations on data stored in the Table using database functions. Totals Queries perform summary calculations based on records stored in the Table. Results of the calculations are displayed in a single row.

Unlike Select Queries, a Totals Query doesn't display records. Instead, it returns a single row of data (Figure 9.9). The data displayed by the Totals Query depends on the functions selected in the Query design grid.

MaxOfPrice	MinOfPrice	AvgOfPrice
€925,000.00	€249,000.00	€511,800.00

Figure 9.9: Output from a Totals Query

Field:	Price	Price	Price
Table:	Property Details	Property Details	Property Details
Total:	Max	Min	Avg
Sort:			
Show:	☑	☑	☑
Criteria:			
or:			

Figure 9.10: Design view of a Totals Query

Figure 9.10 shows the design of the Query displayed in Figure 9.9. Three separate functions are used in this Query. Each function does its calculations on the *Price* field, using all the records in the *Property Details* Table.

1. The Max function displays the price of the most expensive property (€925,000).
2. The Min function displays the price of the cheapest property (€249,000).
3. The Avg function calculates the average price of a property (€511,800).

Totals Queries can also perform summary calculations based on *groups* of records stored in the Table. Results of the calculations are displayed in multiple rows.

Address2	MaxOfPrice	MinOfPrice	AvgOfPrice
Bray	€465,000.00	€379,000.00	€433,000.00
Dalkey	€925,000.00	€525,000.00	€725,000.00
Dun Laoghaire	€595,000.00	€475,000.00	€515,000.00
Glasthule	€895,000.00	€590,000.00	€742,500.00
Killiney	€725,000.00	€499,000.00	€612,000.00
Monkstown	€335,000.00	€335,000.00	€335,000.00
Sandycove	€495,000.00	€495,000.00	€495,000.00
Shankill	€585,000.00	€330,000.00	€446,666.67
Stillorgan	€299,000.00	€249,000.00	€274,000.00

Figure 9.11: Output from a Totals Query grouped by the *Address2* field

The Query in Figure 9.11 has been grouped by the *Address2* field. Instead of displaying a single row of calculations based on all the records in the Table, it now displays nine rows of calculations – one row for each of the nine towns stored in the *Address2* field. The results of the calculations are displayed in ascending order of *Address2*.

Unlike a standard Select Query, a Totals Query is not used to find records.

WORKED EXAMPLE: CREATE A TOTALS QUERY

1. Create a new Query in design view.
2. Add the *Property Details* Table to the Query.

3. Click the *Totals* button in the Design section of the Ribbon. This adds a Total row to the Query design grid. The Total row appears immediately above the Sort row.

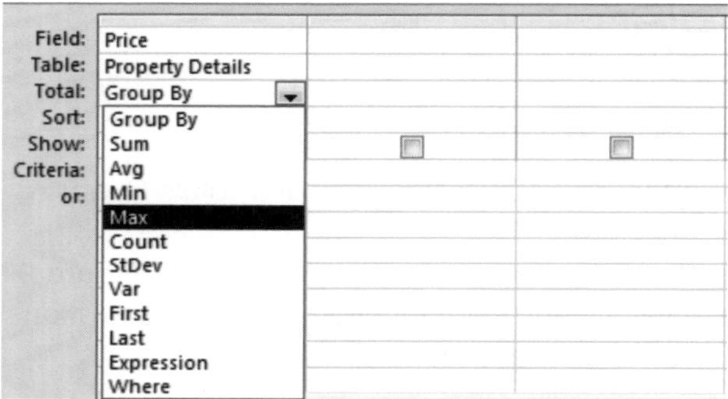

Figure 9.12: Selecting the Max function for the *Price* field

4. In the first column of the Query design grid, select *Price* as the field and then select *Max* from the *Total* drop-down list of functions, as shown in Figure 9.12.

5. Run the Query. A single item – the highest number stored in the *Price* field – is displayed (Figure 9.13). This is the price of the terraced house in Dalkey.

6. In design view of the Query, add Min and Avg calculations for the *Price* field, as shown in Figure 9.14.

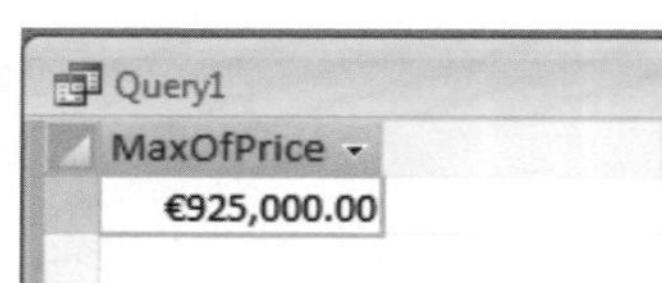

Figure 9.13: Output from the Totals Query

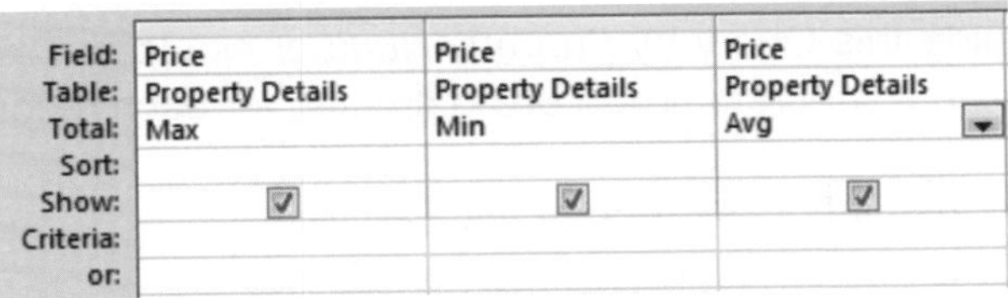

Field:	Price	Price	Price
Table:	Property Details	Property Details	Property Details
Total:	Max	Min	Avg
Sort:			
Show:	☑	☑	☑
Criteria:			
or:			

Figure 9.14: Min and Avg calculations for the *Price* field have been added to the Query design grid

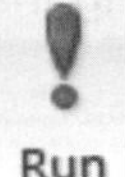

7. Run the Query again. The highest price, lowest price and average price are now displayed, as shown in Figure 9.15.

MaxOfPrice	MinOfPrice	AvgOfPrice
€925,000.00	€249,000.00	€511,800.00

Figure 9.15: Output from the Query design displayed in Figure 9.14

8. In design view of the Query, add the *Address2* field, as shown in Figure 9.16. This time, instead of selecting a function for the *Address2* field, accept the default setting of *Group By*.

Field:	Address2	Price	Price	Price
Table:	Property Details	Property Details	Property Details	Property Details
Total:	Group By	Max	Min	Avg
Sort:				
Show:	☑	☑	☑	☑
Criteria:				
or:				

Figure 9.16: The Query is now grouped by the *Address2* field

9. Run the Query again. The output from the Query should now look like Figure 9.17.

Address2	MaxOfPrice	MinOfPrice	AvgOfPrice
Bray	€465,000.00	€379,000.00	€433,000.00
Dalkey	€925,000.00	€525,000.00	€725,000.00
Dun Laoghaire	€595,000.00	€475,000.00	€515,000.00
Glasthule	€895,000.00	€590,000.00	€742,500.00
Killiney	€725,000.00	€499,000.00	€612,000.00
Monkstown	€335,000.00	€335,000.00	€335,000.00
Sandycove	€495,000.00	€495,000.00	€495,000.00
Shankill	€585,000.00	€330,000.00	€456,666.67
Stillorgan	€299,000.00	€249,000.00	€274,000.00

Figure 9.17: Output from the Totals Query grouped by the *Address2* field

Instead of displaying a single row of calculations based on all the records in the *Property Details* Table, the Query in Figure 9.17 now calculates the highest, lowest and average price for properties in each of the nine towns. This is because the Query has been grouped by the *Address2* field.

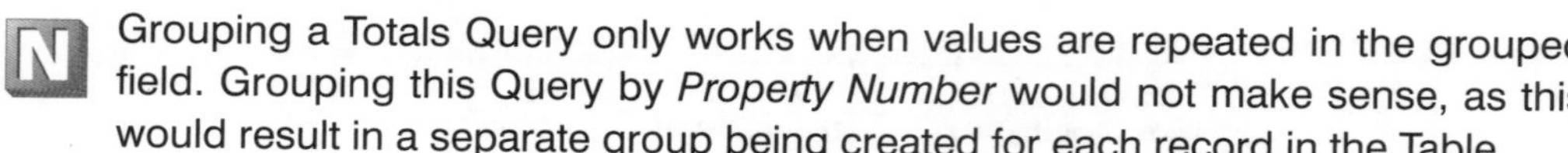

Grouping a Totals Query only works when values are repeated in the grouped field. Grouping this Query by *Property Number* would not make sense, as this would result in a separate group being created for each record in the Table.

10. Save the Query as *Property price analysis*.

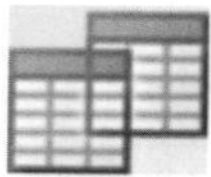

CREATE QUERIES

Create a Totals Query for each task described in Table 9.6. Save each Query using the name provided.

	Purpose of Query	Query Name	Query Results
Task 7	Calculate: ● Min of No of Bedrooms. ● Max of No of Bedrooms. ● Average of Price.	Property size analysis	Min . . . . .1 Max . . . . .5 Average €511800
Task 8	Calculate: ● Sum of price for each property type.	Portfolio value by property type	Apartment . . . .€1243000 Detached House . .€2075000 SD House . . . .€4534000 Terraced House . . .€2384000

Table 9.6

ADD RECORDS

Task 9: Open the *Properties For Sale* Form. Use the *New Record* button to add the records displayed in Table 9.7 to the database.

Property Number	21	22	23	24
Client First Name	Caroline	Joseph	Ekuile	Noel
Client Surname	Brennan	Hannigan	Mulumba	Phelan
Address1	15 Rosemount Lawn	8 Hilltown Grove	75 Woodford Road	Cliff House
Address2	Bray	Greystones	Greystones	Delgany
Address3	Co. Wicklow	Co. Wicklow	Co. Wicklow	Co. Wicklow
Client Contact Number	(085) 8531099	(01) 6680045	(01) 6681133	(01) 6670903
Price	€495,000	€440,000	€395,000	€595,000
Photo	15rosemount.jpg	8hilltown.jpg	75woodford.jpg	cliffhouse.jpg
Property Type	Detached House	Semi-Detached House	Terraced House	Detached House
No of Bedrooms	4	3	2	5

Table 9.7

Parking	Yes	Yes	No	Yes
Alarm	Yes	Yes	Yes	Yes
Description	Lovingly maintained by its present owners, this property comes to the market in show house condition	Nestled in a quiet cul-de-sac yet within walking distance of a wealth of local amenities	Boasting many special features, this property is ideal for the first or second time buyer	Set in an ideal location, this property boasts spacious and well apportioned accommodation

Table 9.7 (continued)

LEARN ABOUT CROSSTAB QUERIES

A Crosstab Query is a more powerful version of a Totals Query. It allows additional levels of analysis that are not available in a Totals Query.

Figure 9.18 displays output from the *Portfolio value by area* Totals Query. Having input four additional records in Table 9.7, this Query is grouped by the *Address2* field. A Totals Query allows a single level of calculation per group. We can calculate the total value of property in Dun Laoghaire, but we cannot see how that total value is split across different property types.

Using a Crosstab Query, we can analyse the data in Figure 9.18 using two fields.

Address2	SumOfPrice
Bray	€1,794,000.00
Dalkey	€1,450,000.00
Delgany	€595,000.00
Dun Laoghaire	€2,060,000.00
Glasthule	€1,485,000.00
Greystones	€835,000.00
Killiney	€1,224,000.00
Monkstown	€335,000.00
Sandycove	€495,000.00
Shankill	€1,340,000.00
Stillorgan	€548,000.00

Figure 9.18: Output from a Totals Query

Figure 9.19 displays output from a Crosstab Query. As well as calculating the total value of properties in each town, each total is broken down into subtotals for apartments, detached houses, semi-detached houses and terraced houses. The *Address2* field is cross-tabulated with the *Property Type* field.

Address2	Total Of Price	Apartment	Detached House	Semi-Detached House	Terraced House
Bray	€1,794,000.00		€495,000.00	€1,299,000.00	
Dalkey	€1,450,000.00			€525,000.00	€925,000.00
Delgany	€0.00		€0.00		
Dun Laoghaire	€2,060,000.00	€495,000.00	€595,000.00	€970,000.00	
Glasthule	€1,485,000.00		€895,000.00	€590,000.00	
Greystones	€835,000.00			€440,000.00	€395,000.00
Killiney	€1,224,000.00	€499,000.00		€725,000.00	
Monkstown	€335,000.00				€335,000.00
Sandycove	€495,000.00				€495,000.00
Shankill	€1,370,000.00		€585,000.00	€455,000.00	€330,000.00
Stillorgan	€548,000.00	€249,000.00			€299,000.00

Figure 9.19: Output from a Crosstab Query

Additional levels of analysis can be added to a Crosstab Query as long as data is repeated in another field. In Figure 9.19, the properties are split between Co. Dublin and Co. Wicklow. This means we can cross-tabulate the data first by *Address3* and *Address2* and then by *Property Type*.

Address3	Address2	Total Of Price	Apartment	Detached House	Semi-Detached House	Terraced House
Co. Dublin	Dalkey	€1,450,000.00			€525,000.00	€925,000.00
Co. Dublin	Dun Laoghaire	€2,060,000.00	€495,000.00	€595,000.00	€970,000.00	
Co. Dublin	Glasthule	€1,485,000.00		€895,000.00	€590,000.00	
Co. Dublin	Killiney	€1,224,000.00	€499,000.00		€725,000.00	
Co. Dublin	Monkstown	€335,000.00				€335,000.00
Co. Dublin	Sandycove	€495,000.00				€495,000.00
Co. Dublin	Shankill	€1,370,000.00		€585,000.00	€455,000.00	€330,000.00
Co. Dublin	Stillorgan	€548,000.00	€249,000.00			€299,000.00
Co. Wicklow	Bray	€1,794,000.00		€495,000.00	€1,299,000.00	
Co. Wicklow	Delgany	€0.00		€0.00		
Co. Wicklow	Greystones	€835,000.00			€440,000.00	€395,000.00

Figure 9.20: Data is cross-tabulated by Addres3, Address2 and Property Type

In Figure 9.20 there are three levels of analysis in the Crosstab Query. Each county has been analysed by town. Each town has been analysed by property type.

WHEN CAN YOU USE A CROSSTAB QUERY?

A Crosstab Query can analyse a Table as long as data is repeated in two or more fields. In the *Property Details* Table, data is repeated in the *Address2* field (Killiney occurs twice, Shankill occurs three times, etc.), the *Address3* field (Co. Dublin occurs 17 times, Co. Wicklow occurs seven times) and the *Property Type* field (Apartment occurs three times, Detached House occurs five times, etc.). A Crosstab Query analyses the data in the Table using a variety of functions, such as Sum, Avg, Count, Max and Min.

In a Crosstab Query, a grid is created where the fields containing repeated data become row and column headings. In the example in Table 9.8, the column headings are generated by the *Property Type* field and the row headings are generated by the *Address2* field.

	Apartment	Detached House	Semi-Detached House	Terraced House
Bray				
Dalkey				
Delgany				
Dun Laoghaire				
Glasthule				
Greystones				
Killiney				
Monkstown				
Sandycove				
Shankill				
Stillorgan				

Table 9.8

Once the structure of the Crosstab Query is established, we can perform a calculation on a selected field for each cell in the grid where data occurs. For example, if we selected the *Property Number* as the field and *Count* as the calculation, the number of apartments, detached houses, semi-detached houses and terraced houses in each location would be calculated, as displayed in Table 9.9.

	Apartment	Detached House	Semi-Detached House	Terraced House
Bray		1	3	
Dalkey			1	1
Delgany		1		
Dun Laoghaire	1	1	2	
Glasthule		1	1	
Greystones			1	1
Killiney	1		1	
Monkstown				1
Sandycove				1
Shankill		1	1	1
Stillorgan	1			1

Table 9.9

Not all cells in the grid contain data. For example, there are no apartments or terraced houses available in Bray, so these cells are empty in the first row. From the results of the Crosstab Query, it can be quickly seen that there are three semi-detached houses for sale in Bray, one semi-detached house and one terraced house for sale in Dalkey and so on. Adding all the numbers in Table 9.9 gives 24, which is the number of records stored in the *Property Details* Table.

By adding conditions to a Crosstab Query, you can specify the type of records you want to analyse.

Field:	Address2	Property Type	Property Number	Total Of Property Nun	Price
Table:	Property Details	Property Details	Property Details	Property Details	Property Details
Total:	Group By	Group By	Count	Count	Group By
Crosstab:	Row Heading	Column Heading	Value	Row Heading	
Sort:					
Criteria:					<=450000
or:					

Figure 9.21

For example, adding the condition shown in Figure 9.21 would give the results displayed in Table 9.10.

	Apartment	Detached House	Semi-Detached House	Terraced House
Bray			1	
Greystones				1
Greystones			1	
Monkstown				1
Shankill				1
Shankill			1	
Stillorgan	1			
Stillorgan				1

Table 9.10

From Table 9.10 it can be seen that there are a total of eight properties for sale for €450,000 or less. These properties are available in Bray, Greystones, Monkstown, Shankill and Stillorgan. No detached houses are available in this price range.

WORKED EXAMPLE: CREATE A CROSSTAB QUERY

1. In the Create section of the Ribbon, click the *Query Wizard* button.
2. Select *Crosstab Query Wizard* in the New Query dialog box. Click *OK*.
3. The *Property Details* Table is highlighted, indicating that it contains the fields that will be used in the Crosstab Query. Click *Next*.

4. Add *Address2* to the Selected Fields box. This will generate row headings from the *Address2* field. Click *Next*.
5. Select *Property Type* as the column heading. This will generate column headings from the *Property Type* field. Click *Next*.
6. Select *Property Number* as the field and *Count* as the function. Click *Next*.
7. Enter *Analysis of market supply* as the Query name.
8. Click *Finish* to view the results of the Query.
9. Check the results of your Crosstab Query. They should match the data displayed in Table 9.9 on page 257.

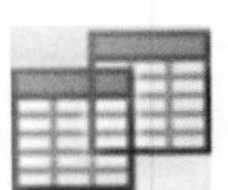

CREATE QUERIES

Create a Crosstab Query for each task described in Table 9.11. Save each Query using the name provided.

	Purpose of Query	Query Name
Task 10	Calculate the average price for each property type by Address2	Average price of property types by area
Task 11	Calculate the lowest price of property types by Address2 for properties worth less than €500,000	Lowest price of property types by area
Task 12	Calculate the total value of each property type by county and then by town	Portfolio value of available property types by area

Table 9.11

In Task 12, add *Address3* and *Address2* as the row headings.

WORKED EXAMPLE: DISPLAY THE RESULTS OF A CROSSTAB QUERY USING A REPORT

In this worked example, we will create a Report to display the results of the *Analysis of market supply* Crosstab Query.

Select the *Analysis of market supply* Query in the Navigation Pane before clicking the *Report Wizard* button.

1. Using the Report Wizard, create a new Report linked to the *Analysis of market supply* Query.
2. Add all fields to the Report except for *Total of Property Number*.
3. Skip Grouping. Sort the Report in ascending order of *Address2*.
4. Select *Tabular* as the layout and *Portrait* as the orientation.
5. Apply the *Urban* style to the Report.
6. Enter *Market Supply Report* as the title. Click *Finish* to preview the Report.
7. Using layout view, adjust the width of the *Address2* text box so that all town names are fully visible. Centre the data in labels and text boxes for each *Property Type*.
8. In the Report footer, enter functions to calculate the total number of properties available in each category. =sum([Apartment]) calculates the total number of apartments available. =sum([Detached House]) calculates the total number of detached houses available. A separate function is required for each property type.
9. Set the background colour of the Report footer to *dark blue.*
10. Select a font colour of *white*, a font size of *12* and a font weight of *bold* for each of the text boxes in the Report footer.
11. Delete the *Address2* label box.

12. Copy the address and logo from the Form header of the *Properties for Sale* Form and paste into the Report header.
13. The completed Report should look like Figure 9.22.

Market Supply Report

Southern Estate Agents
1 Main Street
Ballybrack
Tel: (01) 6679923

	Apartment	Detached House	Semi-Detached House	Terraced House
Bray		1	3	
Dalkey			1	1
Delgany		1		
Dun Laoghaire	1	1	2	
Glasthule		1	1	
Greystones			1	1
Killiney	1		1	
Monkstown				1
Sandycove				1
Shankill		1	1	1
Stillorgan	1			1
Total:	3	5	10	6

Figure 9.22: The completed *Market Supply Report*

CREATE CROSSTAB REPORTS

Task 13: Display lowest prices of property types by area.

- Create a Report linked to the *Lowest price of property types by area* Query.
- Include all fields except for *Total of Price* in the Report.
- Sort the Report in ascending order of *Address2.*
- Apply the *Urban* style to the Report.
- The Report title is *Entry Level Properties.*
- Copy the company name, address and logo from the *Market Supply Report* and position in the Report header, similar to Figure 9.22.
- Add functions to the Report footer to calculate the total number of apartments, detached houses, semi-detached houses and terraced houses.
- Export the *Entry Level Properties* Report to a PDF document.

Task 14: Create a Parameter Query that displays the message "Enter preferred location of property" when it is run. The Query should find records of properties in the location entered by the user, e.g. Bray, Dalkey, etc. Save the Query as *Available properties by location*. Test the Query by running it and entering *Shankill* as the location. Three records should be displayed.

WORKED EXAMPLE: CREATE A DYNAMIC REPORT TITLE

1. Create a Report linked to the *Available properties by location* Query. Include the *Price*, *No of Bedrooms*, *Property Type*, *Address1*, *Address2* and *Address3* fields in the Report.
2. Sort the Report in descending order of *Price*.
3. Apply the *Urban* style to the Report.

4. The Report title is *Properties for Sale by Location.*
5. View the Report in design view.

6. Edit the label in the Report header so that it reads *Properties for Sale in*, as shown in Figure 9.23.

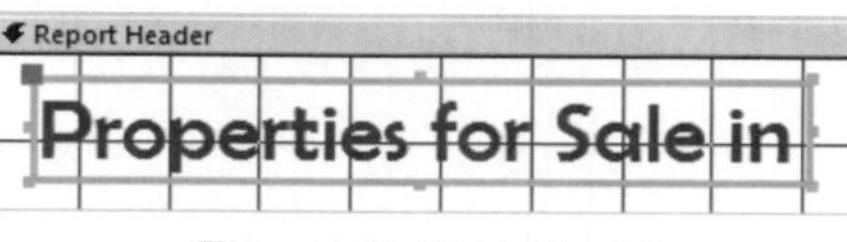

Figure 9.23: Label text has been edited

7. Format the label using a font of *Berlin Sans FB* and a font size of *28*.
8. Display the field list. Drag the *Address2* field from the field list and drop to the right of the label in the Report header. Delete the *Address2* label. Position the *Address2* text box control immediately to the right of the label containing the text *Properties for Sale in* (Figure 9.24).

9. Select the *Properties for Sale in* label. Click the *Format Painter* button in either the Home or Design section of the Ribbon. Now click the *Address2* text box. The text formatting of the label is applied to the *Address2* text box.

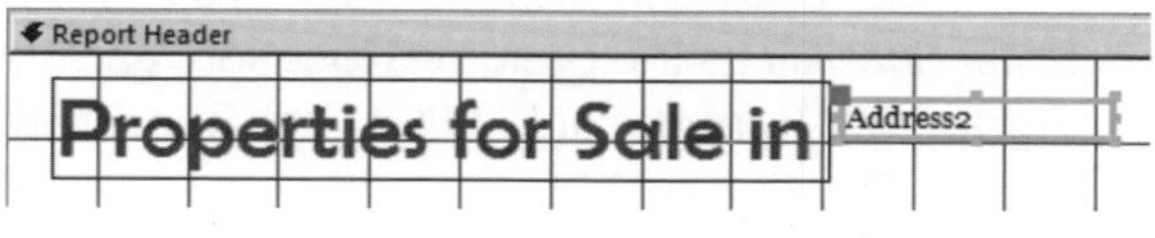

Figure 9.24: *Address2* text box positioned next to the label

10. Adjust the size of the *Address2* text box so that it is the same height as the label. Ensure that the *Address2* text box is wide enough to display the text *Dun Laoghaire*. Position the text box so that it appears like Figure 9.25.

View the properties of the label. Make a note of the height and then enter this height for the *Address2* text box.

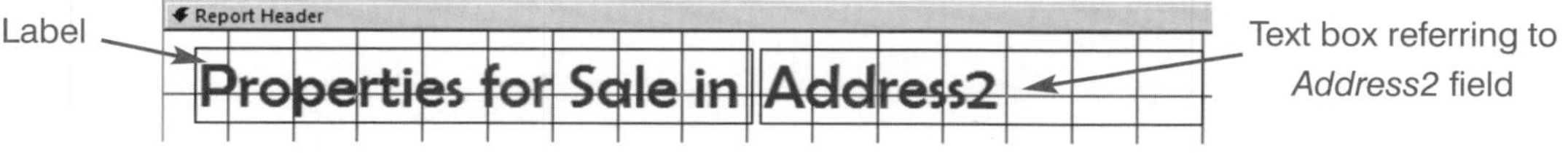

Figure 9.25: Label and text box controls lined up to create an adjusting Report title

11. Increase the height of the Report header and move both the label and text box down to make space at the top of the Report header.
12. Create a Count function in the Report header to count the number of properties available. Position this function above the existing label and text box (see Figure 9.26).

13. The label associated with the Count function is positioned on the left of the text box by default. Move this label to the right of the text box and type the text *Properties Available* (see Figure 9.26).

14. Format the newly created text box and label using a font of *Berlin Sans FB,* a font size of *14* and a font style of *Italic* (see Figure 9.26).

15. Copy the address and logo from the *Properties for Sale* Form. Position the address and logo to the right of the functions (see Figure 9.26).

Report Header

=Count([Address2]) Properties Available

Southern Estate Agents

1 Main Street
Ballybrack
Tel: (01) 6679923

Properties for Sale in Address2

Figure 9.26: Labels and text boxes in the Report header

N Access displays a green triangle in the top left-hand corner of a label that is not associated with a text box. You can safely ignore this.

16. Preview the Report. As the Report is linked to a Parameter Query, the dialog box shown in Figure 9.27 is displayed.

17. Enter *Shankill* as the preferred location, as shown in Figure 9.27, and click *OK*. The Report should appear like Figure 9.28.

18. Use layout view to adjust the positioning of the labels and text boxes so that they appear like Figure 9.28.

19. Edit the *Address1* label so that it reads *Address*. Delete the *Address2* and *Address3* labels.

20. Preview the Report for Dun Laoghaire and ensure that "Dun Laoghaire" fits in the text box in the Report header, as shown in Figure 9.29.

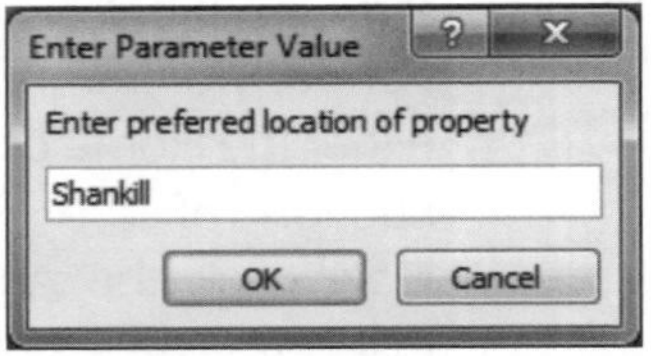

Figure 9.27: As the Report is linked to a Parameter Query, this dialog box is displayed each time the Report is previewed

3 Properties Available

Southern Estate Agents

1 Main Street
Ballybrack
Tel: (01) 6679923

Properties for Sale in Shankill

Price	Number of Bedrooms	Property Type	Address		
€585,000	4	Detached House	16 Wolverton Grove	Shankill	Co. Dublin
€425,000	3	Semi-Detached House	3 Corbawn Terrace	Shankill	Co. Dublin
€330,000	3	Terraced House	122 Plunkett Road	Shankill	Co. Dublin

Figure 9.28: Preview of the *Properties for Sale by Location* Report, having entered Shankill as the preferred location

4 Properties Available

Southern Estate Agents
1 Main Street
Ballybrack
Tel: (01) 6679923

Properties for Sale in Dun Laoghaire

Price	Number of Bedrooms	Property Type	Address		
€595,000	5	Detached House	22 Anville Wood	Dun Laoghaire	Co. Dublin
€495,000	1	Apartment	27 Abbey Lane	Dun Laoghaire	Co. Dublin
€495,000	3	Semi-Detached House	28 Dorney Road	Dun Laoghaire	Co. Dublin
€475,000	3	Semi-Detached House	23 Seaview Park	Dun Laoghaire	Co. Dublin

Figure 9.29: Preview of the *Properties for Sale by Location* Report, having entered Dun Laoghaire as the preferred location

21. Save the *Properties for Sale by Location* Report.

Task 15: Display properties currently on the market using a Report.

- Create a Report linked to the *Property Details* Table.
- Include the *Price*, *No of Bedrooms*, *Property Type*, *Address1*, *Address2* and *Address3* fields in the Report.
- Group the Report by the *Address2* field.
- Sort the Report in descending order of *Price*.
- Select *Stepped* as the layout and *Portrait* as the orientation.
- Apply the *Urban* style to the Report.
- The Report title is *Properties Currently on the Market.*
- Copy the address and logo from the *Properties for Sale* Form to the Report header.
- Insert a function in the Report header to count the number of records in the Report. Combine this function with a label so that it appears as “24 Properties Available”.

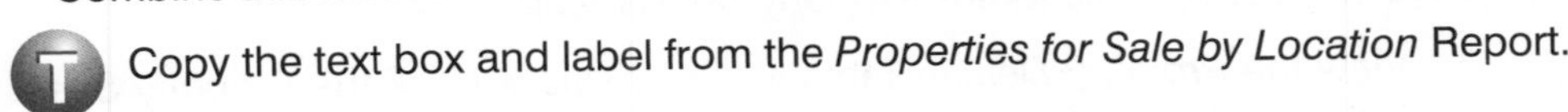

T Copy the text box and label from the *Properties for Sale by Location* Report.

- Draw a label immediately below the function and enter the text “Please phone the office for a viewing time”.
- Apply a background colour of grey to the *Address2* header.
- Remove the alternate shading from the detail section.

H View the properties of the detail section.

- Display the *Address2* footer and insert a function to calculate the average price of a property in each area.
- Delete all labels in the page header and set the height of the page header to *0*.
- Draw a label box in the Detail section between the No of Bedrooms and Property Type text boxes. Enter the text “bedroom” in the label. Position the label using Figure 9.30 as a guide.

Figure 9.30 is an extract from the Report, displaying properties in Bray and Dalkey.

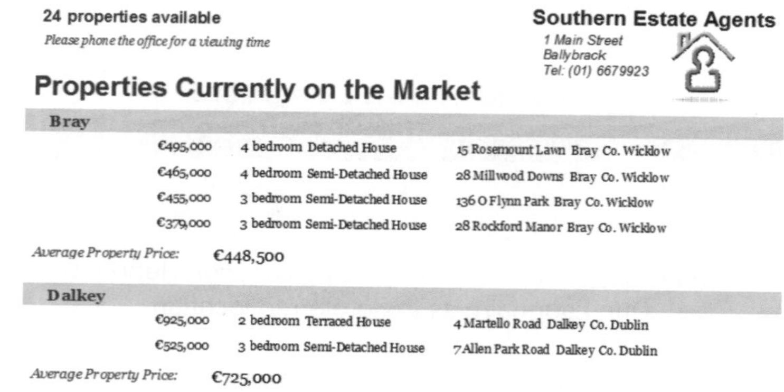

24 properties available
Please phone the office for a viewing time

Southern Estate Agents
1 Main Street
Ballybrack
Tel: (01) 6679923

Properties Currently on the Market

Bray

€495,000	4 bedroom Detached House	15 Rosemount Lawn Bray Co. Wicklow
€465,000	4 bedroom Semi-Detached House	28 Millwood Downs Bray Co. Wicklow
€455,000	3 bedroom Semi-Detached House	136 O Flynn Park Bray Co. Wicklow
€379,000	3 bedroom Semi-Detached House	28 Rockford Manor Bray Co. Wicklow

Average Property Price: €448,500

Dalkey

€925,000	2 bedroom Terraced House	4 Martello Road Dalkey Co. Dublin
€525,000	3 bedroom Semi-Detached House	7 Allen Park Road Dalkey Co. Dublin

Average Property Price: €725,000

Figure 9.30: Extract from the Report created in Task 15

Task 16: Create a new field.
Add a new field named *Date First Advertised* to the *Property Details* Table, using an appropriate data type, field size and format (see Table 9.12 on page 265).

WORKED EXAMPLE: CREATE A VALIDATION EXPRESSION

1. We will create a validation rule to ensure that the date entered in the *Date First Advertised* field occurs *before* the date stored in *the Date Sale Completed* field. This requires the following validation expression:

   [Date First Advertised] < [Date Sale Completed]

   Because this validation rule compares values in two different fields, it cannot be entered as the validation rule for the *Date First Advertised* field. Instead, it must be entered as a validation rule for the *Property Details* table.

2. View the *Property Details* Table in design view. Click the *Property Sheet* button in the Design section of the Ribbon.

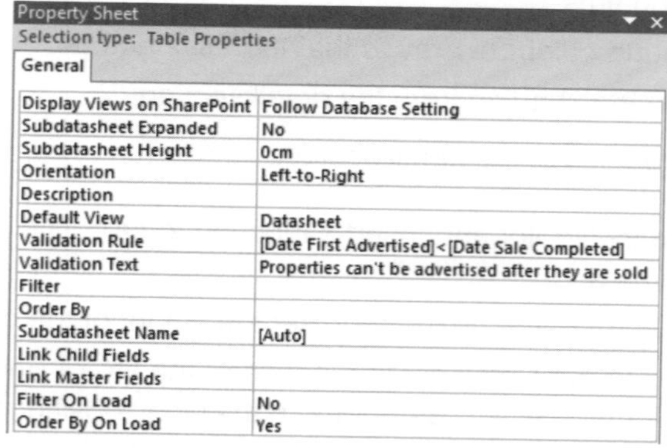

Property Sheet
Selection type: Table Properties
General

Display Views on SharePoint	Follow Database Setting
Subdatasheet Expanded	No
Subdatasheet Height	0cm
Orientation	Left-to-Right
Description	
Default View	Datasheet
Validation Rule	[Date First Advertised]<[Date Sale Completed]
Validation Text	Properties can't be advertised after they are sold
Filter	
Order By	
Subdatasheet Name	[Auto]
Link Child Fields	
Link Master Fields	
Filter On Load	No
Order By On Load	Yes

Figure 9.31: Using a validation rule to compare values in different fields

3. Enter the validation rule and validation text displayed in Figure 9.31.

4. Save the *Property Details* Table.
5. View the Table in datasheet view.
6. Enter yesterday's date in the *Date Sale Completed* field for property number 1. Enter today's date in the *Date First Advertised* field for property number 1. The error message shown in Figure 9.32 should be displayed.

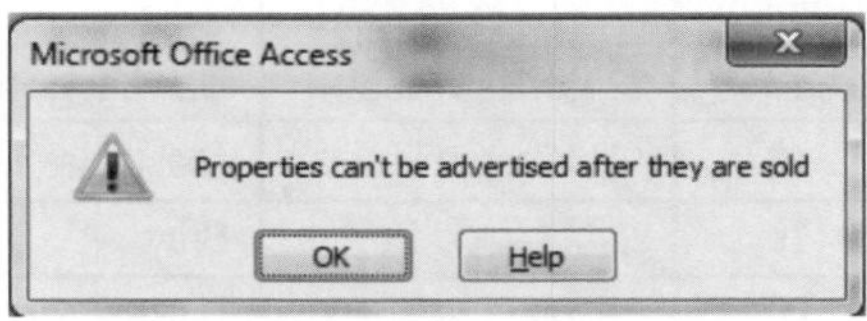

Figure 9.32: Error message displayed having attempted to enter a value in the *Date First Advertised* field that occurs after the date stored in the *Date Sale Completed* field

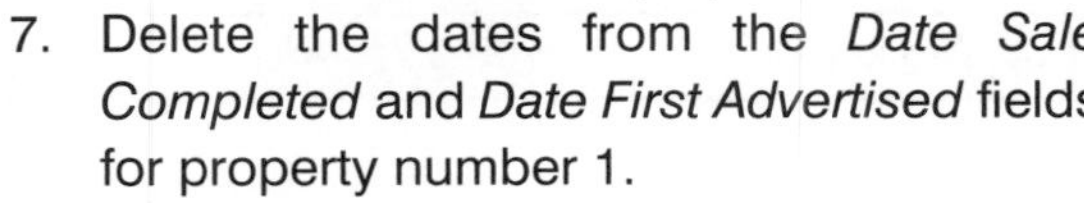

7. Delete the dates from the *Date Sale Completed* and *Date First Advertised* fields for property number 1.

8. Close the *Property Details* Table.

9. Open the *Properties for Sale* Form in design view.
10. Add the *Date First Advertised* field to the Sales Details section of the Form, positioning the new field between the *Client Contact Number* and *Date Sale Completed* fields.
11. Set the alignment of the *Date First Advertised* text box control to centre.
12. Enter the *Highest Offer, Date Sale Completed* and *Date First Advertised* data displayed in the shaded cells in Table 9.12. Press the *Page Down* key to quickly advance to the next record.

Property Number	Address1	Address2	Address3	Highest Offer	Date First Advertised	Date Sale Completed
1	Beachview House	Killiney	Co. Dublin		01/04/2014	
2	3 Corbawn Terrace	Shankill	Co. Dublin	€445,000	05/04/2014	09/05/2014
3	23 Seaview Park	Dun Laoghaire	Co. Dublin		12/04/2014	
4	Rose Lawn	Sandycove	Co. Dublin		26/04/2014	
5	16 Wolverton Grove	Shankill	Co. Dublin		30/04/2014	
6	4 Martello Road	Dalkey	Co. Dublin		04/01/2014	
7	27 Abbey Lane	Dun Laoghaire	Co. Dublin		12/04/2014	
8	12 Bayview Mews	Glasthule	Co. Dublin		03/05/2014	
9	1 Richmond Close	Killiney	Co. Dublin		19/04/2014	
10	3 Eden Terrace	Monkstown	Co. Dublin		10/05/2014	
11	28 Rockford Manor	Bray	Co. Wicklow		10/05/2014	
12	28 Dorney Road	Dun Laoghaire	Co. Dublin		10/05/2014	
13	136 O Flynn Park	Bray	Co. Wicklow	€450,000	01/02/2014	21/05/2014
14	122 Plunkett Road	Shankill	Co. Dublin		19/04/2014	
15	46 Ashlawn Grove	Stillorgan	Co. Dublin		07/09/2013	
16	38 Seaview Court	Stillorgan	Co. Dublin		03/05/2014	

Table 9.12

Property Number	Address1	Address2	Address3	Highest Offer	Date First Advertised	Date Sale Completed
17	22 Anville Wood	Dun Laoghaire	Co. Dublin	€565,000	16/11/2013	28/05/2014
18	101 Westgrove	Glasthule	Co. Dublin		17/05/2014	
19	28 Millwood Downs	Bray	Co. Wicklow		17/05/2014	
20	7 Allen Park Road	Dalkey	Co. Dublin		11/01/2014	
21	15 Rosemount Lawn	Bray	Co. Wicklow		24/05/2014	
22	8 Hilltown Grove	Greystones	Co. Wicklow		24/05/2014	
23	75 Woodford Road	Greystones	Co. Wicklow		07/06/2014	
24	Cliff House	Delgany	Co. Wicklow		14/06/2014	

Table 9.12 (continued)

LEARN ABOUT NULL VALUES

When data hasn't been entered in a particular field, this is referred to as a null value. Searching for null values is an important database task. For example, in a video rentals database, searching for null values in the *Date Returned* field would identify rented videos that have not been returned. In the Southern Estate Agents database, null values occur in the *Highest Offer* and *Date Sale Completed* fields for properties that are currently for sale. As long as a property hasn't been sold, both of these fields will remain empty. Properties that haven't been sold are identified using a Query. The Query searches for null values in the *Date Sale Completed* field.

Field:	Highest Offer	Date Sale Completed	Description
Table:	Property Details	Property Details	Property Details
Sort:			
Show:	☑	☑	☑
Criteria:		Is Null	
or:			

Figure 9.33: *Is Null* finds all properties that have not been sold

In Figure 9.33, *Is Null* has been entered as a condition in the *Date Sale Completed* field. When the Query is run, it will only find records where the *Date Sale Completed* field is empty. Properties 2, 13 and 17 are not found by the Query, as these properties have been sold. The records found by this Query are displayed in Figure 9.34.

In Figure 9.34, a total of 21 available properties are found by the *Is Null* condition in the *Date Sale Completed* field. (The 24 records in the *Property Details* Table minus the three properties that have been sold.)

Searching for records where *no data has been entered* in a particular field requires an *Is Null* condition. An *Is Not Null* condition, on the other hand, is used to find records where data has been entered in a particular field. In the Southern Estate Agents database, *Is Not Null* can be used in the *Date Sale Completed* field to find all properties that have been sold. (For properties that have been sold, a date will be present in the *Date Sale Completed* field.)

P	Client Fi	Client Su	Address1	Address2	Address3	Property Type	Price	Date Sale Completed
1	Adam	Delaney	Beechview House	Killiney	Co. Dublin	Semi-Detached House	€725,000	
3	Pauline	Byrne	23 Seaview Park	Dun Laoghaire	Co. Dublin	Semi-Detached House	€475,000	
4	Daniel	Murphy	Roselawn	Sandycove	Co. Dublin	Terraced House	€495,000	
5	Peter	Looney	16 Wolverton Grove	Shankill	Co. Dublin	Detached House	€585,000	
6	Carl	O Donnell	4 Martello Road	Dalkey	Co. Dublin	Terraced House	€925,000	
7	Fiona	Stapleton	27 Abbey Lane	Dun Laoghaire	Co. Dublin	Apartment	€495,000	
8	Tadhg	Donovan	12 Bayview Mews	Glasthule	Co. Dublin	Semi-Detached House	€590,000	
9	Jack	Dunne	1 Richmond Close	Killiney	Co. Dublin	Apartment	€499,000	
10	Ian	McShane	3 Eden Terrace	Monkstown	Co. Dublin	Terraced House	€335,000	
11	Philip	Donovan	28 Rockford Manor	Bray	Co. Wicklow	Semi-Detached House	€379,000	
12	Gerry	O Neill	28 Dorney Road	Dun Laoghaire	Co. Dublin	Semi-Detached House	€495,000	
14	Roisin	Murray	122 Plunkett Road	Shankill	Co. Dublin	Terraced House	€330,000	
15	Garreth	Moore	46 Ashlawn Grove	Stillorgan	Co. Dublin	Terraced House	€299,000	
16	Geraldine	Walsh	38 Seaview Court	Stillorgan	Co. Dublin	Apartment	€249,000	
18	Andrew	Collins	101 Westgrove	Glasthule	Co. Dublin	Detached House	€895,000	
19	Neil	Conlon	28 Millwood Downs	Bray	Co. Wicklow	Semi-Detached House	€465,000	
20	Tommy	Dunne	7 Allen Park Road	Dalkey	Co. Dublin	Semi-Detached House	€525,000	
21	Caroline	Brennan	15 Roesmount Lawn	Bray	Co. Wicklow	Detached House	€495,000	
22	Joseph	Hannigan	8 Hilltown Grove	Greystones	Co. Wicklow	Semi-Detached House	€440,000	
23	Ekuile	Mulumba	75 Woodford Road	Greystones	Co. Wicklow	Terraced House	€395,000	
24	Noel	Phelan	Cliff House	Delgany	Co. Wicklow	Detached House	€595,000	

Record: 21 of 21 No Filter Search

The *Is Null* expression in Figure 9.39 finds records where the *Date Sale Completed* field is empty

Figure 9.34: Records found by the *Is Null* condition shown in Figure 9.39

In Figure 9.35, *Is Not Null* has been entered as a condition in the *Date Sale Completed* field. When the Query is run, it will only find records where dates have been entered in the *Date Sale Completed* field. These records are displayed in Figure 9.36.

Field:	Highest Offer	Date Sale Completed	Description
Table:	Property Details	Property Details	Property Details
Sort:			
Show:	☑	☑	☑
Criteria:		Is Not Null	
or:			

Figure 9.35: *Is Not Null* finds all properties that have been sold

The *Is Not Null* expression in Figure 9.35 finds records where dates have been entered in the *Date Sale Completed* field

Pr	Client Fi	Client Su	Address1	Address2	Address3	Property Type	Price	Date Sale Completed
2	Joan	Murphy	3 Corbawn Terrace	Shankill	Co. Dublin	Semi-Detached House	€425,000	09/05/2014
13	Anthony	Murphy	136 O Flynn Park	Bray	Co. Wicklow	Semi-Detached House	€455,000	21/05/2014
17	Paul	Mc Carthy	22 Anville Wood	Dun Laoghaire	Co. Dublin	Detached House	€595,000	28/05/2014

Figure 9.36: Records found by the *Is Not Null* condition shown in Figure 9.35

In Figure 9.36, a total of three completed sales are found by the *Is Not Null* condition in the *Date Sale Completed* field.

The effects of using *Is Null* and *Is Not Null* are summarised in Table 9.13.

Logical Operator	Meaning
Is Null	Fields where data hasn't been entered
Is Not Null	Fields containing data

Table 9.13

NULL VALUES – IMPORTANT POINTS

- A primary key field can never have a null value, as Access will not allow you to complete data entry of a record without entering data in the primary key field.
- Fields whose *Required* property has been set to *Yes* cannot have null values.

In Figure 9.37, the *Required* property for the *Client First Name* field has been set to *Yes* in design view of the *Property Details* Table. Access will not transfer a new record from the *Properties for Sale* Form to the *Property Details* Table at the data entry stage unless the data entry operator enters data in the *Client First Name* field. Consequently, the *Client First Name* field can never have a null value. It is worth noting that failure to enter data in the *Client First Name* field will affect the entire record. This is because Access transfers data from a Form to Table record by record and not field by field.

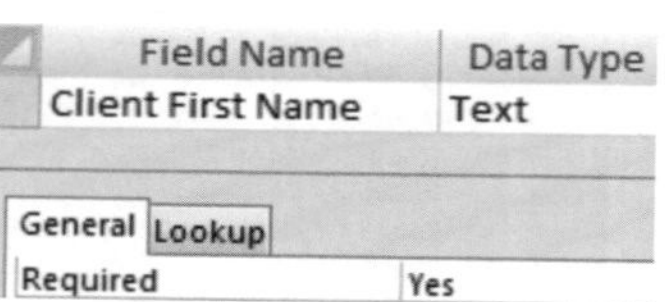

Figure 9.37: *Required* property of the *Client First Name* field has been set to *Yes*

In Figure 9.38, the *Required* property for the *Date Sale Completed* field has been set to *No*. This enables the data entry operator to enter a new record without entering data in the *Date Sale Completed* field.

Field Name	Data Type
Date Sale Completed	Date/Time

General | Lookup

Required	No

Figure 9.38: *Required* property of the *Date Sale Completed* field has been set to *No*

In the Southern Estate Agents database, data entry occurs in two stages. Details of properties have to be recorded in the database when the properties are offered for sale. *Date Sale Completed* data only becomes available at the time of sale, which occurs at a later date. As the *Date Sale Completed* and *Highest Offer* fields will remain empty until a sale is completed, the *Required* property of these fields must be set to *No*. The *Is Null* logical operator can be used in a Query to find records where the *Date Sale Completed* field is empty.

Task 17

1. Open the *Available properties by location* Query in design view.
2. Edit the Query so that it only displays properties that haven't been sold.

3. Preview the *Properties for Sale by Location* Report, entering *Shankill* as the preferred location. The Report should display details of two properties in Shankill. The text at the top left of the Report should read "2 Properties Available". (Originally, three properties were for sale in Shankill.)

4. Close the *Properties for Sale by Location* Report and then preview it again entering *Bray* as the preferred location. The Report should display details of three properties in Bray. The text at the top left of the Report should read "3 Properties Available". (Originally, four properties were for sale in Bray.)

5. Preview the *Properties for Sale by Location* Report, entering *Dun Laoghaire* as the preferred location. The Report should display details of three properties in Dun Laoghaire. (Originally, four properties were for sale in Dun Laoghaire.)

Task 18: Create a Query to find records of properties currently on the market. Save the Query as *Available properties*. Test the Query by running it. The Query should find 21 records.

Use *Is Null*.

WORKED EXAMPLE: CREATE A FUNCTION IN THE FORM HEADER

1. Open the *Properties for Sale* Form in design view.
2. Draw a text box in the Form header to the left of the *Properties for Sale* label box. Delete the label associated with the newly created text box.

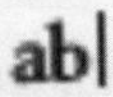

3. Type the following function in the text box:

=count([Property Number])

4. Select the *Properties for Sale* label box. Click the *Format Painter* button in either the Home or Design section of the Ribbon. Now click the text box containing the Count function. The text formatting of the label box is applied to the text box.
5. Increase the font size of the text box containing the Count function to *48*.
6. Adjust the height of the text box to fit the results of the Count function.
7. Position the text box so that it appears like Figure 9.39.
8. View the Form in Form view. The Form title should read *24 Properties For Sale*, as shown in Figure 9.39.

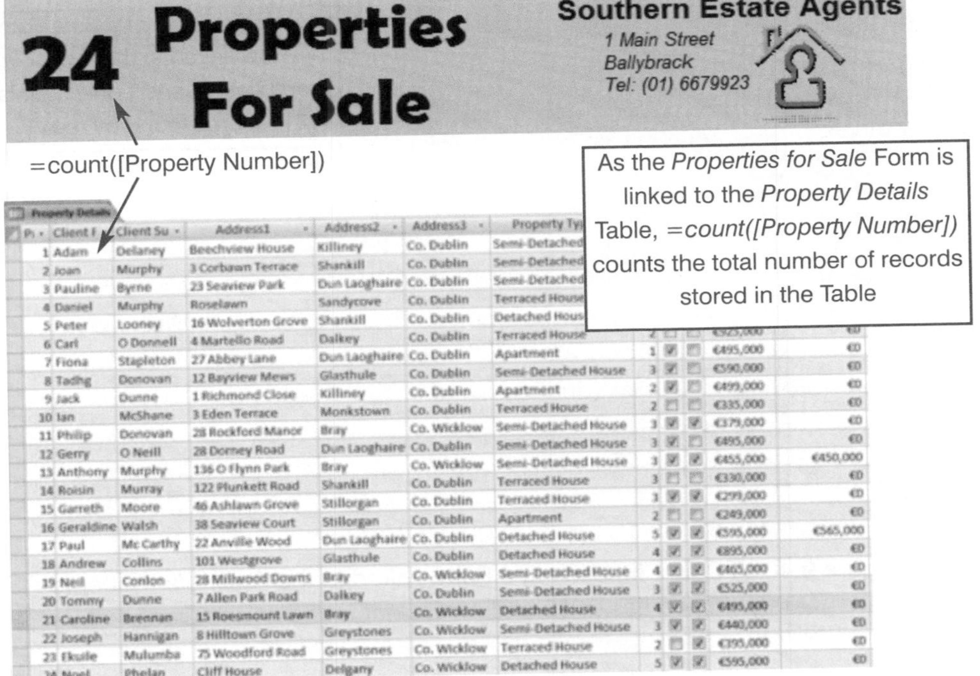

P	Client F	Client Su	Address1	Address2	Address3	Property Ty					
1	Adam	Delaney	Beechview House	Killiney	Co. Dublin	Semi-Detached					
2	Joan	Murphy	3 Corbawn Terrace	Shankill	Co. Dublin	Semi-Detached					
3	Pauline	Byrne	23 Seaview Park	Dun Laoghaire	Co. Dublin	Semi-Detached					
4	Daniel	Murphy	Roselawn	Sandycove	Co. Dublin	Terraced House					
5	Peter	Looney	16 Wolverton Grove	Shankill	Co. Dublin	Detached House					
6	Carl	O Donnell	4 Martello Road	Dalkey	Co. Dublin	Terraced House	2	☐	☐	€325,000	€0
7	Fiona	Stapleton	27 Abbey Lane	Dun Laoghaire	Co. Dublin	Apartment	1	☑	☐	€495,000	€0
8	Tadhg	Donovan	12 Bayview Mews	Glasthule	Co. Dublin	Semi-Detached House	3	☑	☐	€590,000	€0
9	Jack	Dunne	1 Richmond Close	Killiney	Co. Dublin	Apartment	2	☑	☐	€499,000	€0
10	Ian	McShane	3 Eden Terrace	Monkstown	Co. Dublin	Terraced House	2	☐	☐	€335,000	€0
11	Philip	Donovan	28 Rockford Manor	Bray	Co. Wicklow	Semi-Detached House	3	☑	☑	€379,000	€0
12	Gerry	O Neill	28 Dorney Road	Dun Laoghaire	Co. Dublin	Semi-Detached House	3	☑	☐	€495,000	€0
13	Anthony	Murphy	136 O Flynn Park	Bray	Co. Wicklow	Semi-Detached House	3	☑	☑	€455,000	€450,000
14	Roisin	Murray	122 Plunkett Road	Shankill	Co. Dublin	Terraced House	3	☐	☐	€330,000	€0
15	Garreth	Moore	46 Ashlawn Grove	Stillorgan	Co. Dublin	Terraced House	3	☑	☑	€299,000	€0
16	Geraldine	Walsh	38 Seaview Court	Stillorgan	Co. Dublin	Apartment	2	☐	☐	€249,000	€0
17	Paul	Mc Carthy	22 Anville Wood	Dun Laoghaire	Co. Dublin	Detached House	5	☑	☑	€595,000	€565,000
18	Andrew	Collins	101 Westgrove	Glasthule	Co. Dublin	Detached House	4	☑	☑	€895,000	€0
19	Neil	Conlon	28 Millwood Downs	Bray	Co. Wicklow	Semi-Detached House	4	☑	☑	€465,000	€0
20	Tommy	Dunne	7 Allen Park Road	Dalkey	Co. Dublin	Semi-Detached House	3	☑	☑	€525,000	€0
21	Caroline	Brennan	15 Roesmount Lawn	Bray	Co. Wicklow	Detached House	4	☑	☑	€495,000	€0
22	Joseph	Hannigan	8 Hilltown Grove	Greystones	Co. Wicklow	Semi-Detached House	3	☑	☑	€440,000	€0
23	Ekule	Mulumba	75 Woodford Road	Greystones	Co. Wicklow	Terraced House	2	☐	☑	€395,000	€0
24	Noel	Phelan	Cliff House	Delgany	Co. Wicklow	Detached House	5	☑	☑	€595,000	€0

Figure 9.39: A Count function in a Form linked to the *Property Details* Table

In Figure 9.39, the Count function in the Form header calculates a total of 24 records. This is because the record source of the *Properties for Sale* Form is the *Property Details* Table. The Count function counts the 24 records stored in the *Property Details* Table. This is incorrect, as three properties have already been sold. The actual number of properties for sale is *21*. In order for the Count function to correctly calculate the number of properties available, the *Properties for Sale* Form must be linked to the *Available properties* Query instead of the *Property Details* Table.

9. View the *Properties for Sale* Form in design view.

10. Click the *Select Form* icon in the top left-hand corner.

11. Display the property sheet. Click the *All* tab in the property sheet. In the *Record Source* property, select *Available Properties* from the drop-down list. This breaks the link between the Form and the Table and creates a new link to the *Available properties* Query.
12. View the *Properties for Sale* Form in Form view. The total calculated by the Count function is now 21, as seen in Figure 9.40.

21 **Properties For Sale**

Southern Estate Agents
1 Main Street
Ballybrack
Tel: (01) 6679923

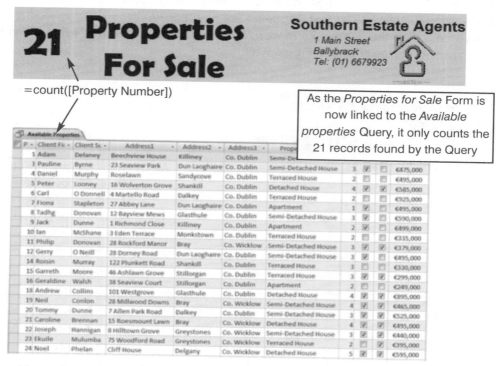

=count([Property Number])

As the *Properties for Sale* Form is now linked to the *Available properties* Query, it only counts the 21 records found by the Query

Available Properties

P	Client Fi	Client Su	Address1	Address2	Address3	Prope				
1	Adam	Delaney	Beechview House	Killiney	Co. Dublin	Semi-De				
3	Pauline	Byrne	23 Seaview Park	Dun Laoghaire	Co. Dublin	Semi-Detached House	3	✓		€475,000
4	Daniel	Murphy	Roselawn	Sandycove	Co. Dublin	Terraced House	2			€495,000
5	Peter	Looney	16 Wolverton Grove	Shankill	Co. Dublin	Detached House	4	✓	✓	€585,000
6	Carl	O Donnell	4 Martello Road	Dalkey	Co. Dublin	Terraced House	2			€925,000
7	Fiona	Stapleton	27 Abbey Lane	Dun Laoghaire	Co. Dublin	Apartment	1	✓		€495,000
8	Tadhg	Donovan	12 Bayview Mews	Glasthule	Co. Dublin	Semi-Detached House	3	✓		€590,000
9	Jack	Dunne	1 Richmond Close	Killiney	Co. Dublin	Apartment	2	✓		€499,000
10	Ian	McShane	3 Eden Terrace	Monkstown	Co. Dublin	Terraced House	2			€335,000
11	Philip	Donovan	28 Rockford Manor	Bray	Co. Wicklow	Semi-Detached House	3	✓	✓	€379,000
12	Gerry	O Neill	28 Dorney Road	Dun Laoghaire	Co. Dublin	Semi-Detached House	3	✓		€495,000
14	Roisin	Murray	122 Plunkett Road	Shankill	Co. Dublin	Terraced House	3			€330,000
15	Garreth	Moore	46 Ashlawn Grove	Stillorgan	Co. Dublin	Terraced House	3	✓	✓	€299,000
16	Geraldine	Walsh	38 Seaview Court	Stillorgan	Co. Dublin	Apartment	2			€249,000
18	Andrew	Collins	101 Westgrove	Glasthule	Co. Dublin	Detached House	4	✓	✓	€895,000
19	Neil	Conlon	28 Millwood Downs	Bray	Co. Wicklow	Semi-Detached House	4	✓	✓	€465,000
20	Tommy	Dunne	7 Allen Park Road	Dalkey	Co. Dublin	Semi-Detached House	3	✓	✓	€525,000
21	Caroline	Brennan	15 Roesmount Lawn	Bray	Co. Wicklow	Detached House	4	✓	✓	€495,000
22	Joseph	Hannigan	8 Hilltown Grove	Greystones	Co. Wicklow	Semi-Detached House	3	✓	✓	€440,000
23	Ekuile	Mulumba	75 Woodford Road	Greystones	Co. Wicklow	Terraced House	2		✓	€395,000
24	Noel	Phelan	Cliff House	Delgany	Co. Wicklow	Detached House	5	✓	✓	€595,000

Figure 9.40: A Count function in a Form linked to the *Available properties* Query (Properties 2, 13 and 17 are not found by the Query)

In Figure 9.40, the *Properties for Sale* Form is linked to the *Available properties* Query. The *Is Null* expression in the *Date Sale Completed* field of the Query excludes the three properties that have been sold. The Query finds 21 of the 24 records in the Table. The Count function in the Form header counts these 21 records.

13. Save the *Properties for Sale* Form.

Task 19: Change the record source of the *Properties Currently on the Market* Report from the *Property Details* Table to the *Available properties* Query. Preview the Report. The text in the Report header should now read "21 Properties Available".

Task 20

You will need to use the *Less than or Equal to* logical operator in this Query.

- Create a Parameter Query that displays the message "Enter the maximum the customer can afford" when it is run. The Query should find records of properties *that haven't been sold* where the price is less than or equal to the number entered.
- Save the Query as *Properties in a customers price range.*
- Test the Query by running it and entering *450000* as the maximum. Seven records should be displayed.
- Check that the Query does not find property number 2 – although the price of this property is less than €450000, it has already been sold.

Task 21: Display property search results using a Report.

- Create a Report linked to the *Properties in a customers price range* Query. Include the *Price, No of Bedrooms, Property Type, Address1, Address2 and Address3* fields in the Report.
- Sort the Report in ascending order of *Price*.
- Apply the Urban style to the Report.
- The Report title is *Properties by Price.*
- Copy the Southern Estate Agents logo and address from the *Properties for Sale* Form and paste into the Report header, as shown in Figure 9.41.
- Edit the Report title so that it adjusts according to the number of records displayed in the Report. If five records are displayed in the Report, the title should be "5 properties matched your search". If 10 records are displayed in the Report, the title should be "10 properties matched your search", and so on.
- Draw a label box in the Detail section and enter the text "bedroom". Position the label box using Figure 9.41 as a guide.
- Edit the labels in the page header so that they appear like Figure 9.41.
- Apply formatting to the Report title so that it appears like Figure 9.41.

- Test the Report by previewing it and entering 400000 as the maximum the customer can afford.
- The completed Report should be similar to Figure 9.41.

Southern Estate Agents

6 Properties Matched Your Search

1 Main Street
Ballybrack
Tel: (01) 6679923

Price	Property Type	Address
€249,000	2 bedroom Apartment	38 Seaview Court Stillorgan Co. Dublin
€299,000	3 bedroom Terraced House	46 Ashlawn Grove Stillorgan Co. Dublin
€330,000	3 bedroom Terraced House	122 Plunkett Road Shankill Co. Dublin
€335,000	2 bedroom Terraced House	3 Eden Terrace Monkstown Co. Dublin
€379,000	3 bedroom Semi-Detached House	28 Rockford Manor Bray Co. Wicklow
€395,000	2 bedroom Terraced House	75 Woodford Road Greystones Co. Wicklow

Figure 9.41: Sample Report from Task 21

Task 22: Using the *Properties for Sale* Form, enter the data displayed in the shaded cells in Table 9.14 in the *Highest Offer* and *Date Sale Completed* fields.

Properties won't always be sold in sequence of their property numbers.

Property Number	Address1	Address2	Address3	Highest Offer	Date Sale Completed
15	46 Ashlawn Grove	Stillorgan	Co. Dublin	€285,000	04/06/2010
6	4 Martello Road	Dalkey	Co. Dublin	€865,000	11/06/2010
20	7 Allen Park Road	Dalkey	Co. Dublin	€575,000	17/06/2010
5	16 Wolverton Grove	Shankill	Co. Dublin	€595,000	25/06/2010

Table 9.14

Click the *Refresh All* button in the Home section of the Ribbon. The Form title should update from “21 Properties For Sale” to “17 Properties For Sale”.

Task 23: Check for updates in Queries and Reports.

1. Edit the *Analysis of market supply* Query so that it only displays properties that haven't been sold.

2. Edit the *Portfolio value of available property types by area* Query so that its calculations are only based on properties that haven't been sold.

3. Preview the *Market Supply Report*. The totals should now be as follows:
   - Apartment: 3

- Detached House: 3
- Semi-Detached House: 7
- Terraced House: 4

4. Preview the *Properties for Sale by Location* Report. Enter *Shankill* as the preferred location. Verify that the number of properties available in Shankill has changed from two to one.

5. Preview the *Properties for Sale by Location* Report again, this time entering *Stillorgan* as the preferred location. Verify that the number of properties available in Stillorgan has changed from two to one.

6. Preview the *Properties currently on the market* Report. Verify that the number of available properties has changed from 24 to 17.

Task 24: Calculate the average price for each *Property Type* by *Address2* for properties that have been sold using a Crosstab Query. Save the Query as *Average selling price by area* and test the Query by running it. The calculations should be based on seven records.

WORKED EXAMPLE: CREATE A FORM FILTER

In previous assignments, we used the *Find* button to search for records with a Form. This method is useful if you want to quickly find a specific record using a single search criteria. Using the *Filter by Form* feature, it is possible to search for multiple records using multiple search criteria.

1. Open the *Properties for Sale* Form.
2. In the *Sort & Filter* group of commands, select *Filter By Form* from the *Advanced* drop-down list (Figure 9.42). Access displays the *Properties for Sale* Form in search mode, as shown in Figure 9.43. All the text boxes are empty and the result of the Count function is no longer displayed in the Form header.

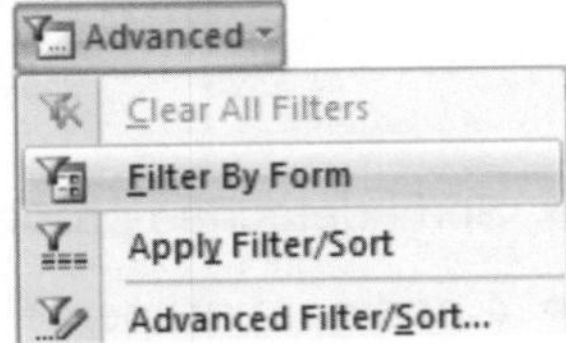

Figure 9.42

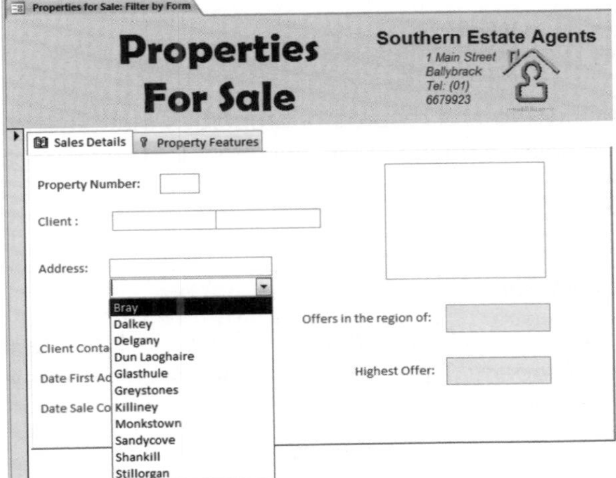

Figure 9.43: Selecting a condition for the *Address2* field

3. Select the *Address2* text box and select *Bray* from the drop-down list, as shown in Figure 9.43.

Look for | Or

4. To add a second condition to the filter, click the *Or* tab, which appears in the bottom left-hand corner of the Form.
5. Create a second condition by selecting *Greystones* in the *Address2* text box.

Apply Filter/Sort

6. In the *Sort & Filter* group, select *Apply Filter/Sort* from the *Advanced* drop-down list. The Form now displays available properties in Bray and Greystones (five in total).

The status bar at the bottom of the screen (Figure 9.44) indicates the Form is in filter mode.

Record: 1 of 5 Filtered

Figure 9.44

Toggle Filter

7. Display all records by clicking *Toggle Filter* in the *Sort & Filter* group.
8. Select *Filter By Form* from the *Advanced* drop-down list in the *Sort & Filter* group.

Clear Grid

9. Delete the Bray and Greystones conditions by selecting *Clear Grid* from the *Advanced* drop-down list.

Task 25: Create filters.

Open the *Properties for Sale* Form if it is not already open. Create filters to display the following records. In each case, check that the number of records found matches the number displayed in the *Records Found* column below. Don't forget to delete conditions before creating the next filter!

	Records Found	Completed (√)
• Semi-detached properties	7	☐
• 4 bedroom properties with parking and alarm	4	☐
• Properties in Dun Laoghaire or Glasthule	5	☐
• Semi-detached properties in Bray or Greystones	3	☐
• Detached properties in Wicklow	2	☐

Task 26: Create a Query to find records of properties that have been sold. Save the Query as *Completed Sales*. Run the Query. It should find seven records.

H Use *Is Not Null*.

Task 27: Create a sales Report.

- Create a Report linked to the *Completed sales* Query. Include the *Highest Offer, Price, No of Bedrooms, Property Type, Address1, Address2, Address3* and *Date Sale Completed* fields in the Report.
- Group the Report by *Date Sale Completed*.

- Sort the Report in ascending order of *Address2*.
- Select *Stepped* as the Report layout and *Portrait* as the orientation.
- Apply the Urban style to the Report.
- The Report title is *Sales Report.*
- Display the *Date Sale Completed* footer. Add functions to calculate the number of properties sold per month, the average selling price and the total monthly sales revenue. Edit the labels for these functions so that they appear like Figure 9.45.
- Create a label box in the Report footer, inserting the text *Report Summary.* Create a second label box immediately below the text *Report Summary* and enter the text *The market is slowly recovering. Sales are currently below target but are expected to improve in the fourth quarter of 2014*. (See Figure 9.45.)
- Add functions to the Report footer to calculate the total sales revenue for the period, the total number of properties sold and the average price received for a property. Edit the labels for these functions so that they appear like Figure 9.45.
- Remove the alternate shading from the *Date Sale Completed* header and the detail section.
- Apply a background colour of light grey to the *Date Sale Completed* footer.
- Delete the label boxes in the page header. Set the height of the page header to *0.*
- Using labels, create the column headings *Selling Price*, *Asking Price, Property Type* and *Address* in the *Date Sale Completed* header, as shown in Figure 9.45.
- Using the *Line* button, draw a horizontal line in the *Date Sale Completed* header above and below the label boxes, as shown in Figure 9.45.
- Copy the *Southern Estate Agents* address and logo from the *Properties for Sale* Form and position to the right of the *Sales Report* label box.
- The completed Report is shown in Figure 9.45.
- Export the *Sales* Report to a PDF document.
- Draw a label box in the Detail section and enter the text "bedroom". Position the label box using Figure 9.45 as a guide.

Sales Report

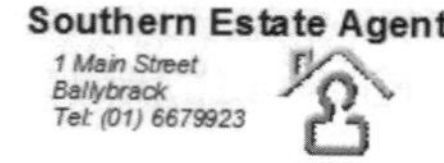

May 2014

Selling Price	Asking Price	Property Type	Address
€450,000	€455,000	3 bedroom Semi-Detached House	136 O Flynn Park Bray Co. Wicklow
€565,000	€595,000	5 bedroom Detached House	22 Anville Wood Dun Laoghaire Co. Dublin
€445,000	€425,000	3 bedroom Semi-Detached House	3 Corbawn Terrace Shankill Co. Dublin

Number of Properties Sold:	3
Average Selling Price:	€486,667
Total Sales Revenue:	€1,460,000

June 2014

Selling Price	Asking Price	Property Type	Address
€865,000	€925,000	2 bedroom Terraced House	4 Martello Road Dalkey Co. Dublin
€575,000	€525,000	3 bedroom Semi-Detached House	7 Allen Park Road Dalkey Co. Dublin
€595,000	€585,000	4 bedroom Detached House	16 Wolverton Grove Shankill Co. Dublin
€285,000	€299,000	3 bedroom Terraced House	46 Ashlawn Grove Stillorgan Co. Dublin

Number of Properties Sold:	4
Average Selling Price:	€580,000
Total Sales Revenue:	€2,320,000

Report Summary

The market is slowly recovering. Sales are currently below target but are expected to improve in the fourth quarter of 2014

Total Sales Revenue for the period:	€3,780,000
Number of Completed Sales:	7
Average price received for a property:	€540,000

Figure 9.45: Sample *Sales Report*

For a detailed explanation of how to set up a mail merge, refer to pages 186–92 in Assignment 8.

Task 28: Create a mail merge for clients whose properties have been sold.

1. Create a new document in Microsoft Word.
2. Type the letter displayed at the top of page 277. Some text is missing from the letter and will be added later on in the mail merge process.
3. Save the letter as *Completed Sale Notification.*
4. Using the mail merge facility, set this document up as a *Letter*. Use the *Completed sales* Query as the *Data Source* and insert the fields shown in bold print on the bottom of page 277.

Southern Estate Agents
1 Main Street
Ballybrack
Tel: (01) 667 9923

Dear ,

We are pleased to inform you that the sale of your property was completed on . The highest offer on your property was € and the sale will now be concluded at this price. Please contact your solicitor for details of contracts to be signed and the closing date of the sale.

It only remains for us to thank you for choosing Southern Estate Agents and to wish you all the best with your new property.

Yours sincerely,

____

Adam Doodle
Managing Director

Microsoft Word will not link to the *Completed sales* Query if the *Photo* field is included in the Query design grid.

«Client_First_Name» «Client_Surname»
«Address1»
«Address2»
«Address3»

Southern Estate Agents
1 Main Street
Ballybrack
Tel: (01) 667 9923

Dear **«Client_First_Name»**,

We are pleased to inform you that the sale of your property was completed on **«Date_Sale_Completed»**. The highest offer on your property was **«Highest_Offer»** and the sale will now be concluded at this price. Please contact your solicitor for details of contracts to be signed and the closing date of the sale.

It only remains for us to thank you for choosing Southern Estate Agents and to wish you all the best with your new property.

Yours sincerely,

____

Adam Doodle
Managing Director

5. Merge the main document with the data source to produce seven individual letters. Save the merged document as *Sales Notification Letters.*

Task 29: Create address labels.

Select the *Completed sales* Query in the Navigation Pane before you create the labels.

Open the Southern Estate Agents database if it is not already open.

- Create address labels for each of the sales notification letters.
- Design the labels so that they appear like Figure 9.46.
- Sort the labels in ascending order of *Client Surname.*
- Enter *Sales Notification Labels* as the Report name.

Tommy Dunne 7 Allen Park Road Dalkey Co. Dublin

Figure 9.46

LEARN ABOUT CALCULATED FIELDS

To date, we have used functions in the Report header, Report footer and group footer to perform calculations on data displayed in a Report. Calculations can also be carried out in the detail section of a Report. For example, we could calculate the number of days that each property was on the market before being sold by subtracting dates in the *Date First Advertised* field from dates in the *Date Sale Completed* field. A text box control that generates new data using data stored in existing fields is called a calculated field. Positioning this text box control in the detail section of the Report ensures that the calculation is carried out for each record in the Report.

WORKED EXAMPLE: CREATE A CALCULATED FIELD

1. Using the Report Wizard, create a new Report linked to the *Completed sales* Query.
2. Include the *Address2, Property Type, Price, Highest Offer, Date First Advertised* and *Date Sale Completed* fields in the Report.
3. Sort the Report in ascending order of the *Address2* field.
4. Apply the Urban style to the Report.
5. The Report title is *Comparison of Time on the Market.*

6. View the Report in layout view. Adjust the width of text box controls to fit the data.
7. Increase the height of the *Date First Advertised* and *Date Sale Completed* label boxes so that the text wraps inside each label box.
8. Adjust labels and text boxes to make space on the right for the new calculated field (Figure 9.47).

Report Header
Comparison of Time on the Market
Page Header
Location | Property Type | Price | Highest Offer | Date First Advertised | Date Sale Completed
Detail
Address2 | Property Type | Price | Highest Offer | Date First Ad | e Sale Compl
Address2 Footer
Page Footer
=Now() | ="Page " & [Page] & " of " & [Pages]
Report Footer

Figure 9.47: Adjust the width of existing labels and text boxes to accommodate the calculated field

9. View the Report in design view.

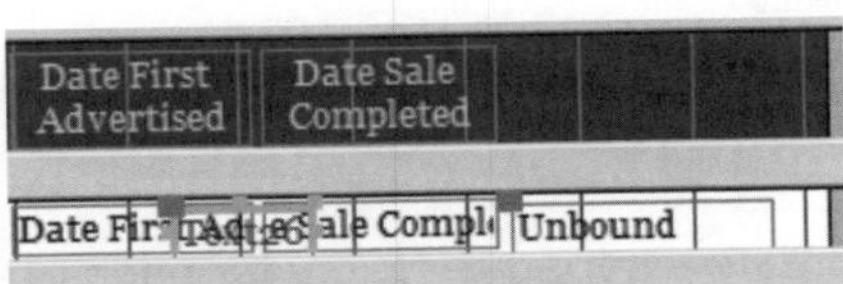

Figure 9.48: New text box positioned to the right of the *Date Sale Completed* text box in the detail section

10. Click the *Text Box* button in the Design section of the Ribbon. Draw a text box in the detail section to the right of the *Date Sale Completed* text box, as shown in Figure 9.48.

A text box created using the *Text Box* button includes both a label and a text box. In Figure 9.48, the label box is selected and is sitting on top of the *Date First Advertised* and *Date Sale Completed* text boxes. The newly created text box contains the text *Unbound*. It is unbound because it is not linked to a specific field in the Table.

11. Delete the label associated with the unbound text box. Click the unbound text box to select it. Click the text box a second time to edit it.
12. Type the following formula:

    =[Date Sale Completed]-[Date First Advertised]

13. Copy the *Date Sale Completed* label box and position the new label box in the page header above the calculated field. Edit the text in the new label box so that it reads *Days on the Market*.

14. In layout view, centre the data in the calculated field.

15. Preview the Report. Figure 9.49 is an example of the completed Report.

The *Days on the Market* values computed by the calculated field are not stored in the Table. They only exist when the Report is previewed. It is not possible to sort the Report by *Days on the Market* as it is not listed in the field list.

Comparison of Time on the Market

Location	PropertyType	Price	Highest Offer	Date First Advertised	Date Sale Completed	Days on the Market
Bray	Semi-Detached House	€455,000	€450,000	01/02/2014	21/05/2014	109
Dalkey	Semi-Detached House	€525,000	€575,000	11/01/2014	17/06/2014	157
Dalkey	Terraced House	€925,000	€865,000	04/01/2014	11/06/2014	158
Dun Laoghaire	Detached House	€595,000	€565,000	16/11/2013	28/05/2014	193
Shankill	Detached House	€585,000	€595,000	30/04/2014	25/06/2014	56
Shankill	Semi-Detached House	€425,000	€445,000	05/04/2014	09/05/2014	34
Stillorgan	Terraced House	€299,000	€285,000	07/09/2013	04/06/2014	270

Figure 9.49: The completed Report incorporating the calculated field

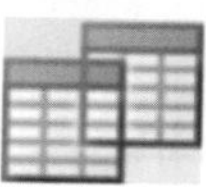

For a detailed explanation of wildcard Queries, refer to pages 206–12 in Assignment 8.

CREATE QUERIES

Create a separate Query for each of the tasks described in Table 9.15. Sort each Query using the sort order specified. Use the *Show* row of the Query design grid to specify the fields displayed by each Query. Save each Query using the name provided.

	Purpose of Query	Sort Order	Fields Displayed in Query	Query Name	Records Found
Task 30	Find records of terraced and semi-detached properties available in Dun Laoghaire, Sandycove and Monkstown	Ascending order of Address2	Address1, Address2, Address3, Property Type, No of Bedrooms, Parking, Alarm, Price, Description	Terraced/ Semi-detached in south Dublin	4
Task 31	Find records of available properties where the garden is a feature	Ascending order of Property Type	Address1, Address2, Address3, Property Type, No of Bedrooms, Parking, Alarm, Price, Description	Properties with featured garden	2
Task 32	Find records of available properties except for those in Bray, Greystones and Delgany	Ascending order of Address2	Address1, Address2, Address3, Property Type, No of Bedrooms, Parking, Alarm, Price	Co Dublin properties	11
Task 33	Find records of available properties that are either semi-detached or have three bedrooms	Descending order of Property Type	Address1, Address2, Address3, Property Type, No of Bedrooms, Parking, Alarm, Price	Family homes	8
Task 34	Display the five most expensive available properties	Descending order of Price	Address1, Address2, Address3, Property Type, No of Bedrooms, Parking, Alarm, Price	Exclusive properties	5

Table 9.15

	Purpose of Query	Sort Order	Fields Displayed in Query	Query Name	Records Found
Task 35	Find records of properties that have been sold in Shankill or Bray	Descending order of Highest Offer	Address1, Address2, Address3, Property Type, No of Bedrooms, Parking, Alarm, Price, Highest Offer, Date Sale Completed	Wicklow border sales	3

Table 9.15 (continued)

EDIT SQL CODE

Task 36

SQL

1. View the *Property Size Analysis* Query in SQL view.
2. Edit the SQL code so that the Query finds the Max of Price.
3. Edit the SQL code so the column heading is *MaxOfPrice* instead of *AVGOfPrice*
4. Run the Query and verify that it displays a maximum price of €925,000.
5. Close the Query without saving it.

Task 37

SQL

1. View the *Properties with featured garden* Query in SQL view.
2. Edit the SQL code so that the Query finds records of properties with a sea view.
3. Run the Query and verify that it finds one record.
4. Close the Query without saving it.

Task 38

SQL

1. View the *Terraced/Semi-detached in South Dublin* Query in SQL view.
2. Edit the SQL code so that the Query finds records of terraced and semi-detached properties available in Bray, Killiney and Shankill.

Copy part of the existing condition.

3. Run the Query and verify that it finds four records.
4. Close the Query without saving it.

Task 39: Create a PivotTable Query linked to the *Available Properties* Query, setting up the PivotTable Grid as follows.

- Add *Address2* as the row field.
- Add *Property Type* as the column field.
- Add *Price* as the detail field.
- Calculate the total value of property by *Address2* and by *Property Type.*
- Add *Address3* as the Filter field.
- Remove Co. Wicklow from the pivot table. Verify that the total value of property for sale has reduced from €8,352,000 to €5,583,000.
- Calculate the number of properties for sale by *Address2* and by *Property Type.* (The overall total should be 17.)
- Remove *Address3* from the filter field. Delete *Address2* and then add *Address3* as the row field.
- View the data in PivotChart view.
- Change the vertical axis title to *Property Value.*
- Remove the horizontal axis title.
- Add a chart title, entering the text *Portfolio Value by County.*
- Save the Query as *Portfolio Value Analysis.*

Task 40: Import data from Excel.

- In the External Data section of the Ribbon, select *Import Excel Spreadsheet.*
- Click the Browse button. Select the *Viewings.xlsw* file that you have downloaded from the Gill & Macmillan website and then click *Open*. Click *OK* to advance to the next step of the Import Spreadsheet Wizard.
- Ensure that the "*First row contains column headings*" check box is ticked. Click *Next*.
- Change the field size of the *Apt No* field to Integer. Change the field size of the *Property Number* field to Byte.
- Select "*Choose my own primary key*" and ensure that this is the *Apt No* field.
- Enter *Viewings* as the name of the Table. Click *Finish* and then close the Import Spreadsheet Wizard.
- Open the *Viewings* Table and verify that it contains 30 records.

WHAT IS A RELATIONAL DATABASE?

In Assignments 1 to 8, we created databases where all the records are stored in a single Table. In a relational database, the records are stored in multiple Tables. Consequently, Queries can find data in more than one Table and Reports can display data from more than one Table. In a relational database, a Form can enter data in one Table while displaying data from other Tables.

Task 41: Set up a relationship between the *Property Details* and *Viewings* Tables.

- In the Database Tools section of the Ribbon, click the *Relationships* button.
- Add the *Property Details* and *Viewings* tables to the Relationships window. Resize both tables so that all fields are visible.
- Drag the *Property Number* field from the *Property Details* Table and drop on the *Property Number* field in the *Viewings* Table.
- Tick the *Enforce Referential Integrity* check box and then click *Create*.
- Save the Relationships layout. It should look like Figure 9.50.

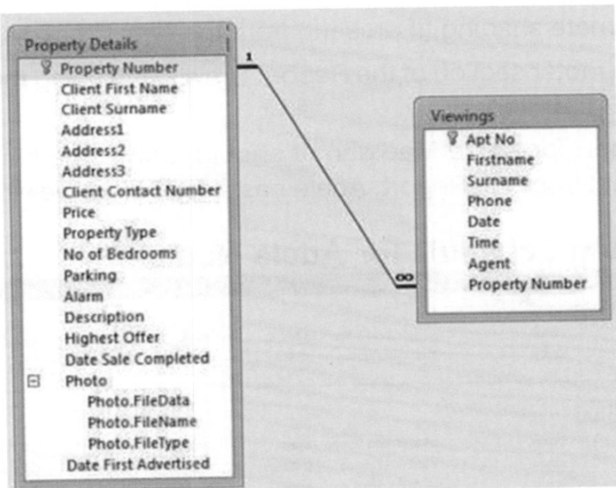

Figure 9.50: One-to-many relationship between the Property Details and Viewings Tables

- Close the Relationships window.

The sideways *8* is the mathematical symbol for infinity.

Task 42: Display appointments by agent.

- Create a new Query and add both the *Property Details* and *Viewings* Tables.
- From the Property Details Table, add the *Address1*, *Address2* and *Price* fields. Add all fields from the Viewings Table except for *Apt No* and *Property Number*.

- Set up the Query so that it displays the message "*Enter agent's full name*" when it is run. The Query should then find all appointments for the agent entered.
- Save the Query as *Viewings by Agent.*
- Create a Report linked to the *Viewings by Agent* Query, including all fields.
- Group the Report by *Date*.
- Sort the Report in ascending order of *Time.*
- The Report title is *Agent Schedule.*
- Using the Group, Sort, and Total Pane, ensure that the *Date* is grouped by *Day*.
- In design view of the Report, select the text box in the *Date* header. View the properties and edit the Control Source property to include the day in the *Format* function as follows: *=Format$([Date],"***dd** *mmmm",0,0)*
- In design view, edit the Report title so that it is displayed either as *Viewing Schedule for Tom Clarke* or *Viewing Schedule for Adele Madigan*, depending on which name is entered when the Report is previewed.
- In the Date footer, calculate the total number of appointments using an appropriate function.
- Remove the alternate shading (if present) from the detail section.
- Expand the Date footer section of the Report. Draw a line using the Line button in the Design section of the Ribbon.
- Preview the Report for Adele Madigan. It should look something like Figure 9.51, which is an extract from the Report. Adele has a total of 16 viewing appointments.

Viewing Schedule for Adele Madigan

Time of Appointment	Address of Property		Client		Phone
12 October					
12:00	28 Rockford Manor	Bray	Aine	O Neill	(085) 6023980
14:00	Beachview House	Killiney	Deirdre	Maloney	(086) 1859745
13 October					
11:00	28 Millwood Downs	Bray	Abbey	Harris	(087) 4571256
12:00	Beachview House	Killiney	Camelia	Laza	(085) 1178458
14:00	15 Rosemount Lawn	Bray	Michael	Scott	(087) 9856233
15:00	28 Millwood Downs	Bray	Andrew	Kileen	(086) 7584632

Figure 9.51: Extract from *Viewing Schedule for Adele Madigan* Report

Task 43: Display appointments by address.

- Create a new Query and add the *Property Details* and *Viewings* Tables.
- From the *Property Details* Table, add the *Address1*, *Address2* and *Price* fields. Add all fields from the *Viewings* Table except for *Apt No* and *Property Number*.
- Save the Query as *Viewings by Property.*
- Create a Report linked to the *Viewings by Property* Query, including all fields.
- Group the Report by *Address1*.

- Sort the Report in descending order of *Date.*
- The Report title is *Property Viewing History.*
- Using an appropriate function positioned in the *Address1* header, calculate the number of viewings by property. (See Figure 9.52, which is an extract from the Report.)
- Using an appropriate function, calculate the overall number of viewings. Display this total after the last record. There are 30 viewings in total.
- Preview the Report. It should look something like Figure 9.52, which is an extract from the Report.

Property Viewing History

12 Bayview Mews	**Glasthule**		**3 Viewings**		
		20/10/2014	Gabriel	Lawlor	(087) 6987558
		19/10/2014	Tony	Spain	(087) 1200583
		17/10/2014	Lynda	Allen	(087) 2258777
15 Rosemount Lawn	**Bray**		**2 Viewings**		
		20/10/2014	Breda	Murdock	(086) 7855989
		13/10/2014	Michael	Scott	(087) 9856233

Figure 9.52: Extract from the completed *Property Viewing History* Report

The One-to-many relationship can be seen clearly in Figure 9.52. Each property can have multiple viewings. The data relating to the property is stored in the *Property Details* Table, while the data relating to viewings is stored in the *Viewings* Table. Data from both tables is brought together in a Query. The *Property Viewing History* Report is linked to this Query, allowing it to display data from both tables.

Task 44: Using Access Help, search for information on grouped Reports. Write a brief report detailing the sections in a grouped Report. Give examples of grouped Reports you have viewed in websites that you regularly use, e.g. a list of songs, grouped by album, on iTunes.

DEFINE DATABASE STRUCTURE

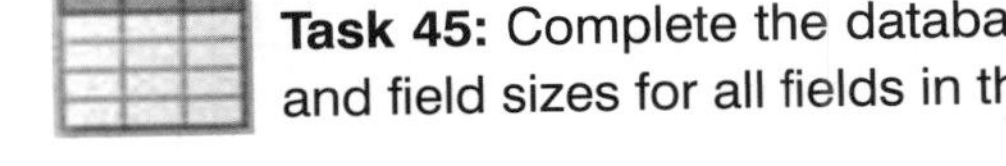

Task 45: Complete the database structure form (Table 9.16) with data types and field sizes for all fields in the *Property Details* Table.

Field Name	Data Type	Field Size
Property Number		
Client First Name		
Client Surname		
Address1		
Address2		
Address3		
Client Contact Number		
Price		
Property Type		
No of Bedrooms		
Parking		
Alarm		
Description		
Highest Offer		
Date Sale Completed		
Photo		
Date First Advertised		

Table 9.16

Ensure that the field sizes of Text fields specified in design view of the *Property Details* Table match those specified in the database structure form.

REVIEW YOUR WORK

Use the checklist below to verify that you have completed all the tasks in the Southern Estate Agents database.

		Completed (√)
Tables:	• Property Details	☐
	• Viewings	☐
Form:	• Properties for Sale	☐
Queries:	• Analysis of market supply	☐
	• Available properties by location	☐
	• Average price of property types by area	☐
	• Lowest price of property types by area	☐
	• Portfolio value of available property types by area	☐
	• Available properties	☐

		Completed (√)
	• Average selling price by area	☐
	• Co Dublin properties	☐
	• Completed sales	☐
	• Exclusive properties	☐
	• Family homes	☐
	• Portfolio value analysis	☐
	• Portfolio value by property type	☐
	• Properties in a customers price range	☐
	• Properties with featured garden	☐
	• Property price analysis	☐
	• Property size analysis	☐
	• Terraced/Semi-detached in south Dublin	☐
	• Viewings by agent	☐
	• Wicklow border sales	☐
	• Viewings by property	☐
Reports:	• Agent Schedule	☐
	• Comparison of Time on the Market	☐
	• Entry Level Properties	☐
	• Market Supply Report	☐
	• Properties by Price	☐
	• Properties Currently on the Market	☐
	• Properties for Sale by Location	☐
	• Property Viewing History	☐
	• Sales Notification Labels	☐
	• Sales Report	☐
Other:	• Database structure form	☐

Log on to www.gillmacmillan.ie to download review questions for Assignment 9.

SECTION 3 REVIEW

Database

A database is used to store, organise and retrieve data. A database can be paper based, e.g. the telephone directory, or computerised, e.g. the iTunes database of artists and songs. Computerised databases are much more efficient, as specific records can be found instantly and records can be quickly sorted into different orders. An Access database consists of four main objects: Tables, Queries, Forms and Reports. Each object carries out a specific function.

Tables

The Table is the most important object in a database. It is responsible for storing data. A database cannot function without a Table. The Table is divided into columns and rows. The columns are called fields. The rows are called records.

Tables – Important Concepts

Data Type

The data type of a field determines the type of data that can be stored in that field. So far we have covered the data types listed in Table 9.17.

Data Type	Purpose	Field Size
Text	Stores field entries made up of letters or combinations of letters and numbers. The Text data type is most commonly used to store names and addresses or codes such as car registration numbers. Access deals with symbols, such as opening and closing brackets, in the same way that it deals with letters. Consequently, phone numbers with area codes must to be stored in Text fields.	Set by the database designer. Ranges from a minimum of 1 character to a maximum of 255 characters. Each character requires 1 byte of storage per record. The default field size is 255. It is good practice to adjust the field size to reflect the data stored. For example, in a *First Name* field the field size could be reduced to 30, as it is highly unusual to encounter a name consisting of more than 30 letters. By adjusting the field size, you will reduce the amount of disk space required to store data. This is particularly important in large databases.
Date/Time	Stores dates or times. Each date must have three sections – a day, month and year, separated by a forward slash, e.g. 23/12/2014. A date can be formatted as a General Date, Short Date, Medium Date or Long Date. Each time must have an hour and a minute, separated by a colon, e.g. 14:45. A time can be formatted as a Short Time, Medium Time or Long Time. The Long Time format includes seconds.	8 bytes per record

Table 9.17

Data Type	Purpose	Field Size
Currency	Stores numbers and displays them with a currency symbol and two places of decimals by default. When the format is set to currency, the currency symbol used depends on the country selected in the Regional Settings of your PC. For example, if the United Kingdom is selected as the country, the pound sign will be used in all Currency fields. Access now has a special euro format.	8 bytes per record
Autonumber	When the data type of a field is set to Autonumber, Access automatically enters numbers in this field in sequence each time a new record is created, e.g. 1 will be entered in the Autonumber field of the first record, 2 will be entered in the Autonumber field of the second record and so on. This is useful in databases that store records of transactions where each transaction must be given a unique number, particularly where there is a high volume of transactions and where the data is entered by more than one data entry operator.	4 bytes per record
Yes/No	Used for fields where the data entered can only be one of the following: 1. Yes or No 2. On or Off 3. True or False A common example of this is a *Paid* field. *Yes* is entered when a customer has paid the amount due. *No* is entered when the customer has not paid. In a Form, Access will automatically display a check box for a Yes/No field. Ticking the box is equivalent to entering *Yes* in the field. Not ticking the box is equivalent to entering *No* in the field.	1 byte per record
Attachment	The Attachment data type allows you to store a file created in another application in an Access database. For example, in a staff database, the Attachment data type could be used to store a digital photo of each employee.	4 bytes per record

Table 9.17 (continued)

Data Type	Purpose	Field Size
Number	The Number type of a field affects three factors. 1. The range of values that can be stored in that field. 2. Whether numbers with decimal places can be stored in that field. 3. Storage space, in bytes, required for each field entry.	

Table 9.17 (continued)

The number types used in this book are summarised in Table 9.18.

Number Type	Description	Max No. of Decimals	Storage Size Entry per Field
Byte	Stores whole numbers from 0 to 255	None	1 byte
Integer	Stores whole numbers from -32,768 to +32,767	None	2 bytes
Long Integer	Stores whole numbers from -2,147,483,648 to +2,147,483,648	None	4 bytes
Single	Stores numbers with decimals	7	4 bytes

Table 9.18

Data Validation

A method of checking the accuracy of data entered in the database by specifying validation rules in the Table. For example, a person's age can't be negative and can't be greater than roughly 110.

Validation Rule	Between 1 And 110
Validation Text	Ages must be from 1 to 110 inclusive

Figure 9.53

The validation rule displayed in Figure 9.53 will prevent numbers outside the range 1 to 110 inclusive from being entered in the *Age* field. When the data entry operator attempts to enter a number outside this range, Access uses the validation text as an error message (Figure 9.54).

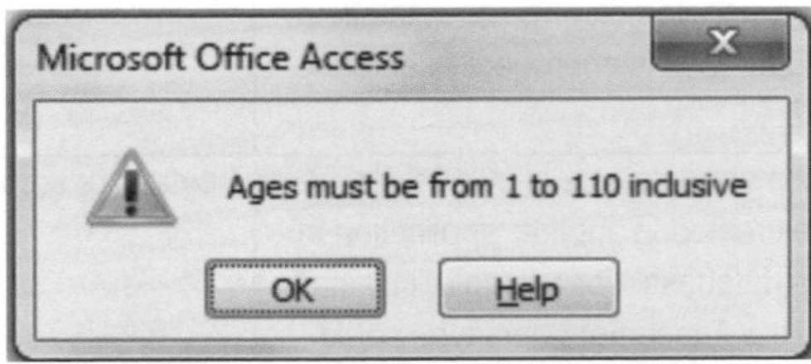

Figure 9.54

The more specific the validation rule is, the better chance it has of trapping errors. In an adult education college, the validation rule for the *Age* field might be similar to Figure 9.55.

Validation Rule	Between 16 And 65
Validation Text	To qualify for the course, students must be aged from 16 to 65

Figure 9.55

Tables – Potential Pitfalls

- A validation rule in a Currency field should never include the euro symbol.
- Access tables are not designed to facilitate easy data entry. When there are a lot of fields in the Table, they won't all be visible on the screen. It is always best to use a Form for data entry.

Queries

The function of a Query is to search for specific records in the Table. Conditions entered in the Query design grid give instructions on how the Query should search for records. A Query searches through the Table record by record. Any records satisfying the Query condition(s) are copied into a separate datasheet, which is then displayed on the screen.

Queries – Important Concepts

Parameter Query

Prompts the user to enter a value each time the Query is run. The Query will display records matching the value entered. For example, in a database of cars for sale, customers could specify their preferred car colour, as shown in Figure 9.56.

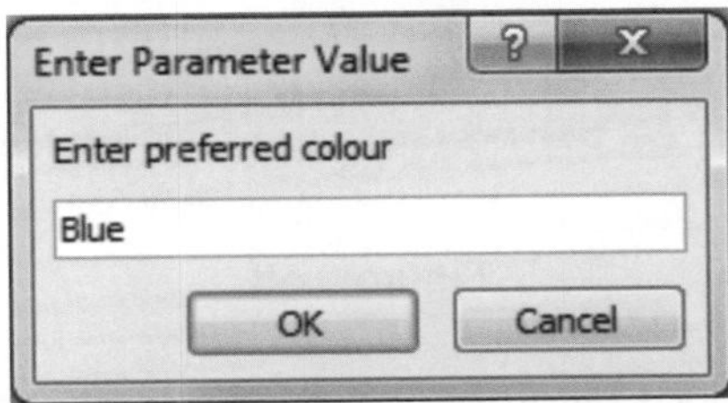

Figure 9.56

In Figure 9.56, clicking *OK* will display blue cars. The advantage of Parameter Queries is that they can be used for multiple values. In Figure 9.56, customers could search for different colour cars simply by entering a different colour each time they run the Query.

Wildcard

Used to search for data when only part of the search information is available. When using wildcards in a Query, data that is missing is represented by the wildcard symbol (*). There are three situations in which wildcards can be used:

1. Data is missing at the beginning, e.g. **Z* finds all PPS numbers ending with *Z*.
2. Data is missing at the end, e.g. *15** finds all car registrations starting with *15*.

3. Data is missing in the middle, e.g. **Mc** finds all names including the letters *Mc*.

Not Logical Operator

Used in negative wildcard Queries. For example, *Not Like "*DL*"* finds all cars except for those registered in Donegal. The *Not* logical operator can also be used instead of <>. For example, *<>23* and *Not 23* achieve the same result.

Joining Conditions

When there are multiple positive conditions in a single field, these conditions are joined using the *OR* logical operator.

Field:	Address1	Address2	Address3
Table:	Property Details	Property Details	Property Details
Sort:		Ascending	
Show:	☑	☑	☑
Criteria:		"Bray" Or "Greystones" Or "Delgany"	
or:			

Figure 9.57

In Figure 9.57, the three conditions are joined with *OR*. Logically, a property cannot be in two locations at the same time, so joining the conditions with *AND* would result in the Query finding no records.

When there are multiple negative conditions in a single field, the conditions must be joined with the *AND* logical operator.

Field:	Address1	Address2	Address3
Table:	Property Details	Property Details	Property Details
Sort:		Ascending	
Show:	☑	☑	☑
Criteria:		<>"Bray" And <>"Greystones" And <>"Delgany"	
or:			

Figure 9.58

The Query in Figure 9.58 finds all properties except for those in Bray, Greystones and Delgany. The negative conditions are joined with *AND*. Joining the negative conditions with *OR* would cause the conditions to cancel each other out. The Query will still work but it will incorrectly find all the records in the table, including properties in Bray, Greystones and Delgany.

Totals Query

Totals Queries are not used to find records. They perform calculations on the records stored in the Table.

A Totals Query can do calculations based on records in the Table.

The output from the Totals Query in Figure 9.59 is from the Southside Motor Tests database. The Query has added all the values in the *Cost* field to calculate the total earned from car tests.

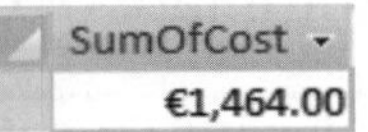

SumOfCost
€1,464.00

Figure 9.59

A Totals Query can also do calculations based on groups of records in the Table.

Make	SumOfCost
Ford	€481.00
Honda	€136.00
Nissan	€272.00
Opel	€277.00
Smart	€47.00
Toyota	€251.00

Figure 9.60

In Figure 9.60, the *Make* field has been added to the Query. This results in the Query calculating six individual totals – one total for each make of car.

Crosstab Query

A Crosstab Query is a more advanced form of the Totals Query. With a Totals Query, data can only be analysed using a single variable. A Crosstab Query allows extra levels of analysis. In Figure 9.61, the total for each *Make* is analysed by *Test Result*.

Make	Fail	Fail Advisory	Pass
Ford	€204.00	€47.00	€230.00
Honda		€136.00	
Nissan	€136.00		€136.00
Opel	€68.00		€209.00
Smart			€47.00
Toyota		€68.00	€183.00

Figure 9.61

Figure 9.61 is a Crosstab Query. The *Make* field is cross-tabulated with the *Test Result* field. Instead of a single total for each make of car, there are now three separate calculations – the totals accruing to failed tests, tests with a result of fail advisory and tests with a result of pass for each make of car.

Summary of Query Logical Operators

Logical Operator	Meaning
<	Less than
<=	Less than or equal to
=	Equal to
<>	Not equal to
Not	Used in negative wildcard Queries. Can also be used as an alternative to <>. *Not 5* and *<>5* achieve the same result in a Query.
>	Greater than
>=	Greater than or equal to
Between	Finds numbers that fall between an upper and lower limit. It is inclusive of the upper and lower limits.
AND	Joins conditions in different fields. When conditions are joined with *AND*, the Query will only find records where *all* the conditions are satisfied. When joining conditions in multiple fields, there is no need to type *AND*. Simply position all the conditions in the same row of the Query design grid. *AND* should only be used to join conditions in a single field when the conditions are negative.
OR	When *OR* is used to join conditions in a single field, the Query will find records that satisfy at least *one* of the listed conditions. An *OR* condition for multiple fields is created by positioning the conditions on different lines in the Query design grid. When *OR* is used to join conditions in multiple fields, there is no need to type *OR*.
Is Null	No data present in the field
Is Not Null	Data has been entered in the field

Table 9.19

Queries – Potential Pitfalls

- A mail merge linked to a Query will not work if the Query includes an Attachment field.
- Joining negative conditions with *OR* has no effect, as the conditions will cancel each other out, resulting in the Query finding all the records in the Table.
- Never join positive conditions in a single field with *AND*.
- <> doesn't work with negative wildcard Queries. Use *Not* instead.

Forms

The main function of a Form is to facilitate data entry. A Form can be linked to a Table or a Query. Data entered in the Form filters down to and is stored in the Table. A Form can also be used to find records, edit records and delete records. When you do this, you are essentially using the Form as an interface to the Table. It is more efficient to use a Form for data entry and record editing, as Tables are not specifically designed for these tasks.

Forms – Important Concepts

Tab Control

Allows a Form to be divided into multiple pages. This is useful where there are too many label and text box controls to fit on a single screen.

Figure 9.62

In Figure 9.62, the tab control has been used to divide the Form into two sections: *Sales Details* and *Property Features*. The data entry operator can switch from one section to another by clicking the appropriate tab.

Form Functions

Functions can be added to the Form header to give extra information. In Figure 9.62, the Count function has calculated that there are 17 properties for sale. The Form in Figure 9.62 is linked to a Query that uses *Is Null* to exclude properties that have been sold. As additional properties are sold, the Count function in the Form header updates. For example, if another property was sold, the Form title would read *16 Properties For Sale*.

Form Filter

Allows you to search for records with multiple search criteria using a Form. Form filters are accessed by selecting *Filter By Form* from the *Advanced* drop-down list in the *Sort & Filter* group of commands. When you do this, the Form changes to a search Form. All the text boxes are empty. Select what you want to search for using the combo boxes.

 Forms – Potential Pitfalls

- When searching for records using a Form, Access will only display records that exactly match the search term. Where separate fields are used to store *Firstname* and *Surname*, searching for *Paul Sheehan* in the *Surname* field won't find any records. Either search for *Paul* in the *Firstname* field or search for *Sheehan* in the *Surname* field.
- You will need to edit the row source of a combo box when new records include data that is not listed the existing combo box. For example, when adding details of new stock in a database of cars for sale, a combo box relating to the colour of the car may not include the latest colours. New colours can be added to the combo box list by editing the row source of the combo box.
- Editing the field name in a text box linked to a specific field in the Table while in design view of a Form will cause an error. Only labels should be edited when you are in design view.
- If a horizontal scroll bar is displayed at the bottom of the Form, it means that the Form is too wide. You should adjust the Form until it exactly fits the width of the screen.
- When a Form has been divided into sections using the tab control, the tab order list will be empty unless you select a text box before displaying the tab order.

Reports

The main functions of a Report are to format, sort and summarise data stored in a database. Reports are usually printed out. You don't need to have knowledge of databases or Microsoft Access to understand and interpret the information contained in a Report. Many businesspeople use Reports to assist them in decision making. A Report can be linked to a Table or a Query. In a database with a single Table, a Report linked to the Table will display all the records in the database. A Report linked to a Query will only display the specific records found by that Query.

 Reports – Important Concepts

Mail Merge

Commonly used in business to combine data from a database with a word processing document, thereby producing an individual personalised document or email for each record stored in the database. Mail merge can also be used to produce address labels. There are four steps in the mail merge process.

1. Type your document using Microsoft Word. This is called the *main document*.
2. Link the document to a Table or Query in your database. The Table or Query you select is called the *data source*.
3. Insert fields from the data source in the main document. These are called *merge fields*.
4. Merge the main document with the data source to produce multiple documents.

Multiple Sort

Using an Access Report, records from a Table or Query can be sorted by up to four fields. A Report can have multiple sort levels as long as data is repeated in one or more fields.

Report Functions

Perform calculations on data displayed in a Report. Functions can be added to the Report header, Report footer or the group footer. Each Report function must refer to a field. The function **=sum([Cost])** adds all the values in the *Cost* field. Positioning this function in the Report footer will calculate a total for *all* the records in the Report. When the same function is positioned in the group footer, a separate total will be calculated for each group of records in the Report. For example, in a Report grouped by Province, four individual totals would be created – a separate total for Munster, Leinster, Ulster and Connaught.

Functions can be used in the Report header to create a dynamic report title.

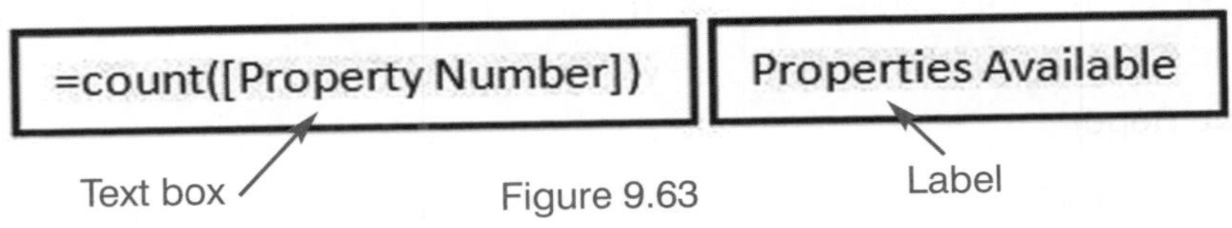

Figure 9.63

For example, the expression in Figure 9.63 creates a Report title that adjusts as properties are sold, i.e. 24 Properties Available, 23 Properties Available, etc.

Grouped Reports

A Report can be divided into groups of records when data is repeated in individual fields. In the Southside Motor Tests database there are three different test results – pass, fail and fail advisory. Consequently, a grouped Report based on the *Test Result* field would consist of three groups. Report functions can be added to the *Test Result* footer to analyse the records in each group. For example, the Count function could be used to calculate the total number of passes, fails and fail advisory results.

Figure 9.64 shows the first two groups of a Report grouped by *Test Result*. A grouped Report has two additional sections: the group header and group footer. As the Report is grouped by *Test Result*, these additional sections are the *Test Result* header and the *Test Result* footer. Each test result (pass, fail and fail advisory) is displayed once in the *Test Result* header. The Count function in the *Test Result* footer calculates the total number of results in each category.

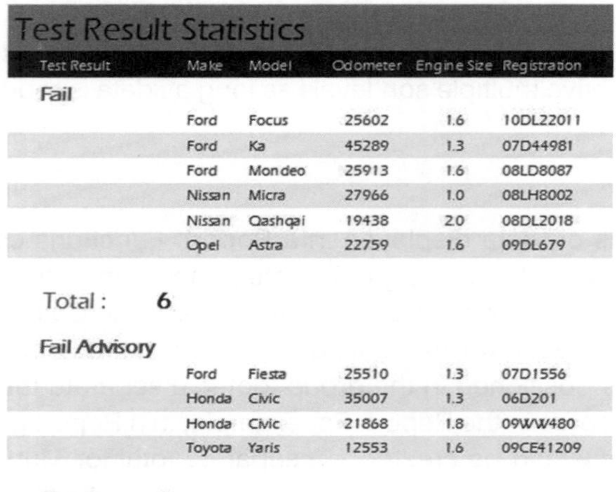

Test Result Statistics

Test Result	Make	Model	Odometer	Engine Size	Registration
Fail					
	Ford	Focus	25602	1.6	10DL22011
	Ford	Ka	45289	1.3	07D44981
	Ford	Mondeo	25913	1.6	08LD8087
	Nissan	Micra	27966	1.0	08LH8002
	Nissan	Qashqai	19438	2.0	08DL2018
	Opel	Astra	22759	1.6	09DL679
Total : **6**					
Fail Advisory					
	Ford	Fiesta	25510	1.3	07D1556
	Honda	Civic	35007	1.3	06D201
	Honda	Civic	21868	1.8	09WW480
	Toyota	Yaris	12553	1.6	09CE41209
Total : **4**					

Figure 9.64

Crosstab Reports

A Crosstab Report is automatically created when a Report is linked to a Crosstab Query.

Test Results by Manufacturer

Make	Fail	Fail Advisory	Pass
Ford	2	1	5
Honda		2	
Nissan	2		2
Opel	1		4
Toyota			3
Total:	**3**	**2**	**4**

Figure 9.65

The Report in Figure 9.65 is a Crosstab Report from the Southside Motor Tests database. The *Make* field is cross-tabulated with the *Result* field, producing a grid similar to a spreadsheet. Access creates new fields when you create a Crosstab Report. In Figure 9.65, three new fields named *Fail*, *Fail Advisory* and *Pass* have been generated from the *Test Result* field. The Count functions in the Report footer refer to these new fields: *=count([Fail])* calculates the number of failed tests, *=count([Fail Advisory])* calculates the number of tests whose result was fail advisory and *=count([Pass])* calculates the number of tests where the result was pass.

Calculated Fields

A calculated field is used to perform an individual calculation for each record in a Report. This is achieved by positioning the calculated field in the detail section.

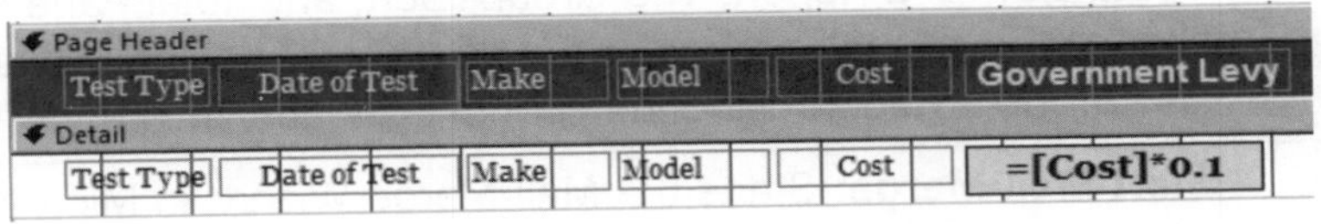

Figure 9.66

Figure 9.66 displays the design of a Report from the Southside Motor Tests database. A government levy of 10% is calculated using a calculated field. The expression *=[Cost]*0.1* is entered in a text box positioned in the detail section. This creates a calculated field. As the calculated field is in the detail section, the government levy is calculated for each record in the Report, as shown in Figure 9.67.

Government Levy Charges

Test Type	Date of Test	Make	Model	Cost	Government Levy
Full	03/06/2014	Ford	Ka	€68.00	€6.80
Full	03/06/2014	Honda	Civic	€68.00	€6.80
Retest	03/06/2014	Ford	Fiesta	€47.00	€4.70
Retest	03/06/2014	Opel	Corsa	€47.00	€4.70

Figure 9.67

Any field names referred to in a calculated field must be enclosed in square brackets. Calculated fields are not stored in the Table. They only exist while a Report is in print preview, layout view or Report view.

Reports – Potential Pitfalls

- Mixing up the brackets in a Report function will cause an error. The square brackets should always be inside the curved brackets.
- When referring to a field with a function, you must use exactly the same spelling as that in the field list. Misspelling a field name will cause an error in the function.
- Report functions don't work when positioned in the page footer.
- When you sort records using the Report Wizard, the sorted fields will always appear on the left of the Report. If you don't want this to happen, sort the Report in layout view or design view once the wizard has finished.
- Before starting the Report Wizard, select the Table or Query the Report is linked to in the Navigation Pane. If you don't do this, you may find that your Report is not linked to the correct object.

TOOLBAR BUTTONS INTRODUCED IN SECTION 3

Group & Sort: Displays the Group, Sort, and Total Pane in design or layout view of a Report. The Group, Sort, and Total Pane is used to change the existing sort order or to add more sorting levels. You can also group a Report using the Group, Sort, and Total Pane.

Start Mail Merge: Starts the Mail Merge Wizard in Microsoft Word, allowing you to link a word processing document to an Access database.

Select Recipients: Click this button to specify first the database and then the Table or Query that you want to link your main document to.

Insert Merge Field: Click this button to insert a field from your Access database into the main document in Microsoft Word.

Preview Results: Displays a preview of the completed mail merge without actually creating a new merged document.

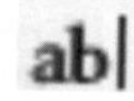

Finish & Merge: Completes the mail merge process by producing a new document containing the merged data. The main document and data source can also be merged directly to the printer or to email.

Text Box: Click this button to create a function or calculated field in a Form or Report.

Property Sheet: Displays the properties of the selected control. Use the property sheet to change the text size, background colour, etc.

Datasheet View: Displays the data stored in the Table. Datasheet view is useful for testing fields and validation rules when setting up a new Table.

Tab Control: Use this button to divide your Form into sections. This is useful when there are too many label and text box controls to fit on the computer screen.

Autoformat: Click this button to format your Form or Report using one of the 25 formats available in Access. The Autoformat option is only available in layout view.

	Totals: When in design view of a Query, clicking this button adds a *Total* row to the Query design grid. Functions such as *Sum* and *Avg* can be selected in the *Total* row.
	Query Wizard: Starts the Query Wizard, which is the most convenient way to create a Crosstab Query. Select *Crosstab Query* in the *New Query* dialog box and follow the steps.
	Format Painter: Copies the formats from the selected control in design or layout view of a Query or Report. These formats will in turn be applied to the next control that is selected.
	Select Form/Report: Selects an entire Report or Form when in design view. Once you click this button, any changes made in the property sheet will be applied to the entire Form or Report.
	Toggle Filter: When a Form is displaying filtered records, click the *Toggle Filter* button to display all the records again.
	Label: Click this button and drag to create a label box. Label boxes are used for descriptive text in Forms and Reports.
	**Line:** Click this button and drag to create a line in a Form or a Report.

SECTION 4

Introduction to Relational Databases

Assignment 10: Exam Management Relational Database System

Tip **Note** **Rule** **Cross-reference** **Shortcut** **Hint** **Important Point** **Theory Section**

10 Exam Management Relational Database System

SCENARIO

Ann Mitchell runs a busy information technology college in Cork. Recently, she has been finding it increasingly difficult to keep track of all the administration work generated by exams, which happen twice yearly. In Assignment 10 you will create a relational database application to manage the administration of student exams.

By completing this assignment, you will learn how to:

- Create a database containing multiple Tables.
- Set up relationships between Tables.
- Create a dynamic combo box.
- Create a Form linked to multiple Tables.
- Create a macro to speed up data entry.
- Develop custom database menus.
- Create a Query linked to another Query.
- Create an Update Query.

This assignment is designed to introduce you to the concepts and practical applications of relational databases. It is not meant to be a comprehensive guide to relational databases. For this reason, less emphasis has been placed on explanation and more emphasis on learning by doing.

PART 1: NFQ LEVEL 5 RELATIONAL DATABASE

NFQ Level 5 students should complete up to Task 9 inclusive.
NFQ Level 6 students should complete all the tasks in Assignment 10.

Task 1: Create a new database named Exam Management System.

Task 2: Create the *Mentors* Table.

- Create a new Table and save the Table as *Mentors.*
- Using the data displayed in Table 10.1, create fields with appropriate data types in the *Mentors* Table.

Mentor Code	RLQN
Mentor Name	Rachel Quinn
Extension Number	2185

Table 10.1

- Set the *Mentor Code* field as the primary key.
- Do not enter data in the Table at this point.

Task 3: Create the *Students* Table.

- Create a new Table and save the Table as *Students.*
- Using the data displayed in Table 10.2, create fields with appropriate data types in the *Students* Table.

Student Code	15CP001
Firstname	Domnic
Surname	Brennan
Address1	The Heath
Address2	Fermoy
Address3	Co. Cork
Course	Computer Programming
Start Date	01/09/2015
Finish Date	
Certificate	No
Mentor Code	RLQN

Table 10.2

- Set the *Student Code* field as the primary key.
- Do not enter data in the Table at this point.

LINKING THE *MENTORS* TABLE AND THE *STUDENTS* TABLE

Each mentor is responsible for a group of students. Each student has only one mentor. The Mentor Code *RLQN* can only be stored in one record in the *Mentors* Table because *Mentor Code* is the primary key, but it can be stored in multiple records in the *Students* Table depending on how many students Rachel Quinn is responsible for. This is called a one-to-many relationship.

REFERENTIAL INTEGRITY

Referential integrity is a system used by Access to ensure that data in related Tables follows the rules of the one-to-many relationship and that data is not accidentally deleted. Referential integrity can be enforced as long as the linking fields have the same data type and one of the linking fields is the primary key.

Enforcing referential integrity means that:

1. A code cannot be entered in the *Mentor Code* field in the *Students* Table unless that code already exists in the *Mentors* Table. In other words, you can't assign a particular mentor to a student unless you have already recorded details of that mentor in the database.
2. The entire record of a particular mentor cannot be deleted from the *Mentors* Table while there are references to the *Mentor Code* of that mentor in the *Students* Table.
3. The *Mentor Code* cannot be altered in the *Mentors* Table while there are references to that *Mentor Code* in the *Students* Table.

WORKED EXAMPLE: CREATE THE RELATIONSHIP BETWEEN THE *MENTORS* TABLE AND *STUDENTS* TABLE

1. Click the *Relationships* button in the Database Tools section of the Ribbon.
2. Add the *Mentors* Table and the *Students* Table to the Relationships window. Close the Show Table dialog box.
3. A one-to-many relationship is set up by dragging the primary key field from the Table on the one side of the relationship (*Mentor Code* in the *Mentors* Table) to the related field in the Table on the many side of the relationship (*Mentor Code* in the *Students* Table).
4. Drag the *Mentor Code* field from the *Mentors* Table and drop on the *Mentor Code* field in the *Students* Table (see Figure 10.1).
5. In the Edit Relationships dialog box, click the *Enforce Referential Integrity* check box. Notice that Access shows the relationship type as one-to-many.
6. Click *Create*. The relationship between the *Mentors* Table and the *Students* Table should appear like Figure 10.1.

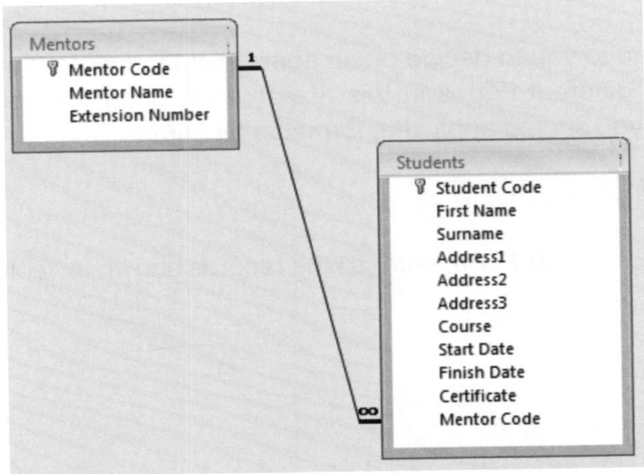

Figure 10.1: One-to-many relationship between the *Mentors* Table and *Students* Table

It is easier to understand the relationship when the Table on the one side of the relationship is positioned on the left.

7. Save the Relationship and close the Relationships window.

Access will not set up the relationship unless the linking fields have the same data type and field size. In this case, *Mentor Code* should be given a data type of Text and a field size of 4 in both tables.

The sideways 8 is the mathematical symbol for infinity.

Task 4: Create the *Mentor Details* Form.

- Create a Form linked to the *Mentors* Table.
- A suggested layout and format for the Form is shown in Figure 10.2.

Holding down the *Shift* key while pressing *Enter* brings you to a new line in a label box.

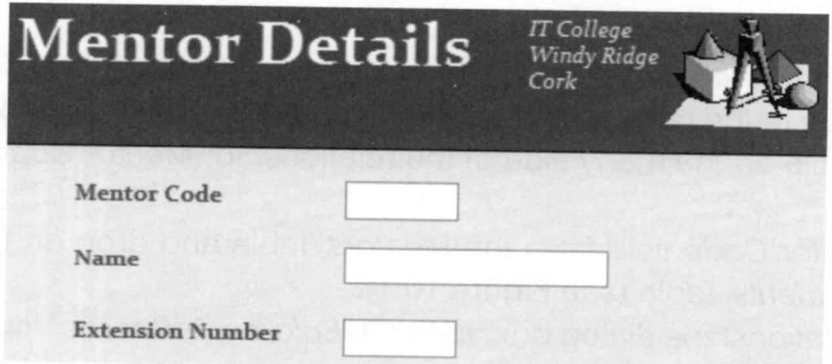

Figure 10.2: Suggested layout for the *Mentor Details* Form

- Save the *Mentor Details* Form.

At this stage, it's up to you to decide on an appropriate format for the Form. As we will use a number of different Forms in this assignment, once you have decided on a particular format, you should apply that format to all Forms.

Task 5: Enter data.

- Using the *Mentor Details* Form, enter all the records shown in Table 10.3.

Mentor Code	Mentor Name	Extension Number
BNSN	Brian Sullivan	2973
JNAG	Jane Armstrong	2601
PRRY	Peter Reilly	2098
RLQN	Rachel Quinn	2185

Table 10.3

Task 6: Create the *Student Registration* Form.

1. Create a new Form linked to the *Students* Table.
   - Add all fields except for *Finish Date* and *Certificate*.
   - The Form title is *Student Registration.*
   - Set up the Form so that it appears like Figure 10.3.
2. Create a combo box for the *Course* field (ensure that the Control Wizard is on). The values to be displayed in the combo box are shown in Table 10.4.

Course (Combo Box)
Computer Programming
Information Technology
Web Design

Table 10.4

3. Set the *Limit to List* property of the combo box to *Yes*.
4. Set the *Allow Value List Edits* property of the combo box to *No*.
5. Create a combo box for the *Mentor Code* field.

Each time the details of a new student are entered in the database, the *Mentor Code* combo box is used to select the code for their mentor. Unlike the *Course* combo box, the *Mentor Code* combo box list is not manually entered using the Combo Box Wizard. Instead, the combo box will find the list of mentor codes and names in the *Mentors* Table. It can do this because the *Mentors* and *Students* Tables are joined with a one-to-many relationship. As new mentors are added to the *Mentors* Table, they will be automatically picked up by the combo box. By contrast, the *Course* combo box is a static list. The only way of adding new courses to the *Course* combo box list is by editing its properties.

6. Select *"I want the combo box to look up the values in a table or query"* and click *Next.*
7. Select the *Mentors* Table and click *Next*.
8. Add *Mentor Code* and *Mentor Name* to the combo box and click *Next.*
9. Sort the combo box in ascending order of *Mentor Code*. Click *Next*.
10. Ensure that the *Hide key column* check box is ticked. Click *Next*.

11. Store the value in the *Mentor Code* field. Click *Next*.
12. Enter *Mentor* as the label for the combo box. Click *Finish*.
13. Test the combo box by selecting *Brian Sullivan*. The combo box displays the text "Brian Sullivan" but has entered the code BNSN in the *Mentor Code* field in the *Students* Table. The relationship between the two tables is working. Once a particular *Mentor Code* is entered in the *Students* Table, Access can display the *Mentor Name* related to this *Mentor Code*.
14. Set the tab order of the *Student Registration* Form to *Student Code, Firstname, Surname, Address1, Address2, Address3, Course, Start Date, Mentor Code*. A suggested layout and format for the Form is shown in Figure 10.3.

Figure 10.3: Suggested layout for the *Student Registration* Form

15. Save the *Student Registration* Form.

Task 7: Enter data.

Using the *Student Registration* Form, enter all the records displayed in Table 10.5.

Selecting Rachel Quinn in the *Mentor Code* combo box results in the code *RLQN* being entered in the *Mentor Code* field in the *Students* Table. This is also the case for the other mentor codes.

There are two students named John Murphy in the *Students* Table. The primary key will be used to ensure the correct John Murphy is selected as the matter arises.

Student Code	Firstname	Surname	Address1	Address2	Address3	Course	Start Date	Mentor
15CP001	Domnic	Brennan	The Heath	Fermoy	Co. Cork	Computer Programming	01/09/2015	Rachel Quinn
15CP002	Brendan	Dunne	87 Earlsfort Mews	Ballinlough	Cork	Computer Programming	01/09/2015	Peter Reilly
15CP003	Tadhg	Scanlan	9 Woodvale Grove	Rochestown	Co. Cork	Computer Programming	01/09/2015	Jane Armstrong
15CP004	Diarmuid	Scott	82 Glendale Park	Clogheen	Co. Tipperary	Computer Programming	01/09/2015	Jane Armstrong
15CP005	Rod	Hogan	The Elms	Ballinlough	Cork	Computer Programming	01/09/2015	Brian Sullivan
15IT001	Maura	Clohosey	31 Hillcourt Park	Killarney	Co. Kerry	Information Technology	08/09/2015	Rachel Quinn
15IT002	Tony	Gallagher	20 Glenbourne Close	Rochestown	Co. Cork	Information Technology	08/09/2015	Rachel Quinn
15IT003	Michael	O Neill	15 Newgrove Avenue	Blackrock	Cork	Information Technology	08/09/2015	Peter Reilly
15IT004	John	Murphy	Woodhaven	Kenmare	Co. Kerry	Information Technology	08/09/2015	Brian Sullivan
15IT005	Deirdre	Moroney	26 Charleville Court	Tralee	Co. Kerry	Information Technology	08/09/2015	Peter Reilly
15IT006	Colin	Evans	The Hollows	Mallow	Co. Cork	Information Technology	08/09/2015	Jane Armstrong
15IT007	Eamonn	Twomey	1 Castlefield Court	Douglas	Cork	Information Technology	08/09/2015	Jane Armstrong
15IT008	Nora	Sheehan	Glenview	Ballinlough	Cork	Information Technology	08/09/2015	Jane Armstrong
15IT009	Susan	Wright	Hillcrest Manor	Glasheen	Cork	Information Technology	08/09/2015	Brian Sullivan
15IT010	Sean	Noonan	13 Eden Park Drive	Douglas	Cork	Information Technology	08/09/2015	Brian Sullivan
15WD001	Ciara	Mooney	48 Auburn Road	Douglas	Cork	Web Design	15/09/2015	Rachel Quinn
15WD002	Robin	Carr	6 Springlawn Park	Dungarvan	Co. Waterford	Web Design	15/09/2015	Rachel Quinn
15WD003	Elaine	Mc Carthy	3 Cairnwood Grove	Raheen	Limerick	Web Design	15/09/2015	Peter Reilly
15WD004	Paula	King	4 Fairview Heights	Macroom	Co. Cork	Web Design	15/09/2015	Brian Sullivan
15WD005	John	Murphy	8 Old Court Road	Douglas	Cork	Web Design	15/09/2015	Peter Reilly

Table 10.5

Once you have entered all the data, open the *Students* Table in datasheet view. Notice that the four character codes have been entered in the *Mentor Code* field even though you selected the *Mentor Names* in the combo box.

Task 8: Create a Report that lists *Students* by *Course.*

- Using the Report Wizard, create a new Report linked to the *Students* Table.
- Add the *Firstname, Surname* and *Course* fields.
- Group the Report by *Course*.
- Sort the Report in ascending order of *Surname*.
- Apply the *Verve* style to the Report.
- The Report title is *List of Current Students*.
- Add a function to calculate the total number of students in each course.
- Copy the college address and logo from the *Mentors* Form and paste them into the Report header.

Task 9: Create a Report that lists students by mentor.

Because this Report will display fields from the *Students* Table and the *Mentors* Table, a Query containing fields from both tables must first be created. The Report will be linked to this Query.

- Create a new Query and add both the *Mentors* Table and *Students* Table. From the *Mentors* Table, add the *Mentor Name* field to the Query design grid. From the *Students* Table, add the *Firstname, Surname* and *Course* fields to the Query design grid.
- Click the *Run* button to view the data found by the Query. Data from both tables is displayed. This data will be used by the Report.

- Save the Query as *Mentors and students.*

- Using the Report Wizard, create a new Report linked to the *Mentors and students* Query. Add all fields to the Report.
- View the Report by *Students.*
- Group the Report by *Mentor Name*.
- Sort the Report in ascending order of *Surname*.
- Apply the *Verve* style to the Report.
- The Report title is *Mentor Groups.*
- Add a label to the *Mentor Name* header so that data appears in the header as follows:
  Mentor: Brian Sullivan
  Mentor: Jane Armstrong
  Mentor: Peter Reilly
  Mentor: Rachel Quinn

- Add a function to calculate the total number of students in each group.
- Copy the college address and logo from the *Mentors* Form and paste it into the Report header.
- Export the *Mentor Groups* Report to a PDF document.

PART 2: NFQ LEVEL 6 RELATIONAL DATABASE

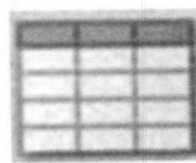

Task 10: Create the *Subjects* Table.

- Create a new Table and save the Table as *Subjects*
- Using the data displayed in Table 10.6, create fields with appropriate data types in the *Subjects* Table.

Subject Code	ICW520
Subject Title	Database Methods
Core Module	0
Vocational Module	1
Elective Module	0

Table 10.6

- Set the *Subject Code* field as the primary key.
- Do not enter data in the Table at this point.

Task 11: Create the *Subject Details* Form.

- Create a Form linked to the *Subjects* Table. Add all fields to the Form. A suggested layout and format for the Form is shown in Figure 10.4.

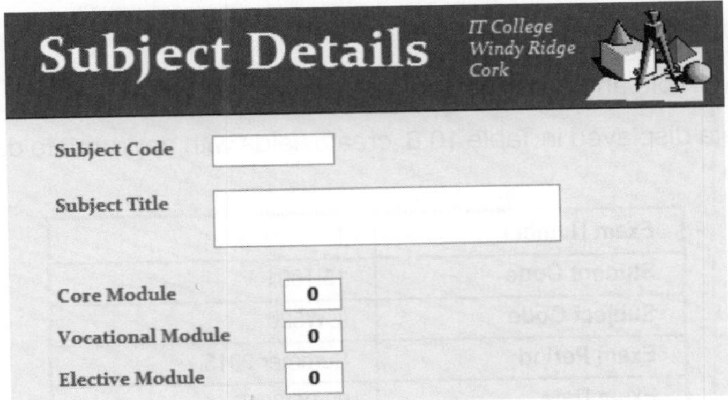

Figure 10.4: Suggested layout for the *Subject Details* Form

- Save the Form as *Subject Details*.

Task 12: Enter data.
Using the *Subject Details* Form, enter all the records displayed in Table 10.7.

Subject Code	Subject Title	Core Module	Vocational Module	Elective Module
C301	Programming	0	1	0
C302	Software Development	0	1	0
C303	Systems Analysis	0	1	0
I201	Computer Maintenance	0	1	0
I202	Information and Communication Systems	0	1	0
IC621	Spreadsheet Methods	0	1	0
ICW400	Communications	1	0	0
ICW401	Work Experience	1	0	0
ICW402	Customer Service	0	0	1
ICW520	Database Methods	0	1	0
IW701	Word Processing	0	1	0
W101	Web Authoring	0	1	0
W102	Graphic Design	0	1	0
W103	eCommerce	0	1	0

Table 10.7

Entering 1 or 0 in the *Core*, *Vocational* and *Elective Module* fields is equivalent to entering Yes or No. By entering 1 or 0 instead of Yes or No, it will be easier to determine which students are eligible for a full certificate later on in the assignment. To be eligible for a full certificate, a student must have a pass, merit or distinction in two core modules, five or more vocational modules and one elective module.

Task 13: Create the *Exams* Table.

- Create a new Table and save the Table as *Exams.*
- Using the data displayed in Table 10.8, create fields with appropriate data types in the *Exams* Table.

Exam Number	1
Student Code	15IT001
Subject Code	ICW520
Exam Period	Summer 2015
Exam Date	02/05/2015
Result	Merit

Table 10.8

- Set the data type of the *Exam Number* field to Autonumber.
- Set the *Exam Number* field as the primary key.
- Ensure that the data type and field sizes for *Student Code* and *Subject Code* are the same as those specified in the *Students* and *Subjects* Tables. This is important so that we can link the Tables.
- Do not enter data in the Table at this point.

Task 14: Set up relationships for the *Exams* and *Subjects* Tables.

1. In the Database Tools section of the Ribbon, click the *Relationships* button, then click the *Show Table* button. Add the *Exams* Table and *Subjects* Table to the Relationships window.

Show Table

2. Position the *Exams* Table to the right of the *Students* Table. Position the *Subjects* Table to the right of the *Exams* Table. (Correct positioning of the Tables makes it easier to understand the relationships.)
3. Set up the relationship between the *Students* Table and the *Exams* Table.
   - The relationship between the *Students* Table and the *Exams* Table is one-to-many.
   - The linking field is *Student Code*.
   - Each student has a unique *Student Code* and that code only occurs once in the *Students* Table.
   - As each student can do many exams, their *Student Code* can occur many times in the *Exams* Table. For example, if student *15IT001* does five exams, then there will be five references to the code *15IT001* in the *Exams* Table.

     To set up the relationship between *Students* and *Exams*, drag the *Student Code* field from the *Students* Table and drop on the *Student Code* field in the *Exams* Table (see Figure 10.5). Click the *Enforce Referential Integrity* check box, then click *Create*.
4. Set up the relationship between the *Subjects* Table and the *Exams* Table.
   - The relationship between the *Subjects* Table and the *Exams* Table is also one-to-many.
   - The linking field is *Subject Code*.
   - Each subject has a unique *Subject Code* and that code only occurs once in the *Subjects* Table.
   - As each subject can be examined many times, its *Subject Code* can occur many times in the *Exams* Table. For example, if there were 10 Database Methods (ICW520) exams, there will be 10 references to the code *ICW520* in the *Exams* Table.

     To set up the relationship between *Subjects* and *Exams*, drag *Subject Code* from the *Subjects* Table and drop on *Subject Code* in the *Exams* Table (see Figure 10.5). Click the *Enforce Referential Integrity* check box, then click *Create*.

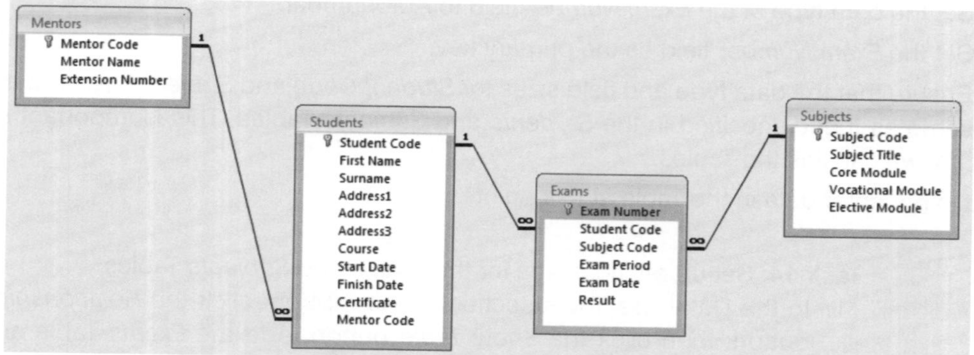

Figure 10.5: Relationships between Tables in the Exam Management database

The Tables should now appear in the Relationships window, as shown in Figure 10.5.

5. Save the relationships and close the Relationships window.

SUMMARY OF RELATIONSHIPS

Tables	Relationship Type
Mentors and *Students*	One-to-many
Students and *Exams*	One-to-many
Subjects and *Exams*	One-to-many
Students and *Subjects*	Many-to-many

Table 10.9

A summary of the relationships in the Exam Management database is displayed in Table 10.9. It is useful to have an overall view of the relationships in a database because data entry always starts on the "one" side of the relationship, i.e. *Students* data entry can't be completed unless data relating to *Mentors* has already been entered. *Exams* data entry can't be completed unless data relating to *Students* and *Subjects* has already been entered.

The relationship between the *Students* Table and the *Exams* Table is called a many-to-many relationship. Each student can do many exams and each subject can be examined many times. In a many-to-many relationship, the two tables (*Students* and *Subjects*) are linked through a third Table, in this case the *Exams* Table. The *Exams* Table contains fields that link it to both the *Students* Table and the *Subjects* Table.

THE *EXAM REGISTRATION* FORM

Each time a student is registered for an exam, data is entered in the *Exam Number, Student Code, Subject Code* and *Exam Period* fields in the *Exams* Table. By entering a

Student Code, we are specifying which of the students stored in the *Students* Table is sitting the exam. By entering a *Subject Code*, we are specifying which of the subjects stored in the *Subjects* Table is being examined.

It would be almost impossible to remember all the student and subject codes. For this reason, we will use combo boxes to look up the codes.

- The *Student Code* combo box will display a list of student codes and student names stored in the *Students* Table. When the data entry operator selects a particular student in the combo box, only the *Student Code* is entered in the *Exams* Table (see Figures 10.6 and 10.7).
- Because there are two students with the same name, it is important that the *Student Code* combo box displays both the *Student Code* and the *Student Name*. So that we know which code relates to which student, we will include the *Firstname* and *Surname* fields in the *Student Code* combo box.

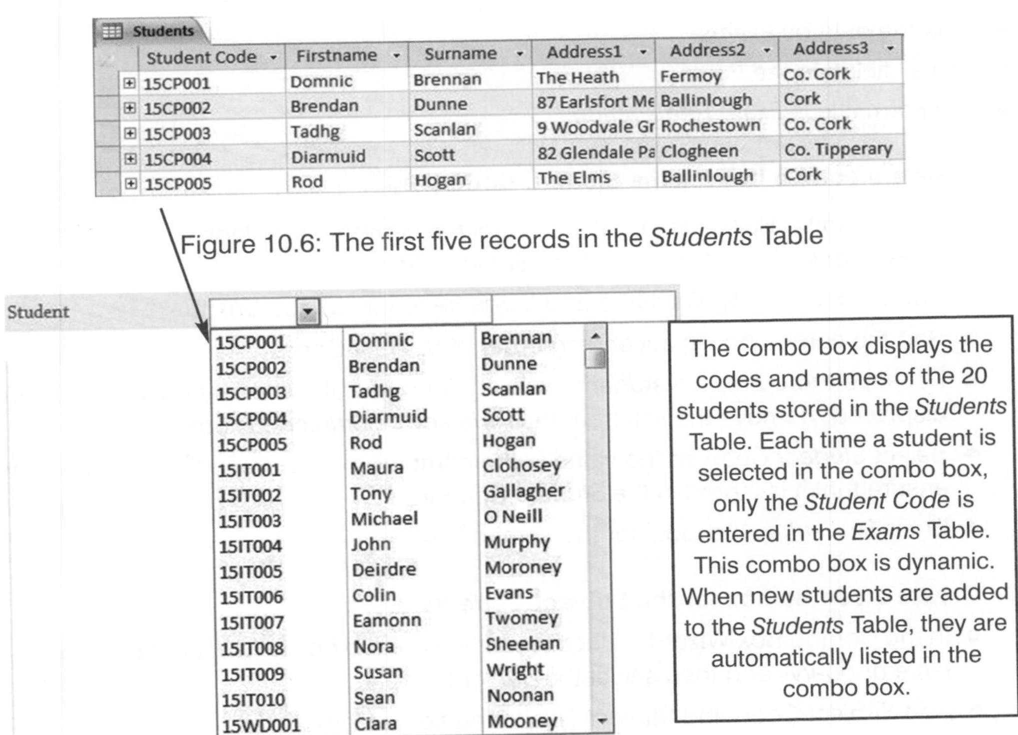

Students

Student Code	Firstname	Surname	Address1	Address2	Address3
15CP001	Domnic	Brennan	The Heath	Fermoy	Co. Cork
15CP002	Brendan	Dunne	87 Earlsfort Me	Ballinlough	Cork
15CP003	Tadhg	Scanlan	9 Woodvale Gr	Rochestown	Co. Cork
15CP004	Diarmuid	Scott	82 Glendale Pa	Clogheen	Co. Tipperary
15CP005	Rod	Hogan	The Elms	Ballinlough	Cork

Figure 10.6: The first five records in the *Students* Table

15CP001	Domnic	Brennan
15CP002	Brendan	Dunne
15CP003	Tadhg	Scanlan
15CP004	Diarmuid	Scott
15CP005	Rod	Hogan
15IT001	Maura	Clohosey
15IT002	Tony	Gallagher
15IT003	Michael	O Neill
15IT004	John	Murphy
15IT005	Deirdre	Moroney
15IT006	Colin	Evans
15IT007	Eamonn	Twomey
15IT008	Nora	Sheehan
15IT009	Susan	Wright
15IT010	Sean	Noonan
15WD001	Ciara	Mooney

Figure 10.7: Student combo box in the *Exam Registration* Form

- The *Subject* combo box will display a list of the subject names stored in the *Subjects* Table. When the data entry operator selects a particular subject in this combo box, the *Subject Code* will be entered in the *Exams* Table (even though the *Subject Code* is not actually displayed in the combo box).

As the *Exam Registration* Form is based on two tables (*Exams* and *Students*), the fields required from each Table must first be added to a Query.

Task 15: Set up the *Exam registration* Query.

- Create a new Query and add the *Students* Table and the *Exams* Table.
- From the *Students* Table, add the *Firstname* and *Surname* fields.
- From the *Exams* Table, add the *Exam Number, Student Code, Subject Code* and *Exam Period* fields.

- Save the Query as *Join tables for exam registration.*

Task 16: Create the *Exam Registration* Form.

- Create a Form linked to the *Join tables for exam registration* Query.
- View the data by *Exams*.
- Add all fields to the Form.
- The Form title is *Exam Registration*.

1. **Create a combo box for the *Student Code* field.**
   - In the Combo Box Wizard, select *"I want the combo box to look up the values in a table or query"* and then select the *Students* Table.
   - Add *Student Code, Firstname* and *Surname* to the combo box.
   - Sort the combo box in ascending order of *Student Code.*
   - Because there are two students named John Murphy, the key column must be displayed. Remove the tick from the *Hide key column* check box.
   - Select *Student Code* as the value in the combo box to store in the database and ensure that it is stored in the *Student Code* field.
   - Enter *Student* as the label for the combo box.

2. **Create a combo box for the *Subject Code* field.**
   - In the Combo Box Wizard, select *"I want the combo box to look up the values in a table or query"* and then select the *Subjects* Table.
   - Add *Subject Code* and *Subject Title* to the combo box.
   - Sort the combo box in ascending order of *Subject Title.*
   - This time, hide the key column (there aren't any subjects with the same name).
   - Store the value in the *Subject Code* field.
   - Enter "*Subject*" as the label for the combo box.
   - View the properties of the combo box. Set the Column Widths to *0 cm; 10 cm* and the List Width to *10 cm*. This makes the list wide enough to display *Information and Communication Systems.*

N Selecting the *Hide key column* box in the Combo Box Wizard sets the width of column 1 of the combo box to 0 cm.

3. Create a combo box for the Exam Period field.

- This time select *"I will type in the values that I want"*. The values to be displayed in the combo box are shown in Table 10.10.

Exam Period (Combo Box)
Summer 2015
Christmas 2015
Summer 2016
Christmas 2016
Summer 2017
Christmas 2017

Table 10.10

- Store the value in the *Exam Period* field.
- Enter *"Exam Period"* as the label for the combo box.
- Set the *Limit to List* property of this combo box to *Yes*.
- Set the *Allow Value List Edits* property of the combo box to *No*.
- Set the *Tab Stop* property to *No* for the *Exam Number, Firstname* and *Surname* fields.
  1. Because the *Exam Number* field has a data type of Autonumber, you will not enter data in this field.
  2. Firstnames and surnames have already been entered in the *Students* Table. The *Firstname* and *Surname* text boxes are not for data entry. Instead, they will display the student name corresponding to the student code selected in the combo box.

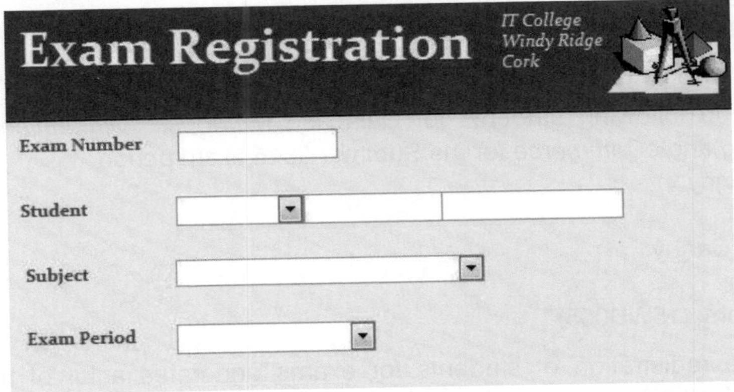

Figure 10.8: Suggested layout for the *Exam Registration* Form

- Ensure that the top three fields in the tab order are *Student Code, Subject Code* and *Exam Period*.

A suggested layout and format for the Form is shown in Figure 10.8.

- Save the Form as *Exam Registration.*

Task 17: Register students for exams.

- Using the *Exam Registration* Form, register the students listed below for *Database Methods, Communications, Word Processing* and *Information and Communication Systems* for the Summer 2015 exam period.

If your exam numbers don't start at 1, it doesn't really matter. What is important is that every record should have a unique exam number.

Maura Clohosey
Tony Gallagher
Michael O Neill
John Murphy (15IT004)
Deirdre Moroney
Colin Evans
Eamonn Twomey
Nora Sheehan
Susan Wright
Sean Noonan

- Register the following students for *Database Methods, Communications, Programming* and *Software Development* for the Summer 2015 exam period.
  Domnic Brennan
  Brendan Dunne
  Tadhg Scanlan
  Diarmuid Scott
  Rod Hogan

- Register the following students for *Database Methods, Communications, Word Processing* and *eCommerce* for the Summer 2015 exam period.
  Ciara Mooney
  Robin Carr
  Elaine Mc Carthy
  Paula King
  John Murphy (15WD005)

Although the registration of students for exams generates a lot of records, the Autonumber field and the combo boxes in the *Exam Registration* Form make the task of data entry much easier. Once you have input all the data, you should have 80 records in the *Exams* Table. Check this by opening the *Exams* Table in datasheet view: "Record 1 of 80" should appear on the bottom left of the screen.

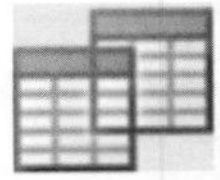

Task 18: Create a Query to find exam registrations by subject and period.

- Create a new Query and add the *Students, Exams* and *Subjects* Tables, in that order. (Adding the Tables in a different order makes it difficult to understand the relationships between the Tables.)
- From the *Students* Table, add the *Student Code, Firstname, Surname* and *Course* fields. From the *Exams* Table, add the *Exam Number, Exam Period, Exam Date* and *Result* fields. From the *Subjects* Table, add the *Subject Title* field.
- Set up the Query so that it displays the message "Enter Exam Period" and then displays the message "Enter Subject Title" when it is run. The Query should then find all exam registrations relating to the *Exam Period* and *Subject Title* entered by the user for which no Exam Date and no Result have been entered.
- Test the Query by running it and entering *Summer 2015* as the *Exam Period* and *Programming* as the *Subject Title*. It should find five records.

- Save the Query as *Find student registrations by subject.*

Task 19: Display exam lists by subject.

- Create a new Report linked to the *Find student registrations by subject* Query. Add the *Subject Title, Exam Period, Firstname, Surname* and *Course* fields.
- View the data by *Exams.*
- Apply the *Verve* style to the Report.
- The Report title is *Exam Lists by Subject.*
- In Report design, move the *Subject Title* and *Exam Period* fields from the detail section to the Report header.
- Edit the *Exam Lists by Subject* label box so that it reads *Exam List.*
- Include the college address and logo in the Report header.
- Draw a label box in the Report header and enter text relating to students who are not registered for the exam, as shown in Figure 10.9, which is an extract from the Report.
- Sort the Report in ascending order of *Student Code*.

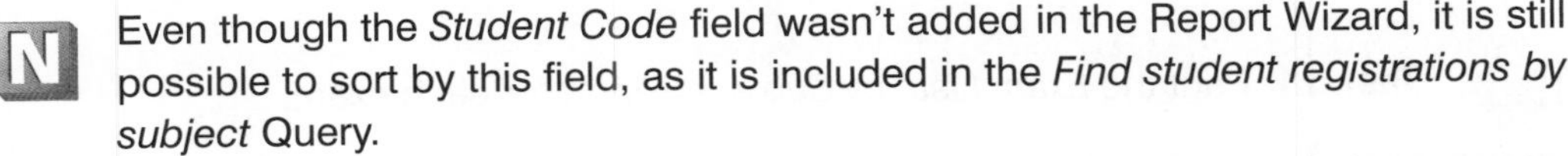

Even though the *Student Code* field wasn't added in the Report Wizard, it is still possible to sort by this field, as it is included in the *Find student registrations by subject* Query.

- Test the Report by previewing it a number of times and entering a different subject each time.

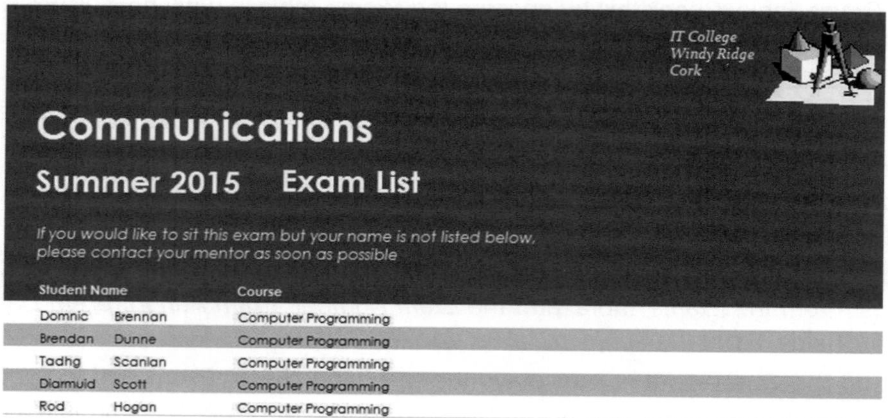

Figure 10.9: Extract from the *Exam Lists by Subject* Report

Copy the college address and logo from one of the Forms and paste it into the Report header.

Figure 10.9 is an extract from the Report, having entered *Communications* as the subject. (Information Technology and Web Design students have also registered for Communications.)

Task 20: Create a summary Report function.

- Create a text box in the Report footer of the *Exam Lists by Subject* Report. Enter the following Report formula in the text box:

  ="There are " & count([Surname]) & " students sitting the "& [Subject Title] & " Exam"

- Delete the label attached to the text box. Preview the Report and enter *Summer 2015* as the *Exam Period* and *Programming* as the *Subject Title*. "There are 5 students sitting the Programming exam" should appear at the bottom of the Report.

Include a space after *are* and *the*. Include a space before *students* and *Exam*.

Save the *Exam Lists by Subject* Report.

Task 21: Print the *Exam Lists by Subject* Report for each exam.

Task 22: Create disk labels.

- Create a Report that produces disk labels by *Subject*.

- When the Report is previewed, the message "Enter Exam Period" followed by the message "Enter Subject Title" should appear.
- The Report should produce disk labels for the subject entered by the user.
- Sort the labels in ascending order of *Student Code.*

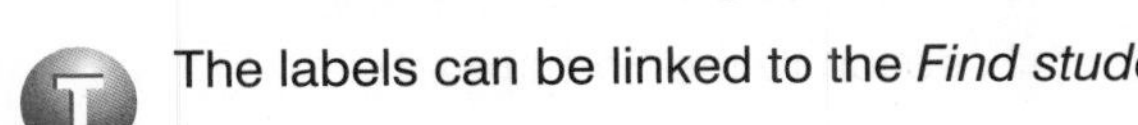

The labels can be linked to the *Find student registrations by subject* Query.

- Save this Report as *Disk Labels by Subject*.

A sample label is shown in Figure 10.10.

Summer 2015
15IT001
Maura Clohosey
Database Methods
Exam Number: 1

Figure 10.10: *Disk Labels by Subject*

ENTERING EXAM RESULTS

To enter exam results efficiently, a number of conditions need to be specified:

1. Only records relating to the subject and exam period selected should be displayed.
2. Only records where the *Result* field is empty should be displayed.

These conditions can be specified in a Query. A Form to enter exam results will be linked to this Query.

Task 23: Find records for exam results data entry.

- Create a new Query and add the *Students, Exams* and *Subjects* tables.
- From the *Students* Table, add *Student Code, Firstname* and *Surname*. From the *Exams* Table, add *Exam Period, Exam Date* and *Result*. From the *Subjects* Table, add *Subject Title*.
- Add parameters to the Query so that when it is run, you are asked to enter an *Exam Period* and a *Subject Title*.
- Enter a condition so that only records where the *Result* field is empty are displayed.
- Sort the Query in ascending order of the *Student Code* field.

- Save the Query as *Exams with no results entered.*

 **Task 24:** Create the *Exam Results* Form.

- Create a Form linked to the *Exams with no results entered* Query.
- Add all fields to the Form. The Form title is *Exam Results.*
- Move the *Exam Period* field from the detail section to the Form header.
- Set the *Enabled* property to *No* for the *Student Code, Firstname, Surname* and *Subject Title* fields.
- Set the *Tab Stop* property to *No* for the *Exam Period* field.
- Create a combo box for the *Result* field. Select "I will type in the values", which are Distinction, Merit, Pass, Fail.

A suggested layout and format for the Form is shown in Figure 10.11.

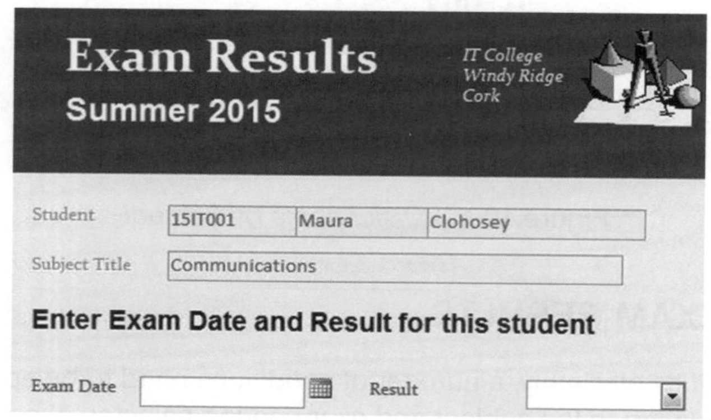

Figure 10.11: Suggested layout for the *Exam Results* Form

 MACROS

A macro is a list of commands, specified by the database designer, that are executed in quick succession by Access each time the macro is run. Macros are linked to events. For example, the event of clicking a button can trigger a macro into action. Macros are created to speed up common database tasks, such as finding and adding records. Macros can also be used to develop a user interface by creating custom menus, making it easier and faster for the database user to carry out tasks. Our first macro relates to the *Exam Results* Form. Because the *Exam Results* Form is linked to the *Exams with no results entered* Query, we are prompted to enter an *Exam Period* and a *Subject Title* each time we open the Form. As the Form displays a very specific set of records, the number of records to scroll through is minimised. Only records relating to a specific exam period and subject are displayed. This speeds up data entry. One downside of linking the Form to a Parameter Query is that we would have to close the Form and open it again, entering a different *Subject Title*, before we could enter results for another subject.

In the following worked example, we will create a macro that has two commands. The first command will close the *Exam Results* Form and the second command will open it again. The macro will be linked to a command button, which will be placed on the *Exam Results* Form. If the database user wants to enter results for another subject, they simply click the button. Once they click the button, the Form will close and immediately open again and they will be asked to enter an *Exam Period* and *Subject Title* so that the next set of results can be entered. This is much faster and easier than manually closing the *Exam Results* Form and then opening it again.

WORKED EXAMPLE: CREATE A MACRO

1. Click the *Macro* button in the Create section of the Ribbon. A new Macro window is displayed, as shown in Figure 10.12.

Macro1

Action	Arguments	Comment

Figure 10.12: Creating a macro

A macro is created by specifying commands in the *Action* column. When the macro is run, the commands will be executed in sequence by the macro. The good news is that you don't have to type the commands – Access provides a list of macro commands that can be selected in each line of the Action column. All you have to do is figure out which commands you need and then put them in the correct sequence.

It is good programming practice to enter comments in your macro. A comment is usually a short statement describing the function of a particular line in the macro. If you don't enter comments, you may find it difficult to remember the purpose of the macro the next time you edit it. Comments have no effect on the operation of the macro.

2. Select the *Close* command in the first line of the Action column (Figure 10.13).

Macro1

Action	Arguments	Comment
Close	Form, Exam Results, Promp	Close the Exam Results Form

Action Arguments

Object Type	Form
Object Name	Exam Results
Save	Prompt

Figure 10.13: Macro commands are selected in the Action column

In the *Action Arguments* section, select *Form* as the Object Type, *Exam Results* as the Object Name and Save=*Prompt*, as shown in Figure 10.13.

3. Select the *Open Form* command in the second line of the Action column. In Action Arguments, select *Exam Results* as the Object Name.

4. Save the macro as *Next set of results*.

WORKED EXAMPLE: RUN A MACRO FROM A COMMAND BUTTON

1. Open the *Exam Results* Form in design view.

Button

2. In the Design section of the Ribbon, check that the Control Wizard is on, then click the *Button* button.
3. Click and drag to draw a rectangle in the detail section to the right of the *Surname* text box.
4. The Command Button Wizard asks you *"What action do you want to happen when the button is pressed?"* Select *Miscellaneous* from the Categories list, then select *Run Macro* from the Actions list. Click *Next*.
5. Select *Next set of results* as the macro that the command button will run. Click *Next*.
6. A picture or text can be inserted in the command button. Select the *Text* option. Delete *Run Macro* and type *Next Subject*. Click *Next*.
7. Type *exam results button* as the button name and click *Finish*.
8. View the properties of the button and set the *Tab Stop* to *No*.
9. Change the font colour of the button text (*Next Subject*) to match the design of your Form. Select a font weight of bold.

10. Save the *Exam Results* Form, then click the *Form View* button. Enter *Summer 2015* as the exam period and *Communications* as the subject title. The Form displays 20 records.
11. Click the *Next Subject* button. Enter *Summer 2015* as the exam period and *Programming* as the Subject Title. The Form displays five records.

Task 25: Edit the *Next set of results* macro.

To ensure that the *Exam Results* Form is maximised when it is opened, we will add another line to the *Next set of results* macro.

1. In the Navigation Pane, right click the *Next set of results* macro and select design view from the pop-up menu.
2. In the next line below the *OpenForm* command, select *Maximize* in the Action column. (This ensures that the *Exam Results* Form occupies all the available window when it is opened.)

3. Save and close the macro.

Task 26: Create a command button to close the *Exam Results* Form.

Access has a Command Button Wizard that can be used to automate simple operations such as opening and closing Forms and Reports as well as record navigation. If the operation you wish to automate is included in the Command Button Wizard, there is no need to create a macro. Once you draw a command button, the wizard brings you through a series of steps asking you what should happen when the button is clicked and writes code in the background to implement this.

Button

1. In design view of the *Exam Results* Form, click the *Button* button and draw a button immediately below the *Next Subject* button.
2. In the Categories list, select *Form Operations*. In the Actions list, select *Close Form*. Click *Next*.
3. Select the text option and replace *Close Form* with *Exit*. Click *Next*.
4. Type *close exam results button* as the button name and click *Finish*.
5. View the properties of the button and set the *Tab Stop* to *No*.
6. Using the Format Painter, copy the format from the *Next Subject* button to the *Exit* button.
7. Set the width of both buttons to 2.275 cm (0.91 inches) and the height of both buttons to 0.714 cm (0.286 inches).

8. Save the *Exam Results* Form.

Task 27: Enter exam results.

- Using the *Exam Results* Form, enter the Database Methods results displayed in Table 10.11.

To speed up entering the date in the *Exam Date* field, enter 02/05/2015 in the *Exam Date* field for Domnic Brennan. Now highlight 02/05/2015 and click the *Copy* button. This date can then be pasted into the *Exam Date* text box each time you are entering an exam result, either by clicking the *Paste* button or by holding down the *CTRL* key and typing *V*.

Exam Period	Summer 2015
Subject Title	Database Methods
Date of Exam	02/05/2015

Student Number	Student Name	Result
15CP001	Domnic Brennan	Merit
15CP002	Brendan Dunne	Pass
15CP003	Tadhg Scanlan	Distinction
15CP004	Diarmuid Scott	Fail
15CP005	Rod Hogan	Merit
15IT001	Maura Clohosey	Merit
15IT002	Tony Gallagher	Merit
15IT003	Michael O Neill	Merit
15IT004	John Murphy	Fail
15IT005	Deirdre Moroney	Merit
15IT006	Colin Evans	Distinction
15IT007	Eamonn Twomey	Distinction
15IT008	Nora Sheehan	Pass
15IT009	Susan Wright	Merit
15IT010	Sean Noonan	Merit
15WD001	Ciara Mooney	Distinction
15WD002	Robin Carr	Distinction
15WD003	Elaine Mc Carthy	Distinction
15WD004	Paula King	Pass
15WD005	John Murphy	Distinction

Table 10.11

Next Subject Click the *Next Subject* button and enter the Communications results displayed in Table 10.12.

Exam Period	**Summer 2015**
Subject Title	**Communications**
Date of Exam	**05/05/2015**

Student Number	Student Name	Result
15CP001	Domnic Brennan	Distinction
15CP002	Brendan Dunne	Merit
15CP003	Tadhg Scanlan	Distinction
15CP004	Diarmuid Scott	Pass
15CP005	Rod Hogan	Merit
15IT001	Maura Clohosey	Pass
15IT002	Tony Gallagher	Fail
15IT003	Michael O Neill	Merit
15IT004	John Murphy	Pass
15IT005	Deirdre Moroney	Distinction
15IT006	Colin Evans	Merit
15IT007	Eamonn Twomey	Merit
15IT008	Nora Sheehan	Merit
15IT009	Susan Wright	Fail
15IT010	Sean Noonan	Pass
15WD001	Ciara Mooney	Merit
15WD002	Robin Carr	Distinction
15WD003	Elaine Mc Carthy	Distinction
15WD004	Paula King	Merit
15WD005	John Murphy	Merit

Table 10.12

Next Subject Click the *Next Subject* button and enter the Word Processing results displayed in Table 10.13.

Exam Period	Summer 2015
Subject Title	Word Processing
Date of Exam	06/05/2015

Student Number	Student Name	Result
15IT001	Maura Clohosey	Distinction
15IT002	Tony Gallagher	Merit
15IT003	Michael O Neill	Distinction
15IT004	John Murphy	Merit
15IT005	Deirdre Moroney	Distinction
15IT006	Colin Evans	Distinction
15IT007	Eamonn Twomey	Distinction
15IT008	Nora Sheehan	Merit
15IT009	Susan Wright	Merit
15IT010	Sean Noonan	Pass
15WD001	Ciara Mooney	Distinction
15WD002	Robin Carr	Merit
15WD003	Elaine Mc Carthy	Merit
15WD004	Paula King	Fail
15WD005	John Murphy	Distinction

Table 10.13

Next Subject Click the *Next Subject* button and enter the Information and Communication Systems results displayed in Table 10.14.

Exam Period	Summer 2015
Subject Title	Information and Communication Systems
Date of Exam	09/05/2015

- Deirdre Moroney did not sit the Information and Communication Systems exam.

Student Number	Student Name	Result
15IT001	Maura Clohosey	Merit
15IT002	Tony Gallagher	Pass
15IT003	Michael O Neill	Distinction
15IT004	John Murphy	Fail
15IT006	Colin Evans	Distinction
15IT007	Eamonn Twomey	Merit

Table 10.14

Student Number	Student Name	Result
15IT008	Nora Sheehan	Pass
15IT009	Susan Wright	Pass
15IT010	Sean Noonan	Fail

Table 10.14 (continued)

Next Subject Click the *Next Subject* button and enter the Programming results displayed in Table 10.15.

Exam Period	**Summer 2015**
Subject Title	**Programming**
Date of Exam	**12/05/2015**

Student Number	Student Name	Result
15CP001	Domnic Brennan	Distinction
15CP002	Brendan Dunne	Pass
15CP003	Tadhg Scanlan	Merit
15CP004	Diarmuid Scott	Pass
15CP005	Rod Hogan	Distinction

Table 10.15

Next Subject Click the *Next Subject* button and enter the Software Development results displayed in Table 10.16.

Exam Period	**Summer 2015**
Subject Title	**Software Development**
Date of Exam	**13/05/2015**

Student Number	Student Name	Result
15CP001	Domnic Brennan	Merit
15CP002	Brendan Dunne	Merit
15CP003	Tadhg Scanlan	Distinction
15CP004	Diarmuid Scott	Fail
15CP005	Rod Hogan	Pass

Table 10.16

Next Subject Click the *Next Subject* button and enter the eCommerce results displayed in Table 10.17.

Exam Period	Summer 2015
Subject Title	eCommerce
Date of Exam	16/05/2015

- Paula King did not sit the eCommerce exam.

Student Number	Student Name	Result
15WD001	Ciara Mooney	Merit
15WD002	Robin Carr	Distinction
15WD003	Elaine Mc Carthy	Merit
15WD005	John Murphy	Distinction

Table 10.17

- Click the *Exit* button to close the *Exam Results* Form.

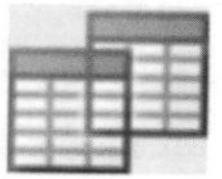

Task 28: Find results by subject.

- Create a new Query and add the *Students, Exams* and *Subjects* Tables. From the *Students* Table, add *Firstname, Surname* and *Course*. From the *Exams* Table, add *Exam Period, Exam Date* and *Result*. From the *Subjects* Table, add *Subject Title*.
- Add parameters to the Query so that when it is run, we are asked to enter an *Exam Period* and a *Subject Title*.
- Enter conditions so that only records where the *Exam Date* and *Result* fields *contain data* are displayed.

- Save the Query as *Find results by subject*.

Task 29: Display results by subject.

- Create a new Report linked to the *Find results by subject* Query. Add all fields except *Exam Date* to the Report.
- View the data by *Exams*.
- Group the Report by *Result*.
- Sort the Report in ascending order of *Surname*.
- Apply the *Verve* style to the Report.
- The Report title is *Results by Subject.*
- Delete the label containing "Results by Subject" in the Report header. Create a text box in its place and enter a formula that creates a different Report title depending on which subject is entered in the Parameter Value dialog box as follows: Communications Results, Database Results, and so on.

Use & to join a field name and text in the text box, e.g. =[SubjectTitle]&"Results".

- Move the *Exam Period* text box from the detail section to the Report header below the main heading.
- Delete the *Subject Title* text box in the detail section.
- Delete all labels in the page header. Reduce the height of the page header to 0 cm.
- Add a function to the Report to calculate the total number of distinctions, merits, passes and fails. An extract from the Report is displayed in Figure 10.14, where *Communications* was entered as the Subject Title.

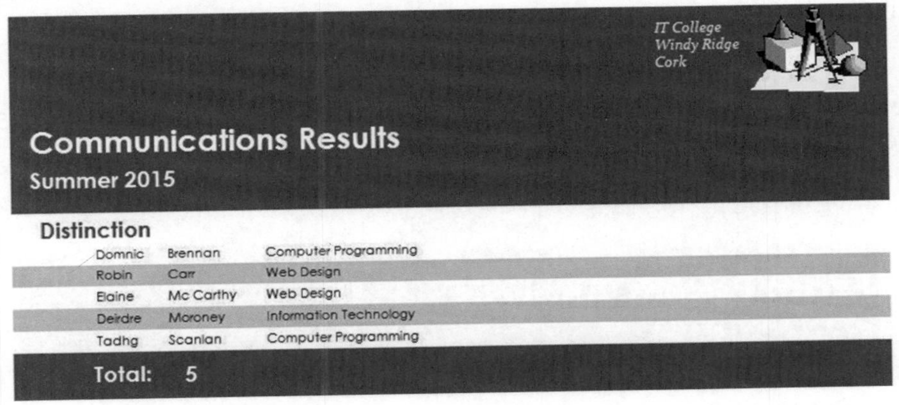

Figure 10.14: Extract from the *Results by Subject* Report

Preview the Report for each of the remaining subjects in which there were exams. Print each Report. The one-to-many relationship between *Subjects* and *Exams* can be seen clearly in this Report. Each *Subject* can generate many *Exams*.

Task 30: Display the number of distinctions, merits, passes and fails in all subjects.

- Create a new Query and add the *Exams* and *Subjects* Tables. From the *Exams* Table, add *Exam Period* and *Result*. From the *Subjects* Table, add *Subject Title*.
- Add a parameter to the Query so that when it is run, we are asked to enter an *Exam Period*.
- Enter a condition so that only records where the *Result* field contains data are displayed.

- Save the Query as *Find results for a specific period.*

- Create a new Report linked to the *Find results for a specific period* Query. Add all fields to the Report.
- View the data by *Exams.*
- Group the Report first by the *Subject Title* field and then by the *Result* field.

- Apply the *Verve* style to the Report.
- The Report title is *Exam Results Analysis.*
- Move the *Exam Period* text box control from the detail section to the Report header below the main heading.
- Add a Count function to the result header to count the number of results per grade.

H Refer to the *Exam Period* field.

- Reduce the height of the detail section to 0 cm (0 inches).
- Add a Count function to the *Subject Title* footer to count the number of results per subject.

H Refer to the *Subject Title* field.

An extract from the Report is displayed in Figure 10.15, where *Summer 2015* was entered as the Subject Title.

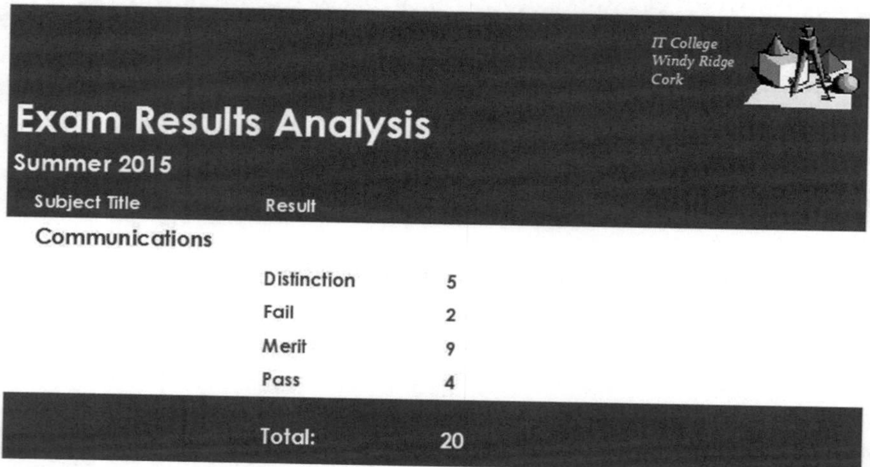

Figure 10.15: Extract from the *Exam Results Analysis* Report

Task 31: Find exam results of current students.

- Create a new Query and add the *Students, Exams* and *Subjects* Tables. From the *Students* Table, add the *Student Code, Firstname, Surname, Course* and *Finish Date* fields. From the *Exams* Table, add *Result*. From the *Subjects* Table, add *Subject Title*.
- Add conditions to the Query so that it only finds records where data has been entered in the *Result* field and where data hasn't been entered in the *Finish Date* field.

- Save the Query as *Results of current students*.

Task 32: Display student results.

- Create a new Report linked to the *Results of current students* Query.
- Add all fields except for *Finish Date* to the Report.
- View the data by *Exams.*
- Group the Report first by *Course* and then by *Student Code*.
- Apply the *Verve* style to the Report.
- The Report title is *Results by Student.*

Group & Sort

- Adjust the group properties to keep *Student Code* groups together on the same page.
- Add a function to the Report that displays today's date beneath the Report title.

- Add a formula to the Report to calculate the total number of exam results for each *Course*. This formula should produce three statements in the Report, as follows: "Number of exams taken by Computer Programming students: 20", "Number of Exams taken by Information Technology students: 39" and "Number of Exams taken by Web Design students: 19". (These totals will increase as more exam results are entered in the database.)
- Move the *Firstname* and *Surname* text box controls from the detail section to the *Student Code* header.
- Delete all label boxes in the page header. Reduce the height of the page header to 0 cm (0 inches).

A suggested layout and format for the Report is displayed in Figure 10.16. This Report was previewed on 06 July 2015.

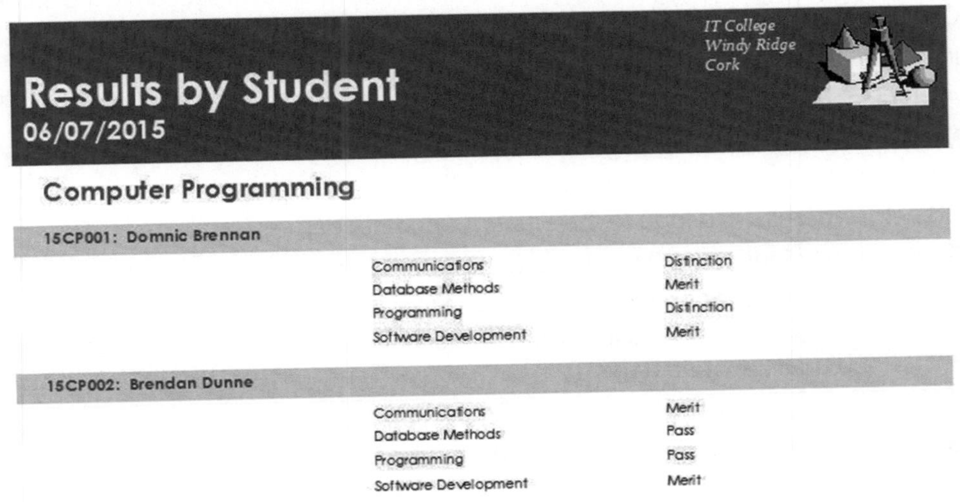

Figure 10.16: Extract from the *Results by Student* Report

The one-to-many relationship between students and exams can be seen clearly in this Report. Each student can do many exams.

Task 33: Design and create student certificates.

- Create a new Query and add the *Students, Exams* and *Subjects* Tables.
- From the *Students* Table, add the *Student Code, Firstname, Surname, Course, Finish Date* and *Certificate* fields. From the *Exams* Table, add *Result*.
- From the *Subjects* Table, add *Subject Title, Core Module, Vocational Module* and *Elective Module*.
- Add conditions to the Query so that it finds records of exams where the result was Pass, Merit or Distinction, where data hasn't been entered in the *Finish Date* field and where Certificate is equal to *No*.

- Save the Query as *Certification query*.

- Create a Report linked to *Certification query* including the *Student Code, Firstname, Surname, Course, Result* and *Subject Title* fields.
- View the data by *Exams.*
- Group the Report by *Student Code*.
- Sort the Report in ascending order of *Subject Title.*
- Apply the *Verve* style to the Report.
- The Report title is *Student Certificates*
- Delete all labels in the page header. Reduce the height of the page header to 0 cm (0 inches).
- Move the *Firstname, Surname* and *Course* fields from the detail section to the *Student Code* header.
- In the *Student Code* header, delete the *Student Code* controls.
- Add a function to the *Student Code* header that displays today's date.
- Move the label box containing the text *Training Certificate* from the Report header to the *Student Code* header (see Figure 10.17).
- Copy the address and logo to the *Student Code* header.
- Reduce the height of the Report header to 0 cm (0 inches).

- View the properties of the *Student Code* footer. Set the *Force New Page* property to *After Section*. This means that details relating to each student will be on a separate page.

To eliminate large gaps between the *Firstname* and *Surname* fields, create a text box in the *Student Code* header and type the following formula:

=[Firstname] & " " & [Surname]

A suggested layout and format for the Report is displayed in Figure 10.17. This Report was previewed on 06 July 2015.

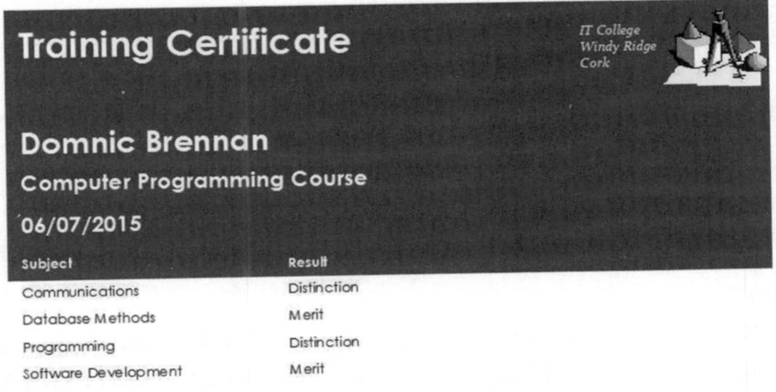

Figure 10.17: Extract from the *Student Certificates* Report

Scroll through the Report. It should contain 20 pages with a separate Training Certificate on each page.

- Export the *Student Certificates* Report to a PDF document.

Task 34: Create a Report summary.

- Create a Report summary, as shown in Figure 10.18, in the *Student Code* footer. (Totals displayed are for Domnic Brennan.)

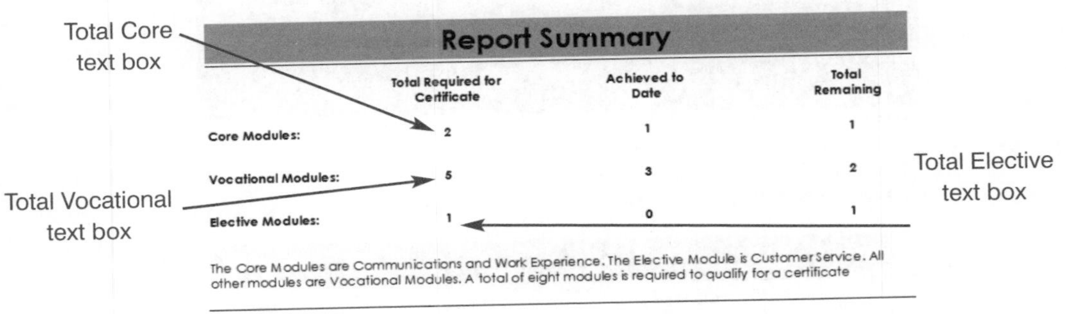

Figure 10.18: Functions in the Report footer of the *Student Certificates* Report

IMPORTANT POINTS

1. *Total Required for Certificate:* The number of core, vocational and elective modules required to qualify for a certificate are fixed numbers. They are not stored anywhere in the database. To display these numbers, create three text boxes positioned as shown in Figure 10.18.

- In the top text box, enter the formula =*2*.
- View the properties of this text box and enter *Total Core* as the Name.
- In the middle text box, enter the formula =*5*.
- View the properties of this text box and enter *Total Vocational* as the Name.
- Enter =*1* in the bottom text box.
- View the properties of this text box and enter *Total Elective* as the Name.

2. *Achieved to Date*
   - The total number of core, vocational and elective modules achieved to date is calculated using the Sum function in three separate text boxes.
3. *Total Remaining*
   - To calculate the total number of core, vocational and elective modules remaining to be completed, subtract the number of modules achieved to date from the total number of modules required.
   - Example: *=[Total Core]-sum([Core Module])* calculates the number of core modules remaining.
   - Similar formulas are required for vocational and elective modules.
4. The explanation at the bottom of the Report summary is entered in a label box. A sample page of the completed Report is displayed in Figure 10.19. This Report was previewed on 06 July 2015.

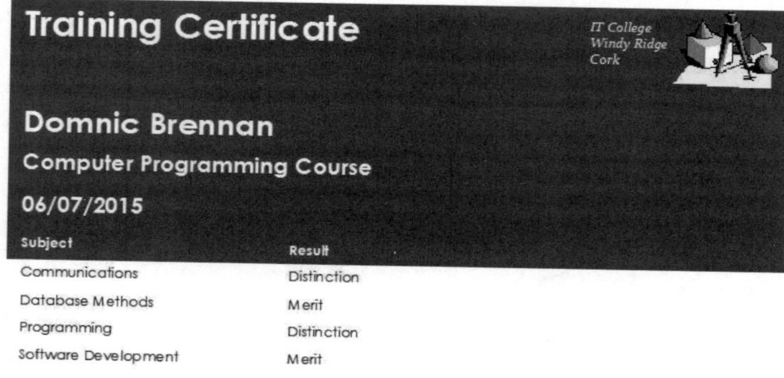

Training Certificate

IT College
Windy Ridge
Cork

Domnic Brennan

Computer Programming Course

06/07/2015

Subject	Result
Communications	Distinction
Database Methods	Merit
Programming	Distinction
Software Development	Merit

Report Summary

	Total Required for Certificate	Achieved to Date	Total Remaining
Core Modules:	2	1	1
Vocational Modules:	5	3	2
Elective Modules:	1	0	1

The Core Modules are Communications and Work Experience. The Elective Module is Customer Service. All other modules are Vocational Modules. A total of eight modules is required to qualify for a certificate

Figure 10.19: Completed *Student Certificates* Report

Task 35: Create a letter to accompany student Reports.

- Create a new Query and add the *Mentors* and *Students* Tables. From the *Mentors* Table, add the *Mentor Name* field. From the *Students* Table, add the *Firstname, Surname, Address1, Address2, Address3, Course* and *Finish Date* fields.
- Add a condition to the Query so that it only finds students who don't have a Finish Date.
- Save the Query as *Students receiving certificates*.

Create the letter displayed below using Microsoft Word. (Don't type the field names, displayed in bold print.)

IT College
Windy Ridge
Cork

«Firstname» **«Surname»**
«Address1»
«Address2»
«Address3»

Dear **«Firstname»**,

Congratulations on completing your exams in the **«Course»** course. Enclosed is your Certificate. Enjoy the holidays!

See you in September.

____

«Mentor Name»

- Save the letter as *Certificate Notice*.
- Using the mail merge facility, set up *Certificate Notice* as a *Letter*.
- Use the *Students receiving certificates* Query as the data source and insert fields from the database, shown in bold print above.
- Merge the main document with the data source to produce a new document containing 20 letters.

- Save the merged document as *Certificate Notifications Summer 2015*.

Task 36: Create address labels.

- In Microsoft Access, use the Label Wizard to produce labels for all students receiving letters.
- Set up the labels as shown in Figure 10.20.
- Sort the labels in ascending order of *Surname*.
- The Report name is *Labels for Certificate Letters.*

Domnic Brennan
The Heath
Fermoy
Co. Cork

Figure 10.20: Sample label

WORKED EXAMPLE: CREATE A CUSTOM MENU SYSTEM

To streamline use of the Exam Management System database and to make it more user friendly, we will create a menu system using a series of Forms containing command buttons. By clicking the command buttons, the database user will be able to access Forms and Reports stored in the database.

The functions of the *Exam Management System* database can be divided into two broad categories:

1. Data entry.
2. Reporting.

To allow easy access to data entry and reporting, we will create three custom menus, as follows:

1. Data Entry Menu.
2. Main Menu.
3. Reports Menu.

Step 1: Create the Data Entry Menu

Blank Form

1. In the Create section of the Ribbon, click *Blank Form*.

2. In design view, increase the size of the detail section until it occupies the entire screen.
3. Set the *Back Color* property of the detail section to *#ECECEC.*

4. Draw a label box at the top left of the Form. Enter the text *DATA ENTRY MENU* in the label box. Format this text to *Arial,* font size *26, bold.*

5. Copy the college address and logo from any of the other Forms and position to the right of the label box (see Figure 10.21).

6. Save the Form as *Data Entry Menu*.

Step 2: Create Command Buttons to Open Forms

1. In design view of *Data Entry Menu*, check that the Control Wizard is on and then draw a command button below the title.

Button

2. Select *Form Operations* in the Categories list and *Open Form* in the Actions list. Click *Next*.
3. Select *Student Registration* as the Form to open. Click *Next*.
4. Select *Open the Form and show all the records*. Click *Next*.
5. Select *Address Book* as the button picture. Click *Next*.
6. Enter *student reg button* as the button name. Click *Finish*.

7. Draw a label box to the right of the button and enter the text *Register New Students* (see Figure 10.21).
8. Format the label text to *Arial, bold, italic,* font size *12.*

9. Save the *Data Entry Menu* Form.

Task 37: Complete the *Data Entry Menu.*

Following the steps described above, create command buttons to open the *Exam Registration* Form, open the *Exam Results* Form and close the *Data Entry Menu* Form using the button pictures displayed in Figure 10.21, which is a suggested layout and format for the *Data Entry Menu* Form.

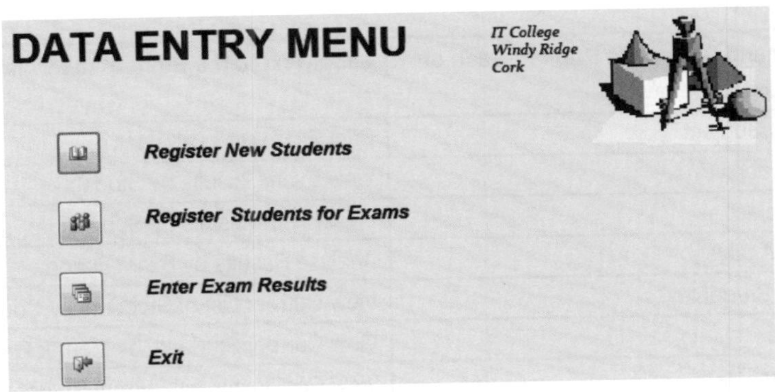

Figure 10.21: Suggested layout for the *Data Entry Menu*

The *Exit* button can be created by selecting *Form Operations* in the Categories list and *Close Form* in the Actions list.

Task 38: Create the *Reports Menu* Form.

1. Rather than creating a new Form, select the *Data Entry Menu* Form in the Navigation Pane. Click the *Copy* button in the Home section of the Ribbon, then click *Paste*.
2. Enter *Reports Menu* as the name for the new Form.
3. In design view of the *Reports Menu* Form, change the title to *REPORTS MENU.*
4. Delete all command buttons and labels except for the *Exit* command button and label.

Create Command Buttons to Preview Reports

1. In design view of the *Reports Menu* Form, draw a command button.
2. Select *Report Operations* from Categories and *Preview Report* from Actions. Click *Next*.
3. Select *Exam Lists by Subject* from the list of Reports. Click *Next*.

4. Select *MS Access Report* as the button picture. Click *Next*.
5. Enter *exam lists button* as the button name. Click *Finish*.
6. Draw a label box to the right of the button and enter the text *Exam Registrations by Subject*.
7. Format the label text to *Arial, bold, italic,* font size *12.*
8. Save the *Reports Menu* Form.

Task 39: Complete the *Reports Menu* Form.
Following the steps described above, create command buttons to preview the reports listed in Table 10.18. Create a label to the right of each button and enter the label text specified in Table 10.18.

Create Command Buttons to Preview Each of the Reports Listed Below	Label Text to the Right of the Command Button
Disk Labels by Subject	Print Exam Disk Labels
Results by Student	View Exam Results by Student
Results by Subject	View Exam Results by Subject
Exam Results Analysis	Analyse Results by Exam Period
List of Current Students	View Current List of Students by Course
Mentor Groups	View Current Students by Mentor Group
Student Certificates	View Certificates for Current Students
Labels for Certificate Letters	Print Mailing Labels for Certificates

Table 10.18

Figure 10.22 is a suggested layout and format for the *Reports Menu* Form.

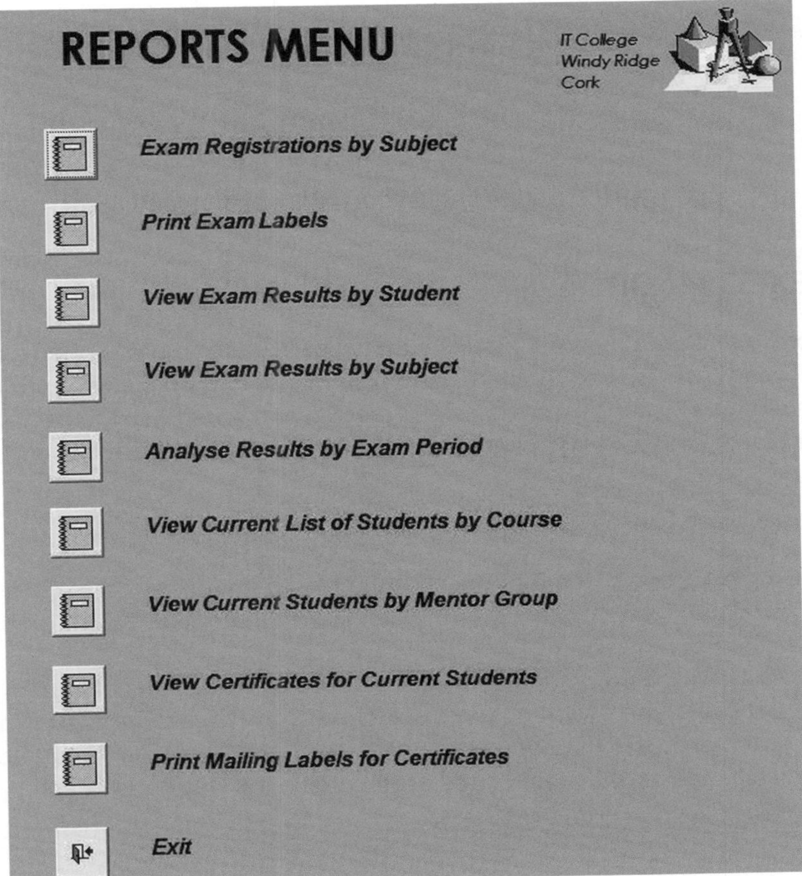

Figure 10.22: Suggested layout for the *Reports Menu Form*

Task 40: Create the *Main Menu* Form.
We will create the *Main Menu* Form by copying an existing Form.

1. In the Navigation Pane, select the *Data Entry Menu* Form. Click the *Copy* button in the Home section of the Ribbon, then click *Paste*.
2. Enter *Main Menu* as the name for the new Form.
3. In design view of the *Main Menu* Form, change the title to *IT COLLEGE EXAM SYSTEM.*
4. Delete all four command buttons and their associated labels.
5. Create separate command buttons to open the *Data Entry Menu* Form and the *Reports Menu* Form, using the button text in Figure 10.23.
6. Format the button text using *Arial*, font size *12, bold.*

Figure 10.23 is a suggested layout and format for the *Main Menu* Form.

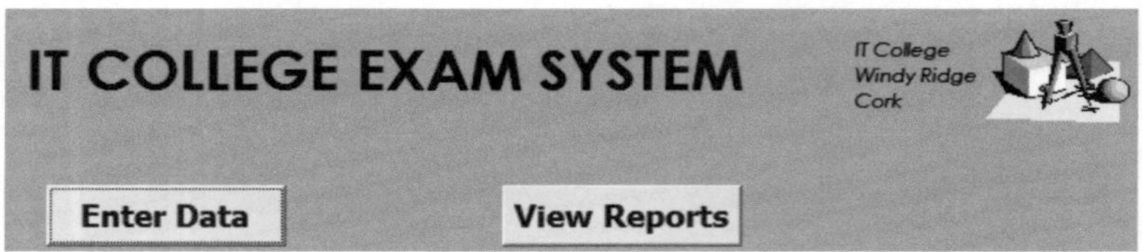

Figure 10.23: Suggested layout for the *Main Menu* Form

AUTOEXEC MACROS

An autoexec macro is a macro that runs automatically each time you open a database. In the following task, we will create an autoexec macro that opens and maximises the *Main Menu* Form. Once the macro has been created and saved with the name *autoexec*, the Exam Management System database will always open with the *Main Menu* Form displayed.

Task 41: Create an autoexec macro.

1. In the Create section of the Ribbon, click the *Macro* button.
2. Select the *OpenForm* command in the first line of the Action column. Select *Main Menu* as the Form name.
3. Select the *Maximize* command in the second line of the Action column.
4. In the third line of the Action column, select the *LockNavigationPane* command. In Action Arguments, set the *Lock* property to *Yes*. (This prevents the database user from deleting Tables, Queries, Forms or Reports in the Navigation Pane.)
5. Save the macro as *autoexec*.
6. Test the autoexec macro by closing the Exam Management System database and then opening it again. The database should open with the *Main Menu* Form displayed.
7. Right click any object in the Navigation Pane. Notice how the *Delete* option is no longer available.

Task 42: Register students for exams.

In the main menu, click the *Enter Data* button and then click the *Register students for exams* button. Click the *New* button and register the students listed below for *Computer Maintenance, Spreadsheet Methods, Work Experience* and *Customer Service* for the Christmas 2015 exam period.

Maura Clohosey
Tony Gallagher
Michael O Neill
John Murphy (15IT004)
Deirdre Moroney

Colin Evans
Eamonn Twomey
Nora Sheehan
Susan Wright
Sean Noonan

Register the following students for *Systems Analysis, Spreadsheet Methods, Work Experience* and *Customer Service* for the Christmas 2015 exam period.
Domnic Brennan
Brendan Dunne
Tadhg Scanlan
Diarmuid Scott
Rod Hogan

Register the following students for *Web Authoring, Graphic Design, Work Experience* and *Customer Service* for the Christmas 2015 exam period.
Ciara Mooney
Robin Carr
Elaine Mc Carthy
Paula King
John Murphy (15WD005)

Task 43: Produce exam labels.

Using the *Print Exam Labels* button in the *Reports* menu, preview and print labels for *Spreadsheet Methods, Web Authoring* and *Graphic Design* for the Christmas 2015 exam period.

Task 44: Print reports.

Using the *Exam Registrations by Subject* button in the *Reports* menu, preview and print exam registrations for each subject in the Christmas 2015 exam period.

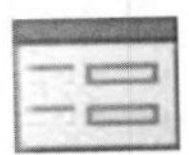

Task 45: Enter exam results.

In the main menu, click the *Enter Data* button, then click the *Enter exam results* button. Enter the exam results displayed in Table 10.19.

Exam Period	Christmas 2015
Subject Title	Computer Maintenance
Date of Exam	05/12/2015

Student Number	Student Name	Result
15IT001	Maura Clohosey	Merit
15IT002	Tony Gallagher	Distinction
15IT003	Michael O Neill	Merit
15IT004	John Murphy	Pass
15IT005	Deirdre Moroney	Distinction
15IT006	Colin Evans	Distinction
15IT007	Eamonn Twomey	Merit
15IT008	Nora Sheehan	Pass
15IT009	Susan Wright	Pass
15IT010	Sean Noonan	Merit

Table 10.19

Next Subject Click the *Next Subject* button and enter the Spreadsheet Methods results displayed in Table 10.20.

Exam Period	Christmas 2015
Subject Title	Spreadsheet Methods
Date of Exam	06/12/2015

Student Number	Student Name	Result
15CP001	Domnic Brennan	Distinction
15CP002	Brendan Dunne	Pass
15CP003	Tadhg Scanlan	Distinction
15CP004	Diarmuid Scott	Merit
15CP005	Rod Hogan	Merit
15IT001	Maura Clohosey	Merit
15IT002	Tony Gallagher	Merit
15IT003	Michael O Neill	Distinction
15IT004	John Murphy	Fail
15IT005	Deirdre Moroney	Distinction
15IT006	Colin Evans	Distinction
15IT007	Eamonn Twomey	Merit
15IT008	Nora Sheehan	Fail
15IT009	Susan Wright	Pass
15IT010	Sean Noonan	Pass

Table 10.20

Next Subject Click the *Next Subject* button and enter the Work Experience results displayed in Table 10.21.

Exam Period	**Christmas 2015**
Subject Title	**Work Experience**
Date of Exam	**08/12/2015**

Student Number	Student Name	Result
15CP001	Domnic Brennan	Merit
15CP002	Brendan Dunne	Fail
15CP003	Tadhg Scanlan	Merit
15CP004	Diarmuid Scott	Pass
15CP005	Rod Hogan	Merit
15IT001	Maura Clohosey	Distinction
15IT002	Tony Gallagher	Merit
15IT003	Michael O Neill	Distinction
15IT004	John Murphy	Pass
15IT005	Deirdre Moroney	Pass
15IT006	Colin Evans	Merit
15IT007	Eamonn Twomey	Distinction
15IT008	Nora Sheehan	Pass
15IT009	Susan Wright	Merit
15IT010	Sean Noonan	Merit
15WD001	Ciara Mooney	Distinction
15WD002	Robin Carr	Distinction
15WD003	Elaine Mc Carthy	Merit
15WD004	Paula King	Fail
15WD005	John Murphy	Merit

Table 10.21

Next Subject Click the *Next Subject* button and enter the Customer Service results displayed in Table 10.22.

- Tadhg Scanlan did not sit the Customer Service exam.

Exam Period	**Christmas 2015**
Subject Title	**Customer Service**
Date of Exam	**12/12/2015**

Student Number	Student Name	Result
15CP001	Domnic Brennan	Pass
15CP002	Brendan Dunne	Merit
15CP004	Diarmuid Scott	Merit
15CP005	Rod Hogan	Pass
15IT001	Maura Clohosey	Merit
15IT002	Tony Gallagher	Distinction
15IT003	Michael O Neill	Pass
15IT004	John Murphy	Distinction
15IT005	Deirdre Moroney	Merit
15IT006	Colin Evans	Fail
15IT007	Eamonn Twomey	Pass
15IT008	Nora Sheehan	Merit
15IT009	Susan Wright	Pass
15IT010	Sean Noonan	Pass
15WD001	Ciara Mooney	Distinction
15WD002	Robin Carr	Merit
15WD003	Elaine Mc Carthy	Distinction
15WD004	Paula King	Pass
15WD005	John Murphy	Merit

Table 10.22

Next Subject

Click the *Next Subject* button and enter the Systems Analysis results displayed in Table 10.23.

Exam Period	**Christmas 2015**
Subject Title	**Systems Analysis**
Date of Exam	**14/12/2015**

Student Number	Student Name	Result
15CP001	Domnic Brennan	Distinction
15CP002	Brendan Dunne	Merit
15CP003	Tadhg Scanlan	Merit
15CP004	Diarmuid Scott	Distinction
15CP005	Rod Hogan	Distinction

Table 10.23

Next Subject Click the *Next Subject* button and enter the Web Authoring results displayed in Table 10.24.

Exam Period	**Christmas 2015**
Subject Title	**Web Authoring**
Date of Exam	**15/12/2015**

Student Number	**Student Name**	**Result**
15WD001	Ciara Mooney	Distinction
15WD002	Robin Carr	Distinction
15WD003	Elaine Mc Carthy	Distinction
15WD004	Paula King	Merit
15WD005	John Murphy	Distinction

Table 10.24

Next Subject Click the *Next Subject* button and enter the Graphic Design results displayed in Table 10.25.

Exam Period	**Christmas 2015**
Subject Title	**Graphic Design**
Date of Exam	**16/12/2015**

Student Number	**Student Name**	**Result**
15WD001	Ciara Mooney	Merit
15WD002	Robin Carr	Merit
15WD003	Elaine Mc Carthy	Merit
15WD004	Paula King	Distinction
15WD005	John Murphy	Pass

Table 10.25

Task 46: Finalise the *Student Certificates* Report.

Edit the *Student Certificates* Report so that each certificate fits on one page. Remove the page footer from the Report.

Task 47: Print Reports.

Using the Reports menu, print all Reports relating to *Exam Results* and *Certificates*.

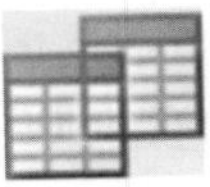

Task 48: Find students who qualify for a full certificate.
To qualify for a full certificate, a student must have achieved a pass, merit or distinction in two core modules, five vocational modules and one elective

module. We have already created a Query named *Certification query* that lists subjects passed by current students. This Query displays a separate record for each exam passed by a student. For example, Paula King passed five exams, so the *Certification query* displays five records for Paula King. To determine which students qualify for a certificate, we must summarise data stored in the *Certification query* so that only one record is displayed for each student with the total number of core, vocational and elective modules passed.

1. Create a new Query linked to *Certification query*. Add *Student Code, Firstname, Surname, Course, Core Module, Vocational Module, Elective Module* and *Certificate* to the Query design grid.

Σ Totals

2. Click the *Totals* button and select *Sum* in the *Totals* row for the *Core Module, Vocational Module* and *Elective Module* fields.
3. Run the Query. It should display 20 records with the total number of core, vocational and elective modules displayed for each student.
4. Add conditions to the Query so that it finds students who have two core modules, five vocational modules and one elective module.
5. Run the Query again. It should now display nine records. Print the records found by the Query.
6. Save this Query as *Certification query part 2*.
7. Create a new Form linked to the *Students* Table. Add the *Student Code, Firstname, Surname* and *Certificate* fields to the Form.
8. Save the Form as *Award Certificate*.

A suggested format and layout for the Form is displayed in Figure 10.24.

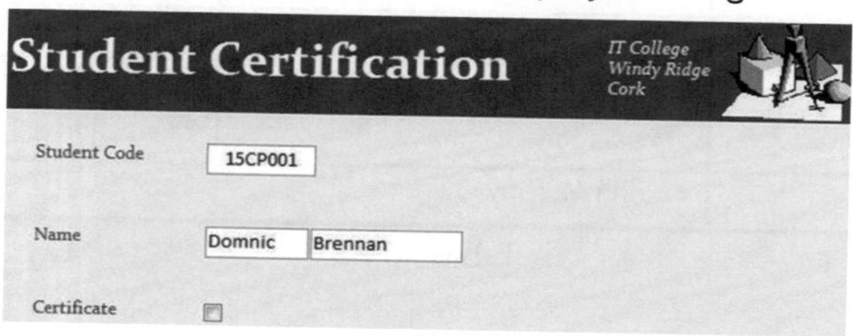

Figure 10.24: Suggested layout for the *Award Certificate* Form

9. In the *Data Entry Menu* Form, create a new command button that opens the *Award Certificate* Form. Position the command button between the *Enter exam results* and *Exit* buttons, as displayed in Figure 10.25.
10. Using the *Award Certificate* Form, tick the *Certificate* check box for each of the nine students found by *Certification query part 2*.

N The *Award Certificate* Form cannot be linked to *Certification query part 2* due to the fact that this Query calculates totals. This problem can only be solved using techniques that are beyond the scope of this book.

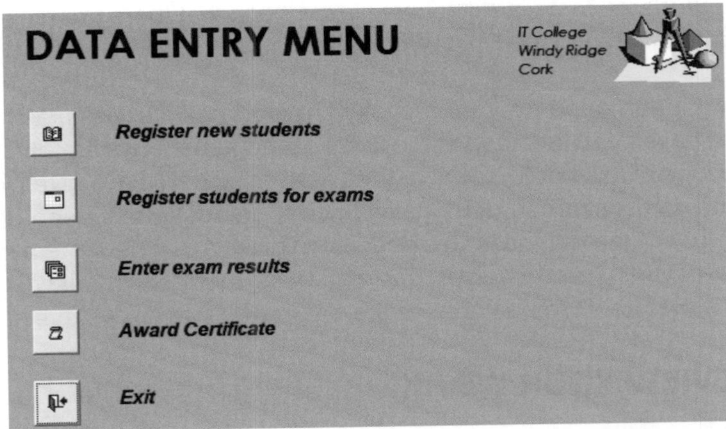

Figure 10.25: Award Certificate has been added to the Data Entry Menu

Task 49: Create an Update Query.

Up to this point, all the Queries we have created have been Select Queries. A Select Query simply finds and displays records. An Update Query, on the other hand, finds records and then updates these records by entering data in one or more fields or by altering existing data in one or more fields. We can create an Update Query to find all records of students who have received a full certificate and then enter today's date in the *Finish Date* field for each of these students.

1. Create a new Query and add the *Students* Table.
2. Add the *Student Code, Firstname, Surname, Start Date, Certificate* and *Finish Date* fields to the Query.
3. Add a condition to the Query so that it only finds records of students who have a certificate.
4. Test the Query by running it. It should find nine records.
5. View the Query in design view. In the Design section of the Ribbon, click the *Update* button.
6. A new *Update To* row appears in the Query design grid.
7. Enter *=date()* in the *Update To* row of the *Finish Date* field. When the Query is run, today's date will be entered in the *Finish Date* field for all students who have a certificate.
8. Save the Query as *Update finish date*.
9. Run the Query. The message "You are about to update 9 rows" is displayed. Click *Yes* to update the records.

If nothing happens when you run this Query, it is because Access has disabled the active content. If this is the case, tick the *Show/Hide* check box in the Database Tools section of the Ribbon. Click the *Options* button in the message bar and then select *Enable this content*. Open the *Update finish date* Query in design view. Click the *Run* button. The message "You are about to update 9 rows" should now be displayed. Click *Yes* to update the records.

10. Open the *Students* Table in datasheet view. Check that there are nine records with today's date entered in the *Finish Date* field.

This assignment has been an introduction to relational databases. Many additional features could have been included in the Exam Management System database but are beyond the scope of this book. Hopefully this assignment will have given you a taste of what relational databases can do. Finally, once a database has been designed and created, the work of the database designer isn't finished. As the system supported by the database develops and evolves, the database must be modified to reflect the changes in the system. Good databases are databases that are always up to date!

REVIEW YOUR WORK

Use the checklist below to verify that you have completed all the tasks in the Exam Management System database.

		Completed (√)
Tables:	• Exams	☐
	• Mentors	☐
	• Students	☐
	• Subjects	☐
Forms:	• Award Certificate	☐
	• Data Entry Menu	☐
	• Exam Registration	☐
	• Exam Results	☐
	• Main Menu	☐
	• Mentor Details	☐
	• Reports Menu	☐
	• Student Registration	☐
	• Subject Details	☐
Queries:	• Certification query	☐
	• Certification query part 2	☐
	• Exams with no results entered	☐
	• Find results by subject	☐

Completed (√)

- Find results for a specific period ☐
- Find student registrations by subject ☐
- Join tables for exam registration ☐
- Mentors and students ☐
- Results of current students ☐
- Students receiving certificates ☐
- Update finish date

Reports:

- Disk Labels by Subject ☐
- Exam Lists by Subject ☐
- Exam Results Analysis ☐
- Labels for Certificate Letters ☐
- List of Current Students ☐
- Mentor Groups ☐
- Results by Student ☐
- Results by Subject ☐
- Student Certificates ☐

Macros:

- Autoexec ☐
- Next set of results ☐

Log on to www.gillmacmillan.ie to download review questions for Assignment 10.

Glossary of Database Terms

Action Query
A Query that finds records and then either deletes the records, copies them to a new Table, appends them onto an existing Table or updates them using a formula.

AND logical operator
Two or more conditions in multiple fields can be joined in a Query by placing all conditions in the Criteria row of the Query design grid. Access interprets the conditions as being joined using *AND*. Only records satisfying all the conditions will be found. Negative conditions in a single field are joined with *AND*.

Attachment data type
Used to store objects such as pictures, Word documents, Excel spreadsheets or sound files in an Access Table. The Attachment data type requires 4 bytes of storage per record.

Autoexec macro
A macro that runs automatically each time the database is opened.

Autonumber data type
A numeric data type where Access automatically enters numbers in sequence. It is very useful as a primary key field in a Table where a high volume of records is generated, e.g. a database that stores records of customer orders. The Autonumber data type requires 4 bytes of storage per record.

Byte number type
A Number data type that stores whole numbers ranging from 0 to 255 in a field. The Byte number type requires 1 byte of storage per record.

Combo box
An expandable list that can be displayed in a Form to assist the data entry operator with data entry. Rather than typing the data, the data entry operator selects an item from the combo box list. In a database with a single Table, the items in the list are static. In a relational database, the items in the list adjust as records are added to or removed from the database.

Command button
Used in a Form to run a macro. Command buttons are frequently used to create custom database menus.

Crosstab Query
A Query that produces a summary based on data that is repeated in two or more fields. The output of the Query is arranged like a spreadsheet, in rows and columns. Each repeated value becomes an individual row or column in the grid.

Currency data type
A data type used to store monetary values in a field. It is accurate up to four decimal places. The Currency data type requires 8 bytes of storage per record.

Data type
The data type of a field should match the type of data that field will store. Field data types are specified in Table design. The main data types are Text, Number, Date/Time, Currency, Autonumber, Yes/No and Attachment.

Database
A database stores data in a specific structure and order. Each record is divided into a number of sections, which are called fields. Records are stored in ascending order of the primary key field. A database is not necessarily computerised. The telephone directory is the most common example of a database.

Date/Time data type
A data type used to store dates or times in a field. A range of formats is allowed. The Date/Time data type requires 8 bytes of storage per record.

Detail section
The main section of a Form. Text boxes used for data entry are normally displayed in the detail section.

Field
The smallest unit of data in a database. Each record stored in a Table is divided into sections, referred to as fields. The fields define the columns in a Table. Fields must be set up in Table design before you can enter data in the database.

Field list
The list of fields available to a Form or Report. If the Form/Report is linked to a Table, all the fields in the Table will be listed in the field list and can be included in the Form/Report. When a Form/Report is linked to a Query, only the fields that were added to the Query will appear in the field list. Fields can be added to a Form/Report by dragging and dropping from the field list.

Field size
The amount of disk space, measured in bytes, required to store data entered in a specific field for each record in the Table.

File tab and Office button
In Access 2007, the File menu was replaced by the Office button, which appears in the top left-hand corner of the screen. The *New*, *Open*, *Save*, *Save As* and *Print* commands are accessed by clicking the Office button. Clicking the Office button also displays a list of recently used databases. In Office 2010, the Office button was replaced by the File tab.

Form
An object whose main function is to facilitate data entry. Controls, such as combo boxes and list boxes, can be used in a Form to make data entry faster and more accurate. Forms can also be used to find and edit records and as menus in a custom menu system.

Form footer
The bottom section of the Form. The Form footer normally contains the date or summary information.

Form header
The top section of the Form. It normally contains the Form title. It can also contain a company logo and address, text box controls referring to fields or text box controls containing formulas or functions.

Integer number type
A Number data type that stores whole numbers ranging from -32,768 to 32,767 in a field. The Integer number type requires 2 bytes of storage per record.

Label box
A label box is used in a Form or Report to display descriptive text. In a Report, label boxes display the Report title and column or row headings. The fields in a Form normally consist of a label box and a text box. The label box displays the field name by default. As labels are not linked to specific fields in the Table, label text can be edited if required. The Form title is also contained in a label box.

Label Wizard
Not to be confused with labels used in Forms or Reports. The Label Wizard guides you through the process of creating address labels, product labels or any other type of label. The output of the Label Wizard is printed on special sheets containing sticky labels.

List box
A list that can be displayed on a Form to assist the data entry operator with entering data in a particular field. Rather than typing the data, the data entry operator selects an item from the list. In a database with a single Table, the items in the list are static. In a relational database, the items in the list adjust as records are added or removed from the database. As all the items in the list are visible, list boxes are not suitable for lists containing a large number of items.

Logical operator
In a Query, logical operators are combined with numbers or text to create conditions. The Query will only find records matching these conditions. The most common logical operators are <, <=, =, <>, > and >=.

Long Integer number type
A Number data type that stores whole numbers ranging from -2,147,483,648 to 2,147,483,647 in a field. The Long Integer number type requires 4 bytes of storage per record.

Macro
Used to automate tasks in a database. The macro stores a sequence of commands. Each time the macro is run, all the commands are executed in quick succession. A custom menu can be created by linking a number of macros to command buttons in a Form.

Mail merge
A facility that links data stored in a Table or Query with a document created in a word processing or email package. By placing fields from the Table or Query in a word processing document, a personalised document can be produced for each record in the Table or Query.

Memo data type
A data type that can be used to store long text descriptions. The Text data type allows a maximum of 255 characters. For field entries longer than 255 characters, the Memo data type should be used. A memo field can store up to 32,768 characters.

Navigation Pane
Lists all the objects in your database. The Navigation Pane is used to open the Tables, Queries, Forms and Reports in your database. It appears on the left of the screen and can be minimised when not in use.

Number data type
Used to store numbers in the Table. The Number data type has a variety of field sizes that determine the range of values that can be entered in the field and whether decimals are allowed. For each Number field, a field size of Byte, Integer, Long Integer, Single, Double, Replication ID or Decimal can be selected.

One-to-many relationship

When Tables are linked in a relational database, the nature of the relationship between the linking fields must be specified. In a one-to-many relationship, the link is between the primary key field on the one side of the relationship and a related field on the many side of the relationship. Data can only occur once on the one side of the relationship, e.g. a customer number, which is the primary key, can only occur once in the *Customers* Table but can occur many times on the many side of the relationship, e.g. if a particular customer has ordered 10 products, their customer number will appear 10 times in the *Orders* Table.

OR logical operator

Two or more Query conditions can be joined in the same field using the *OR* logical operator. For example, in a database that stores data relating to cars, the Query condition "Red" **or** "Blue" **or** "Black" would find red, blue and black cars. Conditions entered in different fields can also be joined using the *OR* operator by entering one condition in the *Criteria* row of the Query grid and another condition in the *OR* row of the Query grid.

Parameter Query

A Query that prompts you to enter a search term and then displays records matching that search term. A different search term can be entered each time you run a Parameter Query.

Primary key

The field in a Table that uniquely identifies each record. Once a field has been set as the primary key, the same data cannot be repeated in that field. Access will not enter a record in the Table if the primary key field is empty. Records are stored in the Table in ascending order of the primary key field, regardless of the order in which the records were entered. In a relational database, the primary key field is used to link Tables.

Query

A database object that allows database users to find records matching certain conditions. By entering conditions in the Query design grid, the database user can specify exactly what type of records they would like to find.

Quick Access toolbar

The Quick Access toolbar contains frequently used commands. It appears above the Ribbon in the top left-hand corner of the screen and can be used to create a new database, open an existing database or save the object you are currently working on. The Undo and Redo buttons also appear in the Quick Access toolbar.

Record

A record contains all the data relating to one item or entity stored in a Table. For example, in a Table that stores data relating to employees, each record would contain all the data relating to a particular employee. Records are stored in rows in the Table. Each record is divided into sections, which are called fields. In the Table, records are listed in ascending order of the primary key field.

Referential integrity

A system used by Access to ensure that data in related Tables follows certain rules and that data is not accidentally deleted. When referential integrity is enforced, you could not, for example, enter an order for a customer in an *Orders* Table unless that customer exists in the *Customers* Table.

Relational database

A database consisting of two or more Tables that are joined together using linking fields. For example, in a sales database, the *Customer ID* field could be used to link the *Customers* Table to the *Orders* Table. Each *Customer ID* will occur once in the *Customer* Table, but will occur many times in the *Orders* Table, depending on how many orders the customer has made. This is called a one-to-many relationship.

Report

Reports are used to present information from the database in printed form. The person reading a Report can understand its content without having any knowledge of databases. Reports are also used to sort records and perform calculations on data stored in Tables and Queries. Data displayed in a Report can be grouped into categories with the option of performing calculations on each group.

Report function

Functions, such as Sum, Avg and Count, can be included in a Report to perform calculations on the records displayed in the Report. Functions can be included in the Report header, Report footer, group header or group footer.

Ribbon

In Access 2007, menus and toolbars were replaced by the Ribbon. In the Ribbon, command buttons and drop-down menu lists are collected together under tabs. The Access Ribbon initially has four tabs representing four different groups of commands. Each tab relates to a particular activity. For example, the Home tab primarily consists of commands related to formatting data. The Ribbon adjusts to reflect the task that you are working on. For example, when you open a Report in design view, three extra tabs are added to the Ribbon.

Select Query

A Query that finds and displays records matching conditions entered in the Query design grid.

Single number type

A Number data type that stores numbers with up to seven decimal places in a field. The Single number type requires 4 bytes of storage per record.

Tab order

The order in which the cursor moves through text box controls in a Form as the Tab key is pressed. The tab order should be set up so that the cursor moves from one text box to the next without skipping text boxes. The order should also match the way in which the source data is laid out on a printed page.

Table

A database object that stores data. The Table consists of records. Each record is divided into sections, referred to as fields. The primary key field uniquely identifies each record. The Table is the most important object in the database. A database cannot function without a Table.

Text box

Fields displayed in a Form or Report consist of a label box and a text box. The text box control contains the field name providing the link back to a specific field in the Table or Query to which the Form or Report is linked. Text boxes can also be used for calculations in Forms and Reports. You should never edit the field name in a text box control, as this will break the link to the field in the Table or Query.

Text data type

The Text data type is used to store text and combinations of letters and numbers, e.g. a car registration number. The field size of a Text field is entered by the database user. Initially it is set to 255, but it should be adjusted to reflect the type of data stored in each Text field. The maximum number of characters that can be entered in a Text field is 255.

Totals Query
A Query that generates a single row of calculations based on records stored in the Table. In a grouped Totals Query, a separate row of calculations is generated for each group of records stored in the Table. Totals Queries are not used to find records.

Update Query
A Query that finds records matching conditions entered in the Query design grid and then updates the data in one or more fields by applying a formula. For example, an Update Query could be used to find all products in a particular category and apply a 10% price increase to those products by multiplying the price field by 1.1. Update Queries don't work unless you allow the active content in the database.

Validation
A method of checking data entered in a database to ensure that it satisfies certain rules. For example, a person's age can't be negative and can't be greater than roughly 110. An error message can be displayed when the data entry operator attempts to enter data that breaks a validation rule.

Wildcard
Used in a Query to find data that matches a pattern or when some of the search information is missing. The * character is included in the Query condition and represents the data that is missing. For example, entering *G* in the *Registration* field would find all cars registered in Galway.

Wizard
Each time you create a new Table, Query, Form or Report, you have the option of information assistance from a wizard. Most of the wizards in Access are very good and can save you a lot of time by doing the basic set-up of an object for you, giving you more time to work on the finer detail. Within a Form or Report, the Control Wizard provides help when objects such as combo boxes and list boxes are created.

Yes/No data type
A data type that will only accept the following values: Yes or No, On or Off, True or False. Set a field's data type to Yes/No where either Yes/No, On/Off or True/False are the only values that can be entered in that field. For example, in an employee database, the data type of a field named *Full Licence* could be set to Yes/No. The Yes/No data type requires 1 byte of storage per record.